Corruption by Design

Corruption by Design

BUILDING CLEAN GOVERNMENT IN
MAINLAND CHINA AND HONG KONG

MELANIE MANION

HARVARD UNIVERSITY PRESS

Cambridge, Massachusetts, and London, England   2004

Library of Congress Cataloging-in-Publication Data

Manion, Melanie, 1955–
    Corruption by design : building clean government in mainland China and Hong Kong /
Melanie Manion.
        p.   cm.
    Includes bibliographical references and index.
    ISBN 0-674-01486-3
    1. Political corruption—China—Prevention. 2. Political corruption—China—Hong
Kong—Prevention. 3. Political corruption—Prevention—Case studies. 4. Political
corruption—China. 5. Political corruption—China—Hong Kong. 6. Political
corruption—Case studies. I. Title.

JQ1509.5.C6M36 2004
364.1'323'0951—dc22   2004047348

For David, my hero

Contents

Acknowledgments

It is my great pleasure to thank those who have helped me in a variety of ways with this book. The chapters on mainland China, which comprise most of the book, benefitted immensely from discussions with a number of officials and ordinary Chinese, here unnamed. In particular, I learned about the importance of beliefs from my interviews on bribery in enterprise licensing conducted there in the early 1990s, while researching "clean government" with support from a grant sponsored by the Committee on Scholarly Communications with China. In the mid-1990s, a year in Hong Kong enriched my understanding of an extraordinary example of transformation from corruption to clean government; it also yielded the discovery of previously unexploited surveys that provided a rare opportunity to chart changes in beliefs about corruption.

In 1995 and years after, intelligence officers in the Hong Kong Independent Commission Against Corruption (ICAC) Operations Department were tremendously helpful, without compromising the duties of office. Their insights, analyses, and opinions greatly furthered my understanding of pivotal issues of anticorruption reform. In the Community Relations Department, Directors Janet Wong and Fanny Wong Lai-kwan elaborated on the department's work and graciously made available important materials, Raymond Ng Kwok-ming generously facilitated my study of survey reports and data books, and Pamela Lau provided invaluable assistance in clarifying question coding and data reporting—and responding to my many queries.

Comments and conversations with a number of people helped make this a better book. In particular, I thank Richard Baum, John Burns, Randall Calvert, James Feinerman, Kuan Hsin-chi, Barry Naughton, Pei Minxin, Susan Rose-Ackerman, Warren Schwartz, and Susan Whiting. I also thank ICAC officials in all three departments, who offered detailed comments on a draft of Chapter 2. Jean Hung at the Universities Service Centre for Chinese Studies at the Chinese University of Hong Kong ensured that my research stays in Hong Kong were both productive and happy. Closer to home in Madison, Wisconsin, Yang Wang and Jiangtao Ge helped with research support.

This book began as a modeling exercise: a game theoretic study of corruption in China, grounded in case study field research. I thank David Weimer for encouraging me to turn it into a study of anticorruption reform and for coaxing me along with his enthusiastic responses to my work. This book is dedicated to him.

Corruption by Design

Anticorruption Reform in a Setting of Widespread Corruption

Countries vary enormously in the extent to which officials abuse public office for private gain. Rapacious kleptocrats, for whom office is essentially an opportunity for plunder, rule a good many countries in which corruption flourishes with particular virulence. Of greater intellectual interest, however, are other countries, more numerous in recent years, in which governments have taken up the challenge of reform to lessen the scope and severity of corruption. How to accomplish the transformation from widespread corruption to clean government is an intriguing generic research question and a formidable practical policy problem. What are the prospects for success in anticorruption reform and what are prescriptions, if any, for hurrying it along?

This book considers the problem of anticorruption reform in contexts where corruption is most problematic—where it is routine, effectively constituting its own "informal political system" (Scott 1972). It argues that where corruption is commonplace, the environment in which public officials and ordinary citizens make choices to transact corruptly (or not) is fundamentally different from that in which corrupt practices are uncommon. A central feature of this difference is the role of beliefs, about both the prevalence of corruption and the reliability of government as an enforcer of rules ostensibly constraining official venality. Anticorruption reform in a setting of widespread corruption is a problem not only of reducing corrupt payoffs, but also of changing the shared expectations of rank venality that define a "folklore of corruption" (Myrdal 1968).

Most of the book examines this problem empirically, in case studies of anticorruption reform in mainland China and Hong Kong. Hong Kong offers an example—probably the best in the world—of successful transformation from widespread corruption in the 1960s to clean government in the 1970s. Over recent decades, new opportunities, new pressures, and new players have tested clean government, but Hong Kong has sustained a consistent ranking as one of the "cleanest" countries in the world since 1980, on a par with established liberal democracies. Mainland China, by contrast, experienced an explosion of corruption in the early 1980s. Chinese leaders have acknowledged that corruption is more serious now than at any time since the communists won power in 1949 and, probably correctly, view it as one of the greatest threats to communist party rule today. Despite two decades of anticorruption reform, including more anticorruption campaigns than in any other country in the world, corruption in China has continued to grow more or less unabated. Mainland China ranks today among the most corrupt countries in the world.[1]

Hong Kong and China, notwithstanding important commonalities such as a shared Chinese culture and an absence of meaningful elections to choose governments, differ greatly in most respects. Many of these differences are surely relevant to anticorruption success. Hong Kong is tiny, populated by fewer than 7 million people. China is huge, with a population exceeding 1.2 billion. Hong Kong's capitalist economy is more open than most and freer than most from government intervention. By contrast, the Chinese government protects its state industries, which are still major economic players after two decades of "reform and opening." Not least of all, Hong Kong, as a British colony and after the transfer of sovereignty from Britain to China in 1997, has been ruled by governments that basically respect civil liberties and uphold the rule of law, both in principle and as a real constraint on political power. In mainland China, the more sophisticated grasp of legal form in recent decades cannot obscure an essentially instrumental perspective on law. And civil liberties remain largely absent, in both rhetoric and reality.

Hong Kong is studied here as an example of the *possibility* of anticorruption reform. A recent statistical inquiry into the causes of corruption concludes that policy alone has "little significant impact on corruption." To the degree that policy decisions have any impact, they work "painfully slowly" (Treisman 2000: 441). Yet Hong Kong achieved, within a few years, spectacular success in overcoming obstacles to reform in a setting of flagrant institutionalized corruption. The government employed policy instruments that reflect an appreciation of the key features of these obstacles, as set out in general form in this chapter.

Moreover, the link between policy instruments and results in Hong Kong is about as clear as can possibly be, considering the extraordinary difficulties of measurement in the study of corruption. Findings from 19 previously unexploited surveys of the Hong Kong mass public, conducted regularly beginning in 1977 and discussed in this book, provide a basis for charting changes in beliefs about corruption.

Mainland China illustrates the *difficulty* of anticorruption reform. Anticorruption measures have largely failed in China, despite basic contextual features that favor success. Three of these features merit particular attention, if only because they distinguish the Chinese effort from anticorruption projects in many other gravely corrupt countries. First, it is a sincere (not merely strategic) endeavor. This does not mean that inclinations toward anticorruption reform trump top Chinese leaders' attachments to power, only that the effort is surely serious, if also seriously flawed. Real tradeoffs produce these flaws. They are not (or not only) the product of cynical maneuvers to bamboozle disgruntled citizens or purge political opponents. Instead, in many countries, longstanding corruption is no puzzle: Occasional "corruption cleanups" are launched to consolidate incumbent power or justify undemocratic regime change (Gillespie and Okruhlik 1991), but many governments have not taken up anticorruption reform in earnest.

Second, the Chinese government has demonstrated, in other arenas, an awesome ability to engineer major transformation and implement difficult policies, even in the relatively less intrusive post-Mao years. That is, anticorruption reform in China is the effort of a comparatively strong state with greater capacity than can be claimed by governments in many developing countries.

Finally, the scope and severity of corruption in China is a fairly recent occurrence. Compared to countries where corruption is long entrenched, it should be more manageable to change payoffs and beliefs to bring about cleaner government. The failure of Chinese anticorruption reform, despite these features that favor success, points to the real difficulty of reform. The fact that the Chinese and Hong Kong efforts have in common a number of anticorruption policy instruments illuminates, to some degree—and strengthened by the theoretical framework presented in this chapter—the source of these difficulties.

Corruption and the Relevance of Rules

In her analysis of the political economy of corruption, Susan Rose-Ackerman (1978) observes that all theories of the state implicitly or explicitly draw a normative line between market and nonmarket mechanisms of allocating scarce resources. Legislative decisions are not supposed to be for sale to the highest bidder in a liberal democracy, for example, even though democracy coexists with markets for many goods. Formal rules, such as those embodied in the law, reflect where this normative line has been drawn. Corruption is one of the most fundamental issues of modern political economy, as reflected in the question: How do market forces undermine whatever normative line has been drawn? In this sense, the study of corruption is truly at the core of the study of government.

In theory, formal rules reflect the government's proclaimed commitment to a predictable, normatively rationalized, social order. The government supplies these rules as a public good and manages their enforcement in its role in maintaining social order. When officials openly and routinely ignore rules about allocation of goods and services requiring their actions, then the system of order that in theory is backed up by the government's coercive power loses its practical meaning. Some alternative system of order then exists, an informal political system. This situation is fundamentally different from the familiar problem of social control. When corruption is widespread, the system of order defined by formal, normatively rationalized rules reflecting a theory of the state coexists alongside an observable pattern of allocation contradicting those rules and following instead the market law of supply and demand (but with the additional transaction costs of illegality). As expectations set in about how public officials normally transact business, the informal system subverts the formal one. In so doing, it subverts the role of government in supplying a social order roughly consistent with a publicly proclaimed theory of the state.

Widespread corruption connotes widespread violations of rules by public officials for private gain. Obviously, not all citizens prefer all rules. The question, however, is not whether particular rules somehow aggregate the most preferred principle of allocation. Nor is it whether they are preferred to rules based on some alternative ideal. The question is whether the replacement of rule-based allocation with what is essentially allocation based on the market principle for all government goods and services is a generally preferred change.[2] In most cases, for most ordinary citizens, the answer to this question is "No." Obviously, no country is free from corruption. Nor is the optimal level of corruption zero—not only is corruption control costly, but the "pursuit of absolute integrity" is quite dysfunctional (see Anechiarico and Jacobs 1996), distorting the purpose of government and its agencies. This is hardly the problem in most countries, however.

In countries with "clean governments," corrupt practices are not unknown, but they are uncommon and widely perceived as such. They can be scandalous, a notion incompatible with routine. What most fundamentally distinguishes these countries from countries with widespread corruption is not the content of laws (or other rules) relating to abuses of official power, but their relevance. When government is relatively clean, ordinary citizens interacting with public officials may argue for exceptions to rules, but the arguments will tend toward rule-conscious exceptions, not arguments (or bribes) against constraint by rules per se. From this perspective, the notion of "legalized corruption" (see Etzioni 1984) totally misses the point. The term refers to practices that some consider unethical but that are nonetheless legal and widespread; campaign contributions observing the letter of the law but undermining its spirit are an example. The point, however, is that such practices do not violate laws. Rather, they exhibit a very conscious observance of the law, necessitated by a concern about maintaining strict legality. Individuals engaging in such practices use the law as their standard in making choices about actions.[3] In countries widely perceived as corrupt, many (and perhaps most) officials commonly flout rules. There, in contrast to countries where cleaner governments govern, rules do not describe official activity well and so are not a useful basis for expectations about official conduct. Corrupt practices are too routine to be the stuff of scandal. The notion of exceptions to rules makes little sense when rules are practically irrelevant.

In this book, corruption is the *abuse of public office for private gain in violation of rules*. The reference to *rules* follows Joseph Nye (1967) and others in applying a formal-legal standard to define "abuse" of office. This perspective contrasts with a public interest or public opinion standard (see Scott 1972; Gardiner 1993). It most closely approximates a positive definition of corruption, but by no means trivializes the role of beliefs. Indeed, beliefs are central to the perspective on corruption presented here. A number of classic studies (Andreski 1968; Huntington 1968; Ekpo 1979) properly and usefully invoke incongruity of beliefs and rules as an explanation for corruption. Respecting this insight means that beliefs cannot, at the same time, serve to define corruption.[4]

The formal-legal standard is not, then, a simpleminded rejection of the importance of culture, but nor is it unproblematic. As the law and other rules reflect some normative theory of the state, the standard simply pushes the normative connotation of corruption back one layer, choosing in effect to ignore it. Nor does it fully resolve definitional ambiguity. As Daniel Lowenstein (1985, 1996) demonstrates, even in the United States, where the legal code is highly developed, the law is not unequivocal about what constitutes corruption. Finally, it is important to be explicit about the implications of the formal-legal standard for comparative analysis. The standard implies that the comparative study of corruption, whether spanning historical periods or countries in the same period, is not necessarily a study of comparable actions. Instead, it is a study of a comparable *relationship,* the contradictory relationship between self-serving actions of public officials and rules designed to constrain them in their pursuit of private gain.

The Persistence of Widespread Corruption

Transparency International, a nongovernmental anticorruption agency based in Berlin, has produced a "corruption perceptions index" (CPI) annually since 1995, including 90 or more countries in its rankings in recent years. The index is essentially a measure of corruption by a public opinion standard, although the general public is absent from a number of rankings. Each country in the CPI is given a score, calculated from three or more surveys of country experts, risk analysts, domestic and expatriate businesses, and (where available) ordinary citizens. In 1996 Transparency International also produced two rankings of 54 countries as "historical perspective," for 1980–85 and 1988–92. These are based on fewer and less diverse sources.[5] The CPI is a measure of perceived corruption, on a ten-point scale, with higher scores signifying less perceived corruption. For example, scores compiled for the 2003 CPI, presented in Table 1.1, range from 9.7 for the cleanest ranked country (Finland) to 1.3 for the country viewed as most corrupt (Bangladesh).

The availability (and increasing acceptability) of subjective measures of corruption, such as the CPI, has given impetus in recent years to cross-national statistical studies of corruption.[6] These analyses have increased our knowledge about consequences of corruption. Ceteris paribus, more corruption is generally associated with less investment, lower growth, lower income, higher child mortality, less government spending on education, and weaker political system support.[7] Progress has also been made using subjective measures to examine causes of corruption. Analysts basically agree that, ceteris paribus, British colonial heritage

Table 1.1 Transparency International 2003 corruption perceptions index

Rank	Country	Score	Surveys	Standard deviation	90 percent confidence range
1	Finland	9.7	8	0.3	9.5–9.9
2	Iceland	9.6	7	0.3	9.4–9.7
3	Denmark	9.5	9	0.4	9.3–9.7
	New Zealand		8	0.2	9.4–9.6
5	Singapore	9.4	12	0.1	9.3–9.4
6	Sweden	9.3	11	0.2	9.2–9.4
7	Netherlands	8.9	9	0.3	8.7–9.1
8	Australia	8.8	12	0.9	8.3–9.1
	Norway		8	0.5	8.5–9.1
	Switzerland		9	0.8	8.3–9.1
11	Canada	8.7	12	0.9	8.2–9.1
	Luxembourg		6	0.4	8.4–8.9
	United Kingdom		13	0.5	8.5–8.9
14	Austria	8.0	9	0.7	7.7–8.4
	Hong Kong		11	1.1	7.4–8.5
16	Germany	7.7	11	1.2	7.1–8.2
17	Belgium	7.6	9	0.9	7.1–8.1
18	Ireland	7.5	9	0.7	7.1–7.9
	United States		13	1.2	6.9–8.0
20	Chile	7.4	12	0.9	6.9–7.7
21	Israel	7.0	10	1.2	6.3–7.6
	Japan		13	1.1	6.5–7.4
23	France	6.9	12	1.1	6.3–7.4
	Spain		11	0.8	6.5–7.2
25	Portugal	6.6	9	1.2	5.9–7.2
26	Oman	6.3	4	0.9	5.8–7.0
27	Bahrain	6.1	3	1.1	5.5–6.8
	Cyprus		3	1.6	4.7–7.2
29	Slovenia	5.9	12	1.2	5.4–6.6
30	Botswana	5.7	6	0.9	5.2–6.3
	Taiwan		13	1.0	5.3–6.2
32	Qatar	5.6	3	0.1	5.5–5.6
33	Estonia	5.5	12	0.6	5.3–5.8
	Uruguay		7	1.1	4.9–6.2
35	Italy	5.3	11	1.1	4.7–5.8
	Kuwait		4	1.7	3.8–6.3
37	Malaysia	5.2	13	1.1	4.8–5.8
	United Arab Emirates		3	0.5	4.6–5.5
39	Tunisia	4.9	6	0.7	4.4–5.3
40	Hungary	4.8	13	0.6	4.5–5.1
41	Lithuania	4.7	10	1.6	4.0–5.6
	Namibia		6	1.3	4.0–5.6

Table 1.1 (continued)

Rank	Country	Score	Surveys	Standard deviation	90 percent confidence range
43	Cuba	4.6	3	1.0	3.6–4.9
	Jordan		7	1.1	4.0–5.3
	Trinidad and Tobago		6	1.3	3.9–5.5
46	Belize	4.5	3	0.9	3.6–5.1
	Saudi Arabia		4	2.0	3.2–5.9
48	Mauritius	4.4	5	0.7	4.0–4.9
	South Africa		12	0.6	4.1–4.7
50	Costa Rica	4.3	8	0.7	4.0–4.7
	Greece		9	0.8	3.9–4.8
	South Korea		12	1.0	3.8–4.8
53	Belarus	4.2	5	1.8	2.8–5.3
54	Brazil	3.9	12	0.5	3.7–4.1
	Bulgaria		10	0.9	3.5–4.4
	Czech Republic		12	0.9	3.5–4.3
57	Jamaica	3.8	5	0.4	3.5–4.1
	Latvia		7	0.4	3.6–4.1
59	Colombia	3.7	11	0.5	3.4–3.9
	Croatia		8	0.6	3.3–4.0
	El Salvador		7	1.5	2.8–4.7
	Peru		9	0.6	3.4–4.0
	Slovakia		11	0.7	3.4–4.0
64	Mexico	3.6	12	0.6	3.4–3.9
	Poland		14	1.1	3.2–4.2
66	China	3.4	13	1.0	3.0–3.9
	Panama		7	0.8	3.0–4.0
	Sri Lanka		7	0.7	3.0–3.8
	Syria		4	1.3	2.4–4.2
70	Bosnia and Herzegovina	3.3	6	0.7	2.8–3.6
	Dominican Republic		6	0.4	3.0–3.5
	Egypt		9	1.3	2.7–4.0
	Ghana		6	0.9	2.9–4.0
	Morocco		5	1.3	2.5–4.3
	Thailand		13	0.9	2.8–3.6
76	Senegal	3.2	6	1.2	2.6–4.1
77	Turkey	3.1	14	0.9	2.8–3.5
78	Armenia	3.0	5	0.8	2.4–3.6
	Iran		4	1.0	1.9–3.5
	Lebanon		4	0.8	2.3–3.3
	Mali		3	1.8	1.4–4.2
	Palestine		3	1.2	2.0–3.8

Table 1.1 (continued)

Rank	Country	Score	Surveys	Standard deviation	90 percent confidence range
83	India	2.8	14	0.4	2.6–2.9
	Malawi		4	1.2	2.0–3.7
	Romania		12	1.0	2.4–3.3
86	Mozambique	2.7	5	0.7	2.2–3.2
	Russia		16	0.8	2.4–3.0
88	Algeria	2.6	4	0.5	2.2–2.9
	Madagascar		3	1.8	1.2–3.7
	Nicaragua		7	0.5	2.3–2.9
	Yemen		4	0.7	2.1–3.1
92	Albania	2.5	5	0.6	2.1–3.0
	Argentina		12	0.5	2.2–2.7
	Ethiopia		5	0.8	2.0–3.0
	Gambia		4	0.9	1.7–3.1
	Pakistan		7	0.9	2.0–3.0
	Philippines		12	0.5	2.2–2.7
	Tanzania		6	0.6	2.1–2.8
	Zambia		5	0.6	2.1–2.9
100	Guatemala	2.4	8	0.6	2.1–2.7
	Kazakhstan		7	0.9	1.9–3.0
	Moldova		5	0.8	1.9–3.0
	Uzbekistan		6	0.5	2.2–2.8
	Venezuela		12	0.5	2.1–2.6
	Vietnam		8	0.8	1.9–2.8
106	Bolivia	2.3	6	0.4	2.0–2.5
	Honduras		7	0.6	2.0–2.7
	Macedonia		5	0.3	2.1–2.5
	Serbia and Montenegro		5	0.5	2.0–2.7
	Sudan		4	0.3	2.0–2.5
	Ukraine		10	0.6	2.0–2.7
	Zimbabwe		7	0.3	2.1–2.4
113	Congo, Republic of the	2.2	3	0.5	2.0–2.8
	Ecuador		8	0.3	2.0–2.3
	Iraq		3	1.1	1.2–2.9
	Sierra Leone		3	0.5	2.0–2.8
	Uganda		6	0.7	1.9–2.8
118	Côte d'Ivoire	2.1	5	0.5	1.8–2.4
	Kyrgyzstan		5	0.4	1.9–2.4
	Libya		3	0.5	1.7–2.5
	Papua New Guinea		3	0.6	1.5–2.5
122	Indonesia	1.9	13	0.5	1.7–2.2
	Kenya		7	0.3	1.7–2.0

Table 1.1 (continued)

Rank	Country	Score	Surveys	Standard deviation	90 percent confidence range
124	Angola	1.8	3	0.3	1.4–1.9
	Azerbaijan		7	0.3	1.6–2.0
	Cameroon		5	0.2	1.6–1.9
	Georgia		6	0.7	1.4–2.3
	Tajikistan		3	0.3	1.7–2.0
129	Myanmar	1.6	3	0.3	1.4–1.8
	Paraguay		6	0.3	1.4–1.8
131	Haiti	1.5	5	0.6	1.1–1.9
132	Nigeria	1.4	9	0.4	1.2–1.6
133	Bangladesh	1.3	8	0.7	0.9–1.7

Source: Transparency International 2003 Corruption Perceptions Index at Internet Center for Corruption Research at http://www.gwdg.de/~uwvw/corruption.cpi_2003data.html.

Note: Each country's score is calculated as an average of standardized scores from at least three surveys of country experts, risk analysts, and domestic and expatriate businesses. It is a measure of perceived corruption on a ten-point scale: *higher* scores signify perceptions of *less corruption*.

and Protestantism contribute to less corruption, as do economic liberalization and higher per capita income. There is support for a relationship between political freedoms and less corruption, but findings disagree on the strength of this relationship and whether or not long experience of democracy is required for any significant impact. There is disagreement on the relationship between corruption and trade openness, administrative centralization, and country size.[8]

To be sure, these impressive results do not mitigate problems inherent in the measures themselves. The CPI is highly problematic in its assumption of a single dimension to corruption and its source bias toward multinational businesses, for example. There are alternative systematic measures, but not many.[9] Here, I adopt a skeptical view of CPI precision and use the index essentially to punctuate a few broad descriptive points. First, countries and regions featured in traditional studies of corruption in the 1960s and 1970s are also among the low scoring (corrupt) countries in corruption rankings two or three decades later: South and Southeast Asia, Sub-Saharan Africa, and the countries of the former Soviet Union feature prominently in this way.[10] Second, this "stickiness" of corruption (and indeed clean government) emerges from a closer examination of this period, too. CPI coverage spans more than two decades (1980–2003). If the CPI is collapsed to form categories defined by thirds of its ten-point scale, few scores change enough to cross categories over this period.[11] Of the 53 countries for which scores are available for the entire period, more than 90 percent have basically consistent high, low, or intermediate scores.[12] Only five are basically inconsistent and clearly cross categories.[13] Third, intermediate corruption scores are much less common than either high or low scores. Of the countries that exhibit basically consistent scores across the period, 70 percent have consistently high (clean) or low (corrupt) scores. Only 11 countries (21 percent) have consistently intermediate scores.[14] To be sure, this result is very much driven by inclusion of the rankings from the 1980s: In more recently produced rankings, the number of countries in the intermediate range grows. In the 2003 rankings, nearly one-third of the 133 countries ranked fall into this range. All but two of the post-communist countries of Eastern and Central Europe appear in this range (just as practically all countries that constituted the former Soviet Union appear in the low-scoring, most corrupt range). Some other countries that experienced major political change (Peru, Mexico, and South Africa, for example) are also found in the intermediate category. Whether intermediate status is typically associated with significant transitions of one sort or another or whether it can persist remains unclear at this point in time. Taiwan, South Korea, Italy, and Turkey are examples of countries that have remained in this category for more than two decades, suggesting at least the possibility of long life for this status. At this point, however, looking across more than two decades of subjective measures as rough empirical categories, it seems fair to conclude that countries can mostly be generally categorized in terms of their widespread corruption or clean government, and that corruption and clean government tend to persist.

Two Equilibria

For many purposes, a distinction between corruption in Bangladesh, Nigeria, Indonesia, and Azerbaijan, for example—all among the most corrupt countries appearing in the 2003 CPI, with scores ranging from a mere 1.3 to a mere 1.9—may be meaningful. Here, however, to elucidate better the relationship between the frequency and persistence of corruption, I collapse the rich variation in the scope, severity, and forms of corruption across different settings into a simple dichotomy, only distinguishing two obviously disparate settings: "clean government" and "widespread corruption." Bangladesh, Nigeria, Indonesia, and Azerbaijan (and many other countries) fall into the latter category.

Clean government and widespread corruption are described here as equilibria. Roughly, this means that once these destinations are reached, no one inside the situation can expect to improve their lot by choosing independently to act differently.[15] This by no means implies that clean government and widespread corruption are equally preferable to everyone caught up inside them. It only means that, whatever the path that led to these alternative destinations, the structure of the situations—in this case, the corruption rate that defines the two equilibria—points to the choices that secure their persistence. While no single player can unilaterally choose the other equilibrium with her actions, an equilibrium shift is certainly conceivable if some way can be found to coordinate the choices of many players to act differently. Indeed, as I elaborate later, this appears to be one of two features in successful anticorruption reform. However, to be sure, equilibria, almost by definition, do not normally (or easily) shift. A number of specific mechanisms work to sustain clean government and widespread corruption as relatively stable equilibria.[16]

First, when most officials are mostly clean, the government's coercive capacity is generally adequate to enforce adherence to rules constraining official venality. When the government only needs to concentrate its limited resources for enforcement on a small minority, its agencies can more easily detect and punish the corrupt. By implication, volume of corruption and average costs of corruption to the corrupt are inversely related: expected payoffs from corruption must take into account the chances of detection and punishment. When corruption is widespread, the corrupt enjoy some safety in numbers as they "compete" for the attention of law enforcers, perhaps even assuming (unrealistically) low corruption in enforcement itself. As there are practical constraints on enforcement resources, corruption in this situation is more profitable because it is more common—as corrupt activity increases, the likelihood of detection and punishment decreases.

Second, the illegality of corrupt transactions produces costs that are higher than those associated with legal market activity. The transaction costs of corruption are especially high in a setting of clean government, where corrupt officials are few in number. The prevalence of clean officials frustrates efforts by the corrupt to coordinate official venality in a number of ways. From one perspective, for non-officials seeking corrupt accomplices, the risks of initiating corrupt transactions are high when there are few officials who can be counted on to acquiesce and cooperate, lower when corruption is widespread. From another perspective, if signals from corrupt officials are too subtle, as they must be in a setting of clean government, then potential accomplices in society are likely to miss them, even if the corrupt transaction would benefit both parties. In a setting of widespread corruption, not only are these sorts of search costs reduced, but corruption may also be more organized. For example, standard bribe prices for various transactions may be informally established. Middlemen may emerge to match corrupt parties in high-risk transactions, such as those involving illegalities other than corruption.

Third, as discussed in an earlier section, what most fundamentally distinguishes countries with rampant corruption from those where corrupt activities are unusual is not the content of rules but their relevance. Corruption, even where it is the norm, is not generally condoned by law or other rules. Moral squeamishness about acting corruptly (and illegally) is likely to be little or great, depending on whether such violations are common or exceptional. If public officials and ordinary citizens obtain their information about social values by observing the pattern of transactions around them, then what is normal (in a descriptive sense) may become acceptable (in a moral sense). Put another way, the psychic costs of corruption are likely to be high for everyone when most officials are evidently clean, but lower when many officials blatantly flout rules in order to pursue private gain and go more or less unpunished.

Moral qualms about acting corruptly are bound to be affected by more particular contexts too. For example, ordinary citizens seeking government services (in limited supply or not) to which they are entitled, but which are allocated by corrupt officials, may actually take the initiative to transact corruptly. If corruption is a usual feature of the world they know (like it or not), then they also know they are at a comparative disadvantage if they do not offer unlawful extra incentives to officials.

Finally, when clean government prevails, ordinary citizens and clean officials contribute to its maintenance by acting voluntarily to assist in enforcement. This includes citizen resistance to official extortion attempts and citizen reports to authorities about officials who make such attempts. Under clean government, there are alternatives to victimization by corrupt officials. Not only are most other officials clean, but also authorities are presumably reliable in responding to complaints with punitive action against the corrupt. Such assistance is premised on beliefs that the public commitment to clean government is genuine and government capacity up to the task. When clean government prevails, ordinary citizens see evidence of that commitment and capacity all around them. By contrast, when corruption is widespread, it is apparent to all (including the corrupt) that the authorities are not reliable or impartial enforcers of prohibitions against official venality. Indeed, law enforcement is perhaps the most commonly exploited opportunity for official extortion.

From the discussion above, it emerges that clean government and widespread corruption are "frequency-dependent" equilibria (Bardhan 1997): the corruption rate not only defines these situations, but also explains their persistence. This feature and, more importantly, the possibilities for change it presents, can be illustrated with a simple Schelling-type tipping model, as shown in Figure 1.1 (adapted from Andvig 1991). Payoff curves are roughly consistent with the discussion above of mechanisms sustaining clean government and widespread corruption.

The players in Figure 1.1 are public officials who choose to act corruptly or not in some identical transaction (or ordinary citizens who choose to act corruptly or not in some transaction with an official). The number of players choosing to act corruptly is represented on the horizontal axis, from 0 to all n players. The vertical axis represents expected payoffs from choices. The two solid curves describe the expected payoffs for a player choosing a corrupt or "clean" transaction, given her beliefs (and their correctness) about the choices of all other players. When she believes that fewer than x players are acting corruptly and this belief is correct, she does best by choosing a clean transaction; when she believes correctly that more are acting corruptly, she does best by acting corruptly too. Whether corruption pays or not depends on the corruption rate. The model features two stable equilibria: ubiquitous corruption at C and completely clean government at A. It also features an unstable tipping point B, at which a player is strictly indifferent between a clean or corrupt transaction.[17] The characterization of A and C is unrealistic, obviously, but the usefulness of the illustration has less to do with these extreme points than with positions relative to B. Below B, the corruption rate generates its own momentum toward A, with payoffs from corruption declining steeply. Above B, the momentum is toward C, as more and more players profit most by choosing to act corruptly.

The discussion of clean government and widespread corruption focuses attention on points far to the left and right of B, but it is clear in

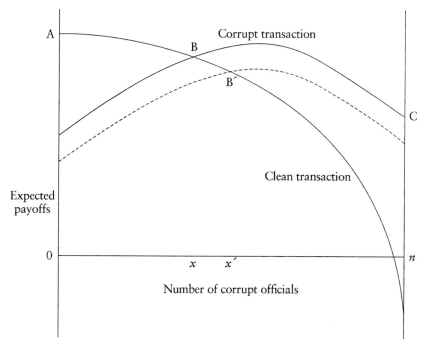

Figure 1.1 Corruption as a frequency-dependent equilibrium

Figure 1.1 that points close to *B* are of much greater interest in their implications for policy interventions. Small interventions can have a big impact when the starting point is close to *B*. Similarly, without timely corrective intervention, an exogenous change that shifts the corrupt payoffs curve only very slightly upward may be enough to accelerate a drive to persistent widespread corruption.

Implications for Anticorruption Reform

The discussion and figure in the preceding section are useful in drawing out clearly three implications for anticorruption reform in countries where corruption already prevails. The first formulates reform as a problem of changing corrupt payoffs, the second as a problem of changing expectations. A third implication is that reform (changing payoffs, changing expectations, or both) need not bear the entire burden of creating clean government. At some point, "clean enough" government generates momentum toward cleaner government.

Reducing Corrupt Payoffs

First and most obviously, a key task of anticorruption reform is to reduce corrupt payoffs—to shift the corrupt payoffs curve downward, in the language of the tipping model. In Figure 1.1, for example, the shift in corrupt payoffs from the solid to the dashed curve moves the tipping point from B (x corrupt officials) to B' (x' corrupt officials), allowing clean government to emerge from a "more corrupt" starting point (with a corruption rate of more than x officials but fewer than x' officials). Of course, when society has already settled at a point close to C, very big changes in the parameters that produce corrupt payoffs are required to disturb it enough to get clean enough government.[18] An intervention that shifts corrupt payoffs downward to the dashed curve in Figure 1.1 does not have nearly enough impact when corruption is widespread.

Corrupt payoffs can be reduced by a number of strategies. The literature mainly draws attention to two: enforcement and institutional design. A third strategy is *education,* to increase the psychic costs of corruption. It is certainly not implausible that moral education about the evils of corruption can help sustain an already low corruption rate, that it can even help clean up "pockets" of corruption in an overall setting of clean government. When the volume of corruption is high, however, moral squeamishness about engaging in corrupt activities is unlikely to be strongly affected by anticorruption publicity. Educational efforts to transform the ethical environment constitute a fairly cheap reform strategy (and probably a necessary one), but they serve best as a complement to other strategies (see Pope 1999).

Enforcement strategies reduce corrupt payoffs by increasing the likelihood that corrupt officials and their accomplices in society are discovered and, when discovered, punished with a severity commensurate to the corrupt act. Enforcement strategies increase resources devoted to monitoring and detection, increase punishments for corruption, or both. Citing the experiences of Hong Kong and Singapore, policy analysts (Langseth, Stapenhurst, and Pope 1999) tout the success of independent anticorruption agencies in discovering and investigating corruption. A few other countries, including Botswana, Tanzania, and Uganda, have in fact established such agencies. Adequate funding is the part of the Hong Kong and Singapore experiences less easily (or less readily) emulated in developing countries, however (Sedigh and Muganda 1999; Sedigh and Ruzindana 1999).

As to increasing punishments, this may seem simple enough. In

China and Vietnam, officials can be executed for corruption. Yet, in both countries, enforcement is uncertain. Even inordinate penalties must be accompanied by an increased likelihood of detection and punishment to be effective. A less extreme way to increase punishments is to alter the legal structure of penalties. In many countries, it is illegal for public officials to solicit or accept bribes, but not for private citizens to offer or pay bribes. Rose-Ackerman (1999) proposes an enforcement strategy that would not only criminalize corruption by private agents, but also make penalties proportionate to the benefits received by at least one party to the corrupt transaction—for the official, the size of bribe received, and for the bribe payer, the amount of excess profit or gains received.

Policy interventions that enhance anticorruption enforcement but leave unchanged the basic conditions that encourage corruption are unlikely to yield lasting results. Changing corrupt payoffs must take into account underlying incentives that foster corruption in its particular context. Anticorruption reform through *institutional design* restructures transactions to lessen incentives (independent of the corruption rate itself) and opportunities to transact corruptly. The most drastic institutional reform is program elimination. It may be warranted for programs with no sound policy justification that operate mainly to generate bribes (Rose-Ackerman 1999). Examples of such programs include many of the licenses and permissions required to set up businesses in developing countries (see Leff 1964; Bates 1981). A recent study of corruption in post-communist countries asked whether traffic police serve any useful purpose there: "Far fewer traffic police and rather more speed cameras might produce more revenue for the state as well as both tighter and fairer control of traffic" (Miller, Grodeland, and Koshechkina 2001: 338). Legalizing activities that generate corruption is another way to redesign incentives: When off-track betting in Hong Kong was legalized, payoffs for police protection were no longer necessary, which helped to reduce syndicated police corruption.

Another institutional design to reduce corruption is the "competitive" reorganization of bureaucracies, so that several officials supply the same government service. When officials lack monopoly power, bribes are driven down as clients seek the least corrupt officials (Rose-Ackerman 1978, 1999), unless the situation offers a possibility of corrupt collusion between clients and officials to deprive the state of revenue (Shleifer and Vishny 1993). Multiple veto points in government—such as separation of executive and legislative powers, legislative supermajority requirements, and constitutional courts—similarly limit the power of any single government institution, making it difficult to exert influence to obtain illegal benefits, as every decision point must be purchased. In government procurement, sealed competitive bidding requirements and the use of private market prices as benchmarks can also reduce corruption. Statutes that provide rewards and protection for whistleblowers can supply incentives for government officials to come forward to reveal corruption (Rose-Ackerman 1999).

The decline of electoral corruption (such as treating and money bribes) from a routine practice in mid-nineteenth-century England to a rare and generally disparaged occurrence by the end of the century reflects the distinct contributions of enforcement, education, and institutional design in anticorruption reform (see Gwyn 1962, 1970; O'Leary 1962; King 1970; Nossiter 1975; Cox 1987).

Enforcement is represented best in the 1854 Corrupt Practices Prevention Act, 1867 Second Reform Act, and 1883 Corrupt and Illegal Practices Act, all designed to reduce corrupt payoffs by improving monitoring and increasing punishments. These statutes created an election auditor in each district to record money spent by candidates, established a practice of decisions by independent judges on petitions protesting electoral corruption, increased penalties for bribery to disqualify candidates from holding office for seven years, and introduced candidate liability for bribery practiced by election agents. The statutes prescribed standards for elections and made more salient the illegality of electoral corruption, thereby also playing a role in educating the mass public about what was appropriate.

Other legal changes reduced corrupt payoffs through institutional design, effectively changing the structure of incentives for electoral corruption. The 1872 Ballot Act introduced the secret ballot, which created uncertainty about the return on particular payments for votes. It also made it difficult to judge the closeness of an election until the end and, therefore, difficult to judge whether bribery was a worthwhile investment. While scholars generally agree that the Ballot Act contributed to the decline of electoral corruption, they view it as only one of a number of structural influences. The persistence of widespread vote buying in the 1880 election is widely acknowledged.[19] The 1884 Third Reform Act and 1885 Redistribution of Seats Act reduced corruption by increasing the size of voting districts. Larger voting districts required extensive vote buying for it to be efficient at all, especially with the uncertainty introduced by the secret ballot, but extensive vote buying was also more easily detected—raising the probability of winning the election but losing the seat (as a punishment for corruption).

Finally, quite apart from the educative role of legal change, explicit democratic *education* contributed to the decline of electoral corruption. At mid-century, voters had "no knowledge or concern to know about the platforms of the political parties but troubled themselves only to discover which side would pay the most," but some fifty years later, "the voter began to value his suffrage as a lever of political power rather than as a privilege for picking the candidate's pocket" (Gwyn 1970: 394, 403). By the beginning of the twentieth century, public opinion in England no longer viewed electoral corruption as a benign practice.

Considering the magnitude of change required when corruption is commonplace (and as demonstrated in the above example), policy interventions that reduce corrupt payoffs are likely to take many years to produce clean enough government. In such a setting, modest interventions that target certain sectors for change may be more successful, although success may be unsustainable without continuous attention. The notoriously corrupt Marcos regime in the Philippines targeted its Bureau of Internal Revenue for reform in an effort to stem declining revenues due to collusive tax evasion and outright embezzlement by bureau officials (see Klitgaard 1988). Under new bureau leadership, grossly corrupt officials were dismissed, strict regulations were introduced, work procedures were reorganized, controls were enhanced, and discretionary authority was reduced. Within a few years, impressive results were achieved: Collected revenues notably increased and corruption in the bureau apparently decreased. Yet, these results were quickly reversed after the bureau experienced another change in leadership.

Changing Shared Expectations

Even if anticorruption interventions shift the corrupt payoffs curve downward by a significant amount, the illegality of corruption delays adjustments of choices because of the information problem it poses. What Gunnar Myrdal (1968) refers to as a "folklore of corruption" reflects actual corruption imperfectly, especially in an environment of change. "Bad guesses" about corrupt payoffs and about the corruption rate can persist long after adoption of anticorruption reforms, particularly where corruption is long entrenched. Commonly shared beliefs about the ubiquity of corruption and the unreliability of the government as anticorruption enforcer may be highly exaggerated, but nonetheless affect choices, feeding corrupt practices (Myrdal 1968; LeVine

1975). In India, for example, Philip Oldenburg (1987) found that peasants widely believed the land consolidation administration was thoroughly corrupt—"the most corrupt in the state"—but it was in fact relatively clean. What largely prevented adjustments in beliefs was the role of middlemen, who actively promoted bad guesses. Middlemen assured peasants that massive bribes were necessary to ensure proper procedure in consolidation of landholdings. Peasants paid bribes to the middlemen, who often simply pocketed them, and land consolidation procedure was generally followed. The activity of these middlemen illustrates one way in which "the folklore of corruption can flourish independently of the practice" (Oldenburg 1987: 532–533).

A more recent study (Miller, Grodeland, and Koshechkina 2001) finds the folklore of corruption at work in everyday citizen encounters with street-level officials in four post-communist countries. Indeed, the issue of corruption emerged spontaneously in focus group discussions, not as an initial focus of the research. Focus groups and representative surveys of the mass public reveal broadly shared perceptions of petty corruption everywhere. Yet these beliefs are greatly distorted. Judging from reported personal experiences, bribe offers are not exceptional, but nor are they so routine.[20] Moreover, bribery appears to be mainly a response to officials "making problems" or "asking for gifts." In addition to documenting a sizable gap between beliefs and actions, the study illustrates the "powerful impact of requests and offers" in a setting where many believe that corruption prevails and that government anticorruption efforts are weak or insincere. In this environment, the researchers argue, bribery requires not two "willing" parties, but one—because popular beliefs enhance "the corruptibility of both citizens and officials in the face of extortion or temptation" (Miller, Grodeland, and Koshechkina 2001: 335). In these sorts of circumstances, anticorruption reform should avoid the message that corruption is an overwhelming problem: It merely encourages submission to extortion (for citizens) and temptation (for officials).

These examples illuminate the crucial role of information (and misinformation) in prompting choices to act corruptly (or not). To be sure, if government interventions reduce corrupt payoffs, then, as more and more officials and ordinary citizens choose to test (with actions based on outdated information) the height of the corrupt payoffs curve and the prevalence of corruption, bad guesses should be self-correcting over time. Anticorruption interventions can accelerate this process, through the strategic supply of information. Rather than waiting for players to discover, in the course of experience, new evidence about reduced corrupt payoffs (and punishing those who discover too late), the government can provide information to prevent players from choosing "incorrectly" to transact corruptly. In so doing, it can also reduce costs of anticorruption enforcement.

Imagine, simply for expository purposes, a widely aired government announcement reporting something like the following: government reforms have abruptly shifted the corrupt payoffs curve downward by a very big amount, and players have adjusted choices so that society is newly located well to the left of x (and tipping point B) on the horizontal axis in Figure 1.1. If enough players find the announcement credible, then the outcome will in fact be a sudden shift to clean enough government, generating momentum to fuel the drive toward cleaner government. With a credible announcement that aligns expectations of enough officials and ordinary citizens away from a pernicious folklore of corruption, the government can "coordinate" an equilibrium shift, even if in fact it takes no other action to support it.[21]

Of course, unless corrupt payoffs are in fact reduced, through a boost in enforcement and a restructuring of institutional designs, officials will eventually rediscover the opportunities and incentives that sustain corruption. The point, therefore, is not that clean government can be wished into being, but that interventions aimed at changing expectations can independently accelerate the anticorruption reform process. Certainly, the transformation to clean enough government is not so easy as a self-fulfilling public announcement, but coordinating an equilibrium shift by changing expectations can accomplish the transformation in less time at less cost. More to the point, perhaps, without changes in expectations, the transformation from widespread corruption to clean government is quite literally unimaginable and, by implication, unattainable.

Anticorruption interventions can take advantage of different preferences over clean and corrupt equilibria. The pool of potential supporters of reform is large. For most ordinary citizens, the choice to transact corruptly when opportunities arise (including opportunities to simply respond to extortion), is a choice to do as well as possible—in the setting in which they find themselves and in the knowledge that clean transactions do not change the environment for choice. Although they cannot alone transform the strategic setting, they can assist in anticorruption enforcement by resisting and reporting corrupt initiatives. They may do so if they believe the environment for corruption has changed.

In sum, there are two ways in which a credible announcement can accelerate anticorruption reform. First, it can coordinate expectations about cleaner government and thereby induce choices to transact cleanly (even without changed payoffs). Second, by boosting anticorruption enforcement with reports from ordinary citizens, it can actually reduce corrupt payoffs. Of course, citizen contributions to enforcement are premised on changes in their expectations, here, expectations about the reliability of the government as anticorruption enforcer.

Problems of Implementation

Where corruption is widespread, implementation of anticorruption strategies are also inherently problematic. Consider first the main strategies to reduce corrupt payoffs: enforcement and institutional design.

Enforcement to detect a higher proportion of officials engaging in corrupt practices strains limited resources. Most important, enforcement strategies assume clean enforcers—a rather fantastic assumption when corruption is widespread. This is especially relevant when the enforcement strategy focuses on increasing the probability of detection and punishment. In Argentina, for example, Luis Moreno Ocampo (2000) points out that increasing the likelihood of punishment requires reversing a history of no legal precedent of conviction for bribery, although the law carries a sentence of up to six years for private agents who give or offer gifts to public officials and a similar sentence for officials who receive gifts to do (or not do) something relating to official duties. Focusing on the other component of the calculus by introducing draconian punishments is not necessarily a feasible alternative if many officials are corrupt. Even in China and Vietnam, notable for both high levels of corruption and extreme penalties for corrupt acts, the government can only execute so many.

Institutional design presents a different sort of problem. Restructuring work procedures to reduce incentives and opportunities for corrupt activities must take into account the elemental irrelevance of rules, which practically defines situations of widespread corruption. The problem here is not that some officials are bound to discover loopholes in redesigned procedures and take advantage. Rather, in a setting of widespread corruption, officials do not need to search for loopholes. It is taken for granted that rules, organizations, and procedures pose few obstacles because their practice is quite unimportant. Put differently, institutional design interventions mostly assume that formal institutions matter in guiding actions, but this correspondence is itself an "informal institution." That is, if institutions are the "rules of the game" that constrain the actions of individuals (North 1990; Calvert 1995), then the emergence of the underlying constraining relationship may be preliminary (or at least integral) to any tinkering with design to reduce corrupt payoffs. This problem of weak institutionalization is also pertinent to enforcement strategies that essentially involve new laws, prohibiting certain activities as corrupt acts (which should not be confused with changes in institutional design). It goes without saying that the relevance of rules cannot simply be mandated. To be sure, some institutional design strategies, such as the introduction of competition as a substitute for regulation, do not depend so much rules that matter. These sorts of designs may be better suited to contexts with weak institutions (Broadman and Recanatini 2002).

Policy interventions aimed at changing expectations about corruption are also problematic in a setting of widespread corruption. The government is not a player outside the setting; indeed, its unreliability in anticorruption enforcement is an integral part of the setting. From a principal-agent perspective, widespread corruption suggests, at best, a monitoring failure of massive proportions. At worst, it suggests a tacit acquiescence (or active connivance) of the principal in providing a "public bad." By implication, even where many (or most) in society prefer clean to corrupt equilibria, the crux of anticorruption reform in a setting of widespread corruption is government credibility. Put simply, it is difficult to change expectations when corruption is widespread. It is also undoubtedly more crucial to anticorruption success.

Preview

The chapters ahead are the richer empirical accompaniment to the bare sketch of the problem of anticorruption reform set out in this chapter.

Chapter 2 elaborates on the experience of corruption and anticorruption reform in Hong Kong, a nonincremental "equilibrium shift" from widespread corruption to clean government, coordinated by the British colonial government. Anticorruption success was accomplished through the efforts of the Independent Commission Against Corruption. The ICAC was created in 1974 as the governor's response to public outrage provoked by a high-level corruption scandal in the police force, the department responsible for anticorruption enforcement but widely perceived as the most corrupt of all government departments. The ICAC implemented a three-pronged anticorrruption strategy. Enforcement was facilitated by extraordinary financial resources and draconian powers of investigation. These allowed ICAC investigators to arrest "big tigers" and break corrupt police syndicates. Highly publicized successful prosecutions formed part of a massive public education effort by community liaison officers, who also used the media to propagate the role of the ICAC and mobilize the community to report corruption. Finally, corruption prevention analysts focused on reducing the opportunities for corruption in the work procedures in government departments and the private sector. The chapter documents the success of the ICAC in reducing corrupt activity to low levels fairly rapidly. It also traces, through surveys of the mass public, a "quiet revolution" in Hong Kong society—the disappearance of a folklore of corruption.

Chapter 3 charts an explosion of corruption in mainland China in the early 1980s, its rapid acceleration to an equilibrium of widespread corruption by the mid-1980s, and its continued growth. The chapter presents a taxonomy of the most common and serious forms of corruption in China today: bureaucratic commerce, predatory exactions, corrupt exchanges, use of public funds as private capital, and illegal privatization of state enterprise assets. It finds the sources of these forms of corruption in specific policies of economic reform. The chapter then considers corruption in terms of the different challenges it presents for the Chinese authorities: how forms of corruption that are the most visible, repugnant, and directly costly to ordinary citizens are not the same forms that produce the most serious state revenue losses. The latter constitute the greater economic challenge, but the former have provoked massive social unrest—including the unprecedented protests in Beijing and other cities in 1989, and major peasant riots in the early 1990s. These forms pose the greater political challenge.

Chapter 4 examines routine anticorruption enforcement in China, focusing on criminal corruption. The design of anticorruption enforcement routinely protects corrupt officials from criminal punishment. One problem has to do with the working relationship between the two main anticorruption agencies: communist party discipline inspection committees and government procuratorates. Party agencies are privileged with a "first-move" advantage over procuratorates in information gathering and sequencing of investigations and punishments. In principle, this permits them to check corruption effectively by holding public officials, who are also party members, to a higher ethical standard than that defined in criminal law. In practice, party agencies protect corrupt officials by routinely substituting milder party disciplinary action for criminal punishment. The main source of this problem appears to be the relationship between the specialist anticorruption agencies and the generalist communist party committees. A second problem inheres in the legal system itself. The slow development of legal standards defining corrupt acts contrasts with the rapid changes in the Chinese political economy, offering opportunities for corruption in forms unimaginable in 1979, when China adopted its first criminal code. Quite apart from this is a problem in legal practice: Procuratorates regularly extend leniency, in exemptions from prosecution, to officials whose crimes of corruption they do investigate. These problems of routine anticorruption enforcement are evident to ordinary Chinese, prompting a widespread cynicism about the reliability (and sincerity) of the authorities as enforcers, exacerbating problems of regime legitimacy that emerge from everyday encounters with corrupt officials.

Chapter 5 describes the main response of Chinese leaders to problems of routine anticorruption enforcement: episodic campaigns. Anticorruption campaigns are short bursts of intensive enforcement set in motion by top leaders to disrupt routines. Campaigns increase demands on communist party committees to boost anticorruption criminal enforcement and escalate anticorruption publicity, including urging ordinary citizens to report corruption and corrupt officials to confess their crimes. Campaigns in 1982, 1986, and 1989 were launched to reduce the volume of corruption overall; campaigns in 1993 and 1995 focused on particularly salient cases of corruption, involving big sums or senior officials. The campaigns produced measurable, often spectacular, short-term results in "enforcement peaks" and "report peaks." Enforcement peaks are above-average numbers of criminal corruption cases that procuratorates file and investigate during campaigns. Report peaks are above-average numbers of corruption reports that ordinary citizens file during campaigns. Between campaigns, however, reports of corruption declined.

Mainland Chinese leaders have chosen to primarily focus their anticorruption effort on reducing corrupt payoffs with enforcement. With laws and other rules, they have increased the severity of punishments for corrupt activities; with campaigns, leaders have increased the likelihood that corrupt officials are discovered and punished. Yet neither campaigns nor routine enforcement appear to have deterred corruption very effectively.[22] Corruption continues to grow, and more than 50 percent of cases investigated in any year are crimes committed in that year—even in 1990, the year after the biggest anticorruption campaign in the post-Mao era. Ordinary Chinese view the anticorruption effort as ineffective. Many believe the vast majority of Chinese officials are thoroughly corrupt, a view that is surely exaggerated and also part of the folklore that coordinates choices of ordinary Chinese and corrupt officials in usual times. In short, leaders have failed to change beliefs about either the high volume of corruption or their reliability as anti-corruption enforcers.

An expression sometimes attributed to veteran revolutionary Chen Yun summarizes anticorruption reform as a dilemma for the communist party: "Fight corruption too little and destroy the country; fight it too much and destroy the party." Chapters 3, 4, and 5 demonstrate that the Leninist party design that frustrates effective corruption control is but one institutional barrier to the emergence of clean government in mainland China. Chapter 6 concludes with a reflection on the choices that explain much of Hong Kong's successful transformation and a consideration of institutional designs for clean government. The chapter asks what generalizable lessons, if any, does the Hong Kong experience offer for mainland China and other countries mired in corruption? Three notions of institutional design are drawn from the empirical accounts in Chapters 2 through 5. They highlight crucial differences between the Hong Kong and mainland Chinese anticorruption experiences—namely, the organization of *agencies* established to combat corruption, the attention to *incentive structures* that facilitate corrupt practices, and not least of all the underlying *constitutional design,* especially the rule of law and civil liberties that survive even today in the special administrative region of Hong Kong.

CHAPTER TWO

Corruption and Anticorruption
Reform in Hong Kong

Qualitative accounts suggest that corruption in Hong Kong in the 1960s was as common as that found in mainland China today. In contrast to mainland China, however, modern-day Hong Kong offers an example of a successful government-coordinated "equilibrium switch" from widespread corruption to clean government. Basically, this success was achieved through the efforts of the Independent Commission Against Corruption (ICAC), created in 1974.

The Hong Kong experience is interesting because it is a story of big changes, with fairly clear causal connections between anticorruption interventions and outcomes. It is even more interesting because the changes were abrupt. Chapter 1 set out a logic of widespread corruption and clean government as equilibria and suggested a possibility of non-incremental equilibrium switches. Hong Kong illustrates this possibility empirically. Corruption in Hong Kong was reduced by means of a three-pronged strategy: enforcement to investigate corruption and prosecute the corrupt, education to mobilize ordinary citizens to report corruption and increase psychic costs of corrupt activities, and institutional design to reduce opportunities for corruption in the organization of work.

Corruption and anticorruption reform in Hong Kong are of obvious interest, then, both practically and in light of the general discussion in Chapter 1. In addition, an unusual data set recommends the Hong Kong experience for study. Of major importance to this chapter are findings from 19 essentially unexploited surveys of the Hong Kong mass public, conducted regularly for the ICAC beginning in 1977.[1] The surveys provide a rare empirical basis for studying changes, over time, in characteristic expectations of ordinary citizens about corruption, that is, change in the "folklore of corruption" in Hong Kong.[2] Quite apart from whatever relevance beliefs about the scope of corruption may have in estimating actual corruption, these beliefs are of intrinsic interest as inputs that help or hinder anticorruption efforts. As described in Chapter 1, they both reflect and sustain equilibria of widespread corruption and clean government.

The chapter begins with a description of widespread corruption in Hong Kong before the mid-1970s, followed by a brief discussion of the events that produced the ICAC in 1974. Most of the chapter is about anticorruption interventions and their impact in the period 1974–2002. To preview, the evidence suggests that the ICAC had reduced corruption to fairly low levels and substantially transformed a folklore of corruption by the mid-1980s or somewhat earlier. Sometime around 1993, however, corruption grew quite rapidly. Beliefs of ordinary citizens about the scope of corruption changed accordingly, although public confidence in the ICAC did not diminish significantly. The erosion reversed itself after the transfer of sovereignty of Hong Kong from Britain to mainland China in 1997. ICAC anticorruption efforts in the 1990s did not change in ways that make sense of these patterns. The last section of the chapter explains the anomalous return of corruption in the 1990s and the subsequent recovery, mainly by taking into account the changing context of anticorruption work. The influence of mainland China, both direct and indirect, is a crucial part of the explanation.

An Equilibrium of Widespread Corruption

While quantitative measures comparable to those available for later periods are lacking, there can be little doubt that widespread corruption and a folklore of corruption characterized Hong Kong in the 1960s—and perhaps as early as a century before then. For example, H. J. Lethbridge (1985: 24, 51) begins and concludes his survey of corruption in Hong Kong from 1842 through 1941 with the comment that corruption was "a customary habit known to all," infecting the middle and lower levels of all government departments that provided any opportunity for its occurrence. E. J. Eitel (1983: 337–338) and Geoffrey Sayer (1975: 23) agree that, at least as early as the 1850s, routine police corruption flourished. A particularly remarkable case of police corruption was discovered in 1897, involving regular payments to protect gambling houses in a network including Chinese and non-Chinese officers junior to senior in rank. Investigation resulted in the dismissal of about half the police force (see Lethbridge 1985: 30–36). Other cases of flagrant regularized corruption investigated by the authorities include corruption in the Public Works Department in 1902 and the Immigration Department in 1941. Corruption evidently did not diminish with the occupation of Hong Kong in 1941. The Japanese administration was intensely bureaucratic, and ordinary citizens engaged in routine bribery of officials to avoid interference in daily life (Endacott 1978: 136–137, 152–153).

By all accounts, corruption in Hong Kong increased in the 1950s and 1960s (see especially Lethbridge 1974). Political change outside Hong Kong seems to have been a main cause. The population grew from 840,500, recorded in the 1931 census, to an estimated two million by the end of 1950, and nearly a quarter of the increase came after 1947, largely due to the influx of mainland Chinese refugees fleeing first the civil war and then the consolidation of communist rule. By the end of 1960, the population of Hong Kong had increased to more than three million, by 1971 to nearly four million. The doubling of the population in twenty years put intense pressure on scarce resources and on the government. Beginning in the 1950s, government regulation and intervention to provide basic social services expanded. Officials pursued new opportunities for "payment for convenience" (see Faure 1981), especially in areas of government monopoly (for example, the distribution of public housing) and the enforcement of standards (for example, for public construction projects). The embargo on strategic goods to mainland China during the Korean War of the 1950s also created lucrative opportunities for entrepreneurs in the private sector and customs officials in Hong Kong to connect with mainland Chinese officials in "a great increase in smuggling . . . and the bribery of revenue officials" (Grantham 1965: 121).

"The whole of Hong Kong operates on a commission basis." So concluded Justice Alastair Blair-Kerr, surveying the island's situation in 1973 for the governor (1973b: 23). Yet, with few exceptions, leading officials, including the governor, trivialized the problem. "The Fixers," published in the *Far Eastern Economic Review* (Goodstadt 1970a), was an early attempt to alert the expatriate community to a potential crisis. It described different forms of corruption in more than a half-dozen government departments (see also Baird 1970; Goodstadt 1970b) and presented corruption as a grave challenge to the presumption of legitimacy based on "good government."[3] Accounts agreed that corruption was particularly serious in the police force.

Police corruption typically took the form of "syndicated corruption," in which a number of officers join together to extort money for abstaining from mandatory duties (Cater 1977; Cheung and Lau 1981; Peter Lee 1981).[4] Syndicated police corruption was localized, situated within Hong Kong's 16 territorial divisions or sub-divisions. The syndicates thrived on regularized protection of illegal businesses (such as gambling houses and illegal drug houses) and harassment of ordinary citizens (for example, professional drivers found guilty of a real or invented traffic infraction). The relatively greater scope of police corruption, compared to other departments, is evident even in the presumably biased (by sector-specific underreporting) figures on reported corruption—reported, that is, to the anticorruption agency within the police force itself (see discussion below). From 1952–1953 (the first year for which such figures are available) through 1972–1973, reports of police corruption in most years (and on average for the entire period) exceeded reports of corruption in all other government departments combined (Royal Hong Kong Police Force 1953–1973).[5]

In the Hong Kong of the 1960s, mass public beliefs about corruption can be fairly encapsulated in expressions popular at the time. Realistically, ordinary Chinese had two choices: "Get on the bus" (actively participate in corruption) or "run alongside the bus" (be a bystander, but not interfere with corruption). Under no circumstances was it practical to "stand in front of the bus" (report or resist corruption) because the bus would surely knock them flat (Cater 1995; Blair-Kerr 1973b: 24).

In the view of many ordinary Chinese, then, it was "futile and unwise, and perhaps even dangerous" to challenge or query government officials:

Many people may not like to pay squeeze but they are even more frightened of *mafan* (trouble). . . . They firmly believe that reporting a corrupt officer will result in reprisals. Even if the corrupt officer is dealt with, the informer's business or application may get on to some black list whereby other members of the same department will seize each and every excuse to prosecute him. It is believed that unless someone intends to wind up his business, it is very unwise to try to fight the corrupt official because usually a syndicate exists. They do not believe that it is useful to report this to some senior officers, because some clever explanation can always be given to justify the officer's course of action. (Blair-Kerr 1973b: 21–22)

The notion that corruption was pervasive may have derived in part from past experience. Most middle-aged and elderly Hong Kong Chinese had lived on the mainland under a regime riddled with corruption. Lethbridge (1985: 14) notes: "They arrived with cultural expectations about how officials were likely to act, and react; they had their own folklore of officialdom." Blair-Kerr (1973b: 20) quotes a Hong Kong Chinese on the effect of deep-rooted impressions of a regime rotting with corruption: "These immigrants believe, without too much critical examination, that many Hong Kong Government officers, like the Chinese officials they knew, may also be corrupt. This belief in itself breeds corruption because it leads to voluntary bribery by people who consider it normal practice in dealing with Governments."

A poor grasp of the (literally) alien language of officialdom and unfamiliarity with rules of evidence and procedure in criminal proceedings exacerbated the problem.[6] Blair-Kerr (1973b: 27) notes: "What members of the public see is a number of corrupt officers retained in the public service. They conclude that Government is unwilling to bring them to trial, unwilling to dismiss them, unwilling to retire them compulsorily; and the public concludes that Government connives at, indeed approves of, corruption in the public service."

Anticorruption Efforts before 1974

A clear obstacle to a credible anticorruption effort was structural. The agency charged with fighting corruption was precisely the one widely perceived (accurately, it seems) as the most corrupt of government departments. The Anti-Corruption Office (ACO), created in 1952, was a specialized unit of the police force for the investigation of bribery and corruption cases. The arrangement was an acknowledged problem. Separation of the ACO from the police force was periodically studied by officials and organizations overseeing the anticorruption effort. As early as 1961, for example, the Advisory Committee on Corruption reported:

There was a strong feeling . . . that the Anti-Corruption Branch should not be a part of the Police Force. . . . The public are reluctant to complain to the Police of whom they are afraid. . . . While there is evidence that in recent years the public have become more willing to approach the police with general problems or complaints, we feel that, partly through fear and

> partly because the police themselves are felt to be corrupt, there still exists in the minds of the public a definite reluctance to become involved with the police in relation to complaints of corruption. (1961: 59)

The Committee nonetheless "reluctantly" advised against separation, seeing little advantage in a civilian organization.

In the early 1970s there was renewed support for separation of the ACO from the police force. ACO leaders countered criticism by arguing that they had not been given sufficient time to prove themselves with their new legal weapon, the 1971 Prevention of Bribery Ordinance, modeled in part on anticorruption laws in Singapore, Malaysia, and Ceylon (Sri Lanka). The new law gave expanded powers of investigation to the ACO and introduced a provision defining "possession of unexplained income or property" as an offense. Barring a "satisfactory explanation," public officials who maintained a standard of living above that commensurate with their present or past official earnings or who controlled funds or property disproportionate to those earnings were to be considered guilty of corruption (Prevention of Bribery Ordinance 1971, Sec. 10). The new provision effectively put the onus of proof on the suspect.[7]

A compromise was reached on structural arrangements: the ACO would be reviewed after the Prevention of Bribery Ordinance had been in effect for three years.

The Godber Incident

Peter Godber cheated the ACO of its chance to prove itself. The Godber incident was the catalyst that ultimately produced the ICAC.[8] Godber had been a member of the police force in Hong Kong since 1952. By 1973 he had attained a position of considerable seniority as second in command in the Kowloon district. For many years he had routinely accepted payments from station sergeants below him, the chief organizers of syndicated police corruption. Most of his corrupt gains were hoarded for his retirement, due to begin in July 1973.

In late April 1973, a routine query from a Canadian bank about the lack of activity in Godber's account came to the attention of the police commissioner, essentially because Godber had misrepresented his official position to the bank (Cater 1995). Now aware of the information that Godber had remitted large sums of money abroad, the commissioner initiated an investigation by the ACO. By the end of May, in response to a warrant requiring nearly 500 banks in Hong Kong and abroad to submit to an investigating officer all accounts, books, or documents relating to Godber, the ACO had ascertained that an amount greatly exceeding his total net salary since 1952 had passed through Godber's hands. In consultation with the acting attorney general, the ACO decided to initiate proceedings against Godber. Although Godber lived relatively frugally, he was clearly "in control of pecuniary resources or property disproportionate to his present or past official emoluments," an offense (barring a satisfactory explanation) under the Prevention of Bribery Ordinance.

The ordinance required the ACO to obtain the consent of the attorney general in order to initiate a prosecution. The ordinance also required the attorney general, before consenting, to notify the suspect that a prosecution for the offense described was under consideration and to provide him reasonable opportunity to offer an explanation in writing. Accordingly, notice from the acting attorney general was served on 4 June. It granted Godber a week to make representations. On the same day, ACO officers searched Godber's residence, where they discovered and seized evidence of financial resources exceeding HK $4 million (about US $780,000). Godber was not put under surveillance, but immigration staff at the airport were instructed to stop and detain him if he attempted to leave Hong Kong.

Godber left Hong Kong by air on 8 June, probably without passing through Immigration Control. He was in London, his wealth intact, the next day—safe from extradition for an offense that did not exist in British law.

The story of corruption and escape was widely reported in the mass media. Within a short time, Godber was notorious in Hong Kong, his name a symbol of police corruption and government impotence or, worse yet, government complacency. Students launched a protest campaign and petitioned the British prime minister to return Godber to face trial. An editorial in the *Hong Kong Law Journal* summarized public reaction: "The ordinary man in the Hong Kong street quite fairly thinks it monstrous that a senior British official should be able to commit a serious criminal offence in the Colony and then be permitted to enjoy his ill-gotten wealth in Britain, safe under the protection of British law" ("Godber" 1973: 249). To be sure, street protests against the government in 1973 were nothing comparable to the antigovernment riots of 1966 or 1967—this owed much to the governor's swift response. There is little doubt that the governor would not have been as responsive in a context that did not prominently include the riots of the 1960s. Ian Scott (1989: 81, 82) refers to these as the "watershed in Hong Kong's political history," exposing the impossibility of being both unrepresentative and unresponsive to social demands and making it absolutely clear to the colonial government that "a new political order and a new basis for legitimacy were urgent requirements."

Anticorruption Reform and Its Immediate Impact

Responding to the Godber incident and public reaction, Governor Murray MacLehose acknowledged endemic corruption in Hong Kong for the first time and conceded his failure to appreciate its seriousness. In a highly publicized address to the Legislative Council (*Hong Kong Hansard* 1973–74: 15–17), he noted that he had previously been aware of "suspicions of high level graft as well as of a certainty of extensive low level corruption," but that Godber's escape had awakened him to the new realization that "suspicion of corruption on a more extensive scale" was better grounded than he had personally imagined, that "outside the public service it is a widespread social problem, and inside it corruption exists in several departments of which the police is only one." The media recorded this change in position.[9] The admission was described as "the frankest commentary on this issue ever heard by the legislature from a Hong Kong Governor" (Goodstadt 1973: 20).

So long as ordinary citizens lacked confidence in the integrity of the ACO, the arguments about whether or not the organization was in fact capable of impartial and vigorous investigation and prosecution were immaterial. The governor took this issue of public confidence seriously. He accepted that an effective anticorruption effort would require active cooperation of the community. He recognized that cooperation would not be forthcoming without a fundamental change in the arrangements governing anticorruption work. "Grave situations call for unusual measures," the governor explained, citing public confidence as a "conclusive argument" for separating anticorruption work from the police. "Clearly the public would have more confidence in a unit that was entirely independent, and separate from any department of the Government, including the police" (*Hong Kong Hansard* 1973–74: 17). Blair-Kerr (1973b: 51), quoting others, characterized the argument as the "political and psychological" rationale for taking anticorruption responsibilities away from the police.

The unusual features of the new arrangements communicated the anticorruption commitment. The Independent Commission Against Corruption Ordinance (1974) established an organization (ICAC) that was not only separate from the police force, but also unique in its administrative status as the only government department accountable solely to the governor. Its commissioner is appointed by the governor, reports directly to the governor, and is empowered to appoint (and remove) subordinate officers. The ICAC is not part of the civil service. ICAC officers undergo more stringent security checks, are subject to stricter disciplinary standards, and enjoy salaries higher than civil servants in positions of comparable rank. Governor MacLehose appointed Jack Cater as the first ICAC commissioner. Cater had served in the Hong Kong civil service for nearly 30 years (never on the police force), and he was known for his moral integrity.

The actions sent an unambiguous signal to ordinary citizens that "the authorities mean business" (Davies 1973: 28). The change was structural, aimed at better enforcement, but it was also designed to challenge views of the government as indifferent. The immediate impact on beliefs cannot be examined directly, as surveys measuring those beliefs were not conducted in Hong Kong until years later (beginning in 1977). There is, however, powerful indirect evidence of a sudden, large shift in mass public beliefs about anticorruption enforcement: figures on reported corruption. The figures suggest enormous public confidence in the ICAC (compared to the ACO) as an anticorruption organization. Another section below discusses various indicators of changing beliefs about corruption over the longer term. Here, the focus is only on a couple of figures to make a simple point: The figures on reported corruption in 1973 and 1974 reflect differences in public confidence in the ACO and the ICAC. These differences show up immediately, even before the ICAC began to distinguish itself in actual anticorruption work.

In 1973, a total of *1,457 reports* of corruption were registered with the ACO, a number not very different from the previous few years. In 1974, reports of corruption registered with the newly created ICAC were more than double that number, at *3,189 reports*.[10]

Figures for the last year of the ACO's existence are not unusually low, compared to previous years.[11] In fact, by comparison with previous years, the early 1970s are relatively successful for police anticorruption work, and reports in 1973 were high for the ACO. Organizational and legal changes significantly reduced opportunities for police corruption and improved conditions for anticorruption work generally (Blair-Kerr

1973b; Kuan 1981; Wong 1981). Additionally, it is worth noting that ICAC figures for 1974 are not simply a one-time outpouring of past grievances or recovery from a lapse in anticorruption work due to public disaffection with the ACO as a result of the Godber incident. As discussed in another section below, reports of corruption were similarly high in 1975.

Obviously, increases or decreases in reported corruption can reflect many things: changing incidence of corruption, changing forms of corruption, changing public awareness of laws on corruption, and the impact of discrete events, for example. Figures on reported corruption in 1973 and 1974 are useful as indirect indicators of changing beliefs about anticorruption enforcement because competing explanations for the huge increase registered in 1974 are simply less plausible, in light of the most relevant salient event that separates the two periods: a commitment to eliminating widespread corruption, signaled most effectively by the creation of the ICAC. With this action, the government transformed the environment in which ordinary citizens (and public officials) considered their choices involving corrupt practices. The creation of the ICAC "announced" an equilibrium switch, from widespread corruption to clean government.

Anticorruption Interventions: A Three-Pronged Strategy

In his address to the Legislative Council in 1973, Governor MacLehose defined the condition for success in anticorruption as nothing short of "a quiet revolution in our society" (ICAC 1975: 17). To achieve success, the ICAC developed a three-pronged strategy, reflected in its internal structure. Enforcement to detect and investigate corruption and bring about successful prosecution of the corrupt is implemented by the Operations Department.[12] Public education to propagate the role of the ICAC, spread knowledge of anticorruption laws, mobilize ordinary citizens to cooperate by reporting corruption, and increase the psychic costs of corrupt activities is implemented by the Community Relations Department. Institutional design to reduce opportunities for corruption presented in the organization of government work (and in the private sector) is implemented by the Corruption Prevention Department.[13] Put another way, the Corruption Prevention Department works on "rendering [corruption] difficult," the Community Relations Department works to "create and sustain a general social climate in which corruption is condemned," and the Operations Department works on "making it [corruption] a high-risk crime" (ICAC 1981: 56).

Despite its political significance and (as shown below) actual impact, the ICAC began as (and has remained) a small department relative to others in the Hong Kong government. Its authorized staff size was about 1,100 in 1980, 1,200 in 1990, and 1,300 in 2000.[14] It has, however, fairly consistently been given budgetary resources that reflect strong governmental support for its activities.

In terms of both authorized and actual size, the Operations Department is (not surprisingly, considering its investigative role) by far the largest of the three departments. On average, its officers have accounted for nearly three-fourths of ICAC officers, with rather higher proportions beginning in the mid-1990s.[15] Indeed, since about 1978, the growth of the ICAC has essentially been growth of the Operations Department, from 600 in 1980 (with more than 500 investigators), to nearly 800 in 1990 (with nearly 650 investigators), to nearly 950 in 2000 (with nearly 800 investigators). This is a huge investigative force. Consider, for comparison, that the Department of Investigation for New York City, which performs the same anticorruption functions (although only for the public sector) had a force of 174 investigators in 2000 (Ellenberg 2000).

The Community Relations Department, the only ICAC department continuously staffed entirely by Hong Kong Chinese, has accounted for about one-fifth of ICAC officers on average. It grew from just over 200 officers in 1980, to nearly 250 in 1990, and by 2000 had returned to its 1980 size. Overall, in terms of size, the relative dominance of the Operations Department, with its basic investigative functions, is less surprising than the large size of the Community Relations Department. This is a concrete sign of the government commitment to public education, not only conventional enforcement, as a policy instrument in anticorruption reform.

The Corruption Prevention Department is the smallest of the three departments, accounting on average for about 7 percent of ICAC officers over the years and stabilizing at fewer than 60 officers since about the mid-1980s. Corruption prevention work was unique in its concept at the time the ICAC was established and, as a consequence, initially least well understood. ICAC Commissioner Cater remarked on this particular lack at the outset: "There is no bank of previous experience to consult or to rely upon for guidance and advice" (ICAC 1976: 4). As the pattern of its work developed in the late 1970s, the department shrank and stabilized in size.

Neither public education nor institutional design was the top ICAC priority in the mid-1970s, however. The Operations Department came first, the Corruption Prevention Department second, and the Community Relations Department last.[16] This reflected a realistic appraisal of both the scope of corruption and the state of public opinion at the time. The ICAC commissioner argued that the momentum of initial community support for the ICAC, reflected in the massive increase in reported corruption, could best be maintained by bringing to justice a "satisfactory volume" of corrupt offenders (ICAC 1975: 22). Prominent early success in enforcement was viewed as key to maintaining anticorruption momentum because it was required to transform the belief (of corrupt officials and ordinary citizens) that widespread corruption was an unchangeable feature in Hong Kong government and society. Through enforcement success, the ICAC sought to demonstrate to ordinary citizens that the government was not complacent about corruption. Rather, it was on their side. Cater explained the strategic function of enforcement as follows: "It was vital to establish a real deterrent quickly, a force capable of striking fear into the hearts of the corrupt in our society. This achieved, and with a Commission credibility established, then it would be possible to undertake the more positive areas of our work—corruption prevention and public education" (ICAC 1976: 1).

Enforcement

Apart from the Independent Commission Against Corruption Ordinance, which established the powers of the ICAC, the main legal basis for an ICAC Operations Department investigation is the Prevention of Bribery Ordinance, discussed briefly earlier. A third basis for ICAC action was the Corrupt and Illegal Practices Ordinance (10 June 1955), which applied to illegal activities during elections. It was superceded by the Elections (Corrupt and Illegal Conduct) Ordinance (24 Feb. 2000).[17]

Most enforcement powers of the ICAC derive from the Prevention of Bribery Ordinance. The definition of corruption in this law includes some activities in the private sector, involving no government officials. Specifically, Section 9 of the law, on "corrupt transactions with agents," considers as corruption any offer, solicitation, or acceptance of an "advantage" to induce or reward action (or inaction) or favor (or disfavor) relating to a principal's business, except when the principal gives permission to the agent to solicit or accept the advantage. This form of corruption, where neither principal nor agent are in the public sector, is beyond the scope of criminal activities considered in this book. The other legal categories of corruption, which are of relevance here, are: (1) offering an advantage to a public servant, (2) soliciting or accepting (by a public servant) an advantage, and (3) possession (by a public servant) of unexplained property, the offense under Section 10, described above.[18] The law is quite clear about the meaning of the term "advantage" (Prevention of Bribery Ordinance 14 May 1971, Sec. 1).[19] It explicitly defines *bribery* as offering an advantage in a variety of circumstances, such as for assistance with contracts, for procuring withdrawal of tenders, and in relation to auctions (Secs. 4–7), and it rules out a defense that an advantage is "customary" (Sec. 19).

The law gives the ICAC extraordinary powers. Its investigators have full powers of arrest without warrant for all offenses described in the three ordinances noted above. A 1987 amendment to the Prevention of Bribery Ordinance expanded these powers: If, in the course of investigating any offenses under this law, investigators discover any other criminal offense reasonably suspected of being connected with the bribery offense, they have full powers of arrest without warrant for this related offense too. Investigators have powers of search, seizure, and detention of anything believed to be evidence of offenses for which they have powers of arrest. They have special powers of investigation—for example, to examine bank accounts, to question people under oath, and to restrict the disposal of property during an investigation. ICAC investigators may carry firearms in situations considered dangerous. The ICAC has its own detention facilities.

In 1994, as a result of widely aired and highly damaging allegations by Alex Tsui Ka-kit, who was dismissed from the ICAC, an independent review board was appointed to examine ICAC powers.[20] The recommendations adopted as a result of this review did not diminish ICAC enforcement powers, but they did introduce greater judicial supervision of the exercise of powers and encourage greater ICAC restraint and cooperation with other agencies in pursuing noncorruption related matters (*Report of the ICAC Review Committee* 1994). This was part of a broad effort spearheaded by legislators to improve accountability and transparency as the transfer of sovereignty approached.

In 1974 and 1975, the Operations Department lacked both the resources for sophisticated investigations and the expertise required for these sorts of investigations. Although the department borrowed some officers from the ACO and recruited others from Britain, it attached great importance to recruiting and training its own. Even in its first year of operation, about 80 percent of officers in the department had a civilian background (ICAC 1975, Appendix 6). The dearth of experienced investigators dictated an initial reactive strategy—the department mostly scrambled to respond to public reports of corruption and did not take the offensive for about two years. An important exception was the priority attached to "major personality" cases—the "big tigers" whose swift well-publicized prosecution was viewed as essential to gain public confidence. The extradition of Godber to face trial was a particularly high priority. This was achieved within a year, and the trial itself was dramatic and very highly publicized. Lethbridge (1985: 112–115) describes it as a "show trial."[21]

At the end of 1975, with more than 400 officers, many of them with significant investigative experience, the Operations Department was able to take the initiative. Cater committed the department "to break the back of organized syndicated corruption within the next year or two" (ICAC 1976: 1). Syndicated corruption was an obvious target because of public outrage about corrupt police syndicates, and also because it is less difficult to investigate than some other forms of corruption. Corruption of the "satisfied customer" form, for example, usually involves only two parties, neither with any incentive to report to authorities. A syndicate, by contrast, is frequently very large, with an organizational identity of its own, although membership may change over time. ICAC investigators sought out the weak links in the chain and offered reduced punishment in return for trial evidence against other syndicate members. In the mid-1970s, practically every police division in the territory had at least one syndicate in operation (ICAC 1977: 2). This changed quickly. In May 1976, the entire middle management of the Wanchai police division was under investigation and had been (at least briefly) arrested and interrogated by the ICAC. In October 1977, the ICAC arrested 140 officers from three Kowloon police divisions for alleged involvement in syndicated corruption. In that same month, ICAC investigators detained 24 police officers, including three British superintendents. Altogether, in 1974–77 the ICAC prosecuted 269 police officers on corruption charges, more than four times the number prosecuted in the four years prior to the organization's creation (Royal Hong Kong Police Force 1970–73; ICAC 1975–78). In mid-1977, Cater reported to the Governor that "no major syndicates were known to exist" (ICAC 1978: 1).

The successful offensive against police corruption set in motion what Cater describes as "shameful and degrading events" (ICAC 1978: 1), the resolution of which raised doubts about the government commitment to anticorruption. During the last week of October 1977, the mental strain and low morale of thousands of rank-and-file police officers due to "oppressive tactics against police officers" escalated from petitions to their commissioner to represent them (to the government against the ICAC), to demonstrations and marches, to a forced entry into ICAC headquarters and a scuffle with officers there, and finally to the call for a police strike. The governor responded immediately to the threat of strike by declaring a "partial amnesty": the ICAC would not normally act on complaints or evidence relating to corruption offenses committed before 1 January 1977.[22] The amnesty was a major victory for the police, and it was widely portrayed as such in the Hong Kong media. As the government's response to an aggressive and very public police challenge, the amnesty was devastating to the prestige of the ICAC and to the morale of its officers. Fearing a strike, the governor had sided with the police against the ICAC.[23]

Certainly, the amnesty dampened public confidence in the anticorruption effort. The community did not support the measure,[24] and reports of police corruption declined immediately due to a revival of concern about the dangers of reporting such abuses.[25] Reporting on the ICAC's work in 1978, Cater's successor noted frankly: "During the year there was a good deal of public concern about the possibility that the Commission was likely to be wound up" (ICAC 1979: 9). As a practical matter, however, the governor had delivered, with a single directive, a big one-time reduction in caseload for the Operations Department. The amnesty relieved ICAC investigators from many lengthy, costly, and difficult investigations into past offenses, allowing the organization to focus its resources on more recent offenses.[26] ICAC investigators could attack ongoing corruption with greater proportionate force, a result by no means undesirable for anticorruption work. The amnesty produced a second desirable practical result: Without the fear of investigation and prosecution for past activities, an increasing number of officials showed a new willingness to assist ICAC investigators (ICAC 1979: 24).

In sum, while the amnesty was obviously a blow to the ICAC, its practical results—more cooperation in investigations and effectively more resources—gave the Operations Department a new start and allowed it to shift direction. The department was able to focus on corruption of the "satisfied customer" type, for example, which involved painstaking collection of intelligence and protracted investigations that often required significant resources. The department had formed an intelligence group in 1977, and in 1978 it added surveillance and bank enquiries groups. It also developed an early-warning system, "external monitoring," as an important part of enforcement work. External monitoring sought to detect signs of revival of corrupt activity in areas where corruption was once known to be prevalent. It involved routine investigation of these areas, unprompted by current corruption reports. Full-scale investigations were launched in the event that routine investigation turned up anything suspicious. The public sector remained the main focus of enforcement work in the late 1970s and early 1980s.

Beginning around the mid-1980s, however, the response to greatly increased reported corruption in the private sector consumed massive amounts of Operations Department resources. Private sector corruption, such as cases of fraud facilitated by corruption in banking and finance, accounted for about one-third of the department's investigative resources in 1986 and about one-half in 1989 (ICAC 1987: 16; ICAC 1990: 23). One reason for this growth was that the cases tended to be more complex than corruption cases in government departments. They demanded more investigative time and substantial technical support, overseas inquiries, and assistance from local accountants. They generally took more than a year to investigate. This had an impact on the "more mundane investigations" of interest here—public sector corruption (ICAC 1991: 19–21).

In 1994, the ICAC reasserted the public sector as its first priority in enforcement. The Operations Department introduced in the 1990s a number of new procedures to ensure that public sector corruption received appropriate attention, even as private sector corruption continued to demand huge investigative resources. This was partly a response to a surprising new surge of corruption, including the reemergence of organized corruption in the police force (ICAC 1995: 10). It was also undoubtedly a response to criticism that the ICAC was using too much of its resources on investigations of crimes only marginally related to corruption, crimes more appropriately transferred to the police Commercial Crime Bureau, for example (*Report of the ICAC Review Committee* 1994: 39–43).[27]

The procedures introduced in the 1990s all involved greater liaison and coordination, either within the ICAC or with outside agencies. In 1994, the Operations Department formed a "quick response team" of eight investigators (later expanded) to handle minor cases. Quick response was facilitated by greater coordination with the Community Relations Department and the reallocation of some responsibilities in minor corruption cases. Community Relations Department officers at regional ICAC offices were trained to conduct initial interviews with complainants on behalf of the Operations Department. If the initial interviews suggest corruption, the file is referred to an Operations Department investigating team. This was key to the quick response by the Operations Department team, and it allowed the ICAC to honor a pledge to address complaints within 48 hours. In 1996, the Operations Department adopted a "pro-active strategy" to identify areas of potential corruption at an early stage, implemented through greater cooperation with other government departments and regulatory bodies such as the Securities and Futures Commission and the Hong Kong Monetary Authority. In 1997, cooperation with other departments was taken a step further: The Operations Department cultivated a new partnership with other law enforcement agencies, government departments, and regulatory bodies to share responsibilities in anticorruption. In that same year, the ICAC adopted a more coordinated anticorruption approach within its own organization. It formed 19 work groups with officers in all three departments to facilitate exchange of information and to deploy knowledge and expertise in specific areas more effectively. The Operations Department continues to take main responsibility for detecting corruption. Except in cases where ongoing investigation might be compromised, investigators coordinate their work with the Corruption Prevention Department, which moves in quickly to identify and remove procedural weaknesses that facilitated corruption. The Community Relations Department then steps in to conduct relevant education. Often the Corruption Prevention Department and the Community Relations Department draw up a joint corruption prevention program that includes training talks and seminars as well as practical guides to advise on prevention and compilation of codes of conduct.

Education

From the outset, the governor recognized that the success of the anticorruption effort could not rely on enforcement and prevention alone. The Independent Commission Against Corruption Ordinance (1974, Sec. 12) charges the commissioner to "educate the public against the evils of corruption" and "enlist and foster public support" in fighting corruption. Broadly, this defines the role of the Community Relations Department. The commissioner understood the special importance of staffing this department with local Chinese and recruiting for its specialist positions (such as press officers) local Chinese who had already made an impact in some form of community work.[28] The commissioner summarized the role of the department in 1977 as "a vast exercise in public education, or re-education" and acknowledged that the exercise would be "a long-term business" (ICAC 1977: 7). Essentially, public education involves four major, closely related responsibilities: (1) to propagate widely the role of the ICAC and its reliability as an anticorruption agency; (2) to educate the Hong Kong community about the legal concept of corruption; (3) to mobilize ordinary citizens and officials to cooperate in enforcement, mainly by reporting corruption to the ICAC; and (4) to increase the psychic costs and social disapproval of corrupt activities. The responsibilities entailed in public education, especially in the early 1970s but also in later years, clearly illustrate the interdependence of enforcement, education, and institutional design in ICAC anticorruption work.

Initially, the first responsibility was the most urgent. Besides the fact that the ICAC was a completely new organization in 1974, there was also a widely shared view in the community that the police ACO was at best incapable of controlling the rampant corruption in Hong Kong and at worst flourishing in active partnership with the corrupt. In 1974, the ICAC had the goodwill of ordinary citizens, as shown by the huge increase in reported corruption in 1974, in no small part because it was independent of the police. To maintain goodwill, it had to measure up, in its actions, to the high public expectations reflected in the outpouring of corruption reports. The Operations Department understood this and worked to achieve swift demonstrable results, as discussed in the previous section. In the Community Relations Department, one of the first units set up was the Press Information Office. It placed ICAC successes prominently in the public eye. It provided the press releases on which the mass media built its dramatic stories of anticorruption actions by Operations Department officers. It held regular press briefings and monitored media coverage of the ICAC. Through intense early publicity, community relations officers worked to transform beliefs of ordinary citizens in Hong Kong about what was possible—by pointing to what was currently happening (emphasizing positive results) in anticorruption work. This role became all the more crucial after the partial amnesty of 1977, when the momentum gained in public support was at great risk.

Supporting (favorable) media coverage of enforcement actions is one way to publicize the ICAC and its reliability as an anticorruption organization. The Community Relations Department has also produced its own television dramas, radio call-in shows, posters, and public announcements to educate the mass public about the ICAC. It has further pursued this goal though community liaison organized out of its district offices—three offices opened by the end of 1975, seven by the end of 1977, and eleven by the end of 1983 (reduced to eight, the current total, in 1991). Community liaison officers establish personal contact with the mass public to explain the ICAC and its aims. They do this by meeting with community groups, visiting door to door, going to factories and schools, and working in a variety of other ways to directly contact ordinary citizens—including squatters, hawkers, taxi drivers, bus drivers, small shopkeepers, housewives, juvenile delinquents, Vietnamese refugees, and Chinese immigrants.

The second responsibility of the Community Relations Department, to educate ordinary citizens about what constitutes corruption, was as crucial as the first responsibility in the early years of the ICAC. One reason for this was that the main legal basis for ICAC anticorruption action, the Prevention of Bribery Ordinance, was fairly new when the ICAC came into being. Also, a weak grasp of corruption (in its legal sense) in the early 1970s was quite compatible with the prevalent view of law enforcers (the police) as the most corrupt government department of all: Nuances of the law were hardly meaningful if those charged with enforcing it were themselves unreliable and self-serving enforcers. A more mundane problem was the lack of a Chinese version of the law, a situation quickly remedied.[29] The Community Relations Department printed and distributed two simple leaflets, one explaining bribery offenses generally, the other focusing on bribery in the private sector. The department also made use of television, producing a series of short programs describing various aspects of anticorruption law relating to daily life.

In 1976, provoked by ICAC prosecution of a large business for offering commissions to other firms, the Chinese Manufacturers Association led the business community in an unsuccessful attempt to pressure the government to remove business commissions from ICAC jurisdiction (see King 1980; Rance Lee 1981). The widely aired argument that business commissions are customary in Hong Kong forced the Community Relations Department to make greater efforts (for example, notices accompanying gas and electric bills) to distinguish bribery in the private sector from the provisions for the offer and acceptance of business commissions recognized by the law. The pressure from the business community in 1976 brought the private sector into the department's work and raised its importance somewhat earlier than was the case in the other ICAC departments. In 1984, with a conference on business ethics organized jointly with the Hong Kong Management Association, the department advanced significantly beyond the effort of explaining the law to promote clean business in Hong Kong. By the end of the 1980s, the private sector accounted for about one-half of all activities of the liaison program in the department. In 1990, the department decided to emphasize corruption in the public and private sectors equally in their educational work. In 1995 and again in 1998, the department launched two-year programs that focused on corruption in government.

In educating the community about what constitutes corruption, community relations officers make special efforts to contact new arrivals from mainland China. New mainland immigrants cannot be expected to know the laws of Hong Kong, and they may also be more susceptible than others to the temptations of corruption in the new competitive environment. New mainland arrivals are introduced to anticorruption laws with ICAC videos (in Mandarin, Cantonese, and Fujian dialects) at the Immigration Department and posters at the Lo Wu train station (their main point of entry). In the late 1990s, the department worked through the nongovernmental organizations that provide services to new arrivals to include an ICAC session in new arrival programs. In 1997, a column in a Chinese newspaper and a Mandarin dialect radio program focused specifically on arrivals from the mainland to give them a better understanding of anticorruption laws in Hong Kong.

The third responsibility, mobilizing the community to cooperate in enforcement, mainly by reporting corruption, depended on success with the first two. The relationship implicit in this third responsibility was also a more complex reciprocal one. Reports on corruption were required for Operations Department actions, especially in the first few years, when the department lacked the resources and investigative experience to take the offensive against corruption. At the same time, ordinary citizens could not be expected to report corruption to the ICAC unless they believed the agency would take effective action. Further, unless they understood the legal standards used as the basis for anticorruption action, they might fail to report corrupt activities they did not recognize as corruption (or report malpractices that did not amount to corruption, a less serious problem).

Mobilization of the community in the early years was in part a by-product of Operations Department success (publicized by the Press Information Office) and gains in public knowledge about anticorruption laws. The Community Relations Department has engaged in significant direct mobilization efforts as well. The department widely publicizes the ICAC corruption hotline (for example, on a fleet of public buses in

1993). Television announcements exhort the mass public to report corruption, as do posters, which report locations of the department's district offices (which are open nine hours a day, every day). The department's television spots, several of which have won awards in Hong Kong and Asia, have used a variety of appeals to encourage reporting. For example, a brilliant (and controversial) series of Orwellian-style announcements, aired beginning in 1995, addressed public anxiety about increasing corruption after the transfer of sovereignty. With the slogan, "Hong Kong: Our advantage is the ICAC," the announcement openly acknowledged the basis for anxiety. It also promoted a solution: Only the mass public could prevent the return of 1960s-style widespread corruption after 1997, by demonstrating personal intolerance of it in Hong Kong through reports of corruption to the ICAC.

The fourth, most ambitious, responsibility of community relations officers was also the most novel for the Hong Kong of the 1970s. Mobilization aims to increase the probability of detecting corrupt activities, but this fourth responsibility attempts to increase expected costs of corruption more directly—by augmenting psychic costs and social disapproval of corrupt activities. This involves moral education, an effort to change private values and their social expression. For the most part, this effort has been conducted in the schools—primary, secondary, and tertiary. Young people are the obvious priority, and the department works to develop attitudes and habits that support the anticorruption effort for the long term. To be sure, the educational effort also aims to communicate accurate notions of what constitutes corruption and to encourage reporting. Moral education is key, however. This has involved different sorts of lessons: the evils of corruption, the importance of honesty and self-discipline, the proper functions of government and attitudes of public officials, the citizen's rights and responsibilities.

Only two years after the ICAC was established, the Community Relations Department had developed teaching kits that quickly became the most widely used of all moral education materials in the territory (Clark 1987). By 1977, the department had in place a systematic program of liaison with schools, and it regularly convened seminars with teachers to produce lesson plans and teaching aids. By 1978, the ICAC was serving on the Education Department's curriculum development committees in social studies, economics, and public affairs, and on the educational television program committee in social studies. In 1983, it worked with instructors to discuss areas where anticorruption messages could be relevant in courses taught at the tertiary level. In 1995, the study of business ethics was introduced into the curricula of business schools at all seven Hong Kong universities.

Most of these moral education activities have aimed to inculcate, at an early age, values that raise the psychic costs of participating in corruption or not reporting it. More than this, however, the ICAC aims to have these values expressed socially, as norms whose violation incurs disapproval in the community. Perhaps the best expression of this goal was in 1976, when the ICAC was under attack from the business community for its enforcement of the law on business commissions. The commissioner's comment on this was the following: "An important manifestation that the new environment has been accepted will be when we, as a community, and especially community leaders and those in authority, begin to indicate to those who are known to be corrupt, to those who indulge in unethical business behaviour, that they and their kind are unacceptable in decent society, that they are without honour and are not wanted in Hong Kong" (ICAC 1977: 8).

Institutional Design

The idea of corruption prevention developed from "an assessment that it was the working environment of many civil servants which not only provided the opportunity for malpractice, but virtually encouraged the weak and greedy to be corrupt" (ICAC 1980: 40). Among the duties of the ICAC commissioner outlined in the Independent Commission Against Corruption Ordinance are the following three:

> [To] examine the practices and procedures of Government departments and public bodies, in order to facilitate the discovery of corrupt practices and to secure the revision of methods of work or procedures which, in the opinion of the Commissioner, may be conducive to corrupt practices; [to] instruct, advise and assist any person, on the latter's request, on ways in which corrupt practices may be eliminated by such person; [and to] advise heads of Government departments or of public bodies of changes in practices or procedures compatible with the effective discharge of the duties of such departments or public bodies which the Commissioner thinks necessary to reduce the likelihood of the occurrence of corrupt practices. (Independent Commission against Corruption Ordinance 1974, Sec. 12)

These duties describe the main current of work by the Corruption Prevention Department over more than 25 years: specific studies of the organization of work in government departments, with a view to understanding the opportunities for corruption in work procedures and suggesting ways to redesign procedures to minimize these opportunities. Standard practice quickly developed for these "conventional studies" and did not change notably over the years. After studying the situation, corruption prevention analysts prepare a report describing opportunities for corruption and recommending remedial measures. The report is presented to the Corruption Prevention Advisory Committee (described in Note 13) and then forwarded to the client department. Next, corruption prevention analysts discuss the report in some detail with the client department, attempting to gain its agreement to implement the recommendations. Finally, assuming agreement is reached and after the recommended measures have been in place for a short time, analysts return to the client department to monitor implementation and assess effectiveness to check that adopted changes have not produced new opportunities for corruption.

Initially, conventional studies were selected on the basis of reports and requests by government department heads in the course of informal visits by corruption prevention analysts, with no sectoral priorities. Mainly, the idea was to give analysts experience in a wide variety of departments. In 1976, the department established priorities for studies based on a number of criteria: the number of people affected by the practices and procedures, the extent to which the procedures give rise to other serious problems (for example, other illegal activities or the substantial loss of revenue), the urgency of the particular study (for example, whether new procedures are about to be introduced), and the particular appeal of the department or procedure (for example, because of media publicity). With experience in a variety of departments, corruption prevention analysts also began to identify recurring characteristics of corruption opportunities, and the commissioner noted in 1979 that: "While there are no standard remedial measures that can be automatically applied to eradicate, or substantially reduce, such opportunities, recommendations to clients often differ on points of detail rather than in the principles involved" (ICAC 1979: 40). Experience also allowed corruption prevention analysts to respond to some departments quickly with written advice based on studies already completed, assuming the problem did not fit the criteria for a top priority area and analysts believed this sort of advice would be a useful substitute for a conventional study (which often took months to complete).

In 1985, the department completed its one thousandth conventional study. Among the completed studies was a long complex study on supervisory accountability in the civil service (1977) and another on disciplinary procedures (1978), also in the civil service. Examples of more specifically focused studies include corruption prevention analyses of clearance procedures for illegal immigrants from mainland China (1974), the Labor Department's policy tolerating illegal factories in residential buildings (1975),[30] certification of exports from Hong Kong regarding origin of goods (1979), birth registration procedures to tighten control because children illegally smuggled in from the mainland presented an incentive to introduce false birth records into the system (1982), the selection process for promotion in the police force (1998), and procedures for monitoring and counseling officials in debt (1999).

In 1981, ICAC corruption prevention analysts joined senior police officers to form a corruption prevention group within the police force. This experience was extended to other government departments throughout the decade. Normally, corruption prevention groups meet a few times annually to decide on a program of corruption prevention studies for the department, concentrating on procedures most likely to provide opportunities for corruption. The groups involve heads of departments and senior officials in routine corruption prevention work with the ICAC, making good use of their intimate knowledge of the work in their departments, without ignoring the expertise and interest (and without relinquishing responsibility) of the Corruption Prevention Department. Although corruption prevention had always involved close work with client departments, the innovation of corruption prevention groups was regular joint involvement of the ICAC and other government departments in identifying problem areas for future corruption studies. The actual studies continue to be conducted by ICAC corruption prevention analysts.

Another role of the Corruption Prevention Department is external training in corruption prevention. Corruption prevention officers organize training sessions in government departments—at the managerial level to communicate the theory of supervisory accountability in the context of countering corruption and at the junior official level to help officials recognize specific corruption-related problems in their work, to instruct them how to avoid or discourage offers of bribes, and to inform them about actions to take if offered bribes. Since the mid-1980s, this function is no longer performed by a specialized group within the department, but has become part of any conventional corruption prevention study.

The increase in private sector corruption in the 1980s affected the work of the Corruption Prevention Department. The impact was not as significant as in the Operations Department, but this was mainly a consequence of policy. According to the ICAC commissioner: "The time and resources involved in the Corruption Prevention Department providing advice or assistance to private organizations is carefully controlled, and is very limited in comparison to that expended on assignment [i.e., conventional studies] and advisory work in Government departments and public bodies. This will continue to be the case" (ICAC 1985: 54).

The vision of corruption prevention work described in the Independent Commission Against Corruption Ordinance, quoted at the beginning of this section, only barely suggests the most interesting (and perhaps most effective) aspect of the department's work: consultation at the stage of policy formulation or legislative drafting. The role of corruption prevention analysts in reviewing draft government legislation was agreed on formally in 1977, and the secretary for administration was given responsibility for communicating the new role of the ICAC to government departments. Under this arrangement, an originator of legislation (in Hong Kong's executive-led system, a government department) seeks the advice of the Corruption Prevention Department so that analysts there can advise on the draft, especially on whether there has been an adequate assessment of enforcement capability in terms of resources in the agencies responsible for implementing the proposed legislation. This advisory role quickly became an important part of the department's work, and government departments now typically request advice at the early drafting instruction stage. Corruption prevention analysts do not leave the initiative to government departments entirely, however. They regularly examine the lists of draft legislation published monthly by the Secretariat and maintain contact with government departments "to ensure that corruption prevention considerations are weighed carefully before new laws or regulations are introduced" (ICAC 1980: 37).

The advisory role of the department grew in the 1980s (especially during the late 1980s), as government departments increasingly requested the advice of corruption prevention analysts in developing new procedures. The advisory capacity was acknowledged as an important priority for the department in the 1990s. Corruption prevention analysts have advised on a wide range of policies, regulations, and legislation. For example, in the 1980s, they participated in the framing of criteria for penalization of textile exporters who evade quota controls, reviewed legislation governing district board elections, and were part of a working group to study and advise on procedures for the mass reissue of Hong Kong identity cards. In the 1990s, they were consulted on draft legislation regulating donations to political parties and candidates standing for public election, and on Immigration Department plans for further computerization and integration of existing computer systems. These examples of corruption prevention work, which aim to preempt the creation of corruption opportunities, are institutional design in the most basic sense of the term. Rather than studying, redesigning, and monitoring existing organizational procedures, corruption prevention analysts are full participants in the initial design of procedures, policies, and legislation. They bring to that process their specialized knowledge and a single concern: the implications for corruption. Requiring their involvement at the early stages of institutional design (for example, legislative drafting) is one of the most remarkable policy instruments the Hong Kong government developed in its anticorruption reform of the 1970s.

Having described the three-pronged anticorruption strategy in this section, the next section turns to the question of impact: Has it been successful?

Impact of Anticorruption Reform

To formulate appropriate strategies to educate and involve ordinary citizens in the anticorruption effort, the Community Relations Department began in 1977 to commission a series of representative sample surveys of public opinion in Hong Kong. The surveys offer an excellent basis for estimating change over time in the characteristic expectations of ordinary citizens about corruption, that is, patterns of change in the folklore of corruption. They also provide some insight into change in the scope and main forms of corruption. This section draws mainly on findings presented in reports and data books for the 19 surveys conducted from 1977 through 2002. Given the relatively few data points—fewer than 19 for many questions of interest—and taking into account sampling error (from 3 to 4 percent), trends are not always easily discernible. Obviously, even when an overall pattern is discernible, there are a number of reasons that may account for observations in any particular survey exhibiting results off the trend line.[31] A salient event occurring shortly before a survey is likely to have some impact on response, for example.[32] Of particular note is the timing of the 1997 survey, conducted the month after the transfer of sovereignty. Comparison between 1996 and 1997 survey findings requires sensitivity to the probable impact of this event and particular caution in reliance on differences between 1996 and 1997 findings alone. Throughout this section, then, the focus is on big patterns of change, especially those on which the ICAC survey data and other evidence appear to agree.

Personally Encountered Corruption

Questions about personally encountered corruption are the most direct basis for estimating changes in the volume of corruption, but these are asked in only 12 surveys. Moreover, different question formats frustrate reliable estimation and comparability. In four surveys conducted in 1993–97, respondents were asked whether they had encountered corruption personally in the past year. The 8 or 9 percent who responded "yes" were asked to indicate whether the encounter had occurred in government, the private sector, or some other sector. In the 1998–2002 surveys, however, the first question, to which 3 to 6 percent responded "yes," inquired about corruption encountered personally or by friends and relations.[33] Taking into account responses to both questions in the nine surveys yields the percentages presented in Table 2.1. In the 1986, 1988, and 1990 surveys, the format was completely different. Respondents who stated corruption was common in at least one or two government departments were asked to name the departments and then to indicate the source of their information. ICAC survey reports present the findings by department. As some unknown number of individuals who personally encountered corruption in government had encounters in more than one department, calculations based on these figures must overestimate the percentage of respondents who encountered corruption in these three years.[34] I attempted a number of calculations, none very satisfactory, to arrive at figures substantially comparable to those of the later surveys. My "best guesses" of proportions of respondents reporting encounters of corruption in government are the ranges presented in Table 2.1. The lower percentages are underestimates, the higher are overestimates.[35]

As the surveys are of representative samples of adults, it is reasonable to think of these figures as changing proportions of the Hong Kong population encountering corruption in government over the years. Obviously, with no relevant data for the 1970s and only guesstimates for the 1980s, figures on personally encountered corruption are not helpful in assessing the impact of the ICAC on the scope of corruption. Nonetheless, the percentages from the available data are all quite small. By the

Table 2.1 Personally encountered corruption in Hong Kong government departments, 1986–2002

Year	Respondents who "personally" encountered corruption recently
1986	1.5–3.0%
1988	1.3–2.3%
1990	1.4–3.0%
1993	1.7%
1995	2.3%
1996	2.7%
1997	2.2%
1998	1.2%
1999	1.4%
2000	1.0%
2001	0.6%
2002	0.7%

Sources: Reports and data books for mass surveys commissioned by the ICAC.

Note: Lower percentages for 1986, 1988, and 1990 are underestimates; higher percentages are overestimates. For estimation methods, see notes 34 and 35 in text. "Don't know" and "no answer" percentages are not reported because figures take into account responses to two or three questions.

Question items: Questions on this issue were not asked prior to 1986 or in 1992 and 1994. Figures are based on responses to the following questions (I presume the variations in question wording are consequential to a comparison of the distribution of responses over time):

1986, 1988, 1990: "Do you think corruption is very common in government departments at present?" (Response categories: in most departments, in a good number of departments, in only one or two departments, or is there no corruption at all? Unless response is "no corruption at all," follow up.) "Do you know which departments? Any others?" (For each department named, follow up.) "How do you know?" (Responses categorized as "personal encounters" are corrupt encounters as a victim or bystander and personal work experience involving the department named.)

1993, 1995, 1996–97: "Have you encountered corruption in the past year?" (If "yes," follow up.) "Was this corruption in business, in government, or in some other sector?"

1998–2002: "Have you, your relatives, or your friends encountered corruption in Hong Kong in the past 12 months?" (If "yes," follow up.) "Was this corruption in business, in government, or in some other sector?"

highest overestimate, about 3 percent of the population directly experienced corruption in any given year since the mid-1980s.

In terms of change over time and ignoring guesstimates, the pattern of corrupt encounters is one of rise and fall, with a 1996 peak at about one and one-half to four times the level of endpoints in 1993 and 2002.[36] This pattern is particularly notable considering that question wording in 1998–2002, which includes corrupt encounters of relatives and friends, overestimates personally encountered corruption, compared to 1993–97.

The pattern of rise and fall in the 1990s, with 1996 as the peak, is also roughly consistent with Transparency International scores. In 1995–2002, years for which annual scores are compiled, Hong Kong corruption rose and then fell, with corruption apparently most widespread in 1996.[37] The assessment of ICAC operations and intelligence officers, interviewed by the author in 1995 and 1998, was that corruption in government was basically under control by the mid-1980s but began to increase around 1992 (ICAC Operations Department 5 July 1995, 21 July 1995, 11 June 1998).

The pattern of personally encountered corruption also aligns with yearly assessments presented to the public in ICAC annual reports. Obviously, it is important to separate out assessments of changes in the scope of corruption, based on intelligence and other evidence, from descriptions of changes in reported corruption. These distinctions are indeed generally quite clear in the annual reports.[38] As early as 1976, the ICAC commissioner reported a decrease in overt corruption. He clarified: "This does not necessarily mean there is less corruption but, judging from information received from local community leaders and members of the public, it seems that corruption may be less blatant and obvious than it used to be. I am told that there is now less ostentation, less show of wealth, by many suspected of being corrupt and perhaps, too, it is becoming less fashionable for the corrupt to boast about their ill-gotten gains" (ICAC 1976: 1). By the early 1980s, the commissioner argued that widespread corruption (not only its overt display) was a thing of the past: "The climate has changed markedly. The majority of Hong Kong people do not have to accept corruption as a day-to-day occurrence" (ICAC 1982: 9), and "it is a commonplace that the large scale syndicated corruption of the sixties and early seventies has gone and that the corruption which now confronts us tends to be concentrated in pockets of criminal activity or of activities where money in large amounts is available" (ICAC 1983: 9). In the late 1980s, while expressing concern about the private sector, the commissioner concluded that the three-pronged attack of the ICAC had achieved success in the public sector, "driving home the point that corruption does not pay" (ICAC 1988: 23).

The first note of concern about a resurgence of corruption in government, not reflected yet in reported corruption, appeared in the report on 1992. Cautioning that intelligence is "an imprecise measure" but "often provides a better 'feel' for what is happening," the commissioner stated that intelligence sources "tend to show that much more corrupt activity is taking place than has been reported, particularly in the Government sector" (ICAC 1993: 9). The following year, remarking on a huge increase in reported corruption during 1992, the commissioner continued: "When we relate this increase in reports to our own intelligence, our assessment is that there is indeed more corrupt activity about than in recent years" (ICAC 1994: 9). Continuing concern about corruption in government is evident in ICAC assessments of corruption in 1994, 1995, and 1996.

In reports on corruption in 1997, 1998, and 1999, continued high levels of reported corruption in government were no longer associated with a continuous rise in the volume of corruption. For example, reviewing anticorruption work at the end of 1997, the commissioner stated: "Earlier in the year, some members of the community expressed concern that corruption might increase. As the year drew to a close, such concern proved to be unfounded. Both reports from the public and intelligence from other sources pointed to the fact that corruption was very much under control" (ICAC 1998: 9). Similarly, in 2000, the commissioner noted that "the increase [in reported corruption] should not be interpreted as equivalent to a corresponding surge in corrupt activities" (ICAC 2000: 10).

Folklore of Corruption

Personally encountered corruption is not the only lever in the ICAC survey data by which to estimate changes in the volume of corruption. Another is data on beliefs about the scope of corruption. This is less direct, but data are more complete. In nearly all the surveys, roughly comparable questions were asked about the extent to which respondents believe corruption is common in government. Of course, using data on beliefs to estimate changes in the volume of actual corruption assumes that corruption is fairly highly correlated with beliefs of ordinary citizens about how much corruption prevails (or, at least, given some baseline, about the extent to which corruption rises or falls). From this perspective, encounters with officials—personal as well as those experienced through stories told by others and in the press—are seen as a sort of ongoing sampling process in which subjective estimates of actual corruption are updated continuously by ordinary citizens. Alternatively, how well beliefs about the changing pattern of corruption match actual changes in the volume of corruption can simply be viewed as an empirical question, by comparing data on beliefs with other sorts of information that shed light on actual corruption.

From an entirely different perspective, however, beliefs about corruption are of enormous intrinsic interest, regardless of how accurately they reflect actual corruption. As described in Chapter 1, they are themselves inputs into the anticorruption effort, helping to sustain clean or corrupt practices.[39] This includes not only beliefs about the scope of corruption but also public confidence in the government's anticorruption commitment. This relationship between actual corruption and a folklore of corruption has been described earlier in two empirical contexts: the 1960s and early 1970s (in qualitative accounts) and 1974 (in a discussion of the rise in reported corruption to the ICAC, compared to the ACO in the previous year). This section examines the changing pattern of beliefs about corruption beginning in the late 1970s.

Table 2.2 summarizes responses to questions about the scope of corruption in government departments. Comparison of responses from the first two surveys, which offered respondents choices between two fairly extreme categories, with those from other years is somewhat problematic. In 1977 and 1978, respondents were asked whether corruption was common in most every government department or in only a few. In 1980–2000 respondents were asked whether they believed corruption was: in most government departments, in a number of departments, in only one or two departments, or in no departments at all. Beginning in 2001, respondents were asked whether they believed corruption in government was: very common, quite common, or uncommon.

For the purposes of this study, it is useful to construct from the full array of responses in Table 2.2 a more easily interpretable version by combining responses that can reasonably be considered as beliefs that corruption is a common practice in government. Included in that category are responses that corruption is very common, quite common, and common in most or a considerable number of government departments. Excluded are responses that corruption is uncommon, nonexistent, or in only one or two departments. The categories of interest are highlighted in column 4 of Table 2.2 and are the basis for the corruption in government pattern in Figure 2.1.

What is the pattern of change in beliefs of the mass public that corruption in government is common? It is one of decline, sharp rise, and second decline.[40] The proportion of respondents stating that corruption in government is common is highest in 1980 (the first year for which

Table 2.2 Mass beliefs about corruption in Hong Kong government departments, 1977–2002

Year	Most, very common	A good number, quite common	Most, a good number and very common, quite common	Only a few, only one or two, uncommon	None	Don't know, no answer
1977	38%	—	—	46%	1%	15%
1978	35%	—	—	46%	1%	16%
1980	16%	24%	40%	31%	7%	22%
1982	8%	21%	29%	40%	13%	19%
1984	6%	19%	25%	37%	13%	25%
1986	7%	21%	28%	34%	10%	28%
1988	2%	14%	16%	38%	13%	34%
1990	5%	17%	22%	33%	15%	31%
1992	3%	13%	16%	30%	14%	40%
1993	5%	26%	31%	37%	8%	25%
1994	8%	32%	40%	34%	6%	21%
1995	7%	27%	34%	42%	9%	17%
1996	7%	31%	38%	41%	6%	15%
1997	4%	20%	24%	48%	12%	15%
1998	4%	21%	25%	51%	8%	17%
1999	3%	17%	20%	57%	8%	16%
2000	3%	21%	24%	55%	5%	17%
2001	1%	20%	22%	67%	—	11%
2002	1%	17%	18%	69%	—	12%

Sources: Reports and data books for mass surveys commissioned by the ICAC.

Note: Percentages may not add up to 100 due to rounding.

Question items: Figures are based on responses to the following questions:
1977–78: "Do you think corruption is common in most every government department, or do you think corruption is in only a few government departments?"
1980, 1982, 1984: "How common do you think corruption is in the government at present? Is it in most government departments, in a good number of government departments, in only one or two government departments, or do you think there is no corruption in the government at all?"
1986, 1988, 1990, 1992–2000: "Do you think corruption is very common in government departments at present?" (Response categories: in most departments, in a good number of departments, in only one or two departments, or is there no corruption at all?)
2001–2002: "How common do you think corruption is in government departments at present?" (Response categories: very common, quite common, or uncommon?)

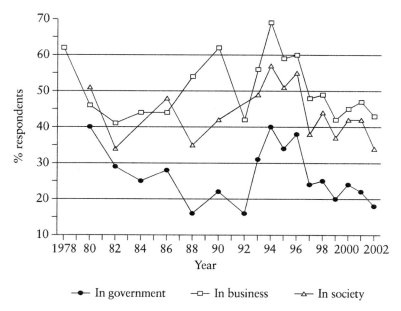

Sources: Reports and data books for mass surveys commissioned by the ICAC.

Figure 2.1 Mass beliefs about corruption as common in Hong Kong, 1978–2002

comparable measures exist) and 1994: 40 percent of respondents indicated corruption is common in most or a considerable number of government departments. That proportion drops fairly steadily after 1980 to a low of 16 percent in 1988 and 1992, before rising to reach its second peak in 1994. The second decline begins in 1997 (with results from the survey conducted shortly after the transfer of sovereignty), and the proportion is fairly low through 2002.

The surveys also probed beliefs about the scope of "under-the-table transactions" and "illegal commissions" in Hong Kong business, which fall under ICAC investigatory jurisdiction as corruption in the private sector (see Table 2.3). Further, in 15 ICAC surveys, respondents were asked about the scope of corruption in society generally (see Table 2.4). Figure 2.1 also shows responses to these two questions. While the definition of corruption adopted in this study excludes these activities, it would be surprising if corruption in government were unrelated to them, as corrupt exchanges that involve officials generally involve non-government players on the other side of the transaction. Indeed, Figure

Table 2.3 Mass beliefs about corruption in the Hong Kong private sector, 1977–2002

Year	Conventional or customary, common, very common	Conventional or customary, common, quite common	Conventional or customary, common, and very common and quite common	Unconventional or uncustomary, uncommon	Don't know, no answer
1977	47%		47%	24%	30%[a]
1978	62%		62%	18%	20%[a]
1980	46%		46%	29%	25%[a]
1982	41%		41%	40%	20%[a]
1984	44%		44%	41%	15%[a]
1986	44%		44%	37%	19%
1988	54%		54%	26%	20%
1990	62%		62%	24%	14%
1992	6%	36%	42%	21%	38%
1993	12%	44%	56%	23%	21%
1994	13%	56%	69%	16%	15%
1995	8%	51%	59%	26%	15%
1996	9%	51%	60%	23%	17%
1997	5%	43%	48%	34%	18%
1998	6%	43%	49%	35%	16%
1999	4%	38%	42%	43%	15%
2000	4%	41%	45%	39%	16%
2001	4%	43%	47%	36%	17%
2002	4%	39%	43%	42%	15%

Sources: Reports and data books for mass surveys commissioned by the ICAC.

Note: Percentages may not add up to 100 due to rounding.

Question items: Figures are based on responses to the following questions:

1977–78: "Some say that under-the-table transactions are a conventional or customary business practice. Do you agree or disagree with this description?"

1980, 1982: "Some say that under-the-table transactions are a common business practice in Hong Kong industry and commerce. Do you agree or disagree with this description?"

1984, 1986: "Some say that under-the-table transactions and illegal commissions are a common business practice in Hong Kong industry and commerce. Do you agree or disagree with this description?"

1988, 1990: "I am going to read you a number of statements. Please say whether you agree or disagree with the statements: 'Illegal commissions are a common business practice in Hong Kong industry and commerce.'" (Response categories: strongly agree, agree, disagree, strongly disagree.)

1992–2002: "How common do you think corruption is in Hong Kong industry and commerce?" (Response categories: very common, quite common, uncommon.)

a. These figures include response "depends," volunteered by 1 to 3 percent of respondents.

Table 2.4 Mass beliefs about corruption in Hong Kong society, 1980–2002

Year	Very common, very serious	Quite common, somewhat serious	Very common, very serious and quite common, somewhat serious	Uncommon, not serious, not a problem	Don't know, no answer
1980	15%	36%	51%	40%	9%
1982	6%	28%	34%	53%	13%
1986	9%	39%	48%	35%	17%
1988	4%	31%	35%	49%	16%
1990	4%	38%	42%	44%	14%
1993	7%	42%	49%	36%	16%
1994	9%	48%	57%	30%	13%
1995	6%	45%	51%	40%	10%
1996	7%	48%	55%	39%	7%
1997	3%	35%	38%	54%	8%
1998	5%	39%	44%	44%	13%
1999	3%	34%	37%	56%	8%
2000	3%	39%	42%	49%	9%
2001	3%	38%	42%	52%	6%
2002	3%	31%	34%	60%	5%

Sources: Reports and data books for mass surveys commissioned by the ICAC.

Note: Percentages may not add up to 100 due to rounding.

Question items: Questions on this issue asked in 1977, 1978, and 1984 are not comparable to those asked in other years. No question on this issue was asked in 1992. Figures are based on responses to the following questions (I presume the question wording change from "serious" in earlier surveys to "common" in later surveys is consequential to a comparison of the distribution of responses over time):

1980, 1982: "There are a number of things happening in Hong Kong these days. Some people may regard these as problems facing Hong Kong at present, while others may not consider them as problems at all. I will mention some of these things and, for each one of them, I would like you to tell me whether or not you personally think it is a problem facing Hong Kong today. Corruption." (If "yes," follow up.) "How serious a problem do you think it is: very serious, somewhat serious, or not a serious problem?"

1986: "Within the past few years or so, do you think corruption is a social problem?" (If "yes," follow up.) "How serious do you think it is: very serious, somewhat serious, or not serious at all?"

1988: "Do you think corruption is *common* in present-day Hong Kong?" (Response categories: very common, quite common, uncommon.)

1990, 1993–2002: "How common do you think corruption is in present-day Hong Kong?" (Response categories: very common, quite common, uncommon.)

2.1 shows a general relationship in mass beliefs about corruption in government, in society, and in the private sector. In all but two years, the proportions of respondents stating corruption in society is common lie between (often halfway between) the proportions stating corruption in business is common and those stating corruption in government is common. Although based on separate measures, the result is similar to a calculated average of proportions for corruption in business and government. This offers reassurance about the reliability of responses of greatest interest here: beliefs about corruption in government.[41]

What do the changing proportions highlighted in Table 2.2 and illustrated in Figure 2.1 suggest about actual corruption? Obviously, proportions of respondents stating corruption in government is common and proportions of corrupt government officials are not the same thing. Fairly apparent patterns of change in the former are quite consistent with changes in the same direction and roughly comparable magnitude in the latter, however. To the extent that belief patterns more or less agree with other sorts of evidence (as they do here) and also "make sense" (as they do here), it is not unreasonable to treat changing beliefs about the scope of corruption as a rough gauge of changes in actual corruption.

The pattern illustrated in Figure 2.1 is perhaps more interesting for what it tells us about the folklore of corruption, however. At the most elemental level, the changing proportions indicate that fewer (or more) ordinary citizens expect encounters with government officials to be corrupt encounters. An "expectation of corruption" means that ordinary citizens believe it is likely that officials will initiate corrupt exchanges, fail to perform their duty absent bribes, or simply be more efficient with illegal inducements. It means they believe other officials in the same departments are also unlikely to be "clean." When large proportions of ordinary citizens enter government offices expecting to encounter corrupt officials, this hinders anticorruption efforts.

The successful transformation (by about the mid-1980s) of a folklore of corruption in Hong Kong was apparently under serious threat in the mid-1990s. In 1993–96, more than a third of respondents expected corrupt encounters in most or a good number of government departments, about the same as in the late 1970s or 1980. Beginning in 1997, the trend reversed itself. Expectations of corruption in government returned to levels of the mid-1980s or late 1980s.

There are few comparable sources on beliefs about the volume of corruption.[42] A survey question asked by the team of scholars for the Hong

Kong Transitions Project is comparable, but it was included in only four surveys—three conducted in 1996–97 and one conducted in 1998. Survey results before and after the transfer of sovereignty are similar to those presented in Table 2.2, although the comparison is by no means straightforward. The proportion of respondents stating corruption in government is somewhat common, fairly common, or very common averages 36 percent in 1996–97 before the transfer and 25 percent in January 1998.[43]

Beginning in 1984, ICAC surveys inquired into beliefs about the scope of future corruption, initially focusing on the transition period ending with the transfer of sovereignty. These findings are presented in Table 2.5.[44] Beliefs about future corruption are consistent with the pattern of beliefs about the current volume of corruption in government, discussed above. The outlook for more corruption in the future is increasingly grim in the 1990s, registering an enormous leap in 1993. In that year, 62 percent of respondents responded that they expected an increase in corruption due to the "1997 issue." The proportion rises to 73 percent in 1994 and remains at about this level until 1997. The change in question wording with the end of the transition period makes responses in the 1997–2002 surveys not comparable to those for previous years.

In 1990, respondents who reported they believed there would be more corruption in the transition years were asked to explain the basis for their pessimism. Sixty-five percent of their responses were coded under the category: "Because of the 1997 issue, many people wish to grab more money before they emigrate."[45]

Surveys conducted by a number of other organizations also attest to the increasing anxiety about future corruption. For example, in four surveys conducted before July 1997, the Hong Kong Transitions Project asked respondents to indicate their level of "worry" about corruption in Hong Kong after the transfer of sovereignty. On average, 49 percent responded they were "very worried" or "fairly worried." In five surveys conducted in 1997–98 (after the transfer of sovereignty), an average of 24 percent offered the same responses, although (as in the ICAC surveys) question wording changed to refer to current corruption. Of seven issues on which respondents were questioned about their worries, corruption figured most prominently in the surveys conducted before July 1997. About one-third of respondents (two or three times the number for any other issue) stated it was their biggest worry. After July 1997, that proportion dropped dramatically and stayed low. By October 1998, respondents worried about corruption less than nearly any

Table 2.5 Outlook for corruption in Hong Kong in the future, 1984–2002

Year	More corruption	Less corruption	More or less the same as now	Don't know, no answer
1984	35%	26%	18%	20%
1986	29%	27%	22%	22%
1990	21%	25%	37%	17%
1992	37%	4%	36%	24%
1993	62%	4%	20%	14%
1994	73%	3%	16%	9%
1995	72%	3%	18%	8%
1996	70%	2%	21%	7%
1997	43%	8%	37%	11%
1998	43%	10%	29%	19%
1999	39%	13%	32%	16%
2000	21%	19%	44%	16%
2001	26%	16%	45%	14%
2002	37%	13%	42%	9%

Sources: Reports and data books for mass surveys commissioned by the ICAC.

Note: Percentages may not add up to 100 due to rounding. Percentages for 1986 are averages of responses about corruption in government and the private sector.

Question items: Questions on this issue were not asked before 1984 or in 1988. Figures are based on responses to the following questions (italics call attention to variation in question wording that I presume is consequential to a comparison of the distribution of responses over time):

1984: "In the years between now and 1997, do you think more or fewer people are likely to use corrupt means to make money?" (Response categories: a lot more, more, more or less the same, fewer, many fewer, none at all.)

1986: "In the years between now and 1997, do you think more or fewer people in government are likely to use corrupt means to make money? How about the private sector?" (Response categories: a lot more, more, more or less the same, fewer, many fewer, none at all.)

1990: "In *the coming few years,* do you think there will be more, less, or more or less the same level of corruption as is present in Hong Kong now?"

1992–96: "Do you think the 1997 issue will cause an increase, decrease, or will not cause any change in the current level of corruption in Hong Kong?"

1997–2002: "Do you think *next year* there will be an increase, decrease, or no change in the current level of corruption in Hong Kong?"

other issue.[46] To be sure, the worsening economic circumstances had begun to dominate worries.

Public Confidence in the ICAC

Anticipation of the transfer of sovereignty also affected public confidence in the ICAC. The six surveys conducted in 1990–96 inquired: "Has the 1997 issue weakened your confidence in the ICAC?" The number reporting weakened confidence in the ICAC averages 34 percent and never amounts to a majority of respondents. Nonetheless, confidence began to erode notably in 1994. On average, 29 percent of respondents reported weakened confidence in 1990–93, but in 1994–96 the proportion averages 38 percent. Of those reporting weakened confidence, a majority attributed it to lack of confidence in the Chinese mainland government or in the Hong Kong government of the future.[47]

Public confidence in the ICAC as an effective organization also deteriorated somewhat in the mid-1990s. Column 4 of Table 2.6 shows lower levels of public confidence beginning in 1994 and extending through 2002 (with a one-time recovery in 1997). Columns 2 and 4 show post-1997 public confidence in ICAC effectiveness as lower than at any other time for which survey data are available.

Generally, however, levels of confidence are high. Even in the post-1997 years, about 70 percent of those surveyed describe the work of the ICAC as effective or very effective. Moreover, in other public opinion polls, the ICAC has consistently emerged as an institution enjoying high public confidence, much higher than the Hong Kong government, civil service, and other government institutions.[48] In sum, while beliefs about increased corruption and fears about even greater increases began to jeopardize the equilibrium of clean government in the mid-1990s, serious doubts about the credibility of the anticorruption effort and the ICAC do not appear to be part of this change.

Reported Corruption

The creation of the ICAC produced an immediate sharp increase in reported corruption in 1974, a change described earlier as evidence of a transformation of the folklore of corruption in Hong Kong. Reports of corruption overall decreased steadily after that, reaching a low of 1,234 reports in 1978. In 1979, reports rose but remained at a fairly constant (higher) level through the 1980s. In 1993, reports increased dramatically, by 45 percent, and remained high through the 1990s. Figures on reported corruption are presented in Table 2.7, and the pattern of change is illustrated in Figure 2.2.

This is accounted for by two quite different patterns of change, however. On the one hand, there is a fairly steady increase in reports of illegal business commissions over the entire period, with the slope significantly steeper in 1993 and 1994. By contrast, reports of corruption in government follow a more complex pattern. They decreased a great deal from 1974 through 1978, increased fairly steadily from the late

Table 2.6 Mass beliefs about the performance of the ICAC, 1977–2002

Year	Very good, very effective	Good, quite good, effective	Very good, very effective and good, quite good, effective	Average	Ineffective and very ineffective	Don't know, no answer
1977	31%	42%	73%	13%	1%	14%
1978	7%	65%	72%	16%	1%	12%
1980	13%	63%	76%	18%	1%	5%
1984	13%	71%	84%	7%	<1%	9%
1986	9%	78%	87%	6%	<1%	8%
1988	10%	78%	88%	6%	<1%	5%
1990	9%	67%	76%	18%	1%	5%
1992	22%	53%	75%	16%	2%	7%
1993	20%	58%	78%	16%	2%	4%
1994	11%	60%	71%	25%	2%	3%
1995	17%	56%	73%	21%	3%	3%
1996	12%	57%	69%	25%	3%	3%
1997	17%	59%	76%	19%	2%	2%
1998	7%	60%	67%	22%	3%	9%
1999	7%	64%	71%	22%	2%	5%
2000	6%	54%	70%	34%	2%	4%
2001	10%	58%	69%	27%	2%	2%
2002	8%	62%	70%	26%	2%	3%

Sources: Reports and data books for mass surveys commissioned by the ICAC.
Note: Percentages may not add up to 100 due to rounding.
Question items: No question about ICAC performance was asked in 1982. Figures are based on responses to the following questions:
1977, 1978, 1980: "What do you think of the performance of the Independent Commission against Corruption since its establishment?" (Response categories: very good, good, neither good nor bad, bad, very bad.)
1984, 1986, 1988, 1990: "On the whole, what do you think of the performance of the Independent Commission against Corruption?" (Response categories: very good, quite good, so-so, quite poor, very poor.)
1992–2002: "Do you consider the anticorruption work of the Independent Commission against Corruption effective or not?" (Response categories: very effective, effective, average, ineffective, very ineffective.)

Table 2.7 Reports of corruption to the police anticorruption office, 1973, and the ICAC, 1974–2002

Year	All reports	Non-anonymous	Government	As a percentage of all reports	
				All government	Police force only
1973	1,457	38%	1,245	85%	49%
1974	3,189	35%	2,745	86%	45%
1975	3,179	39%	2,661	84%	47%
1976	2,433	47%	1,883	77%	46%
1977	1,700	51%	1,271	75%	43%
1978	1,234	55%	887	72%	39%
1979	1,665	58%	1,182	71%	38%
1980	1,772	56%	1,159	65%	30%
1981	2,344	60%	1,554	66%	31%
1982	2,349	59%	1,421	61%	29%
1983	2,516	63%	1,542	61%	31%
1984	2,365	63%	1,406	59%	30%
1985	2,474	61%	1,486	60%	29%
1986	2,545	65%	1,364	54%	25%
1987	2,299	66%	1,160	50%	23%
1988	2,162	65%	1,046	48%	20%
1989	2,388	68%	1,034	43%	19%
1990	2,390	66%	1,125	47%	20%
1991	2,186	65%	978	45%	20%
1992	2,257	68%	1,032	46%	20%
1993	3,276	63%	1,365	42%	19%
1994	3,312	66%	1,381	42%	20%
1995	2,987	65%	1,248	42%	19%
1996	3,086	66%	1,304	42%	19%
1997	3,057	68%	1,288	42%	17%
1998	3,555	68%	1,456	41%	16%
1999	3,561	68%	1,445	41%	14%
2000	4,390	68%	1,732	39%	14%
2001	4,476	71%	1,587	35%	11%
2002	4,371	72%	1,638	37%	13%

Sources: Figures for 1973–99 and 2002 were provided to me by the ICAC, but most can be found in ICAC annual reports. Figures for 2000 and 2001 are from annual reports (ICAC 2001, 2002).

1970s through the mid-1980s, then leveled off to slightly lower numbers—but registered a fairly sharp increase in 1993 and remained high in years after.

Before 1997, the pattern of reported corruption in government is not inconsistent with changes in mass beliefs about the scope of corruption. After 1997, however, the patterns diverge. There is a huge decline in

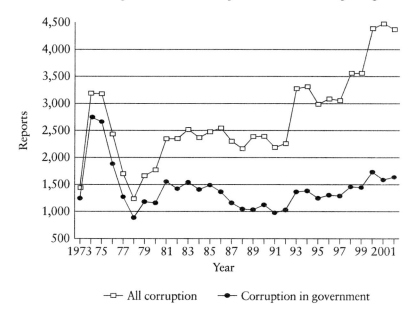

Sources: Figures for 1973–99 and 2002 were provided to me by the ICAC, but most can be found in ICAC annual reports. Figures for 2000 and 2001 are from annual reports (ICAC 2001, 2002).

Figure 2.2 Reports of corruption, 1973–2002

numbers believing corruption in government is common, but corruption reports continued to rise. The pattern of rise and fall in personally encountered corruption in the 1990s roughly mirrors beliefs, not reports. Additionally, ICAC intelligence and public assessments suggest a pattern consistent with personal encounters and beliefs about the scope of corruption, not reports.

That reported corruption seems to follow a different pattern than personal encounters, mass beliefs, or intelligence about the scope of corruption is not surprising. Reports of corruption reflect not only the incidence of corruption but many other things too: public awareness of what constitutes corruption, salience of corruption, availability of channels to report corruption, and public willingness to report corruption, for example.[49] Reports in no small part also reflect enforcement. Big increases in reported corruption *and* little or no apparent increases in actual corruption (after 1997) are an intriguing issue, however. Changes in enforcement, especially the adoption of a proactive anticorruption strategy in 1996, may be part of the explanation. It is also simply possible that reported corruption as a fraction of actual corruption has increased in recent years, a notion taken up in this chapter's conclusion.[50]

Two sorts of changes over time in reported corruption can serve as useful measures of public confidence in the agency charged with anticorruption work. One is the extent to which ordinary citizens are willing to identify themselves in reporting corruption. Proportions of non-anonymous reports of corruption to the ICAC increased in steady increments over the years, with the strongest gains in the 1970s. Certainly, the Operations Department takes the issue of confidentiality very seriously. Its internal computer and filing systems are strictly monitored, with highly restricted, access and its files are systematically culled and shredded to dispose of outdated information (de Speville 1999: 55). Figure 2.3 (and column 6 in Table 2.6) shows that the ICAC had clearly established its reputation by about the mid-1980s, by which time about two-thirds of reported corruption was non-anonymous, suggesting fairly high levels of confidence in the ICAC among those reporting corruption.[51] Also shown in Figure 2.3 is the proportion of corruption reports among all reports to the ICAC. Ordinary citizens appeared to view the ICAC initially as an ombudsman agency. In addition to reports of corruption, the ICAC received many reports about problems completely unrelated to corruption. As shown in Figure 2.3, reports of corruption as a proportion of all reports to the ICAC began to increase sharply in the late 1970s. This may be due to the work of the Community Relations Department to educate the mass public about the content of anticorruption laws and the specialized anticorruption function of the ICAC.

The changing content of these reports is quite informative. In the 1970s, the content of noncorruption reports was very diverse. Ordinary citizens reported marriage problems, legal problems, business disputes, quarrels with neighbors, and housing problems (ICAC 1979: 27). In the mid-1990s, the proportion of reports unrelated to corruption briefly increased again, but noncorruption reports in the 1990s were more often "civil service malpractices . . . not so serious as to amount to a breach of the anti-corruption law" (ICAC 2000: 11).[52] The sorts of problems reported in the early years of the ICAC suggest a naive all-encompassing trust in the ICAC combined with ignorance of the law. Problems reported in the 1990s seem to reflect keener anticorruption vigilance and more active intolerance of abuses of power.

—•— % corruption reports —■— % non-anonymous corruption reports

Sources: Figures were provided to me by the ICAC, but most can be found in ICAC annual reports.

Figure 2.3 Reports, corruption reports, and non-anonymous corruption reports, 1973–2002

Forms of Corruption

Reported corruption also suggests patterns of change in prevalent forms of corruption. For example, reports of corruption in fire departments and government hospitals were not uncommon in the 1970s, but had practically disappeared by the end of the 1980s. Reports of police corruption as a proportion of all reported corruption decreased over the years (as shown in Table 2.6), but the police force has continuously accounted for much more reported corruption than any other government department. In annual reports, beginning as early as the first report, the ICAC commissioner has frequently made an effort to place these numbers in comparative context. For example, the reports provide figures on the large size of the police force relative to other government departments, point out that police officers have relatively more daily contact with the public than other government officials, and note that corruption of the "satisfied customer" type (which typically goes unreported) accounts for a relatively higher proportion of corruption in other government departments, such as housing and public works. Nonetheless, even when figures are adjusted for relative department size, reported police corruption has consistently been a good deal higher than reported corruption in most other government departments.[53]

Other government departments in which reported corruption has been significant over the years are the Housing Department and Urban Services Department. Reported corruption in each of these departments was less than 25 percent of reported police corruption in the 1990s, and absolute numbers of reports for the Housing Department have increased noticeably beginning in 1993. That is, corruption in housing and urban services has been a constant problem and remains a problem. Another government department in which reported corruption suggests an ongoing problem is the Lands Department, although reports of corruption there amount only to about half the number for the Housing and Urban Services Departments. Finally, reports of corruption in the Regional Services Department are only somewhat fewer than those for corruption in the Lands Department.

These patterns are not inconsistent with survey data, although observations are fewer and the time period shorter. As noted above, in surveys conducted in 1980–90, respondents who stated there was corruption in at least one or two government departments were asked to name departments. Not surprisingly, the police department figured most prominently in responses to this question. Seventy-nine percent mentioned the police in 1980, and responses in the years following rarely dropped below 50 percent. Other frequently mentioned sectors are: urban services, health inspection, public works, fire services, and housing—but none is mentioned in more than 20 percent of valid responses (more commonly 10 percent).

A Summary of the Pattern of Change

What pattern emerges from the various sorts of evidence considered to this point? Overall, outcomes suggest the strong impact of anticorruption interventions. An initial boost in public confidence was clearly evident by the end of 1974. Syndicated police corruption was eradicated by the end of the 1970s, and by the mid-1980s (or late 1980s, at worst) corruption in government was no longer a routine practice. A new equilibrium of clean government was established, accompanied and sustained by public expectations of clean officials and public confidence in the ICAC as a credible anticorruption organization. Yet, sometime around 1993, corruption began to rise and continued to rise for about another three years. The equilibrium of clean government was plainly threatened, although confidence in the ICAC never seriously eroded. In 1994–96, more than one-third of survey respondents viewed corruption in government as the norm once more. With the transfer of sovereignty of Hong Kong from Britain to mainland China in 1997, this erosion of past gains ceased. More to the point, despite public and official anxiety about a post-1997 explosion of corruption, Hong Kong as a special administrative region of the mainland quickly regained the equilibrium of clean government attained in the 1980s. To summarize, the overall pattern is one of decreasing corruption since 1974, with an anomalous increase in 1993–96.

Accepting, then, the pattern described above, the puzzle is clear. If ICAC anticorruption efforts reasonably account for the new equilibrium of clean government achieved in the 1980s, what accounts for the short-term rise in corrupt activities and corresponding expectations in the years preceding the transfer of sovereignty in 1997?

Explaining the Anomaly of the 1990s

This section attributes the rise and fall of corruption in the 1990s to the political and economic context of the time. Most important is the influence of mainland China, both direct and indirect. The section begins with a general argument about the role of uncertainty in promoting corruption in the 1990s. This is followed by a discussion of the relationship between corruption and business cycles. Most of the section presents arguments about the specific impact of four processes on corruption: mainland Chinese investment in Hong Kong, migration from the mainland to Hong Kong, migration and return of Hong Kong businessmen, and early retirement in the Hong Kong civil service. Each is offered as a plausible explanation of the anomaly of the 1990s, in the sense that it meets two requirements. First, it supplies a reasonable substantial argument that links each process with corruption. Second, each process explains both the rise of corruption in 1993–96 and the recovery after 1997. Each of these changes is presented as having an independent impact. Of the four, migration from the mainland and early retirement from the civil service were probably the least consequential in terms of impact.

The four specific processes elaborated below are not inconsistent with a more general and fairly obvious explanation having to do with *uncer-*

tainty in Hong Kong about the mainland Chinese regime's willingness and ability to uphold the institutions necessary for continued economic prosperity and political freedom after 1997. The uncertainty was well founded. For example, considering the instrumental view of law on the mainland, investors reasonably feared that property rights were not secure (see discussion in Newman and Weimer 1997). Considering the politicized nature of the mainland bureaucracy and the insensitivity of mainland Chinese statements on the issue, officials properly feared that loyalty tests would substitute for civil service neutrality (see Wong 1997).

That uncertainty about the future of Hong Kong after 1997 affected actions is not in dispute. To cite a couple of key indicators for the 1990s, local investors increasingly incorporated their companies outside the territory rather than in Hong Kong and put increasingly less of their personal capital into new businesses (Newman and Weimer 1997). Increasing numbers of highly educated or fairly wealthy Hong Kong Chinese emigrated to Australia or North America (Skeldon 1994a, 1994b, 1995; Siu-lun Wong 1992). That uncertainty about the future encouraged more risk taking in anticipation of the transfer of sovereignty is not a leap of logic, and that risk taking included corrupt activities is not farfetched. Civil servants uncertain about the security of their positions were likely to be more willing than before to abuse office for personal advantage. Businesses and ordinary citizens were likely to find more officials willing to be their accomplices in corruption, and they may have needed official accomplices more to accomplish their goals before 1997. In fact, the ICAC commissioner alluded to these forms of risk taking when he cited the "1997 quick buck syndrome" as a major impetus for increased corruption (ICAC 1994: 9).

In short, the rise in corruption in 1993–96 can be explained as a product of the "end game" context. The transfer of sovereignty in 1997 was a certainty, and end game strategies were set in motion by the huge uncertainty about the fate of Hong Kong under mainland sovereignty. In real life, of course, most "games" are played more than once. Shared expectations about strategies of other players develop through continuous play, presenting cooperative solutions that do not normally emerge in a one-shot game. In an "end game," players know the game is finite, and this knowledge leads them to adopt strategies as though the game were "one-shot." This shift in strategies of a sizeable number of important players describes Hong Kong in the years immediately preceding the transfer of sovereignty in 1997, with a predictable increase in corruption.

Before moving on to present four specific explanations of changes in corruption in the 1990s, it is important to address (and rule out) a second general explanation: business cycles. Conventionally, economic recession is thought to trigger a rise in corruption and economic growth to bring about a decline.[54] This relationship treats corruption as a sort of second job to which people turn to make up lost income from legal work activities. Alternatively, corruption can be viewed as a product of economic growth, which offers more opportunities for illegal as well as legal economic activity. These arguments point to predictions in opposite directions. More to the point, neither offer predictions consistent with what appears to be the pattern of corruption in Hong Kong in the 1980s and 1990s.[55]

Consider the 1990s, for example. Per capita GDP in Hong Kong grew on average by nearly 5 percent in the early 1990s, by just over 2 percent in the mid-1990s, and by lower (including negative) rates in the late 1990s (with the Asian financial crisis). Undoubtedly, Hong Kong's economic boom in the early 1990s attracted certain mainland Chinese investors who might not otherwise have played a role in the Hong Kong economy and who (as argued below) did indeed contribute to increased corruption. Yet the state of the Hong Kong economy was probably no more important in this regard than the economic liberalization on the mainland that immediately followed the famous "southern tour" by Deng Xiaoping in 1992, signaling a shift away from the post-1989 conservative interregnum. Both of these point to specific sorts of linkages, however. The general arguments noted above, linking economic growth (or decline) and corruption, do not appear to measure up very well.[56]

Mainland Chinese Investment in Hong Kong

With the "reform and opening" of the economy in mainland China in the 1980s, Hong Kong and the mainland became increasingly economically interdependent. The ratio of Hong Kong–mainland China trade to the Hong Kong GDP captures this well. From a mere 0.17 in 1979, it surpassed 1.00 in 1989 (Newman and Weimer 1997). While both sides of this relationship account in some part for the rise and fall of corruption in the 1990s, mainland China's economic presence in Hong Kong is undoubtedly more important.

To be sure, Hong Kong investment in the mainland Chinese economy was (and is) very substantial. By the early 1990s, Hong Kong had contributed more than 60 percent of all direct foreign investment in China (Hsueh and Woo 1994). Much of this was in the directly adjacent southern province of Guangdong, in which Hong Kong businesses relocated industrial capacity in the 1980s, transforming the Hong Kong economy at the same time. In a special survey commissioned by the ICAC in 1993, business executives in Hong Kong companies with a production base in mainland China characterized themselves as "victims" of rampant corruption on the mainland, with little choice but to rely on personal relationships and gifts as a normal means of conducting business there. By their estimation, gifts (including cash and deposits in Hong Kong bank accounts) typically amounted to 3–5 percent of operating costs (ICAC 1993).[57] These practices, taking place on the mainland and involving the private sector, are not strictly relevant here, however. As to the public sector, ICAC intelligence officers interviewed in 1995 commented that Hong Kong government officials routinely made use of relationships with their counterparts in Guangdong to obtain privileged business opportunities there (ICAC Operations Department 5 July 1995, 21 July 1995). Again, however, these practices take place on the mainland, and also do not necessarily meet the definition of corruption.

The other side of the relationship appears more important. The mainland Chinese emerged as Hong Kong's biggest outside investor sometime in 1993 (overtaking Britain, Japan, and the United States), doubling their investment in Hong Kong in 1992–94 (Shen 1993). From about US $9 billion in 1989, Chinese investment in Hong Kong expanded to reach US $20 billion in 1994.[58] By the end of that year, more than 1,800 Chinese companies were in Hong Kong with the official approval of the Chinese government (*Gang ao jingji* 1995, no. 2: 61). Companies operating without approval almost certainly exceeded this official number. Some estimates put the actual number of Chinese companies in Hong Kong at closer to 5,000 (see Lin 1996).

The explosion of Chinese investment in Hong Kong in 1993 also differed qualitatively from two earlier waves of mainland investment (see Chan 1995; Tseng 1996). The earliest investors were four big corporate groups, effectively business arms of the Chinese government, each monopolizing a business in which they specialized and representing mainland China in dealings with Hong Kong companies. With the reforms of the 1980s came the second wave of investors: companies from Guangdong and Fujian provinces and the coastal cities, which had been granted preferential treatment by Beijing to invest abroad. The mainland Chinese investors of the early 1990s had neither trade monopolies nor preferential permits to establish themselves in Hong Kong.

Many were local governments or central ministries investing strategically through the Hong Kong Stock Exchange to raise funds to inject into their mainland companies. As these mainland companies typically did not meet requirements for listing on the stock exchange, they took irregular shortcuts to achieve listed status. They commonly acquired "shells" in Hong Kong, inactively traded companies already publicly listed or companies not listed but which satisfied requirements for listing (see Shen 1993; Chan 1995; Tseng 1996; Cai 1999). This third wave of investors typically sought quick returns on their investments by speculating in the highly volatile Hong Kong property market. Additionally, the heads of many companies investing in Hong Kong in the 1990s were linked personally to top mainland Chinese leaders. The insecurity of these investors, inherent in the fluctuating relative power of various political patrons, gave them incentives to pursue individual interests through quick returns on their investments, usually at the expense of longer-term company interests.[59]

In sum, beginning in about 1993, not only did mainland Chinese investment in Hong Kong expand enormously, but the new mainland investors were also less scrupulous about playing by the rules. It is not farfetched, I think, to argue that the appearance of this new type of economic player in large numbers presented Hong Kong government officials with new opportunities to pursue corrupt gains. That they may indeed have pursued these opportunities is suggested by the increase in reported corruption in government, greater prevalence of beliefs about corruption in government, and ICAC intelligence about a rise in corruption, discussed above.

In 1994, Beijing reacted strongly to the activities of these new investors in Hong Kong because they threatened to undermine "prosperity and stability" in the territory—the maintenance of which was, for Beijing, a major political objective of Chinese investment.[60] The Hong Kong Stock Exchange also reacted, introducing new standards in 1994 for mainland companies attempting to list through the "back door" (see Chan 1995). These included a requirement that mainland companies produce official documents indicating that their plan to list in Hong Kong was approved by the Chinese Securities Regulatory Commission, in effect giving Beijing a new lever to control mainland economic activities in Hong Kong. As 1997 approached, political leaders in Beijing expressed increasing concern about the contaminating effects of corruption from the mainland and its potential to harm the Hong Kong economy. Moreover, only a few years after the transfer of sovereignty, they established a new post at the Xinhua office (which represents Beijing in Hong Kong). While the exact functions of the new deputy director were not disclosed, the person appointed to the post had worked previously in the communist party's anticorruption agency and was widely expected to investigate corruption among mainland companies in Hong Kong and their affiliates (*South China Morning Post*, 7 Jan. 2000).

Chinese Migrants to Hong Kong

Increased immigration presents another direct channel through which mainland Chinese may have contributed to corruption in Hong Kong. Immigrants habituated to the corrupt practices widespread in mainland China and unaccustomed to the notion of rule of law arrived with a set of expectations unsupportive of clean government. Unfamiliarity with relevant specific laws in Hong Kong probably made them easy targets for extortion of bribes. Illegal immigrants had two additional problems. They were more likely than legal immigrants to require favors involving corruption (for work, medical care, or housing, for example), and they could not report complaints if victimized by corrupt officials (for fear of exposing their status as illegals).

Prior to October 1980, a "touch base" policy granted an automatic right to residency to any mainland Chinese who arrived in Hong Kong. Net migration from the mainland was about 400,000 in the 1950s, 120,000 in the 1960s, and 500,000 in the 1970s (official statistics, cited in Siu-lun Wong 1992). After October 1980, by mutual agreement, the mainland Chinese authorities gained control over legal migration to Hong Kong through the use of exit permits, initially issued at the rate of 75 per day. In the 1980s, migrants arriving in Hong Kong with exit permits issued by the mainland authorities totaled about 243,000. In 1990–96, the number was nearly 250,000.[61] Legal migration from the mainland was accelerated in the 1990s by two big increases in the exit permit rate: a 40 percent increase (to 105 per day) at the end of 1993, followed by a 43 percent increase (to 150 per day) in mid-1995. The overwhelming majority of these immigrants (more than 85 percent) were spouses (mainly wives) or children of mainland Chinese already resident in Hong Kong. Just over one-half of the adult migrants entered the labor force, most as employees earning low incomes and without managerial responsibilities (Siu 1999). More likely than not, legal migrants arriving from the mainland in the 1990s did not contribute very significantly to the increase in corruption. The numbers of economically active migrants among them were not very large (about 72,000 in 1990–96), and the nature of their employment was unlikely to bring them into much contact with government officials. Moreover, to the extent that they wanted to sponsor additional relatives from the mainland, they probably tried to observe the law.

Illegal migrants are another matter, however. Ronald Skeldon (1995) estimates that vigilance by the police force has kept the number of illegal mainland immigrants down to somewhere less than 20,000 at any given time. This is a small number, but most are males in the prime economically active age groups; they are most responsive to economic fluctuations such as labor shortages in an economic boom. As argued above, the objective demand for corruption (of the "satisfied customer" sort) is likely to be relatively high and recourse to the law (if victimized) low for illegal immigrants. Skeldon (1991) also presents figures on illegal mainland immigrants detained upon entry and illegal mainland immigrants arrested as "evaders" (that is, arrested some time after successfully infiltrating border security and finding employment as low-income laborers in sectors such as construction). These figures show a trend in the 1980s toward increasing proportions arrested as evaders, that is, a longer stay and higher rate of participation in the labor market. For example, in 1989 and 1990 (the most recent years for which figures are presented), illegals detained as evaders are about twice the number of those detained upon entry; in previous years, the number detained upon entry were about three times the number arrested as evaders. More likely than not, illegal migrants from the mainland, while many fewer in number than legal migrants, contributed more to the increase in corruption in the early 1990s.[62] Furthermore, the economic downturn with the Asian financial crisis in 1998 probably discouraged illegal migration to Hong Kong, which would partially explain the decline of corruption after 1997. Migrants from the mainland, legal or illegal, probably had much less impact on corruption than the economic influences discussed earlier or the indirect influences discussed below, however.

Hong Kong Migrants and Returnees

With the signing of the Joint Declaration in 1984, the transfer of sovereignty over Hong Kong from Britain to mainland China in 1997 became a certainty, setting in motion an end game for many in Hong Kong with opportunities elsewhere. The ICAC commissioner referred to this in 1993 as the "1997 quick buck syndrome," and it included efforts of Hong Kong Chinese and expatriates to make as much money as possible in anticipation of exiting the territory before the transfer of sovereignty in 1997.

Emigration (and return) is prominent in one end game strategy, adopted by a number of Hong Kong Chinese in the business sector. In 1980–86, emigration averaged about 21,000 annually, with little variation over the years. Beginning in 1987, it rose sharply. In 1987–97, average annual emigration exceeded 48,000, with the peak at 66,000 in 1992 (Skeldon 1990–91; Siu 1999). Skeldon (1990–91) reasons that 1987 was the year when people began to look seriously for alternatives to Hong Kong, as part of a "ten-year countdown." Those who emigrated from Hong Kong as 1997 approached tended to be educated, highly skilled, and quite prosperous. The numbers with vast wealth were a minority, but many had substantial assets. Between one-fourth and one-third of Hong Kong Chinese migrating to Canada in the 1990s entered under business migration programs for entrepreneurs, investors, and the self-employed (Smart 1994). Hong Kong contributed nearly one-half of the people who entered Canada under the investor program in 1986–93. Indeed, over US $4.2 billion flowed from Hong Kong to Canada in 1992 alone (official Canadian estimates, cited in Skeldon 1994b). Business programs also accounted for significant proportions of migrants to Australia and New Zealand.

The migrants of interest here are those who returned to Hong Kong in the 1990s to work with a foreign passport or residence status in some other country. No accurate data are available on these returnees, but official government estimates put their number at 10 to 12 percent of migrants who left Hong Kong beginning in the mid-1980s (Skeldon 1991, 1995).[63] Skeldon (1995) views this estimate as too conservative. He estimates that at least one-third of migrants who left for Australia in the early 1990s may have returned, although rates for Canada and the United States were probably somewhat lower. By returning to Hong Kong, often leaving families behind to ensure citizenship, these migrants hedged their economic and political risks, with a foothold in two economies at different stages of the business cycle and the legal right to leave Hong Kong permanently if the political situation deteriorated (Skeldon 1994b). Returnees with the right of abode elsewhere numbered in the hundreds of thousands of Hong Kong residents in 1994 (Skeldon 1994a).[64] Paul Kwong (1993: 155) comments, on the basis of essentially anecdotal evidence, that returnees were not a "stable force" in Hong Kong, that they gave themselves three to four years to accomplish one mission: "Make as much money as possible, and then either stay after 1997 to make more money or pull out from Hong Kong and China."

As with migrants from mainland China, nothing conclusive can be said about the contribution of returnees to the rise of corruption in the early 1990s. Returnees differ from migrants, however, in that they are wealthier, more likely to interact with government officials in their work, have a shorter time frame, and probably many (if not most) exited Hong Kong shortly before 1997. In the mid-1990s, their numbers were also probably greater than illegal mainland migrants. For these reasons, returnees may better explain both the rise and fall of corruption in the 1990s.

Hong Kong Civil Service Retirements

Turning from businesses and ordinary citizens to government officials themselves, trends in the civil service also suggest another possible contribution to the corruption in the 1990s that diminished after 1997. This has to do with retirements from the Hong Kong civil service.

From the late 1980s to the mid-1990s, overall annual attrition rates in the civil service remained quite low (4 to 6 percent in 1988–96), but two new trends began to emerge in 1992–93 (see Lee 1997). First, the rate of retirement increased enormously, from 12 percent of total attrition in the late 1980s to 50 percent by the mid-1990s. Second, the attrition rate in the thousand or so directorate posts (the most senior civil servants, who essentially run the government departments) increased greatly over previous years, reaching a rate of about 10 percent beginning in 1992–93. Fanny Wong (1997) notes that early retirement overall and among senior officials in particular was more noticeable in some government departments, including the police department, than in others. Financial incentives (discussed below) played a major role. Yet, these should be understood in the context of two views that gained currency among civil servants in the 1990s: unease about the changing role of the civil service in the new period of Hong Kong legislative politics (Lee 1997) and anxiety about whether mainland China actually understood the culture of neutrality in the civil service (Wong 1997).

Early retirement among civil servants, especially senior civil servants, had much to do with financial incentives in a new pension scheme introduced in 1987. Under the old scheme, civil servants retired at age 55 (with an option to retire at 50) and could draw up to 25 percent of the pension as a lump-sum gratuity. Under the new scheme, the normal age of retirement was raised to 60 (with an option to retire at 55) and 50 percent of the pension could be drawn as a lump-sum gratuity. Senior civil servants could retire with a much higher gratuity payment under the new pension scheme, and many officials in posts at the directorate level (in particular, expatriates, who occupied nearly one-half of all these posts in 1987) opted for early retirement rather than risk not being able to draw on their pension benefits after the transfer of sovereignty. While some retired officials then emigrated from Hong Kong, others joined the private sector. Indeed, retired civil servants formed a consulting firm to sell their expertise on government matters. As Grace Lee (1997) argues, a large-scale movement of civil servants into the private sector must subject the civil service to outside influences. In part, officials work to establish relations with future employers while in office.[65] While her argument is intended as a prospective one that anticipates the consequences of retirements to the private sector after 1997, she presents evidence pointing to the trend of early retirement beginning in 1992, well before the transfer of sovereignty. Moreover, she offers evidence that significant proportions of officials and former officials intended to emigrate upon the transfer of sovereignty.

Two arguments, then, link civil service retirement trends to the rise of corruption in the 1990s. Both take into account a rise in the early retirement rate—prompted by the new pension scheme, worries about pension and job security after 1997, anxiety about the changing role of the civil service, and fears about mainland Chinese politicized notions of bureaucracy. First, officials planning early retirement to the private sector may have anticipated their move by cultivating less scrupulous relationships with potential future employers in the private sector. Second, officials who retired to the private sector may have made use of their government contacts to seek favors, including corrupt advantages. Taking into account the exodus of government officials and former officials when sovereignty over Hong Kong was transferred from Britain to mainland China, the actions can be viewed as part of the "1997 quick buck syndrome" and are also consistent with the decline of corruption after 1997.

Conclusion

In the early 1970s, corruption was endemic in Hong Kong and worst of all in the government department charged specifically with anticorruption work: Police corruption was organized in flourishing, apparently invulnerable syndicates. Syndicated corruption was found in other government departments too, as was individualized "satisfied customer" corruption, "gratuities" to junior officials, and the blatant or subtle extortionist "squeeze" that exploited the ignorance, resignation, and despair of ordinary citizens in their dealings with government. The

Hong Kong mass public viewed corruption as an unchangeable feature of daily life. This is no longer so. The transformation from widespread corruption to clean government was basically achieved by about the mid-1980s. The equilibrium of clean government has persisted, despite challenges in the years leading up to 1997. Today, there is more cause for optimism than pessimism about the continued persistence of clean government in Hong Kong. This owes much to the past and ongoing work of the ICAC, an anticorruption organization that enjoys high popular confidence and strong government support.

This chapter has documented the transformation that began in 1974 with the creation of the ICAC, its independence from the police, subordination only to the governor, exemplary leadership, and draconian powers sending (what was viewed as) an immediately credible signal that the "quiet revolution" of clean government had begun. This chapter has also described the ICAC's three-pronged anticorruption strategy: enforcement, education, and institutional design. The link between anticorruption interventions and results in Hong Kong is about as clear as it can possibly be, considering the usual difficulties of measurement in the study of corruption.

Despite a rise in corruption beginning in 1993, two more recent trends offer a reasonable basis for optimism about the ongoing and future anticorruption effort in Hong Kong. On the one hand, it appears that corruption in government has returned to the historically low levels of the 1980s and that increased corruption was an anomaly explained mainly by unique circumstances preceding the transfer of sovereignty in 1997. On the other hand, it appears that ordinary citizens are reporting corruption in greater proportions than before. This may be due to a new vigilance now that Hong Kong has become part of China, known for its widespread corruption. It may be due to a new critical scrutiny and higher demands of government now that Hong Kong is no longer a British colony. Whatever the cause, the Hong Kong community appears more, not less, willing than before to contribute as "voluntary enforcers" to the anticorruption effort.

CHAPTER THREE

An Explosion of Corruption in Mainland China

As early as 1982, Chinese leaders publicly acknowledged that corruption had reached crisis levels. By their own account, corruption continued to grow more or less unabated through the 1980s and 1990s, despite drastic measures to control it. A senior researcher at the Central Discipline Inspection Commission (CDIC), the communist party anticorruption agency, described in the late 1990s the following trends:

> Not only is corruption widespread in the economic spheres of finance, securities, real estate, land leasing, and construction, but it also has emerged and is growing in politics, culture, and all aspects of social life—in the party, government, and [nonpolitical] organizations. A second trend is more collaborative corruption and corruption at high levels of authority. Cases tend to involve more people, some cases as many as tens or even hundreds of individuals. More cases involve close collaboration and bigger amounts of money, rising to the billions [of yuan]. More cases involve leading officials at and above the division level of administration. Cases involving middle-ranking and high-ranking officials have tripled in the past few years. A third trend, surfacing despite the major anticorruption effort by the party and government in recent years and some abatement of some sorts of corruption, is the continued growth of corruption overall. Crimes continue to be committed in great numbers: More than 50 percent of cases investigated in a year are crimes committed in that year. The number of cases involving big sums *(da an)* and senior officials *(yao an)* rises yearly. Improper conduct is repeatedly prohibited, only to reappear in new forms. The spread of corruption to executive departments of the party and government and departments responsible for law enforcement and discipline becomes more serious by the day. (Li 1997: 21–22)

This chapter charts and explains the rapid acceleration in China past a "tipping point" to an equilibrium of widespread corruption by the mid-1980s. It first establishes that the volume of corrupt activities in China exploded in the early 1980s, continued to grow in the 1980s and 1990s, and increasingly involved large sums (probably increasingly larger sums) and probably a greater number of senior officials too. It then describes the most common and serious forms of corruption in China and examines their general and specific sources in post-Mao policy. The chapter concludes with a consideration of these different forms of corruption in terms of the political and economic anticorruption challenge for the Chinese authorities.

Interestingly, the forms of corruption that are the most visible, repugnant, and directly costly to ordinary citizens are not the forms that produce the most serious state revenue losses. Chinese authorities have responded to the anticorruption challenge by defining the forms of corruption that produce major state revenue losses mostly as crimes. The forms of corruption most offensive and directly costly to ordinary citizens have been defined as mere irregularities. This practical emphasis on corruption as an economic problem has exacerbated corruption as a political problem, that is, as a problem of regime legitimacy. This chapter's discussion of the anticorruption challenge and regime response prepares the way for Chapters 4 and 5, which explore anticorruption strategies adopted in the 1980s and 1990s.

The Growth of Corruption

Anecdotal evidence and legal casebooks in China are rich with disclosures of corruption involving huge sums or very senior officials (or both) and its reach to practically every party and government department. Corruption reaches to the highest level of leadership. Politburo member and Beijing Party Secretary Chen Xitong was found guilty in 1998 of embezzlement and dereliction of duty, after a lengthy investigation that implicated other senior officials and provoked the suicide of Beijing Deputy Mayor Wang Baosen. Corruption is prominent in law enforcement, including anticorruption enforcement at high levels. Anticorruption Bureau Chief Luo Ji was removed from office in 1998 for diverting embezzled funds recovered by his bureau. Public Security Deputy Minister and Antismuggling Leading Group Deputy Chief Li Jizhou was found guilty in 2001 of accepting bribes and obstructing justice to facilitate major smuggling operations. These stories and countless others suggest the seriousness of corruption in China.

Estimates put losses of state revenue due to corruption at approximately 4 percent of GDP annually at the end of the 1990s (Hu 2001). Corruption is a highly volatile issue in Chinese society. Increasing income inequality in the 1980s and 1990s has exacerbated this volatility because of a perception that the wealthy have attained their status corruptly. For example, 60 percent of ordinary Chinese surveyed by People's University Social Survey Center in the mid-1990s believed that "hardly any" or "not many" of those with wealth had obtained it by legitimate means (He 1997: 259). The official Chinese news agency put the Gini coefficient at 0.458, "greater than the international warning line," in March 2001, more than twice the figure provided by the State Statistics Bureau for 1978 (*Economist* 2–8 June 2001: 39, 44).[1]

Since the mid-1980s, corruption has ranked at or near the top of every public opinion poll as the most urgent problem confronting the country. Citizens describe it as serious and its growth as unabated or more rapid than ever.[2] As recently as 2002, in an Internet survey conducted by the *Renmin ribao,* the communist party newspaper, corruption emerged at the top of ten social, political, and economic concerns (see *Straits Times* 28 Feb. 2002). The National People's Congress, which rarely dissents in its votes, reflected this dissatisfaction by presenting the chief procurator with the lowest rates of approval on record for his reports on the anticorruption effort in 1997 and 1998. In 1998 the report barely passed.[3]

It is difficult to quantify the real magnitude of corruption, but its growth can be substantiated reasonably well. This section draws inferences about growth from the most conservative sort of evidence: criminal corruption enforcement statistics. To be sure, corruption revealed by these sorts of statistics may indeed be but "a single hair on nine oxen" (Hu 2001: 34), hardly suggestive of the scope of the real problem. The official figures are quite adequate, however, to support the conclusion that corruption exploded in the early 1980s and grew very significantly in the 1980s and 1990s.

Many specific economic crimes can be committed by public officials or ordinary citizens, but Chinese law gives the procuracy, a government investigative and prosecutorial agency, exclusive authority to investigate crimes of officials.[4] Not surprisingly, given this division of labor, unlawful abuses of public office to pursue private gain comprised a very large subset of economic crimes investigated by procurators in the 1980s and 1990s. For the most part, criminal corruption involves embezzlement of public assets *(tanwu),* acceptance or solicitation of bribes, or misuse of public funds—all crimes which, by legal definition, can only be committed by public officials (see Chapter 4 on the legal definitions of these and other crimes of corruption). These three crimes accounted for 80 percent of all economic crime cases filed for investigation by procurators in the 1980s and 1990s. In the 1990s, they accounted for 85 percent of all economic crime cases involving "big sums" and 95 percent of all "senior officials" investigated for involvement in economic crime.[5] Aptly, the Economic Crime Bureau of the Supreme People's Procuratorate (SPP) was renamed the Anticorruption Bureau at the end of the 1980s.

Table 3.1 presents official figures on the three main crimes of corruption—which together totaled more than 700,000 cases filed for investigation in 1979–2000. Some of the big patterns of change over time are more apparent in Figure 3.1. The figures understate revealed criminal corruption by some unknown magnitude: Procurators conducted preliminary reviews of perhaps double this number of cases, but ultimately did not conduct a criminal investigation.[6] Of all criminal corruption investigated in the 1980s and 1990s, embezzlement of public assets accounts for 56 percent of cases, bribery for 28 percent, and misuse of public funds for 16 percent.[7] Senior officials, defined as officials at and above the county or division level *(xian chu)* of administration, comprised a mere 3 percent of officials investigated in the 1990s.[8] Criminal corruption involving big sums comprised one-third of all cases investigated from the late 1980s through the 1990s, although a change in legal definition, effective in 1998, significantly reduced the number of such cases.[9] Before 1998, "big sums" referred to bribery and embezzlement of public assets involving sums of 10,000 yuan or more and misuse of public funds in sums of 50,000 yuan or more. These sums were raised to 50,000 yuan and 100,000 yuan, respectively.

Certainly, the official figures are unreliable estimates of the actual volume of criminal corruption. Most obviously, in mainland China, as elsewhere, much corruption goes unreported. Ordinary citizens who are victims of corruption that results in lower state revenues or shoddy construction in public works are unlikely to be aware of a specific crime to report. Outright theft of state assets, kickbacks in government procurement, and any corrupt exchanges of the "satisfied customer" variety will also go unreported by those involved. Additionally, in contexts where officials routinely flout the law, as they do in China, ordinary citizens are likely to view the authorities as unreliable anticorruption enforcers. Official extortion may then go unreported too, even if the ex-

Table 3.1 Cases of bribery, embezzlement, and misuse of public funds filed and investigated by procuratorates, 1979–2000

Year	All cases	Bribery	Embezzlement of public assets	Misuse of public funds
1979	598[a]	—	—	—
1980	6,941	454	6,487	—
1981	9,879	1,306	8,550	23
1982	22,913	6,547	16,348	18
1983	16,440	2,763	13,667	10
1984	17,304	2,224	15,065	15
1985	22,301	3,775	18,516	10
1986	34,382[a]	6,047[a]	28,335[a]	—
1987	23,581	4,804	18,777	—
1988	21,441	4,840	16,292	309
1989	60,494	25,245	33,681	1,568
1990	61,929	22,185	29,188	10,556
1991	57,260	17,668	28,551	11,041
1992	47,451	11,964	24,569	10,918
1993	44,540	10,019	20,858	13,663
1994	50,074	14,797	21,674	13,603
1995	51,089	16,831	21,642	12,616
1996	46,314	15,945	19,520	10,849
1997	42,762	12,916	18,782	11,064
1998	29,951	8,759	12,909	8,283
1999	32,620	8,192	14,372	10,056
2000	36,807	9,872	16,765	10,170

Sources: I found no figures on criminal corruption for 1979 and none on misuse of public funds for 1980, 1986, or 1987. Figures for 1980–85 are from He with Waltz (1995: 271). Figures for 1987–99 are from yearbooks published by the procuracy since 1989: *Zhongguo jiancha nianjian 1988* (1989: 351), *1989* (1991: 410), *1990* (1991: 327), *1991* (1992: 342), *1992* (1992: 361), *1993* (1994: 417), *1994* (1995: 550), *1995* (1996: 382), *1996* (1997: 396), *1997* (1998: 486), *1998* (1999: 506), *1999* (2000: 511), *2000* (2001: 645), *2001* (2002: 504). The 1979 figure on economic crime used for the 1979 estimate in col. 2 is from Gong (1991: 1).

Notes: The 1997 Criminal Law no longer considers managers in enterprises that are not state enterprises in defining crimes in these three categories, with the result that cases greatly diminish in number beginning in 1998. See *Zhonghua renmin gongheguo xingfa* (14 March 1997, Arts. 163, 271, 272). I found no statistics to construct comparable figures for recent years. The 1986 estimates in cols. 2, 3, and 4 are calculated by subtracting all cases of bribery and embezzlement of public assets filed for investigation by procuratorates in the six-year period 1982–85 and 1987–88, for which data are available, from the figure provided by Liu Fuzhi (SPP, Chief Procurator 29 March 1989) on cases of bribery and embezzlement of public assets filed for investigation by procuratorates in the seven-year period 1982–88; we know that cases of misuse of public funds filed in these years were infinitesimal. The 1979 estimate in column 2 is 85 percent of all cases of economic crime filed for investigation by procuratorates in 1979; we know that bribery, embezzlement of public assets, and misuse of public funds amount to this percentage of all economic crime cases filed for investigation by procuratorates in 1980.

Campaign years are in bold.

a. Estimated.

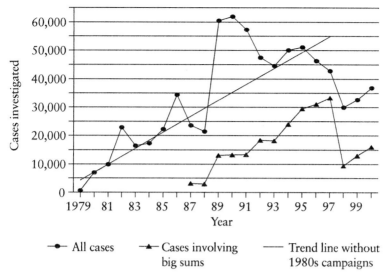

Figure 3.1 Criminal corruption cases investigated, 1979–2000

Sources: I found no figures on criminal corruption for 1979 and none on criminal corruption involving big sums for 1980–86. Figures for 1980–85 are from He with Waltz (1995: 271). Figures for 1987–99 are from yearbooks published by the procuracy since 1989: *Zhongguo jiancha nianjian 1988* (1989: 351), *1989* (1991: 410), *1990* (1991: 327), *1991* (1992: 342), *1992* (1992: 361), *1993* (1994: 417), *1994* (1995: 550), *1995* (1996: 382), *1996* (1997: 396), *1997* (1998: 486), *1998* (1999: 506), *1999* (2000: 511), *2000* (2001: 645), *2001* (2002: 504). The 1979 figure on economic crime used for the 1979 estimate is from Gong (1991: 1).

Notes: Big sums are defined, until 1998, as money and assets valued at 10,000 yuan or more for bribery and embezzlement of public assets, 50,000 yuan or more for misuse of public funds; beginning in 1998, values are 50,000 yuan and 100,000 yuan, respectively.

See Notes for Table 3.1 for more information.

change involves a good to which individuals are legally entitled. Victims of extortion are likely to view reporting the crime as an unproductive nuisance or, worse yet, an invitation to official retaliation, a matter taken up in Chapter 5. All this implies that enforcement figures on corruption greatly *underestimate* its actual volume—because of the inherent nature of the crime, particularly where corruption is relatively widespread.

Additional problems attend the Chinese figures. First, the organization of Chinese anticorruption work is biased against criminal procedure. Much criminal corruption that is detected does not reach procurators at all, but rather is investigated by communist party agencies and punished with party disciplinary action. In the 1980s and 1990s, the party investigated and punished nearly 3 million communist party members, among whom more than 500,000 were punished with expulsion.[10] (As described in Chapter 4, some proportion of these are cases of criminal corruption not investigated as such.) Second, blatantly predatory actions by local governments and government agencies, which violate government regulations usually in pursuit of narrow collective gains, are treated as improprieties or irregularities, rather than crimes, a point taken up in a later section of this chapter. In sum, for a number of reasons, figures on criminal corruption in China underestimate actual corruption, probably hugely.

Assuming systematic bias, this sort of underestimation does not pose a problem for the question of interest here: change over time. The bias in Chinese figures involves not only systematic underestimation, however, but also significant measurement change and enforcement variation. As noted above, a redefinition of big sums deflated corruption figures in this category beginning in 1998. Also in 1998, a more restrictive understanding of the three main crimes of corruption began to exclude crimes by officials working strictly outside the state sector, in collectively-owned enterprises, for example.[11] In Figure 3.1, these changes in measurement are reflected in an apparent big drop in corruption in 1998 (by 30 percent, compared to 1997) and especially in corruption involving big sums (by 72 percent). As to enforcement variation, the main subject of Chapter 5, Chinese leaders adopted a "campaign" style of enforcement in the 1980s and 1990s, promoting an intensive anticorruption effort in some years and not others. Figure 3.1 reflects this with apparent peaks of corruption in 1982, 1986, and especially 1989. The Chinese enforcement focus was also uneven, with a much stronger emphasis on corruption involving big sums or senior officials after 1993. Cases involving big sums comprised 14 percent of all cases investigated in 1987, but 83 percent in 1997—an emphasis reflected in Figure 3.1 with an apparent steady, steep rise of corruption involving big sums in the 1990s.

Accepting that the figures hugely underestimate actual corruption and also conflate corruption and enforcement, the pattern of growth in the 1980s and 1990s is nonetheless evident. Ignoring campaign years of intensive enforcement in the 1980s, Figure 3.1 clearly illustrates a strong trend of increase in all cases.[12] Corruption has also apparently increasingly involved bigger sums and a greater number of senior officials over time. This trend, asserted publicly by Chinese leaders and procurators, is completely plausible. Given the campaign focus in the 1990s on big sums and senior officials, however, the figures nearly completely conflate corruption and enforcement. It is practically impossible to assess the trend of corruption involving a greater number of senior officials (and officials at more senior levels), but some levers exist for gauging growth in corruption involving big sums.

Figures for corruption cases involving big sums and senior officials are unavailable for the 1980s, but they are available for the larger set of all economic crime cases investigated by procurators, and these are a reasonable proxy for corruption (see Manion 1998). Ignoring campaign years of intensive enforcement, the number of economic crimes involving big sums or senior officials investigated by procurators increases from about 100 in 1980, to 700 in 1981, 2,000 in 1983 and 1984, and more than 5,000 in 1985, 1987, and 1988—all without the upward enforcement bias of the 1990s (see Table 3.2).[13] As senior officials are only a tiny proportion of these numbers, this suggests very significant increases in corruption involving big sums, although not necessarily increasingly bigger sums.

To gauge roughly (but with a measure more contaminated by enforcement bias) the increasingly bigger sums involved in corruption, we can consider growth in the value of assets recovered by the procuracy in their investigations. According to reports to the legislature by the SPP chief procurator, this amounted to less than 10,000 yuan per case in 1985, about 15,000 per case in 1990, nearly 60,000 per case in 1995, and more than 100,000 yuan per case in 2000.[14]

Alternatively, we can consider cases of bribery and embezzlement of public assets involving very big sums. This is less satisfactory because figures are not available for the early and mid-1980s, undoubtedly in part because such cases were less common, and this means that available figures completely conflate enforcement and actual corruption. In any case, in 1988–92, only 203 cases involved sums of more than 500,000 yuan, and only 81 involved sums of more than one million yuan. By contrast, in 1993–97, 1,414 cases involved sums of more than 500,000 yuan, and 617 involved sums of more than one million yuan— a substantial increase, notwithstanding inflation.[15] Acknowledgment of these increasingly bigger sums appeared in the redefinition of big sums in the 1997 Criminal Law, with fivefold increases for bribery and embezzlement of public assets, far outpacing inflation. In his report on anticorruption results in 1998–2002, the chief procurator discussed cases involving big sums of more than one million yuan (not 500,000 yuan): He aggregated cases of bribery, embezzlement, and misuse of

Table 3.2 Economic crime cases filed and investigated by procuratorates, 1979–99

	All economic crime			Bribery, embezzlement of public assets, and misuse of public funds as % of:		
Year	All cases	Cases involving big sums or senior officials		All cases	Cases involving big sums or senior officials	
1979	703	7		—	—	
1980	8,184	103		85%	—	
1981	15,753	717		63%	—	
1982	29,563	2,682		77%	—	
1983	22,531	2,120		73%	—	
1984	22,490	2,243		77%	—	
1985	28,812	6,249		77%	—	
1986	49,557	13,888		69%[a]	—	
1987	31,737	5,392		74%	63%	
1988	32,626	5,450		66%	58%	
1989	77,432	17,842		78%	78%	
1990	71,881	16,346	1,386	86%	81%	97%
1991	68,437	17,009	1,015	84%	78%	99%
1992	61,424	24,920	652	77%	74%	97%
1993	56,491	22,359	1,037	79%	81%	95%
1994	60,312	28,626	1,768	83%	84%	97%
1995	63,953	32,408	2,285	80%	91%	96%
1996	61,099	34,863	2,700	76%	89%	87%
1997	53,534	36,548	2,222	80%	91%	97%
1998	30,670	9,715	1,674	98%	97%	99%
1999	32,911	12,969	2,019	99%	100%	98%
2000	37,183	16,121	2,556	99%	99%	98%

Sources: Figures on all cases of economic crime filed for investigation in 1979–84 are from Gong (1991: 1), which are essentially the same as those in Wei and Wang (1992). (Although the latter study identifies the figures with cases of bribery and embezzlement of public assets, there is no doubt, from a comparison with several sources, that, except for 1988 and 1989, the figures in this study are for economic crime. Procuratorates began to report figures on corruption cases as a separate category in 1988. The only real discrepancy between the two studies is in figures for 1988 and 1989.) Figures on cases of economic crime involving big sums or senior officials filed for investigation in 1979–85 are from Wei and Wang (1992). Figures on all cases of economic crime filed for investigation in 1985 and 1986 and on cases involving big sums or senior officials in 1986 are from Supreme People's Protectorate (SPP), Chief Procurator Yang Yichen (8 April 1986, 6 April 1987). Both Gong (1991) and Wei and Wang (1992) provide figures on economic crime for 1979–89 and are the only sources I found that provide figures for 1979–81. For 1982–89, where a comparison with figures in annual reports by the chief procurator or procuratorial yearbooks is possible, the only notable discrepancy between figures in the two studies and those reported by the procuracy is in figures on all cases of economic crime filed for investigation in 1982. (The figure for economic crime cases filed for investigation in 1989 reported in Gong [1991: 1] is somewhat lower than that reported in the procuratorial yearbook on 1989, which did not appear until November 1991, but it matches the partial statistics provided by SPP, Chief Procurator

Table 3.2 (continued)

Liu Fuzhi [29 March 1990] in his report on activities in 1989.) For 1983–85 I chose to use the figures from the studies by Gong (1991) and Wei and Wang (1992) only because figures reported by the chief procurator on the activities of the past year are rounded to the nearest thousand (for all economic crime cases) or hundred (for cases involving big sums or senior officials). These figures do accord with the more precise figures reported in the two studies. For 1982, however, SPP, Chief Procurator Huang Huoqing (7 June 1983) reported that "more than 33,000" cases of economic crime had been filed for investigation, about 12 percent higher than the figure reported in the two studies. I chose to use the more conservative figure from the two studies because 1982 was a campaign year, the first since the reestablishment of the procuracy in 1978. Mechanisms for efficient compilation of economic crime data, if in place by 1982, were undoubtedly challenged by the massive increase in procuratorial activity in that year. The studies by Gong (1991) and Wei and Wang (1992) were produced many years after the campaign. Further, both studies acknowledge the review of the manuscript by organizations with access to relevant data: Officials in the Central Committee General Office reviewed the former study, and officials in the SPP reviewed the latter. Figures on bribery, embezzlement of public assets, and misuse of public funds for 1980–85 are from He Jiahong with Waltz (1995: 271). Figures for 1987–99 are from yearbooks published by the procuracy since 1989: *Zhongguo jiancha nianjian 1988* (1989: 351), *1989* (1991: 410), *1990* (1991: 327), *1991* (1992: 342), *1992* (1992: 361), *1993* (1994: 417), *1994* (1995: 550), *1995* (1996; 382), *1996* (1997: 396), *1997* (1998: 486), *1998* (1999: 506), *1999* (2000: 511), *2000* (2001: 645), *2001* (2002: 504).

Notes: Campaign years are in bold.

Big sums are defined, until 1998, as money and assets valued at 10,000 yuan or more for bribery and embezzlement of public assets, 50,000 yuan or more for misuse of public funds; beginning in 1998, values are 50,000 yuan and 100,000 yuan, respectively.

Senior officials are those at the county or division (*xian chu*) level and higher, with figures expressed as number of officials, not cases. Senior officials are essentially a subset of individuals investigated in cases involving big sums.

a. Estimated. This figure was calculated by subtracting all cases of bribery and embezzlement of public assets filed for investigation by procuratorates in the six-year period 1982–85 and 1987–88, for which data are available, from the figure provided by Liu Fuzhi (SPP, Chief Procurator 29 March 1989) on cases of bribery and embezzlement of public assets filed for investigation by procuratorates in the seven-year period 1982–88; we know that cases of misuse of public funds filed in these years were infinitesimal.

public funds, which makes comparison difficult, but the sum for the five years was a staggering 5,541 (SPP, Chief Procurator, 11 March 2003).

In sum, we can be quite sure that the volume of corrupt activities grew in the 1980s and 1990s, and the real sums involved grew too. It is more difficult to verify the Chinese assertion that corruption increasingly involved senior officials, but it is certainly not implausible.

Policy Roots of Corruption

As Ting Gong (1994) argues, the explosion of corruption in mainland China is essentially a policy outcome: It is the unintended consequence of the policies of reform, mainly economic reform, adopted by communist party leaders in the 1980s and 1990s (see also Ostergaard 1986).

The section after this one provides a taxonomy of corruption in post-Mao China, tracing specific forms of corruption to specific reform policies that have offered new opportunities and incentives for corrupt activities. This section discusses the policy roots of corruption in a broader sense. Economic reform, driven by the new priority of economic growth adopted as party policy in December 1978, has provided an overall context for the growth of corruption. This context features more opportunities, higher payoffs, weaker enforcement, and lower psychic costs for officials choosing to engage in corruption.

This is not to suggest that corruption first appeared in the 1980s. The Nationalist government that ruled China before 1949 was notoriously corrupt. Corruption certainly existed in the Maoist era, too. The Chinese traditional reliance on social connections (guanxi) provided a basis for a "gift economy" of instrumental relationships of exchange and the cultivation of guanxi networks to meet a variety of needs long before the 1980s (see especially Yang 1989, 1994). This was not only common practice for individuals in pursuit of private goals, but also for organizations. Guanxi between workplaces existed long before the reform era, in informal practices of "commissions" and payment of "managerial fees" (Solinger 1984: 124–153; Lee 1990). These were regarded as acceptable in relationships of supply, procurement, sales promotion, and contracting. Wojtek Zafanolli (1988) also describes these sorts of "institutional offenses" in the Maoist era, mainly by industrial enterprises but also by the bureaucratic agencies that administered the industrial economy.

Corruption was also common in the Chinese countryside. For example, it was not uncommon for production team leaders to conceal grain or sell produce on the black market to boost collective consumption in times of need. Higher authorities generally turned a blind eye to these activities, knowing they were carried out to support actual needs of the collective that could not be met if regulations were strictly observed (Chan and Unger 1982).

In the 1980s, however, there was "a fantastic increase in these irregularities" (Zafanolli 1988: 139) as well as the emergence and growth of new forms of corruption. Quite apart from the impact of reform policies on opportunities for corruption, discussed below, the rejection of Maoist economic policy in 1978 transformed the normative environment. Reform replaced the Maoist rhetoric of economic equality with a "trickle-down" economic strategy that unabashedly encouraged some to get rich first (and others later).[16] In the post-Cultural Revolution context, the "transformation of economic ethics [was] nothing short of astonishing" (He 1997: 195). Andrew Nathan (1990: 103) describes a "general blurring of boundaries between legitimate and illegitimate economic and social behavior" and "an increasing sense of normlessness." Alan Liu (1983: 618) notes the emergence of a "climate of corruption" in the 1980s, subjecting "a few honest officials to isolation and public ridicule." Economic reform was biased against officials, reversing a centuries-old tradition of superior status. In the 1980s, salary gains of Chinese officials were meager, at a time when incomes of entrepreneurs grew to exceed by far those of middle-ranking officials (see Ma 1989; He 2000). To be sure, if corruption reasserted official superiority, it also neutralized bureaucratic resistance to reform (Ma 1989; Sun 1999; Fan and Grossman 2000). In short, the new value system promoted in what the Chinese ultimately referred to as the "socialist market economy" was, at best, incoherent (Ostergaard and Petersen 1991; Rocca 1992; White 1996). Economic reform gave impetus to a context in which it was easier than before to be confused about the standards defining appropriate (indeed, legal) conduct (see Myers 1985, 1989). In the new normative climate, officials who chose to engage in corruption had less cause for moral qualms about it.[17] Indeed, many officials apparently viewed corruption as an income supplement (see Burns 2003).

The normative climate promoted by economic reform has had implications for the policy instruments the Chinese authorities can use effectively in their anticorruption interventions (see Einwalter 1998). The Maoist era witnessed massive projects of social engineering to transform the thoughts and conduct of ordinary Chinese. These projects were often coercive, but they also included normative appeals and moral education. Chinese communist leaders have not entirely abandoned the notion of building social norms to implement public policies (see Manion 1993). Nonetheless, in the environment of reform, it has been more difficult for them to define clearly their expectations of moral conduct for public officials, most of whom are also communist party members—and much more difficult to rely on moral suasion to convince officials to do the right thing (see especially Ostergaard 1986; Myers 1987; Ostergaard and Petersen 1991; He 2000).

More generally, the old instruments for exacting compliance with whatever standards Chinese leaders choose to put forward are fewer and weaker. Citing Chinese analyses of this problem, Yan Sun (1991: 772) writes: "The old methods [have lost] efficacy after reform. Administrative command collides with ideas that reform seeks to promote;

ideological education is made difficult by the confusion over changing values. The method of mass campaigns, during which random investigation and prosecution were common, was discredited with the end of the Cultural Revolution, and while this has made it more difficult to exert moral and political controls over corruption, adequate legal reforms have not been established to take their place."

It is not only easier for officials to choose corrupt payoffs in the post-Mao normative environment, there are more opportunities for lucrative choices. The explosion of corruption in mainland China is conditioned by an explosion of new opportunities for such choices, many described in the following section. Overall, reform policies of economic decentralization have been especially important catalysts of both corruption and economic growth. Decentralization of administrative powers over finances, resource allocation, and investment decisions has given local officials (mainly, local communist party committees) a bigger stake in the local economy. It has also increased the number of officials with monopoly discretionary powers (Oi 1989; Stone 1993; Shaoguang Wang 1995; Baum and Shevchenko 1999). For China's top leaders, the tension between unleashing entrepreneurial initiative and controlling corruption has proven difficult to resolve by relying on the leadership of these local party generalists, a point taken up in chapter 4. Decentralization has also made detection and punishment of abuses more difficult.

A Taxonomy of Corruption

This section presents a taxonomy of the most common and serious forms of corruption in post-Mao China and identifies, where relevant, their specific roots in new opportunities and incentives created by policy. It describes corruption as bureaucratic commerce, predatory exactions, corrupt exchanges, use of public funds as private capital, and illegal privatization of state enterprise assets. The Chinese authorities do not view all these activities as criminal corruption, but do recognize the abuses of official power inherent in them.[18] The authorities appear more tolerant of abuses that are essentially distortions of official policy (rather than clear violations) and situations in which corrupt gains are distributed within a formal government organization as collective benefits.

Much of the corruption in contemporary China is not the widely studied variant of corruption in the general literature—exchanges between different parties in the public and private sectors, including rent seeking. As Ting Gong (1997: 287) notes, corruption in China frequently involves only a single agent, a "cadre entrepreneur": "One agent is sufficient to execute a successful transaction between public power and private wealth because, sanctioned by the reform, government officials themselves now have direct access to the market."

The discussion below should not obscure an important fact about corruption in contemporary China: It is very widespread, extending to practically every sort of official activity in every sector. Zhong Jiwen (1997) and Wen Shengtang (2003) note a very troubling trend of increased corruption in law enforcement and the judiciary beginning in the late 1990s. It does appear, however, that a great deal of corruption in China in recent decades occurs in enterprises and involves individuals who would not be construed as public officials in capitalist market economies. In 1990, Sun Qian (1990) noted that about 70 percent of officials involved in corruption cases were factory directors, managers, financial officers, or procurement agents in state or collective enterprises. At the end of the 1990s, Lu Yun (1998) cited evidence from a survey of cases in a number of cities, which put 76 percent of bribery and embezzlement cases in enterprises. These figures undoubtedly reflect some enforcement biases, but the importance of enterprise corruption is also suggested by the drop (discussed earlier) of about 30 percent in corruption and bribery cases filed in 1998, compared to 1997. Most observers agree that state enterprises are very active players in enterprise corruption; the drop in enforcement figures, associated with the redefinition of these crimes to exclude nonstate enterprises, indicates the importance of corruption in these enterprises and implies its importance in state enterprises.

Bureaucratic Commerce

"Bureaucratic commerce" refers to the business activities of companies created by party and government departments, including law enforcement agencies, in the 1980s and early 1990s for the purpose of generating profits.[19] Bureaucratic agencies of the State Council in Beijing down to local government departments set up and usually directly manage the businesses as economic subsidiaries. For example, in interviews in Tianjin, a provincial-level municipality, Jane Duckett (2001) found that government departments had *each* created as many as half a dozen bureaucratic businesses by 1993. Most bureaucratic businesses are officially registered as independent, for-profit companies under state or collective ownership.[20] Their operation lies outside the scope of the formal state budgetary process and personnel management process. Bureaucratic commerce by law enforcement agencies and the People's Liberation Army was explicitly prohibited in the early 1990s (see Mulvenon 1998, 2001). In a series of regulations issued in 1993–97, senior party and government officials were prohibited from holding concurrent positions in bureaucratic businesses (and any profit-making enterprise). Other than this, bureaucratic businesses are not illicit per se. They are relevant to a discussion of corruption because some of their rent-capturing activities are illegal and many are only semi-legitimate. Moreover, a number of bureaucratic entrepreneurs take advantage of bureaucratic business opportunities to engage in illegal trade or to appropriate bureaucratic business profits for themselves.[21]

Bureaucratic businesses developed in three waves: in 1985, when they numbered more than 300,000; in 1987–88, when their numbers grew to nearly 500,000; and in 1992, when more than 900,000 such businesses operated (Gong 1994: 1996). The first wave of bureaucratic businesses included many "shell companies" created for speculation, with informal links to state agencies mainly through personal connections, such as retired officials or children of incumbent officials. It was partly a product of a new retirement policy for Chinese officials, widely implemented beginning in 1982 (see Manion 1993). The second wave was businesses that were mostly directly operated by the state agencies and employed many officials, some of very high administrative rank, working concurrently in these agencies. By contrast, many bureaucratic businesses created in the third wave, which was stimulated mainly by the "southern tour" of Deng Xiaoping in early 1992, promoting market activity, are neither formally affiliated with government agencies nor managed by incumbent officials. Their bureaucratic character lies in the close financial, administrative, and personal links of bureaucratic entrepreneurs with their former government agencies and in their reliance on government agencies as the source of initial capital funds (Gong 1996). They are bigger, better organized, and more diversified than their predecessors of the 1980s. Some are joint stock companies that span provinces, and others include foreign partners (Wong 1994). Nationwide, each "company wave" has been followed by an effort by the authorities to screen, consolidate, or eliminate large numbers of businesses, depending on their activities and their relationship to state agencies and officials.

Essentially, bureaucratic businesses transform "the public assets and regulatory authority" under the command of their sponsoring official agencies into "capital for individual and collective gain" (Lin and Zhang 1999: 204). Their most common means of generating profits in the 1980s was through arbitrage in materials controlled by government agencies. Arbitrage in the form of official profiteering *(guandao)* constituted the dominant form of corruption from the mid-1980s to the early 1990s (Ostergaard and Petersen 1991; Gong 1997; Sun 1999). A main cause was price regulation through the two-track pricing system, introduced to dismantle economic planning gradually. The system created new opportunities for agencies with access to price-regulated goods to capture huge rents (see Sands 1990; Shan 1992; Kar-Yiu Wong 1992; Liew 1993).[22] Through their sponsoring agencies, bureaucratic businesses obtained materials at (lower) controlled prices and resold them to collective or private enterprises at (higher) market prices. The Textile Ministry, for example, used its authority to require certain factories to sell their textiles, at controlled prices, to its Textile Industry Products Company, which resold them to garment factories at much higher (roughly double) market prices (Stone 1993). Bureaucratic trade in controlled resources also included the reselling of purchase quotas and permits issued by government agencies to allow state enterprises to obtain production inputs. The demand for industrial materials came mainly from township and village enterprises in the collective sector. Encouraged to expand by permissive reform policies, these smaller and more adaptive enterprises nonetheless lacked the formal access to inputs enjoyed by the state sector, which enjoyed reliable access to cheap inputs. The corrupt exchanges in material (and financial) resources for production forged a trade alliance between the most dynamic enterprises in the reform economy and the government bureaucracies most closely associated with the old planned economy (see Sun 1999; Gilley 2001).

Other bureaucratic businesses generated profits by exercising exclusive rights to provide certain government services. Their sponsoring agencies granted them these monopolies via their regulatory responsibilities and authority, which actually increased in the 1980s and 1990s with the emergence of new economic activities. For example, a municipal government construction commission, prohibited from charging for project inspections, set up an inspection center as a bureaucratic business and charged for inspection. A municipal government finance department opened a vehicle servicing center and issued an official document requiring all government agencies that relied on the department for appropriations to have their vehicles serviced there. A credit consulting firm sponsored by a state bank told clients that seeking its advice before going to the bank for loan requests would help them in securing loans (Gong 1996; Lu 2000b).

A third form of bureaucratic business engaged in profit-making activities without monopoly rights. They competed with non-bureaucratic businesses in the market, operating with an advantage over competitors because of favorable allocation of resources and opportunities by the sponsoring government agency (Francis 1999; Lin and Zhang 1999; Duckett 2001). Taxi services, retail outlets, hotels, and restaurants are examples owned and managed as bureaucratic businesses.

Bureaucratic commerce has its roots in specific reform policies and the overall environment of market reform. Obviously, the two-track pricing system, in place for most raw materials and producer goods from the mid-1980s until the early 1990s, created major opportunities for official profiteering. The more interesting point, however, is that the rents created by price discrepancies were captured not only by individuals but also by government agencies. Moreover, official profiteering was not the only form of bureaucratic commerce. Bureaucratic businesses have policy roots other than price discrepancies. Economic liberalization encouraged entrepreneurship and new economic activities outside the planned economy. The diminution of the planned economy as a proportion of economic activity overall was accompanied by the rise of an increasingly complex regulated economy. Government bureaucracies were assigned new sorts of powers involving business licenses, enterprise leasing arrangements, stock exchange registration, and leasing of government land, for example. These powers were another important source of rents captured by government bureaucratic businesses.

Price discrepancies and increased regulatory powers provided specific opportunities for capturing rents, but bureaucratic commerce was explicitly condoned by policy. In 1979, the Finance Ministry introduced a cap on administrative expenditures for party and government agencies, but the ministry granted bureaucracies more flexibility in the disposal of the budgetary surplus they could save. At about the same time, an explicit policy of "creative earning" *(chuang shou)* actively urged bureaucratic agencies to supplement their administrative budgets through profit-making activities and to use profits for the welfare of their employees (Gong 1994, 1996; Lin and Zhang 1999). These new policy directions were the catalyst for bureaucratic commerce as the main institutional form through which rents were captured in the 1980s and 1990s.

For the most part, government bureaucracies set up businesses to enhance the collective welfare of their employees in a context of flat or reduced supply of budgetary administrative revenue and drastically increased demand for more of it. Reforms in 1982, 1988, and especially 1993 abolished or merged government agencies at the center and below, creating official redundancies without reducing government functions. Government bureaucracies retired many officials but also left large numbers in place as "extra-establishment" personnel. At the same time, new officials were steadily hired to meet higher recruitment standards, implemented in the 1990s through an experiment with competitive civil service examinations. Furthermore, a policy of administrative decentralization increased responsibilities of local governments, and many responded by recruiting more staff. Despite the successive efforts at bureaucratic streamlining, the overall number of officials grew, from 18 million in 1978 to 40 million by the end of the 1990s.

Bureaucratic businesses enhance collective welfare in a number of ways. They provide sponsoring agencies with employment for retired or retained extra-establishment officials. Profits from bureaucratic commerce provide discretionary resources that meet shortfalls in administrative revenue for their sponsoring agencies, as extra-budgetary revenue or unregulated slush funds *(xiao jinku)*. They support a wide range of collective consumption. Cash bonuses to supplement income and housing are probably the most important, but funds are also used to supplement income with free or subsidized consumer goods, to provide or improve collective facilities (such as bathhouses, dining halls, and kindergartens), for collective consumption in banquets or junkets, to upgrade office equipment (such as telephones and photocopiers), and to purchase vehicles for use by agency officials (Lin and Zhang 1999).

Predatory Exactions

"Predatory" exactions refers to excessive compulsory and irregular non-tax charges exacted mainly from peasants by county and township governments, local government agencies, and village authorities in the wake of decollectivization in the 1980s. In 1985, the central authorities set overall limits on non-tax charges. Combined, they were not to exceed 5 percent of the township average per capita income in the preceding year. In fact, exactions grew well beyond this limit, mainly through the "three arbitrary practices" *(san luan)*—imposing a variety of arbitrary fees, arbitrary fines, and arbitrary apportionments. In 1991, a nationwide survey by the Ministry of Agriculture found two sorts of peasant payments to the village and township amounted to an average 8 percent of income (Lu 1997). In the mid-1990s, a 100-county survey by the ministry found fees, fines, and apportionments amounted to 10 percent of income (Bernstein and Lu 2000). Effectively, rural taxes exceeded 20 percent in these counties. They were as high as 40 percent in others (Wedeman 2000). There was huge variation across localities, but everywhere the exactions were highly regressive (Lu 1997; Bernstein and Lu 2000).

Predatory exactions are especially common in central and western China, where rural industry has grown more slowly than in other areas, and local governments rely mainly on agriculture for administrative support and to carry out developmental projects imposed by higher levels. Xiaobo Lu (1997: 119) describes 136 varieties of non-tax fees, exceeding 15 percent of annual income, paid by peasants in a county in Henan province in 1991: "A large proportion of the payments went to government agencies at county and township levels: finance, land management, town planning, water conservation, farming machinery, public health, veterinarian services, seeds service, forestry, family planning, civil affairs, court, police, culture, postal service, power generation, and environmental protection, among others. In other words, all essential public services provided to peasants were fee-based, and almost no governmental service was free." Local government agencies also deducted for services from procurement payments for crops or paid peasants with IOUs (see Wedeman 1997b).

While some "arbitrary practices" involve clearly illegal charges, central government regulations specifically authorize many of the non-tax charges by local governments and their agencies. In these cases, the problem is not the exactions per se, but that their cumulative excess produces a undue burden on peasants *(nongmin fudan)*. In this respect, predatory exactions resemble bureaucratic commerce: they have legitimate premises in official policy or administrative regulations.

The root causes of predatory exactions are decreases in local government revenues and increases in local government responsibilities in the fiscal decentralization of the 1980s and 1990s. In this sense too, predatory exactions resemble bureaucratic commerce. They are driven not only by new opportunities but also by a real shortage of funds (especially administrative funds) in the reform era. Relative to total local government expenditures, the revenue yielded by predatory exactions is not all that large. It amounts to a huge proportion of local government *administrative* expenditure, however—about 80 percent in 1995 (Wedeman 2000). Predatory exactions generate additional revenue, performing a function similar to bureaucratic commerce at higher levels, and revenues exacted are spent in much the same way as bureaucratic business profits: on bonuses, housing, offices, and banqueting—in short, collective consumption by local governments and their agencies (Zhonghui Wang 1995; Wedeman 2000; Lu 2000a).

Corrupt Exchanges

Neither bureaucratic commerce nor predatory exactions involve corrupt exchanges of the sort common in most countries. Corrupt exchanges, often prosecuted as bribery or illegal commissions, are also an important form of corruption in post-Mao China, however. Officials with discretionary power exchange advantages arising from the use of this discretion for some material gain for themselves. Capturing rents through exchanges of advantage for material gain comes in a variety of forms. It involves officials from the highest level to lowly clerks, and the gains range from hundreds of millions to a few dollars. Advantages exchanged for material gain range from collusion in illegal activities, to favoritism in government allocation, to expeditious clerical service. Some forms of corrupt exchanges are similar to predatory exactions, as they are close to extortion. The difference is that victims of corrupt exchanges are typically less vulnerable than Chinese peasants, and payment is generally for some real (or perceived) advantage— which distinguishes it from arbitrary "shakedowns" and charges for essential government services. In the 1980s, corrupt exchanges between rural enterprises and local government officials with discretionary authority over tax rates, allocation of supplies, or favorable credits sometimes took the form of profit sharing (see Sun 1999). This was not the same as bureaucratic commerce. Officials were offered shares of profits, but did not participate in the profit-making activities of the enterprise.

Officials who capture rents from official discretion in corrupt exchanges typically consume the gains as individuals. The parties paying for advantage are often organizations. According to a *Jingji ribao* article (30 April 1997), most bribery cases under investigation by procurators at the time featured organizations seeking collective gains. The "organizational bribery" of the mid-1980s and 1990s contrasts with bribery of the 1970s and early 1980s. In the earlier period, bribes rarely exceeded a thousand yuan and were typically offered in secrecy by ordinary citizens to ordinary officials, usually with the aim of solving personal matters. By contrast, organizational bribes involve tens of thousands (even several million) of yuan and are offered to leading officials in exchange for decisions directly profiting the workplace. Local governments compete for state-funded projects with "pilgrimages to the capital, bearing precious gifts," sometimes offering 5–10 percent of total investment as a kickback to officials with authority to decide on project allocation. Construction companies compete to build and remodel apartments and offices for government departments by bribing decision makers. Organizational bribery may even be discussed openly at workplace meetings as part of competitive strategy.

Beginning in the 1990s, real estate constituted one of the most common sources of rents in corrupt exchanges. Land in China is owned by the state, but in the early 1990s the central authorities decided to lease land—creating market competition for land development rights and ownership rights of developed properties. The market developed quickly, with especially fierce competition in areas such as Beijing, where strict urban planning restrictions limit hotel development within the old city area, for example (Bo 2000). The real estate market opened up new opportunities for officials in certain positions to capture rents from their discretionary authority over whether, when, how, to whom, and at what price to lease government land for development (Gong 1997; He 1997). Officials exchange decisions on these matters for material gain, which often includes "gifts" of private houses for themselves. Indeed, the case of Chen Xitong, the highest-ranking official prosecuted for corruption (discussed in Chapter 5), partly involved exchanges of this type (see Wedeman 1996; Gilley 1998; Bo 2000).

Advantage in real estate decisions can also be resold by successful businesses subcontracting to other firms. As businesses winning advantage in public projects are often state enterprises, commissions for subcontracts might be considered bribes. Zhang Peitian (1995) describes bribery in subcontracting as very common in the construction market (see also Ren 1992). He traces the rise of the practice to a widely publicized 1992 decision of the Supreme People's Court to reverse the judgment of "guilty" to "not guilty" in the bribery case of Li Fuxing. In the early 1990s, Li, a manager of a state enterprise in Hubei province, had accepted large bribes from Hong Kong businessmen in exchange for subcontracting construction works in Shenzhen. In the latter half of 1992, the Supreme People's Court held a work meeting in Shanghai to discuss the issue of commissions in economic activities. The meeting concluded that accepting commissions did not constitute a crime if it did not harm the state or collective interest.

Corrupt exchanges can also involve payments to officials to facilitate illegal activity, such as smuggling foreign-made goods into China. From detected cases, the value of goods smuggled rose from less than US $1 million in 1979 to nearly US $2 billion in 1998 (*Jingji ribao,* 26 January 1999, cited in Hu 2001). One of the biggest corruption cases in recent years is the Yuanhua smuggling case. It aroused great interest in the West because Lai Changxing, owner and manager of the company, escaped to Canada and was the subject of widely publicized extradition proceedings. Lai's Xiamen Yuanhua Company, based in the coastal province of Fujian, smuggled highly profitable goods such as cigarettes and automobiles. The criminal case against Lai involved smuggling goods valued at 53 billion yuan, evading taxes amounting to about 30 billion yuan, and bribing hundreds of party and government officials in his network of support. Officials bribed in exchange for their cooperation included customs officials, police officers, bank officers, deputy mayors of the Xiamen municipality, and the deputy secretary of the political-legal committee of the Xiamen party committee.

Paying for advantage also takes place on a much smaller scale quite routinely. "Speed money" to expedite bureaucratic procedures is one form of routine payment. In interviews with entrepreneurs and enterprise licensing officials in 1992–93 (Manion 1996), I found that entrepreneurs often made payments to officials for standard processing of applications to set up enterprises. Payment for standard service rested on two basic premises. First, information asymmetry in enterprise licensing allows officials to reject as "unacceptable" (that is, incorrect or incomplete) applications that were in fact acceptable, and applicants do not know whether the rejection was well founded or not. Second, entrepreneurs believe a high proportion of officials are corrupt and will offer them advantage in exchange for payments. In this context, faced with a rejected application, many entrepreneurs pay for perceived advantage, which is often simply standard service.

A particularly damaging arena for corrupt exchanges is law adjudication. Corruption in the judiciary appears to have increased in the mid-1990s, perhaps as the sums involved in corruption cases became high enough to justify a substantial enough investment to tempt judges and other judicial staff. By the late 1990s, investigations of judicial corruption regularly numbered more than 1,000 cases annually. Corrupt exchanges in the judiciary became a cause of major concern for Chinese leaders. These exchanges were sometimes relatively small in value. Randall Peerenboom (2002: 295) writes: "Stories abound of various forms of judicial malpractice such as judges demanding bribes, meeting *ex parte* with parties in restaurants or Karaoke bars, and demanding that parties fund lavish 'investigation trips.' Lawyers have recounted instances where they received calls late at night to go to settle a bill run up by judges and their friends at restaurants and saunas or to pay for the shopping expedition of a judge who 'forgot' her purse." The sums involved are not the crucial issue, of course. When corruption is rampant in the judiciary, the entire anticorruption effort is at risk because ordinary citizens no longer believe in impartial justice, even where politics do not affect outcomes.

Public Funds as Private Capital

Another form of corruption, especially common in the 1990s, is financial corruption: specifically, the misappropriation of public funds as interest-free capital for private investment. The main perpetrators are officials in the state-monopolized financial institutions, which offer the best opportunities for this form of corruption. State enterprises, local governments, and state procurement agencies also misuse public funds as private assets, however. Funds are usually invested in the stock market or real estate. These areas are highly speculative and offer the possibility of quick returns: Officials who secretly "borrow" public funds can withdraw quickly from their investment once a profit is made, returning the funds without exposure (Sun 1999; Gong 1997; Ding 2000c). Essentially, only failures are exposed—big losses of public funds, borrowed and not returned over a considerable period of time. Very big losses in investments of public funds in stocks and real estate are somewhat avoided, because much of the financing and organization involves the state banks and financial officials have privileged information that allows them to engage in insider trading on the stock market. Nonetheless, losses can be spectacular. In 1999, the deputy manager of a securities company in Fujian province diverted over US $100 million of company funds to speculate in stocks, ultimately losing more than US $2 million (Ding 2000c).

The diversion of public funds to interest-free loans occurs outside the financial sector too. X. L. Ding (2000b: 139) describes how managers of Chinese state enterprises based in Hong Kong give large sums of enterprise funds to brokers for investment, with instructions that a portion of gains (normally 20 percent) be put aside secretly for themselves in private accounts. The transactions are exposed only if very significant losses arouse suspicion. In most cases, managers can only gain, without personal financial responsibility for losses: "Communist speculators from China . . . are guaranteed a big share of the profits while the state is guaranteed all the costs and risks." Public funds are also gambled away by Chinese officials in Macao casinos. Nearly 100 cases of officials gambling a total of US $12 million have been documented up to the mid-1990s.

Looting public funds to generate earnings through investment also occurs outside the formal banking system. Andrew Wedeman (1997b) describes the diversion of funds designated for agricultural procurement to capital construction and real estate in the development boom of the early 1990s. The funds were looted "layer by layer," by central government financial bureaus, local banks, and agricultural procurement agencies. Procurement agencies borrowed funds from banks, at rates discounted for the purpose of agricultural loans and subsidies, then invested speculatively or extended the funds as illegal loans at the higher commercial rate or much higher market rate in the credit-short overheated economy. The Agricultural Bank reported that over US $1 billion was siphoned out of procurement accounts nationwide for speculative investment, unauthorized loans, or simple embezzlement by local government agencies and officials. One result was an "IOU crisis" in 1992, which left hundreds of millions of peasants without cash to pay routine living expenses or to invest in agricultural production and led to enormous rural discontent.

The underlying causes of financial corruption are many. Most important is the weakness of regulatory and monitoring mechanisms in financial institutions, combined with new opportunities for investment as real estate and stock markets opened up in the late 1980s and 1990s. Efforts to strengthen financial regulation in the late 1990s have targeted problems such as loans without feasibility studies, but the misappropriation of public funds for private investment capital does not appear to have been significantly affected by these efforts.

Illegal Privatization of State Enterprise Assets
Corruption in state-owned enterprises, which comprises the highest proportion of cases handled by Chinese procuratorates in the 1980s and 1990s, takes on a variety of forms. Descriptions have focused on three common forms, all of which can be subsumed under a general heading of illegal privatization of state enterprise assets. One variant is corruption in the process of legally authorized enterprise privatization. A second is fairly direct embezzlement of enterprise profits. A third is a more complicated form of asset stripping that links state enterprises and other enterprises by fudging organizational boundaries. Observers of these

different forms of corrupt privatization of state enterprise assets (He 1997; Sun 1999; Ding 1999, 2000a, 2000b) generally agree that corrupt gains are distributed among only a small circle of officials (including enterprise managers) or individual enterprise managers, usually to the detriment of most ordinary enterprise workers. That is, corrupt gains are generally consumed individually, not as collective welfare benefits for the enterprise.

Chinese authorities have not embraced wholesale privatization of state enterprises. They experimented with corporatization of some small state enterprises in the mid-1980s and endorsed this as policy in 1987. By 1995, more than 25,000 joint stock companies existed, with total capital stock in excess of US $46 billion, and nearly 600 stock trading institutions had emerged, with more than 67,000 brokers (Ding 1999). It was not until 1997, however, that communist party leaders legitimated an expansion of corporatization to include all but major state enterprises. Corruption in the process of legally authorized privatization in the late 1980s and 1990s resembles *nomenklatura* privatization (insider privatization) in the former communist countries. Enterprise managers make corrupt payments, in the form of free shares or low-priced shares, to government officials to obtain authorization to corporatize. Managers undervalue enterprise assets before restructuring, then take advantage of big differences between face value and premium prices of stocks to acquire large blocks of shares as enterprise employees or as "corporate shares," which they effectively control. To purchase shares, managers appropriate enterprise funds as private capital. Describing these and other illegal practices in privatization, Ding (1999) points out the ineffectiveness of monitoring by accounting agencies, which are typically not professional agencies but associated with government departments. Accounting agencies often collaborate in fraudulent asset valuation, induced by bureaucratic pressure or offers of financial gain.

State enterprise profits are also embezzled by managers in a number of fairly direct ways (Ding 2000a, 2000b). The previous section has already described the diversion of a portion of profits from enterprise investments to private accounts by managers of Chinese companies operating outside the mainland. Managers operating domestically or outside the mainland also set up their own private businesses, which exist only on paper, and pay themselves with enterprise funds for services not actually provided. For example, a provincial trade corporation manager registered a shell company owned by him, appointed it an agency of the trade corporation, and then paid it commissions from the trade corporation—although the company handled none of the exports. Managers also siphon off enterprise assets by conspiring with outside businesses, offering attractive business propositions conditional on the issue of inflated invoices (or deflated bills of payment), with the difference deposited in private accounts. These sorts of arrangements are not uncommon in transactions between mainland Chinese enterprises and Hong Kong businesses.

There are also more complicated methods by which managers strip state enterprises of valuable assets, appropriating them as private gains. Taking advantage of the endorsement of new forms of management and ownership in the 1980s, state enterprise managers created new businesses, usually registered as collective enterprises, that took up some operations formerly performed by the state enterprises (He 1997; Sun 1999; Ding 2000a). The businesses usually employed a subset of the state enterprise workforce, with salaries and benefits paid by the enterprises. From an organizational perspective, the new businesses created superfluous market networks, increasing state enterprise costs by transforming transactions within enterprises into interfirm transactions. On paper, the businesses and state enterprises operated independently. In reality, business profits were inseparable from the state enterprise relationship. Effectively, the businesses drained state enterprises of valuable assets and channeled them into the accounts of enterprise managers, who also managed (and effectively owned) the businesses. Ding (2000b) cites the example of managers of a state enterprise specializing in producing energy equipment who created three new businesses to purchase production inputs for the enterprise, market enterprise products, and transport them to consumers. These operations, previously assigned to units within the enterprise, were now contracted out, with higher than prevailing market prices paid by the state enterprise to the new businesses. The businesses employed a workforce of 200, of whom 80 were transferred from the enterprise with their salaries and most benefits paid by the enterprise. Not surprisingly, despite monopoly power and business opportunities, the original enterprise suffered heavy losses. At the same time, the new businesses (and their managers) made big profits. The example illustrates the "systemic unequal exchange" between state enterprises and new business auxiliaries, an exploitative relationship that "routinely transferred physical, financial and proprietary assets from the state to the nonstate auxiliary companies, and simultaneously transferred operational costs and market risks from the latter to the former" (Ding 2000a: 6).

The enforcement figures presented at the beginning of this chapter draw particular attention to embezzlement of public assets. This crime accounts for 56 percent of corruption cases investigated by procurators in the 1980s and 1990s and 48 percent of cases involving "big sums" in the 1990s. This, however, is partly an artifact of legal definition. Compared to the other two main crimes of corruption, embezzlement of public assets encompasses a much wider range of activities (see Luo 1996: 41–43). Essentially, Chinese criminal law defines embezzlement of public assets as the exploitation of public office or the public trust to appropriate, by some illegal means, public assets for private gain.[23] Common activities legally viewed as embezzlement of public assets include: taking advantage of official position to purchase price-controlled materials at low prices to profit privately by selling at higher prices, negotiating private kickbacks from outside contractors, earning private income from work done during regular work hours, retaining for private consumption gifts accepted in the course of official duty, selling at reduced prices fixed assets of a enterprise or warehoused production materials, appropriating for private use confiscated assets or fines collected in law enforcement, submitting false claims for reimbursement from public funds, reporting as waste or missing materials that are actually resold for private profit, and insider purchase of corporate shares at parity prices and sale at high prices for private profit.[24] In the taxonomy presented here, embezzlement encompasses all illegal privatization of state enterprise assets and some corrupt exchanges (for example, arranging kickbacks for government procurement decisions).

Anticorruption Challenge and Regime Response

In this section, the forms of corruption discussed in the previous sections are considered in terms of the different types of challenge they pose. For the Chinese communist regime, as for most governments, corruption is both an economic and a political problem. In China, the form of corruption that poses the most serious economic problem is not the same as the forms that pose the most serious political problem. In terms of losses of state revenue, illegal privatization of state enterprise assets is the most serious problem. Bureaucratic commerce and predatory exactions have greater popular salience, however. Consequently, they pose the most serious political problem.

Table 3.3 presents the different forms of corruption in terms of four features that can be correlated with regime response. Chinese authori-

Table 3.3 Structure of the Chinese anticorruption challenge

Form of corruption and key features	Bureaucratic commerce	Predatory exactions	Corrupt exchanges	Use of public funds as private capital	Illegal privatization of state enterprise assets
State revenue losses	Low	Low	Moderate	Moderate	High
Popular salience	High	High	Variable	Low	Low
Legitimation in policy	High	Moderate	Low	Low	Low
Allocation of gains	Mainly organizational	Mainly organizational	Mainly individual[a]	Mainly individual	Mainly individual
Regime response	Irregularity	Irregularity	Crime	Crime	Crime

a. Mainly individual for bribe recipients; often organizational for bribe givers.

ties have defined corrupt exchanges, use of public funds as private capital, and illegal privatization of state enterprise assets as crimes. Corruption in bureaucratic commerce and predatory exactions are viewed as irregularities.

With as many variables as cases, it is difficult to say what drives regime response, but the pattern of variation is suggestive. Legitimation in policy is one obvious basis for such a distinction. It distinguishes bureaucratic commerce and predatory exactions from the other forms of corruption. Bureaucratic commerce is a policy solution to the problem of budgetary inadequacies and downsizing in government agencies. Predatory exactions are often based in legal categories of exactions, but are excessive in amounts.

A second feature that distinguishes bureaucratic corruption and predatory exactions from the other forms of corruption is allocation of corrupt gains. For both forms of corruption defined as irregularities, the allocation is mainly organizational, not individual.

Specific features of Chinese criminal law also suggest that allocation of corrupt gains is important. For example, in the elaboration of punishments for crimes of "organizational corruption," the 1997 Criminal Law specifies a fine for the workplace, while the individuals directly responsible are considered to have committed a crime and are punished with criminal punishment (such as imprisonment).[25] This presents obvious incentives for everyone in the workplace to protect the individuals directly responsible, even if they profit more from the crime. The more important point, however, is that the mere fact that corrupt gains are distributed among many in a workplace does not transform the legal status of the act. It remains a crime, punishable as such.

In this context, it is also instructive to consider legal practice in cases of corrupt exchanges where the bribe payer is a workplace and the party accepting the bribe is an individual, which is not uncommon. Legally, the individual has accepted a bribe (a crime), and the workplace has offered a bribe (also a crime). If the bribe is funded from public funds (such as government or state enterprise funds), then the workplace has also embezzled public assets. As noted in the discussion of corrupt exchanges earlier, organizational bribery featured in most bribery cases investigated by procurators at the end of the 1990s. Apparently, the prevalence of this form of bribery owes much to a practical emphasis on punishing those who accept the bribes rather than the workplaces that offer them. Procurators have a high standard for prosecuting workplace bribe payers. Usually it requires a case involving several tens of thousands of yuan. Officials who accept bribes of a few thousand yuan are much more likely to be prosecuted. In the strict legal sense, organizational bribery is a crime for both parties. Practically, however, when the bribe is not offered for private gain by an individual, it is treated as less serious (*Jingji ribao*, 30 Apr. 1997).

Variation in losses of state revenue may also be a consideration in regime response. Whatever drives response, the pattern that emerges clearly from Table 3.3 is particularly problematic for the regime. The two forms of corruption that are most salient to ordinary citizens are the forms that the regime has treated as least serious in its anticorruption effort.

Losses of State Revenue
The overall magnitude of corruption in China in terms of losses of state revenue is difficult to estimate, obviously, but available estimates suggest it is considerable. A recent study includes categories that do not strictly (or necessarily) involve unlawful abuses of official power—for example, the underground economy, tax evasion, and inefficient but legal regulatory activities of the state. By this definition, which is much too broad to be considered corruption, losses of state revenue are in the range of US $120–150 billion annually in the last half of the 1990s, a staggering 15 percent of China's GDP (Hu 2001). Taking a narrower view and considering only those activities that meet the definition of corruption introduced in Chapter 1, estimated losses of state revenue are nonetheless very substantial. They are in the range of US $30–40 billion annually, which is about 4 percent of China's GDP.[26] This level of losses accords roughly with official estimates presented in the Chinese media (see Pei 1999). It is somewhat higher than a recent estimate of 2–3 percent of GDP, offered by Andy Xie (cited in Callick 2001), an economist at Morgan Stanley Dean Witter.

What do we know about the relative seriousness of the different forms of corruption described above? In terms of magnitude of state losses, Ding (2000a) identifies illegal privatization of state enterprise assets as arguably the most serious form of corruption in China today. He cites estimates from research staff in Chinese governmental and consulting bodies that place losses of state revenue from asset looting in state enterprises in the range of US $6–12 billion annually in the first half of the 1990s. Considering the growth of corruption and the estimate above of losses from corruption overall in the last half of the 1990s, it seems quite plausible that illegal state enterprise privatization accounts for as much as half of all losses of state revenue due to corruption in the 1990s. By this standard, it is the most serious form of corruption. It represents a much greater loss of state revenue than illegalities in the financial sector, estimated at less than US $2 billion for the entire 1988–97 period and no more than US $8 billion when financial irregularities short of crimes are included (Ding 2000c).

The losses due to illegal privatization of state enterprise assets appear to be surpassed by predatory exactions, however, which Wedeman (2000) estimates at about US $12 billion annually in the early and mid-1990s. In terms of sums involved, then, these two forms of corruption present the most serious problems for the regime. They differ in important ways, however. Perhaps most crucially, predatory exactions are direct theft from ordinary citizens (and not mainly a loss of state revenue), while illegal privatization of state enterprise assets is direct theft from the state (and only indirectly from ordinary citizens). Consequently, if the latter poses the most serious corruption challenge to the Chinese state in economic terms, then the former poses the most serious challenge in political terms. This point also emerges independently from a consideration of the popular salience of different forms of corruption.

To be sure, these and other forms of corruption can have implications that indirectly produce losses of state revenue. For example, corrupt exchanges, whether routine or irregular, big or small, may bias decisions in ways that not only distort public policy but also produce inefficient outcomes that cost the state in revenue. By the same token, of course, some forms of corruption may contribute to economic growth, even if they produce direct losses of state revenue.

In this connection, it is worth noting the apparent anomaly of simultaneous economic growth and rampant corruption in mainland China.[27] (As discussed in Chapter 1, with few exceptions, the literature on corruption indicates that corruption hinders growth, mainly through a dampening effect on investment, including foreign investment.) Obviously, the coincidence of the two by no means implies that the net impact of corruption on economic growth in China has been positive. Indeed, Wei (2000) concludes that China is an "underachiever" in attracting foreign investment. Investment is significantly lower than predicted by his model, and he attributes this to the impact of corruption.

Probably most important of all, the simultaneous growth of corruption and the economy both arise from roughly the same sorts of causes: initiative released by new opportunities, compared to the past. These opportunities include the new normative environment that condones profit making, the replacement of planning with market mechanisms, and the decentralization of economic powers to regions and enterprises. It is no surprise that this liberalization has encouraged entrepreneurial Chinese to make profits—legally and illegally. That is, the parallel explosion of corruption and economic growth share the same root causes, but this does not mean corruption and growth are themselves causally linked.

It is also useful to consider that the greatest loss of state assets from corruption appears to be due to the diversion of assets and profits of state enterprises into the private hands of enterprise directors and government bureaucrats charged with their management. The gains generated from this form of corruption have serious distributive consequences: Public assets are put into private hands, without monitoring. Industrial workers may go unpaid as less profitable state enterprises are squeezed to promote "collective" firms. At the same time, the large public sector of the economy is generally not the most efficient. Many of the new enterprises are not in the underground economy but rather officially registered in the collective sector. They contribute to GDP, operating under an incentive system quite different from the public sector. Furthermore, considering the current investment environment in China, some nontrivial portion of corrupt gains is reinvested into the economy rather than stashed in foreign bank accounts. Even those forms of corruption that have harmful efficiency consequences may be less harmful than would be the case if the Chinese economy were less healthy—such as in Russia or the Ukraine, for example.[28]

Popular Salience

Particularly egregious instances of each of the forms of corruption described in the taxonomy have, at one time or another, provoked public outrage. It is illuminating, however, particularly when juxtaposed with regime response, to consider the following question: What is the relative popular salience of different forms of corruption in their most common manifestations?

In October 1994, the State Council Office to Rectify Improper Work Conduct (1995) and the State Statistical Bureau jointly conducted a major survey that examined the abuses of offices most intensely resented by ordinary citizens.[29] Not surprisingly, perhaps, they tend to be the forms of corruption that involve direct, open, or conspicuously consumed takings from ordinary citizens. According to these survey findings, the abuse that inspires the most resentment is the use of public funds for extravagant banqueting. Other abuses that particularly anger ordinary citizens are the refusal to perform official duties without an advantage and the imposition of arbitrary fees. These abuses involve relatively petty sums and little loss of state revenue. Among the forms of corruption described in the taxonomy, predatory exactions and bureaucratic commerce appear to be the most salient to ordinary Chinese—as registered by public demonstrations. The former provokes resentment in the cities, the latter in the countryside.

Consider first the problem of predatory exactions. Thomas Bernstein and Xiaobo Lu (2000, 2003) argue that peasants have clear ideas about which sorts of exactions are legitimate and which are not. For example, agricultural taxes and fees to support poor families in the community are viewed as legitimate, but exactions to pay salaries of village teachers and village officials are seen as costs the state should disperse more broadly than the locality. Arbitrary fees, fines, and apportionments inspire particular resentment. Bernstein and Lu cite a Central Committee document on rural instability that indicates more than 6,000 instances of rural unrest in 1993. More than 800 involved at least 500 people and extended across several townships. In many hundreds of instances, the public security forces, the armed police, or local army units had to restore order and suffered thousands of casualties, including deaths. In all, more than 8,000 deaths or injuries of officials or peasants resulted. Similar outbreaks of rural unrest occurred in the mid-1990s and after—all with the same dominant complaint, the peasant burden. These protests and riots catalyzed by predatory exactions may constitute the most serious threat to regime stability in decades.

By contrast, the corruption most reviled in the cities is bureaucratic commerce. Corruption was the major issue of the 1989 protest movement, and not only for strategic reasons (see Manion 1990; Ostergaard and Petersen 1991; Sun 1991; Mason 1994). Clemens Ostergaard and Christina Petersen (1991) cite public opinion polls to argue that corruption generally, and "official profiteering" in particular, was the most explosive issue of the 1989 protests. Protests directed their strongest critiques against bureaucratic commerce, especially when linked to nepotism (see Tanner and Feder 1993). A notice distributed at Peking University (reproduced in Han 1990: 28) phrased it this way: "What does it mean when people talk about 'profiteering by government officials?' To describe it simply, it refers to officials using their power to acquire things such as goods at low state-fixed prices, import and export licenses, loans, and foreign currency at cheap rates, so they can reap huge profits. These officials do business in the name of their companies. These companies can be categorized into two kinds: those run by government organs and those run by the sons and daughters of high-level officials."

Any case of corruption that produces obvious, big, direct losses for ordinary citizens can become salient. For example, there was a major public outcry in 1999 when the Rainbow Bridge in the Chongqing municipality collapsed, killing 40 people, because party and government officials had tolerated substandard work in exchange for big bribes from a construction company. But exchange corruption has normally been less salient in the 1980s and 1990s. When corrupt exchanges are salient, it is often because the authorities have chosen to publicize punitive action targeting exchanges of very big sums involving very senior officials. The salience arises not so much from the corruption per se, but from the attendant publicity to demonstrate regime anticorruption commitment. Death sentences meted out (and actually carried out) in 2001 fall into this category. Similarly, illegal privatization of state enterprise assets and use of public funds as private capital are salient mainly when corrupt gains are consumed conspicuously, arousing resentment.

For the Chinese authorities, then, the biggest economic problem of corruption is illegal privatization of state enterprise assets. Politically, however, bureaucratic commerce and predatory exactions are more significant. That is, it is precisely the corruption that is most visible and most directly costly to ordinary citizens that is of the least relevance in reducing losses of state revenue. In fact, the most politically salient and potentially destabilizing forms of corruption are, for the Chinese authorities, policy solutions to problems of revenue shortfalls for governments and public agencies.

Conclusion

At the height of the 1989 protests, an article in a student newspaper commented: "Corruption in China falls into two categories: corruption that involves a violation of the country's laws, and corruption that goes on within the limits of the law; the latter is more dangerous" (reproduced in Han 1990: 32). Anticorruption reform in mainland China is surely more than a program of "asset recovery," but throughout the 1980s and 1990s the Chinese authorities implicitly defined the problem of corruption mainly as the loss of state revenue—and only secondarily as the loss of political support. Corrupt exchanges, illegal privatization of state enterprise assets, and use of public funds as private capital are crimes. By contrast, the forms of corruption that, for most ordinary Chinese, directly call into question the legitimacy of state agents and agencies (namely, corrupt bureaucratic commerce and excessive predatory exactions) are irregularities. This situation poses a problem for involving ordinary Chinese in the anticorruption effort.

Returning to the language of Chapter 1, having moved past a "tipping point" to arrive at an equilibrium of widespread corruption, what can Chinese authorities do to coordinate an equilibrium shift? In particular, how can they coordinate supportive anticorruption actions of the Chinese mass public? Peasant riots and urban protests are not passive acquiescence, but they do not constitute "voluntary enforcement" in cooperation with the authorities. Indeed, they suggest a lack of confidence in regular channels and anticorruption agencies. Chapters 4 and 5 take up the issue of regime response, the anticorruption effort, in detail.

CHAPTER FOUR

Problems of Routine Anticorruption Enforcement

Since the beginning of the 1980s, top Chinese leaders have voiced alarm about the rise in volume and severity of corruption in China, acknowledging it as the gravest threat to the survival of communist party rule. Major anticorruption efforts include the revival of specialized agencies to investigate and punish official venality as well as the promulgation of many hundreds of communist party rules and legal provisions defining corrupt acts and stipulating punishments. Chinese leaders describe the current struggle against corruption as a "protracted war." Yet, as charted in Chapter 3, several times in the course of this war, leaders have sought (and apparently won) big victories in short, intense skirmishes—anticorruption campaigns that produced notable peaks in criminal enforcement figures. In the broader context of solving problems by building "sound organizational and working systems," which generally characterizes mainland China in the 1980s and 1990s, the frequent turn to campaigns is a puzzle.[1] By studying the problems of routine anticorruption enforcement, this chapter answers the question: Why have Chinese leaders also used campaigns to control corruption? At the same time, by pointing out some of the less obvious features that distinguish routine from campaign anticorruption enforcement in China, this chapter begins to answer a more fundamental question: Why have the campaigns failed to become building blocks for clean government? The specific mechanisms, successes, and failures of the anticorruption campaigns are explored in detail in Chapter 5. Problems with routine anticorruption enforcement are examined in this chapter as problems of organization, coordination, and "punishment according to law" *(yi fa chufen).*

Chapter 1 discussed anticorruption interventions in terms of enforcement, education, and institutional design. This chapter and the next focus on enforcement, which contrasts with the more comprehensive discussion of anticorruption reform in Hong Kong in Chapter 2. It is accurate to characterize the anticorruption effort in mainland China as inattentive to institutional design, until the late 1990s. Anticorruption education cannot be similarly dismissed, however. In fact, moral education (and exhortation) has been an integral part of the Chinese response to corruption. This is reflected in the early reinstatement of communist party discipline inspection committees, charged with restoring "party style" *(dang feng*—essentially, party ethics) to regain and maintain communist party moral legitimacy to rule. Yet, as Graham Young (1984) notes, although Chinese communist party orthodoxy traditionally rejected a "legalistic," "purely technical," or "mechanical" conception of party discipline in favor of a view that emphasized consciousness and commitment to the party, the narrower investigative and punitive aspects of party discipline ultimately consumed most resources of the discipline inspection committees. An enforcement orientation is a response to the failure of party discipline to prevent abuses of official power. Top Chinese leaders acknowledged this failure when they learned in 1982 of the involvement of senior officials in massive smuggling operations in the Guangdong province. They reoriented the anticorruption effort accordingly. For most of the 1980s and 1990s, party discipline inspection committees have promoted party ethics mainly by monitoring compliance with hundreds of prohibitions for communist party members and punishing millions for violations. In short, party discipline, initially about education to rectify party style, was largely reinterpreted in the early 1980s through a paradigm of enforcement.

Problems of Organization

Throughout the 1980s and 1990s, Chinese leaders at the center of authority in Beijing created a large number of provisional agencies to deal with specific problems of ideological laxity, organizational indiscipline, and economic crime on an ad hoc basis. Most important, however, was the reinstatement by authorities at the center of two permanent agencies that developed specialized anticorruption functions: party discipline inspection committees and government procuratorates.[2]

These two agencies had first emerged in the 1950s, but their operations had been disrupted for more than a decade during the Cultural Revolution launched in 1966. As Mao Zedong had evidently located a "new class" of oppressors within the communist party organization itself, the party could not be entrusted with its own rectification. From top to bottom, the party organization found itself under attack. The Cultural Revolution was characterized in its methods by legal nihilism, ideological radicalism, and mass violence. Students and workers were mobilized to bring newly labeled oppressors to brutal "revolutionary justice," and a constitution adopted in 1975 confirmed that government procuratorates had been abolished, their powers transferred to public security agencies.

In 1977, a new party constitution formally reinstated discipline inspection committees, and a year later the Central Committee appointed a Central Discipline Inspection Commission (CDIC), with the powerful veteran Chen Yun as its first secretary.[3] Law schools were reopened at about the same time, and a new state constitution reestablished the government procuratorates. By the early 1980s, then, two specialized agencies were in place to handle the explosion of corrupt practices. By the mid-1990s, the number of full-time party discipline inspection officers had grown to about 300,000, and government procurators numbered more than 150,000.[4] While their jurisdictions overlap significantly, their professional orientations differ in important ways.

Government Procuratorates

By the constitution and the law, the Chinese procuracy is an independent branch of government, equal in authority to the executive and judicial branches. The system is highly centralized. The Supreme People's Procuratorate (SPP) is at the top of a hierarchy of procuratorates extending down three levels of government. Formally, it is accountable to the National People's Congress (NPC). At lower levels, each provincial, municipal, and county procuratorate is under dual leadership, formally accountable to the local people's congress and the procuratorate one level up in the hierarchy.[5] At each level, the chief procurator is formally elected by the people's congress. Deputy chief procurators and ordinary procurators are formally nominated by the chief procurator and appointed by the people's congress standing committee. Within each procuratorate is a procuratorial committee that discusses and decides on important or complicated cases.[6] More routine decisions, such as whether to proceed with an investigation or prosecution, are normally left to the chief procurator (He with Waltz 1995: 194–195).

Procurators supervise criminal investigations, approve arrests, and prosecute cases investigated by the public security agencies. They also have exclusive authority to investigate some categories of criminal cases, essentially crimes involving officials. The 1979 Criminal Procedure Law and various regulations passed between 1979 and 1997 explicitly granted to procurators the exclusive authority to investigate and prosecute more than two dozen specific crimes involving officials. These include major economic crimes such as bribery, embezzlement of public assets, misuse of public funds, possession of unexplained assets, and tax evasion.[7]

Investigation and prosecution of corruption is certainly not the only function of procuratorates, but it has been the main focus of their work since the early 1980s. As early as 1980, annual reports of the SPP chief procurator to the Chinese legislature discussed criminal corruption. In the first half of the 1980s, criminal corruption accounted for a very large share of cases of economic crime filed for investigation by procurators.[8] In 1989, economic crime departments in procuratorates were reconfigured as specialized anticorruption departments, modeled on the recent experience of an anticorruption agency established in the Guangdong Provincial Procuratorate. Each year since their formation in 1989, these departments have accounted for at least three-fourths of all cases filed for investigation by government procurators. In 1995, the central authorities enhanced the administrative status of the Anticorruption Bureau under the SPP, upgrading it to deputy ministerial level and renaming it the Anticorruption General Bureau.

In the early 1980s, most procurators were new and inexperienced, recruited mainly from among demobilized military officers, most with no legal education. However, procuratorates quickly established training institutes to provide basic law courses as well as specialized courses on investigation, prosecution, and procuratorial technology. By the mid-1980s, about 60 percent of procurators had received some formal legal training (He with Waltz 1995: 221). This includes thousands of law graduates.

Party Discipline Inspection Committees

The party constitution adopted in August 1977 initially reinstated party discipline inspection committees as fully subordinate agencies of communist party committees, elected by them and working under their leadership. With this arrangement, the effectiveness of discipline inspection work depended crucially on the priorities of local party leaders, a situation that had posed problems in past years (Young 1984). The arrangement did not align with the major new anticorruption role that top party leaders assigned to discipline inspection committees in the early 1980s. For this reason, a new party constitution adopted in 1982 strengthened the discipline inspection system organizationally.[9]

The key change in 1982 was the introduction of dual leadership. At the top of the system, the CDIC works under the leadership of the Central Committee. At the provincial, municipal, and county levels, discipline inspection committees work under the leadership of the party committee at the same level and the discipline inspection committee one level up.[10] A second nontrivial change was expansion of the discipline inspection network. The 1982 Party Constitution introduced the possibility of grassroots discipline inspection committees in rural villages, urban neighborhoods, and basic-level workplaces, and it empowered the CDIC to dispatch ad hoc discipline inspection groups to party or government departments at the center in Beijing, as needed.[11] Another change was election of discipline inspection committee members by the full party congress, not the party committee, at each level. However, as in 1977, discipline inspection committee members elect their own standing committee, secretary, and deputy secretaries, and this is subject to party committee approval.[12]

In investigatory work, the vertical integration of discipline inspection committees was also strengthened in 1982—and again in 1992. In cases where a local discipline inspection committee disagrees with decisions of its leading party committee, the 1982 Party Constitution authorizes it to request the discipline inspection committee one level higher to re-examine the case. It can also appeal to its superior agency in cases of violation of laws or party discipline by its leading party committee (or members) that are not properly handled. The revised 1992 Party Constitution (*Zhongguo gongchandang dangzhang* 18 Oct. 1992, Art. 44) further authorizes local discipline inspection committees to conduct a preliminary investigation in such cases and, if a full investigation is warranted and the case involves a party committee standing committee member, to notify its superior discipline inspection committee at the same time as it requests approval from its leading party committee to file the case. In 1995, party leaders also agreed to a role for discipline inspection committees at an early stage of vetting of officials for any positions of leadership.[13]

The party constitutions adopted in 1977, 1982, and 1992 all assigned the same broad tasks to discipline inspection committees: to uphold the party constitution and party regulations, to assist party committees in strengthening party style, and to monitor implementation of the party line, guidelines, policies, and decisions. To this end, discipline inspection committees are required to educate party members regularly on their duty to observe party discipline, adopt decisions to promote party discipline, investigate important or complicated cases involving violations of the party constitution or party regulations, and decide on disciplinary actions against party members or party organizations.

In the Central Committee meeting that produced the CDIC in 1978, Deng Xiaoping emphasized the problem of party style: "Discipline inspection committees . . . at all levels have the task not only of handling cases, but even more important of upholding party norms and party regulations *(dang gui dang fa)* to really promote party style" (quoted in Chen 1993: 157). One month later, the first meeting of the CDIC set a number of priorities: education to strengthen discipline among party members and to strengthen party style, urgent cases of mistaken political verdicts from the Cultural Revolution and the 1950s, "letters and visits" work, and rebuilding the discipline inspection committees.[14] The primacy of party style was clear in its first document, Guiding Principles for Inner-Party Political Life, drafted at that January 1979 meeting.[15]

As Young (1984: 35) notes, top Chinese leaders did not decide until April 1982 that the struggle against economic crime was one of the "'most realistic and effective measures' for rectifying party style." With this decision, pronounced in a joint document of the Central Committee and State Council (13 April 1982), discipline inspection committees assumed a role that grew throughout the 1980s and 1990s: as party anticorruption enforcement agencies.

Party Leadership of Anticorruption Agencies

Hierarchically organized party committees exercise leadership in anticorruption enforcement in many ways. In the broadest sense of setting priorities and determining the resources devoted to investigation, prosecution, and punishment in corruption cases, local party committees have considerable discretion. Party committees also exercise specific leadership in anticorruption enforcement through political-legal committees that coordinate and direct work related to investigation, adjudication, and punishment of any officially unacceptable actions.[16] At the very top, the Political-Legal Commission includes the CDIC first secretary, the chief procurator, the president of the Supreme People's Court (SPC), the minister of public security, and the minister of state security.[17] At lower levels, political-legal committees are constructed similarly. Through the political-legal committees, party committee secretaries coordinate actions among the various agencies. For example, in politically sensitive cases and most important criminal cases, the political-legal committee conducts a pretrial review (He with Waltz 1995: 374).

At higher levels, the party committee exercises leadership over procuratorates through the party group *(dangzu)*, which discusses cases involving big sums or senior officials and decides whether or not to proceed to formal investigation. The party group often meets jointly with the procuratorial committee to make these decisions, but most members of the party group are also members of the procuratorial committee in any case (Zhang 1995).

Party committees exercise leadership over both party and government anticorruption agencies through the *nomenklatura* system. This is the system by which party committees, with information collected and kept on file by their organization departments, vet and approve the appointments of all officials holding positions of any consequence (Manion 1985; Burns 1989, 1994). The *nomenklatura* system makes party committees the effective "bosses" of all party and government officials one level down. A 1985 Chinese law journal article (cited in Clarke and Feinerman 1995: 153) quotes a county party secretary flaunting this authority to members of the local political-legal committee: "All of you sitting here, I ask you—you, the court president, if I hadn't put your name up, could you serve? You, the chief procurator, if I hadn't put your name up, could you serve? You, the public security chief, if I hadn't put your name up, could you serve? If you ask me, none of you could serve!"

Chief procurators are only nominally elected by the local people's congress. The party committee one level up vets the prospective chief procurator, deputy procurators, and ordinary procurators through its organization department and approves them as candidates before their election. For procurators not on the procuratorial committee, the procuratorate's party group proposes names to the party committee at the same level for vetting and approval (Zhang 1991: 40). Party discipline inspection committee secretaries are also vetted and approved through the *nomenklatura* system. At each level, the local discipline inspection committee standing committee, secretaries, and deputy secretaries are nominally elected by the discipline inspection committee at its plenary session, but the local party committee develops a candidate list prior to this and submits it to the discipline inspection committee for its agreement and then to the party committee at the next higher level for its approval (He with Waltz 1995: 218–219, 234).[18]

Finally, all discipline inspection committee officers and (almost certainly) all procurators are communist party members.[19] As such, they are constrained to observe party discipline, which includes conformity to the decisions of the party committee. He Jiahong and Jon Waltz (1995: 235) note that this can put procurators in an awkward position. Professionally, they are required to protect the rights of citizens and to investigate and prosecute officials who violate the law, but they must at the same time observe the leadership of the communist party.

Overlapping Jurisdictions

Party discipline inspection committees have the authority to investigate and punish party members for a wide range of ideological, organizational, and moral misconduct. A set of prohibitions (Central Committee 27 Feb. 1997) on activities of communist party members includes prohibitions on political misconduct (such as organization of factions within the party, participation in antiparty demonstrations, failure to promote policies of "reform and opening"), moral misconduct (such as visits to prostitutes, perusal of pornographic material, drug abuse, extravagant wedding celebrations or funeral ceremonies, refusal to provide for parents in their old age), and misconduct relating to personnel actions (such as refusal to submit to decisions on appointments or transfers, extending help to candidates in the recruitment process by providing information about examinations, overstaying while conducting business in foreign countries, helping family members go abroad). The rules also prohibit various forms of dereliction of duty and infringement of rights of ordinary citizens, but they devote most attention to various forms of economic misconduct (such as embezzlement of public assets, accepting or soliciting bribes, misappropriation of public funds, smuggling goods or facilitating smuggling, tax evasion).

Nearly three million party members were investigated and punished by the party for some form of misconduct in 1979–2000.[20] Probably another half-million party members were investigated but not punished in the same period.[21] By contrast, government procurators investigated more than 850,000 officials and their accomplices for criminal corruption, that is, about one-fourth the number investigated by discipline inspection committees in this period.[22] In principle, there is a division of labor between party discipline inspection committees and government procuratorates. The party agencies investigate violations of party discipline, most of which are not so serious as to constitute crimes; the government agencies investigate crimes involving officials, most of whom are also party members. In practice, the division of labor is not so clear because investigatory jurisdictions overlap.

Empirically, the extent of overlap is difficult to estimate, due to data limitations. In 1994, it seems that the majority of cases investigated by discipline inspection committees involved abuses of power for private gain, rather than ideological deviations or moral lapses, for example (Hou 1995).[23] It also appears that strictly economic violations constitute a sizeable proportion of cases investigated and party members punished. Nearly one-fourth of party members subjected to party disciplinary actions in 1982–1988 were punished for economic violations, mostly theft, embezzlement of public assets, and bribery ("Dang Jian Cites Statistics" 1989).[24] Economic violations almost certainly account for a higher proportion of misconduct punished with expulsion, the harshest party disciplinary action. In 1987, not an anticorruption campaign year, the party expelled nearly 9,000 party members for economic violations, more than one-third of all party members expelled in that year (*Renmin ribao* 12 Oct. 1988).[25] These sets of figures do not distinguish between party members holding public office and ordinary party members, who constitute the overwhelming majority in the party. Among officials, whose positions offer more opportunities for corruption, such offenses are probably more common. For example, of the 420 officials at and above the county level who were punished by the party in a single province in 1994–1996, nearly 60 percent were punished for economic violations (Song 1998: 20).[26] Party regulations on disciplinary action also suggest the extent to which economic violations may prevail. The 1997 Central Committee prohibitions cited earlier (27 Feb. 1997) detail economic violations far more than any other sort of misconduct, devoting nearly half of the discussion to these sorts of violations.

Obviously, not all economic violations are corruption, and not all meet the standard of crimes elaborated in the Criminal Law, although bribery and embezzlement of public assets do appear to account for a high proportion of economic offenses punished by the party. It is useful to consider, however, that party anticorruption agencies follow the track of "person to offense" in their investigations.[27] That is, unlike public security agencies, which begin with a crime and investigate to discover a criminal, party agencies begin with a report that some party member has engaged in some sort of misconduct. In the case of an economic violation, the circumstances and sums can rarely be completely transparent before the investigation has begun. Strictly speaking, party agencies do not conduct criminal investigations, although crimes do violate communist party discipline.[28]

In sum, not only is the criminal nature of economic transgressions rarely immediately apparent, but economic crimes are at the same time violations of party discipline. Party anticorruption agencies have a legitimate professional interest in economic offenses, including economic crimes, by communist party members. Simply put, insofar as corruption is concerned, the investigatory jurisdiction of procuratorates is practically a subset of that of discipline inspection committees.

Criminal Punishments and Party Disciplinary Actions

As indicated above, the communist party has its own system of adjudication and punishments for members who violate party discipline. Guided by party regulations, party organizations at workplaces decide on disciplinary action. Their decisions are based on results of investigations conducted and reported, with recommendations, by discipline inspection committees. Disciplinary actions, in order of increasing severity, consist of warning, serious warning, dismissal from party positions, probation within the party, and expulsion from the party.[29] All actions are noted in confidential personnel dossiers held by party organization departments that are consulted for appointments, promotions, transfers, and dismissals. Expulsion from the party, the harshest punishment, is nonetheless mild compared to main criminal punishments, excepting perhaps short sentences of control (guanzhi) and criminal detention.[30] Main criminal punishments are fixed-term imprisonment, life imprisonment, death penalty with suspension of execution, and death penalty.

What is the relationship between criminal punishments and party disciplinary actions for economic violations such as corruption? First, legal provisions, including the Criminal Law, explicitly specify the circumstances in which disciplinary actions may substitute for criminal punishments. For example, in cases of bribery or embezzlement of public assets, legal provisions issued over the years assign responsibility for administrative disciplinary action (xingzheng chufen) to the workplace or relevant administrative agency where the sums involved amount to less than 1,000 yuan (in 1982) unless the circumstances are "particularly serious," less than 2,000 yuan (in 1985 and 1988) in "minor" circumstances, and less than 5,000 yuan (in 1997) in "minor" circumstances (SPP 25 December 1982; SPC and SPP 8 July 1985; NPC

Standing Committee 21 January 1988; *Zhonghua renmin gongheguo xingfa* 14 March 1997, Art. 383).[31] That is, in written law and in practice, the criminal adjudication process includes, as one possible outcome of criminal prosecution, a decision that the circumstances of the crime do not justify criminal punishment, but rather less harsh disciplinary action.

Second, all relevant party regulations issued over the years stipulate expulsion from the party for any party member who commits an economic crime and is sentenced to a criminal punishment (CDIC 10 March 1983, 30 June 1987, 1 July 1990; Central Committee 27 February 1997).[32] In cases of bribery and embezzlement of public assets, for example, this would typically require expulsion for crimes involving sums of more than 2,000 yuan in the early 1980s through the late 1990s, and more than 5,000 yuan beginning in 1997 (SPP 25 December 1982; SPC and SPP 8 July 1985; NPC Standing Committee 21 January 1988; *Zhonghua renmin gongheguo xingfa* 14 March 1997, Art. 383). Moreover, the most detailed party regulation, issued in 1990, explicitly stipulates expulsion for party members who accept bribes or embezzle public assets valued at more than 2,000 yuan, which is consistent with legal guidelines for criminal punishment in effect at the time (CDIC 1 July 1990). The regulation also stipulates expulsion for party members who steal, swindle, smuggle, speculate, or misappropriate public funds—and it specifies a minimum sum at which each sort of economic violation justifies expulsion (for example, 300 yuan in cases of theft, 500 yuan in cases of swindling). These minimum sums are consistent with standards for criminal punishment specified in legal provisions. In cases of other economic violations, the party regulation recommends expulsion only in "serious circumstances."

Of course, party regulations also provide specific guidelines on disciplinary actions for the large number of cases of misconduct that do not amount to crimes. For example, the detailed 1990 CDIC regulation noted above recommends a warning or serious warning for bribery or embezzlement involving sums of under 500 yuan, but advises that party members may be exempted from disciplinary action altogether in mitigating circumstances. For sums of 500 to 1,000 yuan, it recommends a serious warning or dismissal from party positions; it recommends probation within the party or expulsion for bribery or embezzlement in sums of 1,000 to 2,000 yuan (CDIC 1 July 1990). Specific sums are not given in the 1997 party regulation issued a few weeks before passage of the 1997 Criminal Law, only recommendations based on circumstances.

For example, the regulation recommends dismissal from party positions or probation within the party in cases of bribery or embezzlement with "somewhat serious" circumstances and expulsion in cases with "serious circumstances" (Central Committee 27 February 1997).

In general, then, party disciplinary actions are explicitly linked to criminal punishments in cases of corruption, insofar as officials punished with criminal punishments for their corrupt acts are thereby normally expelled from the party, according to party guidelines. Further, for the most common forms of corruption, party guidelines also explicitly specify standards for expulsion (regardless of circumstances) that parallel legal standards for criminal punishment. This suggests a constraint on the party, even a particular sanctioning sequence. Yet, as discussed in the next section, the linkage actually constrains procuratorates and courts, not party agencies. In practice and by provision, party disciplinary actions regularly precede (and sometimes supplant) criminal punishments.

Problems of Coordination

In cases of corruption, jurisdictional overlap requires discipline inspection committees and procuratorates to share information and coordinate investigations so that both can perform effectively in their capacities as anticorruption agencies. Discipline inspection committees are at an advantage in the investigatory process, however. Their relatively broader jurisdiction, organizational location, and close relationship with government supervisory departments generally allows them to learn first about corruption.[33] As a result, the involvement of procuratorates in most cases of criminal corruption depends on the initiative of the party organization. Discipline inspection committees routinely pursue their investigations of party misconduct to completion before cases are transferred to procuratorates, a delay that can be detrimental to the subsequent criminal investigation. Many cases of criminal corruption are not transferred at all, but are appropriated by the party organization, with officials punished only for party disciplinary infractions. Party appropriation of anticorruption enforcement is not necessarily due to discipline inspection committees, however. It can be attributed to the role of party generalists, the party committees in localities and workplaces. Their cooperation or obstruction, often exercised through the political-legal committees, is the key determinant of whether, when, and how corrupt officials are punished according to law.

Information about Corrupt Activities

In principle, the elaboration of high standards of conduct for party members, a group which includes most officials, and the existence of a separate party agency to monitor and punish misconduct is a promising means to control official corruption. The broader net that defines the jurisdiction of discipline inspection committees gives these party agencies authority to investigate and punish misconduct that is not so serious as to constitute crime. The broad jurisdiction of discipline inspection committees allows them to pursue a broader range of misconduct, compared to procuratorates, and this means it is likely that party anticorruption agencies will discover, on their own, criminal violations by officials.

Broader jurisdiction has another, probably more important, advantage. Anticorruption agencies rely greatly on reports of misconduct, often from party members or ordinary citizens, to initiate investigations of corrupt officials. Discipline inspection committees have a practically all-encompassing jurisdiction, while procuratorates are constrained to pursue criminal liability only in their investigations. The notion of the law as an appropriate instrument to resolve conflict is fairly new to the Chinese. Decisions to report official misconduct to procuratorates imply conclusions about criminality. And while there may be doubt about the criminal nature of misconduct, practically all misconduct violates party discipline (or administrative ethical guidelines elaborated after 1987). For this reason, more reports of corruption come to party anticorruption agencies and the closely affiliated government supervisory departments than to procuratorates.

How many more is unclear. Annual figures on reports of corruption and bribery to procuratorates are readily available, at least up through 2000.[34] The CDIC does not make comparable figures publicly available, however. Instead, available figures on public reports to discipline inspection committees tend to combine letters, visits, and reports. Reports of corruption are only a subset, although perhaps a sizeable subset. Comparing the numbers of letters, visits, and reports to the party agencies with those to procuratorates suggests differences may be quite large. For example, in the last quarter of 1993, an anticorruption campaign period, procuratorates received only 15 percent the volume of letters, visits, and reports received by discipline inspection committees and supervisory departments. In 1994, not a campaign year, procuratorates received only 18 percent (CDIC Research Office 1996: 276; Wei 20 January 1995).

There is also a practical explanation behind these percentages: organizational location. Discipline inspection committees are functional departments of local party committees, just as procuratorates are agencies of local governments. However, discipline inspection committees are also located at the grassroots level, in rural villages, urban neighborhoods, and within workplaces—offices, factories, hospitals, and schools, for example. Discipline inspection groups may be found in party and government offices at the center. Where grassroots party organizations are too small to form full party committees, a party deputy secretary is assigned responsibility for discipline inspection work. In short, party discipline inspectors are as pervasive as the party itself.

In contrast, procuratorates are separate government organizations, extending only to the county level. There are some procuratorial offices at the township level (the lowest formal level of government), but these are strictly branch offices that do not function as independent procuratorates. More to the point, they are few in number. Just over 1,000 existed in 1993, in more than 45,000 townships and towns (He with Waltz 1995: 166). In 1988, procuratorates made reporting easier by establishing reporting centers and hotlines. Nonetheless, the location of party anticorruption agencies within workplaces as well as the close working relationship between discipline inspection committees and supervisory departments privileges party agencies over government procuratorates as recipients of reports of official corruption.

Sequencing of Investigations and Punishments

Reports about misconduct trigger a preliminary investigation in which discipline inspection officers assess the validity of complaints and determine whether or not to pursue them by filing a case for investigation. Discipline inspection committees conduct full-scale investigations only after a party committee approves. Under normal circumstances, discipline inspection committees are allowed two to three months for preliminary investigations and three to four months for full-scale investigations. Approval to file cases may take as long as one month. Disciplinary actions are decided by party committees, which normally have a month to reach such decisions. At what point in this process, which may be as long as nine months (longer for cases involving complications), does the party invite procurators to investigate criminal corruption?

Reflecting on his experience in the investigation and prosecution of a major bribery case in the mid-1990s, Zhang Peitian (1995) writes that there is no clear instruction to discipline inspection committees on their choice to transfer cases to procurators. The discipline inspection committee transferred the bribery case that he investigated only after it became complicated by a suicide attempt by the official being investigated. The complaint had come to the party agency, and procurators had no authority to investigate without the transfer of case materials by the party. Zhang's experience of party agency discretion reflects guidelines in party documents issued throughout the 1980s (see Kolenda 1990) and 1990s. At best, the documents are ambivalent about sharing case materials with procurators.

For example, even in 1988, when a short-lived policy to separate party and government dictated a greater than usual attention to procuratorial independence, interim party regulations on routine investigation of disciplinary infractions stated that discipline inspection committees "may recommend" cases be transferred to procurators if they discovered, in the course of investigation, that violations of party discipline also involve crimes (CDIC 12 May 1988).[35] In the same year, the CDIC and SPP created the basis for a system to coordinate the work of the two main party and government anticorruption agencies. They enjoined discipline inspection committees to transfer cases to government procurators "promptly," but other language in the regulation indicates this means promptly after the committees have completed their investigations and determined that criminal liability should be pursued. It does indicate that in cases involving big sums or senior officials, the government procurators "may get involved in the case at an earlier point" (CDIC and SPP 21 November 1988).[36]

Documents issued in late 1989, after reversal of the policy to grant government agencies greater independence, go further. They instruct discipline inspection committees and procuratorates to ensure that decisions on party disciplinary actions precede criminal punishments in cases where violations involve both disciplinary infractions and crimes. For cases investigated and decided by the CDIC and the SPP, they state that party and criminal punishments should ideally be announced at the same time, but that party disciplinary actions can precede decisions on criminal punishment if the judicial system cannot handle the case expeditiously (CDIC, SPC, SPP, and Ministry of Public Security 17 September 1989; CDIC 28 October 1989).

In 1994, revised regulations on discipline inspection work are more ambiguous. They state that if an investigation reveals both violations of party discipline and crimes, discipline inspection committees should transfer case materials to procurators "at an appropriate time" (CDIC

25 March 1994). That this was not standard practice by mid-1995 is suggested in a speech by Qi Peiwen (1995: 567), a CDIC official, at a national conference on investigatory work. Qi noted that joint investigations by discipline inspection committees and procuratorates had been common practice in cases involving big sums or senior officials in recent years. He advised conference participants from provincial discipline inspection committees on methods to promote better coordination of their work with procuratorates: "The key point is to create conditions for judicial agencies to get involved, to allow them to handle cases according to legal procedures. . . . Seize on one or two issues of criminal violations, ascertain the facts quickly, and gather evidence. In this way, [discipline inspection committees] can transfer [cases] to judicial agencies so that they [i.e., procuratorates] can reasonably and legally get involved in handling them using the methods of law and, according to legal procedure, begin their investigatory work."

In sum, party and government regulations governing investigation of official corruption offer guidelines that allow cases to remain with discipline inspection committees for a long time, as long as nine months, before procurators begin criminal investigations. Complicated cases may stay within the party system for much longer. For example, Chen Xitong, the most senior official ever to face criminal corruption charges, resigned from his position as Beijing party committee secretary in April 1995, during a CDIC investigation of serious financial misconduct by Beijing political authorities. In September 1995, Chen was dismissed from the Politburo and Central Committee and from all other offices. In September 1997, after completion of the investigation into violations of party discipline, the Central Committee expelled Chen from the party. Only then was the case formally transferred to the SPP for criminal investigation. Chen was prosecuted in June 1998 and sentenced in July 1998. In all, communist party agencies investigated and considered the case for more than two years before finally taking disciplinary action and formally transferring it to procurators.

Consequences of the Party's First-Move Advantage

Failure to involve government procurators in the early stages of investigation can irreparably harm criminal investigations. Criminal punishments are reserved for serious offenses in China, and so criminal investigations can feature harsh methods. Criminal law is often described as a "weapon," which is most appropriately used to handle "antagonistic contradictions" in the exercise of the people's democratic dictatorship (see "Concepts of Law in the Chinese Anti-Crime Campaign" 1985). In contrast, discipline inspection committees were revived mainly to resolve "nonantagonistic contradictions" within the party organization. The ethos of discipline inspection work is evident in the regulations governing investigations. Investigations are guided by the principles of "learning from past mistakes to avoid future mistakes, curing the illness to save the patient" and "educating both the individual party member [under investigation] and party members generally." In this context, it is normal procedure for discipline inspectors to begin investigations with a "talk" with the party member under investigation. Before investigations are completed, the party member under investigation is presented with the evidence collected in the course of the investigation, so that he or she may respond with opinions—which are taken into consideration by the party organization when deciding on disciplinary action (CDIC 25 March 1994).[37]

Obviously, these sorts of investigatory methods can bungle the case for procurators. Gong Xiaobing (1991: 16) complains that when disciplinary inspection committees receive reports about violations that clearly constitute crimes, they do not transfer the case to procurators in a timely way, but instead work on their own investigations first and turn the case over only once they have finished. As the party agencies lack both investigative experience and investigative skills, criminals are able to cover their tracks and destroy evidence so that the criminal investigation results in "half-cooked cases," "unresolved cases," or troublesome "ill aftereffects." Additionally, the practice of deciding party disciplinary actions before criminal punishments prejudices outcomes in criminal investigations, as the party organization has already weighed in with its judgment.

Party Appropriation of Anticorruption Enforcement

A more serious infringement on the anticorruption role of procurators occurs when party organizations completely appropriate cases of criminal corruption, substituting milder party disciplinary actions for harsher criminal punishment. Wen Shengtang (1996: 109), a procurator with the Anticorruption General Bureau, complains about this failure to respect the proper jurisdiction of procuratorates:

The major problem is that certain cases of criminal violations, which ought to be transferred to the criminal justice system so that criminal charges can be pursued, are instead handled as disciplinary matters, with disciplinary action replacing criminal punishment. Corrupt actions are extremely covert to begin with, and a considerable number of cases cannot be detected. Even cases for which clues do exist are difficult to sort out in a timely way. To these circumstances, add excessive leniency and excessively light [penalties] in cases for which the facts are clearly established. All of this greatly harms the anticorruption effort.[38]

From the perspective of procuratorates, a case filed and investigated concludes in one of three ways. It is dropped for lack of sufficient grounds to prosecute, it is prosecuted, or it is exempted from prosecution. With an exemption from prosecution, procurators conclude a case entirely within the procuratorial system, without going to court.[39] They report the decision to the procuratorate at the level directly above them. According to the Criminal Procedure Law, exemption from prosecution is granted only when the circumstances are minor, the harm not great, and the act therefore considered not serious enough to constitute a crime meriting criminal punishment (*Zhonghua renmin gongheguo xingshi susong fa* 1 July 1979, Art. 11; *Zhonghua renmin gongheguo xingshi susong fa* 17 March 1996, Art. 15). In such circumstances, procurators generally recommend the substitution of disciplinary action for criminal punishment. As described earlier, legal provisions provide guidelines that specify sums and circumstances when criminal punishment may be replaced by disciplinary action without a miscarriage of justice.

In principle, then, party organizations do not have the authority to substitute disciplinary actions for criminal punishments. To the extent that government procurators would arrive at decisions to substitute disciplinary actions too, outcomes are not affected if the party subverts legal procedure. To the extent that investigations by discipline inspection committees are less thorough and professional than criminal investigations, however, party decisions to substitute disciplinary actions for criminal punishments can subvert legal outcomes. Obviously, this is also the case when political influence motivates the failure to transfer cases to government procuratorates.

Party appropriation of cases and the substitution of party disciplinary actions for criminal punishments is a sort of plea bargaining outside the legal system. It punishes party members for violations of discipline only, completing cases without allowing procurators to investigate criminal liability. As party disciplinary actions are milder than most criminal punishments, the failure to transfer cases of corruption that amount to crimes protects party members from the law. In this sense, it reverses the higher standard of conduct to which communist party members are ostensibly held.

It is impossible to estimate the extent to which the party appropriates and punishes cases of criminal corruption.[40] CDIC figures indicate that about 80,000 party members, less than 6 percent of those investigated and disciplined by the party, were prosecuted and punished for crimes in 1988–97.[41] This figure seems absurdly low from two perspectives. It seems low if it is correct, considering earlier figures that economic violations accounted for about 25 percent of misconduct investigated and punished by the party in the 1980s.[42] In this sense, it suggests significant party appropriation of punishments. But it also seems too low to be correct, considering the number of individuals prosecuted for criminal corruption in this period, probably more than 300,000.[43] It is improbable that only one-fourth of those prosecuted for criminal corruption are communist party members, considering that these are, by legal definition, crimes of public officials.[44]

Some mundane organizational features contribute to party appropriation of anticorruption enforcement. A key feature is the workplace location of party anticorruption agencies. As discussed earlier, party discipline inspection committees at the grassroots level work under the leadership of workplace party organizations. Exposing criminal corruption sullies the reputation of the workplace. Moreover, as local procuratorates tend to be resource poor, workplaces are usually required to subsidize criminal investigations. Many procuratorates are so financially constrained that they require workplaces to pay for personnel, transportation, and subsidies to investigate workplace corruption (Gong 1991: 96–97). In short, workplaces incur real financial costs in criminal investigations that also bring their problems to the attention of authorities at higher levels. For these reasons, workplace leaders, including workplace party leaders, may prefer not to report criminal corruption to procuratorates. Instead, what are clearly official crimes may be investigated and punished within the workplace as less serious matters, requiring only party disciplinary action. Clearly, the crux of this issue is less the financial costs incurred by the workplace than the distinction between specialist agencies and generalist leaders. It applies as well to an explanation of party appropriation of enforcement by local party committees.

Party Generalists and Anticorruption Specialists
Discipline inspection committees and procuratorates operate in a Leninist political framework. As discussed in earlier sections, local and workplace party committees exercise leadership over anticorruption enforcement through a number of different arrangements. These include

political-legal committees, party groups, the *nomenklatura* system, and party member organizational discipline.

Even in the dual leadership structure of the discipline inspection system, party committees exercise "main leadership" *(wei zhu)*. Rules about approval to file cases for investigation reflect this. Although authority to approve filing a case for investigation typically resides with the discipline inspection committee one level higher, standard procedure requires it to solicit the opinion of its leading party committee first.[45] That party generalists and anticorruption specialists may have conflicting views was made evident by CDIC First Secretary Wei Jianxing (9 August 1995: 582), who cautioned discipline inspection committees against excessive investigatory zeal and asserted the principle of party committee leadership:

> There are times when we [i.e., discipline inspection committees] want to file a case for investigation, but leaders consider various aspects of the situation and decide provisionally against investigation. . . . From one perspective, investigation may make sense, but in the larger scheme of things it may make sense to put the issue aside for a while. Indeed, it may produce even better results. We should have confidence that party committees . . . view problems from a more comprehensive perspective than we do. We cannot be overly confident, thinking that whatever case we want to investigate must be investigated, that not to do so reflects a failure to assign high priority [to the anticorruption effort] or suppression of an investigation. We cannot be so simplistic in our inferences. The same goes for decisions on disciplinary actions. In some cases, we think there should be expulsion from the party, but the party committee discusses it and decides on probation within the party. They do not follow our recommendation. We cannot then say that this is the party committee not assigning high priority [to the anticorruption effort] or being overly lenient in meting out punishment. We must recognize that, after all, our discipline inspection committees have their own biases.

In the Leninist framework and with the weak tradition of legal authority in China, communist party committees have the specific and general powers to make or break investigations of discipline inspection committees and procuratorates, especially in cases involving senior officials or that span localities. Zhang Peitian (1995), reporting on the bribery investigation in which he participated, acknowledges violations of procuratorial independence: For example, procurators reported directly to the local party committee for approval of their actions. He argues that party committee support was essential to successful prosecution of the case. When party committees have an interest in protecting suspects, they can withhold approval for investigatory actions, obstruct prosecution, or leak information to affect the case adversely. Yan Yuhe (1995: 34), a county party committee secretary in Henan, points out that officials are not ordinary criminals: "Investigations encounter considerable resistance. If party committees do not attach a [high] priority to the effort (or in fact obstruct it), then naturally the difficulties in getting the work done are enormous. [For many party committees], when procurators investigate criminal abuses of authority in party and government, they are setting themselves up as rivals to party committees and embarrassing party committees and the government."

In sum, to the extent that there is leniency in anticorruption enforcement due to the substitution of party disciplinary actions for harsher criminal punishments, responsibility probably rests with the generalist party committees, not the specialist discipline inspection committees. Indeed, judging by complaints and cautions, the party generalists also seem to be the source of some obstruction of discipline inspection committee investigations. One advocate of greater autonomy in the discipline inspection system complains: "Some problems already exposed [within the party] and of a very serious nature [meet] with endless intercession for mercy from all quarters, so that it is impossible for investigation and disposition of cases to go forward" (Yan 1997: 24). Discipline inspection committees have pressed top authorities for greater coercive powers to investigate corruption, so that they can put in place a stronger anticorruption effort, not a weaker one (see Qi 1995).

Some have criticized the dual leadership arrangement, arguing that the party committees issue recriminations against discipline inspection committees for performing their assigned anticorruption duties. Yan Tao (1997: 23) articulates a bold alternative:

> A number of comrades have suggested that, at an appropriate time, the current system of local party committees exercising main leadership over discipline inspection committees at the same level be changed to the higher-level discipline inspection committees exercising main leadership. Staffing of local discipline inspection committees leadership positions would have the higher-level discipline inspection committees coordinating with the local party committee, but with the views of the higher-level discipline inspection committees as primary. [These measures] would make discipline inspection organizations an integral system, with its own leadership hierarchy as the main leadership.

Local protection of corrupt officials undoubtedly explains some obstruction of investigations. It is not necessary, however, to invoke protectionism to explain why party committees may be less diligent in pursuing investigations than anticorruption agencies—party or government. Party committees are generalist organizations, evaluated for their performance in a number of different dimensions, of which the anticorruption effort is only one. For most of the 1980s and 1990s, top Chinese leaders have evaluated (and rewarded) local generalist leaders mainly for successful economic performance. Indeed, an officially refuted, but apparently common, view among local officials in the mid-1980s held that anticorruption efforts stifle economic initiative.[46] Even without protectionist influences, then, party committees routinely lack strong incentives to attach a high priority to anticorruption efforts. Another related disincentive may be that anticorruption success is considerably more difficult to measure than the achievement of most economic performance targets.

Problems of "Punishment According to Law"

Quite apart from the problems of organization and coordination detailed earlier in this chapter are problems within the legal sphere itself, many having little or nothing to do with the Leninist political framework within which the law operates. A Leninist framework and Maoist political history has created a situation in which, for ordinary citizens as well as public officials, the role and relevance of law is questionable. The remarkably slow development of a criminal code to define the corruption evident to all did not help to change this situation.

A big part of the problem was the difficulty in defining legally what constituted criminal corruption in a rapidly changing political economy. The country's first Criminal Law, adopted in 1979, was not very helpful in this regard. To be sure, the normative line defining acceptable pursuit of private gain shifted quickly after its passage, but the law was also too vague and general to distinguish and punish economic crime. The development of a more useful legal standard was necessarily slow, not only because the lawmaking role of the legislature was new, but also because the "socialist market economy" of the 1980s and 1990s offered continually new opportunities for unanticipated forms of economic crime.

Nearly two decades passed before adoption of a revised criminal code. While Chinese lawmakers worked to define corruption and other crimes for the 1997 Criminal Law, corruption exploded across China. The legislature and government promulgated legislative acts and provisions assigning criminal responsibility according to the 1979 Criminal Law and other civil, economic, and administrative laws, but these were not formal amendments to the criminal code.[47] Even if law had been a more relevant reference point in China, in the 18 years between 1979 and 1997, there was no criminal code to provide a relatively unambiguous, salient standard defining corruption and associated sanctions. Nor could there have been, under the circumstances.

What Is Criminal Corruption in China?

In 1952, the Chinese government (Central People's Government Council 18 April 1952, Art. 2) introduced a broad notion of criminal corruption, describing it as a crime for a public official to appropriate public assets through embezzlement, theft, fraud, or deception; to extort or accept a bribe; or to engage in any other unlawful action that exploits public office to pursue private gain.[48] In 1954, after passage of the Constitution, the NPC Standing Committee began to craft a comprehensive criminal code. It published a draft in 1955 to generate discussion and in 1956 presented a revised version to the full legislature, which passed it as a provisional law for trial implementation. Maoist radicalism intervened to end further progress, however. First, with the Anti-Rightist Campaign of 1957–58, implementation of the provisional law ended. Then, in the early 1960s, the NPC Standing Committee presented another draft of the law to party leaders for review, but Cultural Revolution politics intervened and issues of legality were put aside. Essentially, then, the communist party ruled for 30 years, until 1979, with few statutes relevant to criminal justice and no effective criminal code (see Luo 1998: 1–21).

Work on major revisions to the 1979 Criminal Law began a few years after its adoption, but nearly two decades passed before passage of the vastly revised version in 1997. In the early 1990s, the legislative plan of the NPC Standing Committee included the drafting of an anticorruption law (SPP Chief Procurator 28 October 1993), but lawmakers focused ultimately on incorporating changes into a new criminal code.

For questions of criminal corruption, drafting a new criminal code presented three sorts of challenges: catching up with greater legal sophistication after decades of legal nihilism, drawing a legal line to accurately reflect the continually changing normative line in the economy, and describing new crimes that did not exist in the former political economy. The 1997 Criminal Law achieved most of this. It refined and clarified the broad definitions of corruption in the 1979 Criminal Law. Some sorts of corruption were redefined to take into account economic

Table 4.1 Corruption in the Criminal Law, 1979 and 1997

Crime	1979 Criminal Law	1997 Criminal Law
Embezzlement of public assets	Art. 155	Arts. 382, 396; see also Arts. 165, 166, 168, 169
Bribery	Art. 185	Arts. 385, 387, 388, 389, 391, 392, 393
Misuse of public funds	—	Art 384; see also Arts. 185, 272
Unexplained assets worth huge sums	—	Art. 395
Failure to report and turn in gifts received in official business	—	Art. 394
Retaliation against complainants	Art. 146	Art. 254
Malfeasance of judicial officials	Art. 188	Arts. 399, 401, 402
Malfeasance of taxation officials	—	Arts. 404, 405
Malfeasance of customs officials	—	Art. 411
Malfeasance of state commodity inspection officials	—	Art. 412
Malfeasance of quarantine officials	—	Art. 413
Malfeasance in hiring practices	—	Art. 418
Malfeasance in land transactions	—	Art. 410
Malfeasance in company registration and initial public offerings	—	Art. 403

Sources: Zhonghua renmin gongheguo xingfa (1 July 1979); *Zhonghua renmin gongheguo xingfa* (14 Mar. 1997).

changes.[49] A separate chapter on crimes of embezzlement of public assets and bribery appears in the 1997 Criminal Law, expanding the two articles on these crimes in the 1979 Criminal Law into 15 articles. Other chapters in the 1997 Criminal Law also contain articles on corruption, that is, actions by an official exploiting public office to pursue private gain illegally. Table 4.1 summarizes basic differences in the treatment of corruption in the criminal codes passed in 1979 and 1997.

As described in Chapter 3, the major form of criminal corruption is embezzlement of public assets *(tanwu)*. Chinese criminal law defines this by a particular combination of subject, object, and manner of embezzlement.[50] Only state functionaries or other individuals entrusted with the authority to manage public assets can be charged with embezzlement of public assets. The former category is fairly clear. It extends well below the various levels of communist party and government leadership to include essentially anyone on the state payroll in a position of responsibility ranking above an ordinary clerk in the administrative hierarchy.[51] The latter category, those entrusted to manage public assets, depends crucially on the definition of public assets, the object of corrupt embezzlement. The 1979 Criminal Law defined public assets by excluding all but obviously private property—it explicitly included assets of collective enterprises, for example. This remained in force until the 1997 Criminal Law introduced the substantially narrower definition of the object of corrupt embezzlement, "state-owned assets," which took the crime out of the collective economy.[52] Finally, embezzlement of public assets does not simply subsume the variety of means of illegal appropriation (such as outright theft and swindling), but necessarily includes the exploitation of official position to embezzle the assets.[53] Also, a separate chapter of the 1997 Criminal Law describes the crime of illegal asset stripping by a director of the board or manager of a state-owned company or enterprise. Although not defined as such, this crime has the features of corrupt embezzlement as redefined in 1997.[54]

The second major form of criminal corruption is bribery. Article 185 of the 1979 Criminal Law makes it a crime for a state functionary to take advantage of public office to accept a bribe and for any individual to offer or introduce a bribe to a state functionary. The 1997 Criminal Law (Arts. 385, 389, 392) offers a more detailed description. Instead of "accept a bribe," bribery is "to solicit or accept money or property or unlawfully accept money or property in exchange for favors." It also defines accepting a kickback or commission in violation of state regulations as accepting a bribe. Separate articles in the 1997 Criminal Law make it a crime to offer a bribe to a state functionary or act as a bribe broker. They also clarify that it is the crime of offering a bribe only when illegitimate benefits are sought, but not as a response to extortion or when no illegitimate benefits are gained.

The 1997 Criminal Law (Arts. 387, 391, 393, 396) also introduces an important notion absent from the 1979 Criminal Law: "organizational corruption."[55] It is a crime for a state agency, state-owned company or enterprise, or people's organization to solicit or unlawfully accept money or property in exchange for benefits. It is a crime for any of these organizations to collect or accept and conceal from public accounting a kickback or commission in the course of a business transaction. It is also a crime for an organization to offer money or property to these organizations in pursuit of illegitimate benefits or to offer a kickback or commission in violation of state regulations. It is a crime for any organization to bribe a state functionary in pursuit of illegitimate benefits or to offer a state functionary a kickback or commission in violation of state regulations. Finally, it is a crime for a state agency, state-owned company or enterprise, or people's organization to allocate state-owned property to a group of private individuals in the name of the organization and in violation of state regulations.

Three crimes that appear in the 1997 Criminal Law do not appear in the 1979 Criminal Law: misuse of public funds, unexplained assets, and failure to report gifts received in the course of official business. The first two crimes reflect positions presented in a legislative provision issued in 1988. The third is a new crime: Article 394 makes it a crime to accept gifts in the course of official business and, in violation of specific regulations or where the value of the gifts is large, fail to report them or turn them over to the state.

Article 384 on misuse of public funds makes it a crime for a state functionary to misappropriate public funds for private use to engage in illegal activities, to misappropriate relatively large sums of public funds to invest in profit-seeking activities, or to borrow illicitly relatively large sums of public funds without returning them for more than three months. This is basically the definition presented in an NPC Standing Committee provision (21 January 1988), issued after many years in which legal authorities either did not investigate or prosecute misuse of public funds or handled it as embezzlement of public assets.[56]

Unexplained assets was introduced as a crime in the same 1988 legislative provision (NPC Standing Committee 21 January 1988), which states that when the assets or expenditures of a state functionary clearly exceed his legal income and the difference is huge, he can be required to explain the source. If he cannot demonstrate that the source is legal, the difference is considered illegal assets. Article 395 of the 1997 Criminal Law makes it a crime for a state functionary to possess assets or make expenditures that obviously exceed his legitimate income by a very large amount and be unable to demonstrate that the sources are legal. It also makes it a crime for a state functionary to have relatively large concealed or undeclared savings deposits in a foreign country. In a discussion of Article 395, Hu Kangsheng and others (1997: 559–560) define a "very large amount" as sums in the order of at least several hundreds of thousands of yuan. They also state that if an investigation reveals the sums are illegally obtained from some crime, then the official is charged with that crime, not with unexplained assets.[57]

Finally, the 1997 Criminal Law offers a more extensive elaboration of criminal malfeasance, mostly in a chapter on crimes involving dereliction of duty *(duzhi zui)*, where a public official exploits office for personal considerations (for example, practicing favoritism toward a friend or relative). The 1979 Criminal Law considered criminal malfeasance by judicial officials. The 1997 Criminal Law considers crimes of malfeasance by judicial officials, taxation officials, customs officials, state commodity inspection officials, and quarantine agency officials. It also elaborates on crimes of malfeasance in civil service hiring, in granting permission to register a company or issue an initial public offering of a company stock or bond, and in approving the seizure or lease at very low prices of land use rights for state-owned land.

By 1997, then, the Chinese criminal code had developed a working definition of "criminal corruption," one that would continue to develop as corrupt practices developed, but would undoubtedly never again entail the major crafting operation of the previous 18 years. All the same, the slow pace of its development meant that it had not served, for the public or for public officials, as a standard or reference point while corruption flourished and adapted in the 1980s and 1990s. Surely, it must be acknowledged, the Chinese political framework would not have accommodated this role earlier, but criminal law was not in any position to play it in any case.

A Double Standard of Criminal Justice

At the same time as Chinese law was working toward a clearer definition of criminal corruption, it was developing a notion of the normative weight of official crime relative to ordinary crime. A number of Chinese legal scholars and practitioners argue that the spirit of the 1979 Criminal Law holds officials to a higher standard than it does ordinary citizens, but that this relationship was completely reversed through the various provisions giving concrete meaning to descriptive categories in the law (see Sun 1990: 27–28; Wei and Wang 1992: 184–191; Wen 1996: 97–111). The more tolerant view of "white-collar crime" may not surprise us, but it is viewed as important by Chinese scholars. They see it as an issue of legal inconsistency—one that promotes understandable public cynicism about official anticorruption efforts and thereby hampers those efforts.

The new tolerance is best illustrated in the virtual reversal of disproportionate punishments for roughly similar crimes: ordinary theft (of public or private property) and embezzlement (theft of public assets by a state functionary who exploits public office). The 1979 Criminal Law (Arts. 151, 155) does appear to consider the embezzlement of public assets as essentially more serious than ordinary theft.[58] This view is suggested in the law's specification of minimum, maximum, and supplementary punishments. The minimum punishment for embezzlement of public assets is criminal detention; the minimum punishment for theft is control.[59] The maximum punishment for embezzlement is the death penalty; the maximum punishment for theft is life imprisonment. Supplementary criminal punishments (such as confiscation of property and payment of compensation) can be attached to embezzlement of public assets quite routinely. No such punishments are attached to theft unless the circumstances of the crime are "particularly serious."

Punishment for a crime takes into account the general value of property affected by the crime (where relevant) and the seriousness of the circumstances of the crime. The 1979 Criminal Law does not associate punishments with specific monetary values for any crime. Instead, punishments are assigned to descriptive categories: a crime involving a "particularly huge" or "huge" amount of money is assigned harsher punishment than the same crime where the amount is only "relatively large," for example. For both theft and embezzlement of public assets, the 1979 Criminal Law specifies punishment of up to five years imprisonment or criminal detention (or, for theft, control) where the crime involves a "relatively large" amount (that is, an amount sufficiently large to merit criminal punishment). Other categories are not strictly comparable because circumstances specified in the law differ for the two crimes.

If the intent behind the 1979 Criminal Law was to hold officials to a higher standard than ordinary citizens, this principle was implicitly repudiated in provisions introduced after 1979. Taken in their entirety, they view the ordinary crime of theft more harshly than the official crime of embezzlement. This view is expressed in specifications of monetary values associated with the descriptive categories employed in the law. In 1982, the Central Committee General Office specified monetary values for embezzlement of public assets. Six years later, the legislature issued its set of provisions, which basically restated those in the 1982 party document. Both documents set 2,000 yuan as the "relatively large" amount that defines an embezzlement of public assets as a crime (meriting criminal punishment) and 10,000–50,000 yuan as the minimum standard for embezzlement involving a "huge" amount. In both documents, embezzlement involving amounts less than 2,000 yuan does not merit criminal punishment unless the circumstances are "relatively serious." By contrast, the SPC and SPP set 200–300 yuan as the "relatively large" amount defining a theft as a crime and 2,000–3,000 yuan as the minimum standard for theft of a "huge" amount. In 1992, these theft amounts were raised to 300–500 yuan and 3,000–5,000 yuan respectively (Central Committee General Office 13 August 1982; NPC Standing Committee 21 January 1988; SPC and SPP 2 November 1984, 11 December 1992).

These specifications effectively reversed the double standard implied in the 1979 Criminal Law: The imputed standard of conduct for officials became *lower* than that for ordinary citizens. By these rules, ordinary theft in the sum of 500 yuan was punishable by up to five years imprisonment, but embezzlement of public assets in any amount under 2,000 yuan was not normally subject to criminal punishment at all. With the exception of changes in effect for a brief period during the 1989 anticorruption campaign, which offered amnesty or leniency to officials who gave themselves up, the standards adopted in the 1980s remained essentially in force until 1997.

The 1997 Criminal Law (Arts. 264, 382, 382) associates specific monetary values with punishments for some crimes, including embezzlement of public assets, but not theft.[60] The law raises the minimum standard defining an act of embezzlement of public assets as a crime from 2,000 yuan to 5,000 yuan. It raises the minimum standard for embezzlement involving a "huge" amount from the previous 10,000–50,000 thousand yuan to the much higher 50,000–100,000 yuan. At the same time, the law reduces punishments in most categories of theft, but adds the death penalty in a new category. It reduces punishment for theft of a "relatively large" amount from five or fewer years imprisonment, criminal detention, or control to three or fewer years. It also permits imposition of a fine as an additional or exclusive punishment. It reduces punishment for theft of a "huge" amount (or theft with "serious" circumstances) from five to ten years imprisonment to three to ten years imprisonment. Theft of a "particularly huge" amount or where the circumstances of the crime are "particularly serious" is punishable by longer periods of imprisonment, including life imprisonment. Theft of a "particularly huge" amount from a financial institution or theft of precious cultural artifacts where the circumstances of the crime are "serious" is punishable by the death penalty or life imprisonment.

Comparing the view of theft and embezzlement of public assets in the 1997 Criminal Law and taking into account the specific definitions pronounced by the SPC and SPP in 1992, there can be no doubt that the criminal law implicitly views ordinary theft more harshly than official theft. As Chinese critics have argued, this double standard is not a new situation in 1997. It can no longer, however, be considered as a conflict between "law" and "policy," as critics asserted before passage of the 1997 Criminal Law. That is, considering the specification of minimum, maximum, and supplementary punishments for the two crimes, the 1997 Criminal Law views embezzlement of public assets as essentially less serious than ordinary theft.

In redefining standards in 1997, Chinese authorities were likely more concerned about how criminal corruption was actually being handled in the criminal justice system than about any contradiction between the widely professed higher standard of conduct for officials and the relationship in criminal law of disproportionate punishments for similar crimes of officials and ordinary citizens. The 1997 standards were intended to demonstrate a new realism and serious willingness to prosecute criminal corruption, not an official tolerance of higher levels of the crime. This entailed redefining standards in ways that seem to reflect more tolerance than before of corruption—but previous standards had been routinely breached for some years. A good parallel is the 1982 redefinition of standards, which increased the minimum standard defining a crime of embezzlement of public assets from 1,000 yuan (the 1952 standard) to 2,000 yuan. The change was explained as follows: "It seems lenient, but actually we are being harsh. For many years now the one-thousand-yuan standard in the [1952] 'Regulations on Punishing Corruption' has not been strictly implemented. In quite a number of instances of embezzlement in amounts of several thousand yuan, even ten or twenty thousand yuan, [individuals] either have not been prosecuted for a crime or have had criminal punishment waived" (Central Committee General Office 13 Aug. 1982: 533).

Similarly in the 1980s and 1990s, for crimes involving the abuse of public office to pursue private gain, the Chinese criminal justice system appears to have regularly practiced greater leniency than the regulations permitted. Wen Shengtang (1996: 109) of the Anticorruption General Bureau complained: "The criminal justice system is excessively lenient in some cases of embezzlement, to the extent of rashly allowing individuals to go free." Leniency has apparently sometimes taken the form of prosecuting officials for other crimes with lesser punishments. For example, according to Wei Pingxiong and Wang Ranji (1992: 187), the relatively less harsh view of embezzlement and bribery in provisions introduced in the 1980s was accompanied by a tendency in practice to prosecute as embezzlement or bribery crimes that were in fact theft or swindling by officials. The practice was a logical extension of the unequal treatment reflected in the law: "The criminals in these cases are officials. It has been considered necessary to prevent a struggle against all [officials], to punish a minority, to educate and admonish the majority, to make the greatest possible effort at redemption, and to assign the least possible criminal responsibility. In our view, this orientation clearly violates the principle of equality before the law."[61]

Exemptions from Prosecution

To the extent that a more tolerant notion of official crime relative to ordinary crime, reflected in punishments for similar crimes, was used strategically by procurators in the way suggested above, officials enjoyed even greater leniency in practice. The degree to which the criminal justice system routinely extended greater leniency toward officials is best illustrated in figures on exemptions from prosecution *(mianyu qisu)*. From the perspective of procurators, a case filed and investigated concludes in one of three ways: the case is dropped for lack of sufficient grounds to prosecute, the case is prosecuted, or the case is exempted from prosecution.[62] With an exemption from prosecution, procurators conclude a case entirely within the procuratorial system, without going to court. They report the decision to the procuratorate at the level directly above them. According to the Criminal Procedure Law, exemption from prosecution is granted only when the circumstances are minor, the harm not great, and, therefore, the act considered not serious enough to constitute a crime, meriting criminal punishment.[63] In such cases, procurators generally recommend the substitution of disciplinary action for criminal punishment.

Figures on exemption from prosecution are interpretable as leniency toward officials in light of characteristic features of the Chinese legal system. The criminal justice system is generally identified with serious crime and severe punishment. The usual outcome of criminal prosecution is criminal punishment. Although Chinese criminal law acknowledges violations that are minor, they are typically punished outside the criminal justice system with milder disciplinary actions. As such violations are considered not serious enough to merit criminal punishment, they do not strictly constitute crimes. In short, exemption from prosecution generally represents a procuratorial decision to substitute relatively mild disciplinary action for harsher criminal punishment.[64]

In this light, it is instructive to compare the use of exemption from prosecution in cases of similar crimes committed by public officials and ordinary citizens. Table 4.2 presents figures on exemptions from prosecution in cases of criminal property violation for 1987–96.[65] This com-

Table 4.2 Exemptions from prosecution, 1987–96: Cases of criminal property violation investigated by public security agencies and procuratorates

Year	Investigated by public security agencies	Exempted from prosecution	As % of cases investigated	Investigated by procuratorates	Exempted from prosecution	As % of cases investigated
1987	125,279	5,171	4.1%	19,767	8,300	42.0%
1988	147,671	5,992	4.1%	16,248	7,673	47.2%
1989	211,179	9,443	4.5%	24,445	13,318	54.5%
1990	235,527	10,189	4.3%	24,503	12,055	49.2%
1991	200,849	8,831	4.4%	21,886	7,901	36.1%
1992	189,075	10,225	5.4%	27,502	13,554	49.3%
1993	188,341	10,012	5.3%	20,913	9,214	44.1%
1994	233,953	10,154	4.3%	16,762	3,974	23.7%
1995	237,445	9,807	4.1%	23,248	7,326	31.5%
1996	294,335	13,169	4.5%	15,479	4,833	31.2%
Average	206,365	9,299	4.5%	21,075	8,815	41.8%

Source: Zhongguo jiancha nianjian for the following years: 1988 (1989: 353–354), 1989 (1991: 412–413), 1990 (1991: 329–330), 1991 (1992: 344–345), 1992 (1992: 363–364), 1993 (1994: 419–420), 1994 (1995: 552–553), 1995 (1996: 384–385), 1996 (1997: 398–399), 1997 (1998: 488–489).

Note: Criminal property violation is comprised of crimes of theft, swindling, extortion, forcible seizure, and embezzlement of public assets. Cases investigated by procuratorates include all cases of embezzlement of public assets, which is under the exclusive investigatory purview of procuratorates.

prises all cases of theft, swindling, extortion, forcible seizure, and embezzlement of public assets. The figures exclude the fairly small proportion of cases dropped in the course of the investigation; that is, they represent only cases resulting in either prosecution or exemption from prosecution.[66] The table compares exemptions from prosecution in two categories of cases: those investigated by public security agencies and those investigated exclusively by procuratorates, a distinction roughly equivalent to that between cases involving ordinary citizens and cases involving public officials.[67]

Most crimes of property violation are ordinary crimes, investigated by public security agencies. In these cases, exemptions from prosecution as a percentage of cases investigated for such crimes average about 5 percent and are quite stable over the years. Cases investigated by procurators provide a stark contrast. Exemptions from prosecution as a percentage of cases investigated are much higher, 42 percent on average. They also exhibit more variation over the years—ranging from a low of 24 percent in 1994 to a high of 55 percent in 1989, the year of the biggest anticorruption campaign in the post-Mao period.[68]

The difference in average proportions exempted from prosecution—42 percent compared to 5 percent—is huge. Obviously, it largely reflects the routine application of more permissive standards for officials. Simply put, if corrupt officials and ordinary thieves stole public property worth under 2,000 yuan in similar proportions over the years, a much higher proportion of officials would be exempted from prosecution according to the rules in force.[69] For exemption from prosecution in the two categories to approach similar proportions, cases of theft of about 200–300 yuan or less (after 1992, 300–500 yuan or less) would have to equal roughly, as a proportion of all theft, cases of embezzlement of public assets involving amounts of about 2,000 yuan or less as a proportion of all such cases. It is certainly possible that petty embezzlement accounts for a higher proportion of embezzlement than does petty theft as a proportion of theft. The proportion would have to be enormously higher, however, to produce differences of the magnitude shown in Table 4.2. Alternatively, procuratorial investigation of embezzlement of public assets would have to be relatively disproportionately focused on petty cases. A procuratorial investigatory bias toward cases of petty corruption is an implausible explanation. Indeed, as discussed above, the bias appears to have been in exactly the opposite direction, with a tendency for less serious crimes of officials to be handled outside the criminal justice system altogether. The differences shown in Table 4.2, then, seem to reflect much greater leniency toward officials, compared to ordinary citizens, in the application of (already more lenient) standards in the criminal justice system.

The relative volatility of exemptions from prosecution in cases investigated by government procurators is a second interesting contrast with ordinary crime. Ten observations are very few indeed for statistical inference, but some simple analysis yields results that are consistent with plausible (but not necessarily obvious) causal relationships. First, the volume of cases investigated is significantly correlated with exemptions from prosecution. Not surprisingly, the more cases investigated, the more cases exempted. More interestingly, the more cases investigated, the higher the proportion of cases exempted. Second, neither absolute numbers nor proportions exempted from prosecution are, in a statistical sense, significantly different in anticorruption campaign years than in noncampaign years.[70] That is, to the extent that anticorruption campaigns affect exemptions from prosecution, they appear mainly to increase exemptions (absolutely and proportionately) by increasing the number of cases investigated.

The analytical results suggest significant capacity constraints of procurators. In discussing misconduct in exemptions from prosecution, He and Waltz comment that procurators may decide to exempt if they find a case too difficult to prove. Exemptions from prosecution allow procurators to complete cases *(jie an)* more quickly (He with Waltz 1995: 314). Case completion statistics are routinely kept and reported as performance measures. When procuratorates are flooded with a higher than usual volume of cases and when they are under pressure to complete cases, as a measure of anticorruption performance, it is quite plausible that exemptions may be artificially boosted. These situations tend to obtain during anticorruption campaigns. Certainly, campaigns also boost exemptions from prosecution by relaxing rules.[71] The biggest influence on exemptions, however, seems to be the volume of cases that present themselves to procurators for investigation.

Conclusion

Up to this point, problems of routine anticorruption enforcement in mainland China have been examined as problems of structure and authority. One set of problems, having to do with organization and coordination, inheres in the coexistence of two tracks of enforcement. Presumably, the communist party discipline inspection system, with its broader jurisdiction, stronger monitoring capacity, and advantaged investigatory and sanctioning position, was designed to check corruption by holding public officials to a higher ethical standard as party members. Yet it has routinely served to keep much official crime out of the criminal justice system. This appears to be due mainly to the party committee leadership structure. Party generalists, less zealous anticorruption enforcers than discipline inspection committees, have viewed corruption more comprehensively (as a lower priority) and have exercised their prerogative to appropriate cases so that milder party disciplinary action substitutes for harsher criminal punishment.

A second set of problems inheres in the criminal justice system. On the one hand, the unavoidably slow development of a legal notion of criminal corruption has deprived the law of a significant role as a "focal point" for anticorruption enforcement. Legal standards to define corruption proliferated in provisions and regulations, alongside hundreds of party disciplinary standards and government administrative ethical standards offering their own continually changing definitions of official venality. At least as important are problems in the practice of law as it relates to anticorruption enforcement. In assigning punishments, the law has held officials to a lower standard than ordinary citizens who commit similar crimes. In implementing punishments, procurators have routinely exempted officials from prosecution at much higher rates than ordinary citizens for similar crimes.

In sum, biases that have protected officials from harsh punishment for corruption by routinely failing to transfer cases to procurators have been reproduced in a criminal justice system that has routinely failed to punish corrupt officials harshly when cases are transferred. The result of both sets of problems is the same: routinely, milder disciplinary action has replaced harsh criminal punishment for corrupt officials.

To the extent that Chinese leaders are concerned about controlling corruption, these conclusions are troubling—even more so when the failure is a source of cynicism and dissatisfaction among ordinary Chinese. That is, routine anticorruption enforcement has also created a problem of legitimation for the regime. To disrupt this routine and reclaim legitimacy to rule, Chinese leaders have turned to anticorruption campaigns. How campaigns work is the subject of the next chapter, but it is useful to preface that discussion by highlighting a dilemma that has already emerged from the discussion here.

If, as described in Chapter 1, the problem of anticorruption reform in a setting of widespread corruption requires reducing corrupt payoffs and changing shared expectations, then the cycles of routine and campaign anticorruption enforcement in mainland China are seriously flawed. It is a huge irony that punishment according to law of corrupt officials is most strongly emphasized when enforcement is most highly politicized—in campaign periods. Party committees have been most reliable as anticorruption enforcers during campaigns, spearheading intensified efforts to bring about punishment according to law by bringing corrupt officials to the agencies charged with enforcing the law.

Routine anticorruption enforcement has not worked to institutionalize the relevance of law, but has instead undermined it at nearly every turn with the primacy of party disciplinary action and the principle that the communist party can correct its own mistakes—even when those mistakes involve serious abuses of official power. Routinely, party committees and discipline inspection committees have not acted in ways to build expectations of impartial adjudication and proportionate punishment according to knowable standards (much less laws). In sum, routine anticorruption enforcement has failed to enforce the law, and the mere fact of campaign anticorruption enforcement has failed to routinize the law.

If the cycles of routine and campaign anticorruption enforcement have fallen short in the effort to change shared expectations, they have not done much better to reduce corrupt payoffs either. Campaigns increase the volume of cases for procurators, but this produces less, not more, punishment according to law. In the politicized campaign context, procurators work to complete the higher number of cases as best they can without comparable increases in resources. The result is not so different as that obtained in periods of routine enforcement: for a great many officials, disciplinary action replaces criminal punishment.

CHAPTER FIVE

Anticorruption Campaigns as Enforcement Mechanisms

Chapter 4 suggests why Chinese leaders often turned to anticorruption campaigns as enforcement mechanisms in the 1980s and 1990s. Put simply, the organization and coordination of corruption control routinely spares corrupt officials from criminal punishment. This exacerbates problems of legitimacy for the regime, fueling popular disquiet about growing income inequality and promoting widely aired cynicism about the effectiveness and sincerity of regime anticorruption efforts. Campaigns disrupt routine anticorruption enforcement, produce the results that show up as "enforcement peaks" in Chapter 3, and allow Chinese leaders to claim credit for these and other successes. How the disruptions produce the successes is the main subject of this chapter.

The chapter begins with a description of a Maoist-era anticorruption campaign, launched in 1951. Examining this early campaign helps to illuminate the successes and shortcomings of campaigns launched more recently. The chapter goes on to describe features of post-Mao anticorruption campaigns. It then more closely examines the role of ordinary Chinese in the campaigns—something that easily distinguishes recent campaigns from the "mass movements" of the Maoist era. Most of the chapter describes the post-Mao campaigns: three in the 1980s (1982, 1986, and 1989) and two in the 1990s (1993 and 1995). Campaigns in the 1980s exhibit a logic that Mark Kleiman (1993), in a different context, has analyzed as "enforcement swamping." Campaigns in the 1990s reflect a change in strategy, to a more focused "enforcement targeting."

The evidence presented in this chapter points to an unhappy conclusion, prefaced in Chapter 4: The anticorruption campaigns of the 1980s and 1990s achieved some spectacular enforcement results, but they failed substantially in three key ways. First, their frequency was probably counterproductive to long-term deterrence. Second, it seems the campaigns did not go far enough in mass mobilization to boost regime legitimacy as anticipated. Finally, and perhaps most important of all, the campaigns undermined nascent institutionalization in specialized enforcement agencies and especially in criminal law.

Maoist Precedent: The 1951–52 Campaign

A Maoist-era precedent for the anticorruption campaigns of the 1980s and 1990s is the campaign launched in December 1951. The Chinese communists had gained power in 1949 after a protracted war, fought for nearly two decades from bases in the countryside and remote interior. They had been supported mainly by the peasantry, mobilized through agrarian reform and anti-Japanese nationalism. When the communists began to enter the cities as a ruling force at the close of the civil war, Mao Zedong (5 Mar. 1949) warned of a new battle. Revolutionaries who had demonstrated extraordinary courage in years of armed struggle now faced a more insidious enemy: "sugar-coated bullets," namely, the temptations of a comfortable lifestyle, which many veterans evidently considered their entitlement in victory.

The high priority assigned to economic recovery in the early years of communist rule actually encouraged close working relationships between communist officials and the urban bourgeoisie. A policy of a broad "united front" promoted cooperation with the industrial capitalists and former government officials who had stayed behind to gamble on their chances with the new regime. The regime badly needed the contributions of these groups. Communists with the experience, education, and skills to reinvigorate the urban economy or staff the government bureaucracy were few in number. For these reasons, and in contrast to the violent excesses instigated against landlords during rural land reform, the communists were quite conciliatory in the cities.

In December 1951, the Central Committee launched a campaign against corruption, waste, and bureaucratism—the "Three Anti" *(san fan)* campaign.[1] It lasted for almost a full year, merging with the "Five Anti" *(wu fan)* campaign (against bribery, tax evasion, theft of state property, cheating on government contracts, and stealing state economic secrets) in January 1952. The latter was an outgrowth of the former, due to links between corrupt officials and the private economic sector. Evidence and confessions gathered in one campaign were often the basis for action in cases investigated in the other. Both campaigns signaled a major policy shift away from economic recovery and political conciliation toward all-encompassing political mobilization. The campaigns were limited mainly to urban areas. All state enterprises and government offices from the county level up to the central ministries in Beijing participated in the Three Anti campaign. By far, the most important focus of the campaign was corruption.

The campaign relied on party leadership, mass mobilization, and no precise definition of corruption. Nor were legal guidelines available until the campaign was well under way.[2] Communist party leaders set up (and headed) committees within state enterprises and government offices to direct the campaign. Party leaders also set up special courts within each workplace, with powers of subpoena, detention, arrest, and sentencing of workplace officials. These ad hoc committees, led by regular party leaders at the workplace, dominated the campaign, essentially usurping the functions of regular enforcement agencies (such as supervisory departments).

The campaign proceeded in three stages: confession, denunciation, and "tiger hunting." Initially, leaders pressured officials to confess their corrupt activity. Top leaders set examples with public self-criticism. Officials were urged to confess in specially convened meetings: in Shanghai, one such confession meeting brought together more than 10,000 officials. Corrupt officials were warned that they would suffer harsher penalties if they were exposed by the mass public in the second stage of the campaign, but were promised mild punishment if they cooperated and confessed in this first stage.

The second stage of the campaign featured extensive mass mobilization. Party members and ordinary citizens were roused to participate in proceedings that completely disrupted routine production and administrative work. These included denunciation meetings at which leaders encouraged ordinary citizens to demonstrate their "revolutionary enthusiasm" by informing on corrupt officials publicly. They also encouraged people to report corruption through letters and set up special mailboxes for this purpose.

The third stage, tiger hunting, was a search for officials suspected of corruption involving sums of 1,000 yuan or more who had not confessed in the first stage of the campaign.[3] Tiger hunting was greatly affected by pressures from the top. Mao sent telegrams to provincial leaders, insisting that every government office handling significant sums of money or production materials must have many corrupt officials. He instructed the provinces to search especially for "big tigers," those whose corruption involved sums of 10,000 yuan or more. There were also pressures from below, as mass mobilization became difficult to control; this led to escalation of the campaign, with leaders at lower levels classifying minor corruption as more serious crimes. Frederick Teiwes (1978: 132–133) describes the severity of tiger hunting:

> Struggle meetings within units were frequent and intense; psychological pressure and verbal abuse were sometimes accompanied by physical blows. As a result, suicides by those suffering humiliation were frequent. Moreover, during this stage many institutions stopped work entirely, others worked half-day shifts, and still others kept only skeleton staffs at work so that as many as possible could participate in the movement. The result was considerable disruption of production and administrative routine. Severity was also manifested in mass trials and harsh criminal punishments.

If sheer numbers are the sole concern, the Three Anti campaign must be judged tremendously successful. Through confession by the corrupt, denunciation by ordinary citizens, and tiger hunting by the authorities, the campaign exposed 1.23 million officials guilty of corruption in some form. This constituted nearly a third of officials in all offices and enterprises that participated in the campaign. It included more than 100,000 officials guilty of corruption involving sums of 1,000 yuan or more.[4] Among these "tigers," about 4 percent received criminal punishment, about 21 percent received other disciplinary action, and about 76 percent were exempted from criminal punishment. Forty-two were executed (Lu 2000b: 56, 57).[5] The yield of tigers among the corrupt was higher than central leaders had expected (or prescribed), which is not surprising considering the intensity of the campaign.[6]

The campaign was also a huge exercise in mass political education. The main lesson of the campaign was political: to highlight the link between corruption and the bourgeoisie. It is mostly in this sense that the campaign constituted a turning point in policy orientation. According to official estimates presented in 1952, most "bourgeois elements" were law abiding or basically law abiding, but many (25 percent) violated the law about as often as they observed it, and a small minority (5 percent) rarely observed the law or were guilty of serious violations of law in their business dealings (Central People's Government Council Political

Legal Committee Deputy Director Peng Zhen 18 Apr. 1952). Most corruption discovered during the campaign involved collusion of officials with the private sector.

The exposure of nearly a third of all officials as corrupt did not undermine support for the new regime. To the contrary, the campaign was an excellent legitimating device. It demonstrated that the communists were committed to the morality that had won them popularity as soldiers. To be sure, communist party members made up a fairly small proportion (less than 16 percent) of officials exposed as corrupt in the campaign. The main targets of the campaign were officials from the old regime. Indeed, in some accounts, the removal of "retained personnel" and their replacement by communist loyalists were the real aims of the campaign (see Teiwes 1978: 140–141). Yet, the party did subject more than 190,000 of its members to disciplinary action in 1952, expelling more than 47,000 of them (Sun and Zhang 1995: 122).

The campaign not only mobilized ordinary citizens to expose corrupt officials, it was also a recruitment mechanism for the new regime, an opportunity for ordinary citizens to demonstrate their revolutionary zeal and be rewarded accordingly. The later stages of the campaign prominently featured calls for "bold promotion" of new people to replace corrupt elements dismissed from government offices and state enterprises. Activists who emerged in the campaign apparently exceeded in number the officials ousted for corruption (Teiwes 1978: 136). In addition to recruiting activists to new positions, the party used the campaign to recruit new members.

Campaigns epitomized an important aspect of the Maoist approach to corruption control: deterrence through unpredictability. A great boon to the communists in the 1951–52 campaign was the simultaneous purge of officials associated with the old regime, identification of loyal activists to take their place, and public approval of a new intolerance for official venality. The constant threat of purge in campaigns also had a deterrent effect on various forms of misconduct by public officials. Mass mobilization campaigns were frequent in the Maoist years. As Lynn White (1989: 18) notes, unpredictability about the next campaign kept officials off balance, inspiring compliance by raising fears of punishment.

Campaigns were the quintessential form of mass political participation in the Maoist years. Participation was practically compulsory: In the highly politicized environment that characterized all campaigns, lack of active enthusiasm was equated with lack of support for regime goals. For many, however, campaigns were not (or not only) a burdensome distraction. At a time when communist party membership constituted the only channel of upward mobility, they presented opportunities for the ambitious to rise. Campaigns were processes of political credentialing. They encouraged the emergence of activists, who demonstrated in the campaigns their enthusiasm for regime goals and thereby earned membership in the communist party or promotion to office or a higher position. For many, of course, campaigns were opportunities to settle personal scores by playing them out as political struggles. In short, campaigns in the Maoist years elicited mass participation not only with coercion, but also with opportunities.

What Is a Campaign in the Post-Mao Era?

Maoist-style political leadership is associated with the greatly disruptive and often violent "mass movements" *(qunzhong yundong)* or "mass mobilization campaigns" launched intermittently from the early 1950s through the mid-1970s, of which the Three Anti and Five Anti campaigns are examples. Maoist-style campaigns mobilized ordinary Chinese to participate in intensive, large-scale, and practically compulsory collective action to achieve a variety of regime goals, often aimed at identified categories of enemies, from sparrows and rats to "capitalist roaders" (see Bennett 1976; Cell 1977). The Great Leap Forward launched in 1958 and the Cultural Revolution launched in 1966 were essentially mass campaigns on a gargantuan scale, both of them disastrous in their consequences for Chinese society and the economy. In 1979, only three years after Mao's death, Chinese leaders officially repudiated mass campaigns (Ye 1979), rejecting their intrinsic social disruption as antithetical to the party's new top priority of economic growth.

Anticorruption campaigns of the 1980s and 1990s were not Maoist-style mass movements. Chinese leaders clearly understand they must rouse ordinary citizens to report corruption to the authorities, but they explicitly reject the practice of mass mobilization to expose and punish corruption collectively. Liu Sheng (1996: 21), chief procurator in Anhui province, expresses the new perspective well:

> In the current transitional stage of transformation to a market economy, the development of democracy and the law has made major progress. If we continue with the mass movement methods of the past, we will not achieve

results. Also, it will disrupt the normal functioning of society, produce serious disorder in the country, and lead to paralysis in development of the law. . . . We want to continue to rely on the masses in our anticorruption struggle, but under no circumstances do we want to promote a mass movement. . . . When we talk about mass participation in the anticorruption struggle, we mean mobilizing the mass public to use legal channels to expose [the corrupt] and provide evidence about criminal corruption. This is the concrete manifestation of the principle of relying on the mass public in law enforcement in the new period of the anticorruption struggle. It is fundamentally different from mass movements of the past.

The Chinese refer to their anticorruption effort as a *fan fubai douzheng,* literally "anticorruption struggle"—not "mass movement" or "mass campaign." In 1982 and 1986, they described their efforts as "struggles against economic crime," although they now present these as an integral part of an ongoing anticorruption struggle. They use this term, "anticorruption struggle," to refer to both a continuous effort spanning many years and an intensified effort occurring in several particular years.

The term "campaign" is used here to contrast routine anticorruption enforcement with the several short bursts of intensive enforcement set in motion by top party and government leaders in the 1980s and 1990s. Although anticorruption campaigns produce measurable outcomes, such as the enforcement peaks described in Chapter 3, campaigns are not defined here by their outcomes. Rather, they are defined by two features: a major escalation of anticorruption publicity, including publicity encouraging ordinary Chinese to report corruption and urging corrupt officials to confess their crimes, and new demands by generalist leaders at the center for greatly increased anticorruption criminal enforcement.

The latter feature of anticorruption campaigns is interesting for what it reveals about perceptions of top leaders. During a campaign, top leaders in Beijing instruct subordinates in the localities and central departments to discover and investigate *as criminal offenses* more cases of corruption. This means they interpret enforcement figures as political performance targets: they view increased cases as evidence of greater anticorruption commitment, not more corruption. By this interpretation, more cases connotes enforcement success, not deterrence failure. In the 1995 campaign, for example, this view is reflected in a rebuke issued by Central Discipline Inspection Commission (CDIC) First Secretary Wei Jianxing (9 Aug. 1995: 580) a few months after exposure of corruption in Beijing municipality:

I must point out that the investigation and handling of cases involving very big sums is uneven. There are provinces and localities with nothing to show for several years—they have handled no such cases. That they have handled none does not mean there are no cases involving very big sums [in these provinces and localities]. For many years, Beijing had no cases involving big sums, but this by no means signifies that all was well in Beijing, that the work was being done well. Rather, the problems were being covered up. Beijing is not an isolated case, there are many such examples. . . . If a large locality or large department has no such cases for a long time, it is hard to believe that it has done such a good job. In some ministries, the discipline inspection group has had no cases for many years. I, for one, do not believe there are no problems [in these ministries]. It has to be that the problems are being concealed or that they have been discovered but not investigated. Every locality, every workplace should handle several influential cases.

Anticorruption campaigns are launched in speeches by top party and government leaders or central documents issued by generalist party and government agencies—or both. A shift in language is usually evident. Top leaders intensify (or relax) the anticorruption struggle by varying their emphasis on economic growth and corruption control. They often refer explicitly to the exhortation issued by Deng Xiaoping in 1982 to work with "two hands" (see Li 1993: 204): uphold economic reform and battle economic crime at the same time. When launching a campaign, leaders cite Deng to denounce a single-minded focus on economic growth and to signal their renewed interest in battling corruption. When ending a campaign, a more balanced tone is evident. For example, Party General Secretary Jiang Zemin, speaking at the CDIC Sixth Plenum after the 1995 campaign had ended, used the following language: "We are gradually finding a way, centered on the task of economic construction, to integrate the anticorruption struggle with reform, development, and stability" (*Renmin ribao* 27 Jan. 1996).

Identifying initiatives by top generalist leaders is the key to sorting out when campaigns begin and end. It is practically impossible to discern the same very significant shifts in intensity by looking only at materials issued by party and government anticorruption agencies or speeches by their leaders. Most of the time, these are about the vital importance of the anticorruption struggle. After examining initiatives, I identified five anticorruption campaigns in the 1979–2000 period, which is not much different from most other accounts. Significant differences of opinion are Yang Shuang (1996), who refers to seven or eight major anticorruption "actions" *(xingdong),* and He Zengke

(2000), who presents the 1990s as one continuous anticorruption campaign beginning in 1993 and ongoing as he writes. Most recent official Chinese sources also present this latter view of the 1990s. This opinion essentially ignores the 1995 campaign and assigns greater prominence to an August 1993 speech by Jiang Zemin that launched both the 1993 campaign and a change in anticorruption strategy. This view is not altogether inconsistent with enforcement outcomes, as discussed in late sections.

Establishing when campaigns begin and end is not guesswork, nor is it an exact science. The premise of this chapter obliges an attempt at the exercise. If campaigns are in fact policy choices that amount to deliberate disruptions of routine anticorruption enforcement, then campaigns cannot themselves be "routine." For how much of the 1980s and 1990s were the Chinese engaged in anticorruption campaigns? In all, by my estimate, the campaigns took up about 28 months.[7] That is, nearly 90 percent of 1979–99, was taken up with routine anticorruption enforcement.

Campaigns and Reported Corruption

Although China's post-Mao leaders have strongly rejected involvement of the mass public in collective denunciation and punishment of errant officials (such as the organized "struggle sessions" of past years) they know they need the active cooperation of ordinary citizens to expose official abuses. New "letters and visits" offices in local governments and government agencies, including procuratorates, offer one channel for complaints. In March 1988, the Shenzhen Municipal Procuratorate went one step further. It opened a crime reporting center to receive specific information from ordinary citizens about crimes by officials. The experience was quickly affirmed in a Central Committee notice (1 June 1988) that promoted the example to procuratorates across the country. By the end of 1988, 70 percent of the approximately 2,500 procuratorates in China had established reporting centers or hotlines, and the Supreme People's Procuratorate (SPP) had issued draft regulations on reporting work. The impact was sizeable. Before the end of the year, procuratorates in many localities experienced a doubling of reports of official crimes since opening the reporting centers. In some localities, reports increased by five or six times (Tong 1991). Widespread publicity accompanied the establishment of the centers and hotlines, to make people aware of a special new channel through which to air complaints as victims of official abuses and participate as informants in the anticorruption struggle. Procuratorates soon came to rely significantly on reports from ordinary Chinese to learn about corrupt activities. In the early 1990s, reports were the source of about 60 percent of bribery and embezzlement cases procuratorates filed for investigation. By mid-decade, the proportion had increased to 70 or 80 percent (SPP Chief Procurator 28 Mar. 1992, 28 Mar. 1993, 11 Mar. 1997).[8]

By providing an outlet for involvement of the mass public in anti-corruption enforcement (albeit strictly individual and highly circum-scribed involvement, compared to past forms), reporting centers and hotlines also reinforce the claim that the regime is an ally of ordinary citizens against corrupt officials. Public opinion findings noted in Chapter 3 suggest ordinary Chinese view corruption as one of the most serious problems the country faces. Moreover, the mass public is gener-ally dissatisfied with the anticorruption effort. These views have not changed very much since the mid-1980s. How are they reflected in day-to-day cooperation with authorities? Do ordinary Chinese act as though they view the regime as a reliable anticorruption enforcer? Reported corruption is a window on regime legitimacy, a behavioral measure to consider alongside polling results.

What do we expect to see? Chapter 3 described an explosion and growth of corruption in China, beginning in the early 1980s. We might expect this growth to be accompanied by an increase in reports of cor-ruption over the years. At the same time, increased anticorruption pub-licity and mobilization of ordinary citizens to report official abuses is a feature of anticorruption campaigns. A campaign can boost reports almost immediately. For example, Jiang Zemin launched an anti-corruption campaign in late August 1993, and procuratorates received more than 68,000 reports of bribery and embezzlement of public assets in September alone, about twice the number received in the first eight months of the year (*Zhongguo falü nianjian 1994* 1994: 117). There-fore, in addition to a trend of increasing reports of corruption over time, we expect to see "report peaks" that coincide with campaign years.

Annual figures on corruption reported to party agencies are missing for most years, but comparable figures on reports to government pro-curatorates are available through 2000 (not before 1988, however). Fig-ure 5.1 presents figures on reported bribery and embezzlement of public assets to procuratorates.[9] The 1987 figure is simply an average for re-ports received in 1983–87, included to illustrate the impact of the re-porting centers and hotlines introduced in 1988.

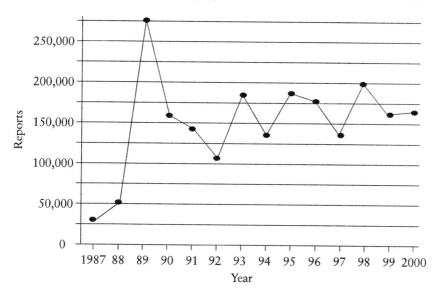

Sources: *Zhongguo falü nianjian 1989* (1990: 13), *1990* (1990: 44), *1991* (1991: 25), *1992* (1992: 39), *1993* (1993: 95), *1994* (1994: 122, 130), *1996* (1996: 146, 155), *1997* (1997: 182–183), *1998* (1998: 155), *1999* (1999: 143), *2000* (2000: 154), *2001* (2001: 184).

Note: Number of reports for 1987 is an annual average for 1983–87 based on a report in *1994* (1994: 130) stating that procuratorates received 806,000 reports of bribery, embezzlement of public assets, and misuse of public funds in 1988–92, representing an increase of 5.3 times the reports received in 1983–97. I found no figure on reports of bribery and embezzlement of public assets in 1994; the figure plotted here subtracts figures for 1991–93 from a figure for 1991–94 reported in *Zhongguo falü nianjian 1996* (1996: 155).

Figure 5.1 Reports of bribery and embezzlement of public assets to procuratorates, 1987–2000

Figure 5.1 suggests two conclusions. First, campaigns (and anti-corruption publicity) matter. Corruption reports increased measurably in every campaign year. The impact of the 1989 campaign is especially sizeable. The report peak for this campaign dwarfs others, mirroring the 1989 enforcement peak shown in Chapter 3. The 1993 and 1995 campaigns also generated notably higher numbers of reports. Reports increased by 431 percent, 73 percent, and 38 percent respectively in the three campaign years represented in Figure 5.1. More to the point, after 1988, the pattern is one of clear increases in reported corruption *only* in campaign years (1989, 1993, and 1995) *and* 1998 (not a campaign year).[10] Declining reports in 1990 and 1996 are not surprising, of course, following increases in 1989 and 1995, but reported corruption continues to drop in 1991 and 1992 and in 1997. The year 1998 is the anomaly. It is the tenth anniversary of corruption reporting centers, however, and the occasion was celebrated with a huge flurry of publicity about the centers, similar to that accompanying campaigns. This may account for the higher number of reports that year.

The second conclusion focuses on trend. Despite a growth in scope, frequency, and seriousness of corruption in the 1980s and 1990s, there is no obvious rise in reported corruption over the years. In 2000, there were about 164,000 reports of bribery and embezzlement of public assets, more or less the same as in 1999 (162,000) and 1990 (about 159,000) and not all that much higher than in 1994 and 1997 (about 136,000). The 1989 campaign appears to have effectively delivered the message about the reporting centers, but reports then hover around 160,000 for the next decade.

To put these conclusions another way, the Chinese have acted as though campaigns are windows of opportunity, during which the officially proclaimed commitment to punish the corrupt is credible—or at least more credible than in times of routine anticorruption enforcement. They have responded to sporadically increased publicity and mobilization with increased reports of corruption. This cooperation is essential to achieve enforcement results, which are essential to demonstrate to a cynical mass public that the authorities are sincere and effective enforcers. At the same time, the trend is consistent with less sanguine findings of public opinion polls. The trend is generally flat. Overall, ordinary Chinese have not reacted as though they believe the regime is a reliable ally in anticorruption enforcement.[11]

Although the enforcement results that campaigns produce may bolster the reputation of authorities, the publicity that accompanies campaigns can exacerbate public dissatisfaction. It is counterproductive, argue Xu Shaowei and Nie Shaolin (1994), to tout anticorruption successes when ordinary citizens see counter-examples all around them in their everyday lives. Even mobilization to involve the mass public in reporting corruption, clearly essential to the anticorruption effort, can have adverse effects, if preliminary investigations do not lead to prosecutions. Gong Xiaobing (1991: 62–63) writes:

> There are . . . many [cases] that prosecutors are unable to follow up or for which they have difficulty obtaining evidence . . . but the masses see absolutely clearly the acts of corruption and bribery. . . . In localities where corruption and bribery among grassroots party and government leaders is se-

rious but difficult to investigate for one reason or another, the masses conclude: "As the small officials at the grassroots are all so corrupt, [how can it be that] the big officials [at higher levels] are ignorant of the extent of this corruption?" The result is a disaffection from the party and government, a belief that from top to bottom it is "say one thing and do another," . . . "all officials looking out for one another," and "swatting flies but not hunting tigers." The masses mistakenly infer that the overwhelming majority of officials today are corrupt.

Exploring the reasons for dissatisfaction with the regime anticorruption effort, Xu and Nie (1994) comment that ordinary citizens see the battle as "loud thunder but little rain." One problem, in their view, is the restriction of the enforcement effort to involvement of a small number of people. Anticorruption enforcement is largely the work of specialized agencies with too few resources to capably contain corruption. The authorities have not effectively mobilized ordinary citizens to fight corruption, and so their participation rate is low. Xu and Nie argue that it is possible (and necessary) to involve ordinary citizens to the greatest degree, without violation of the principle of "no mass movement." They also note the greater importance of killing "tigers" compared to swatting "flies"—for ordinary citizens, one tiger can be worth 10,000 flies.

Anticorruption publicity and exhortation are not the only means used to elicit reports. On a routine basis, the Chinese also encourage the mass public to report corruption by commending and materially rewarding them.[12] Qin Xingmin (2000: 100), reviewing corruption reporting work in the 1988–98 period, indicates that more than 12,000 people were rewarded for their reports, with a total sum of more than 10 million yuan. This amounts to a less than 1 percent probability of a reward amounting on average to about 800 yuan (about US $100).[13] It does not appear that campaigns increase (or decrease) chances of being rewarded.[14] Nor does size (or expected value) of reward appear systematically higher (or lower) in campaign years.[15]

Undoubtedly, the trivial prospect of a nontrivial (but not huge) reward has some impact on corruption reports—but there is also a risk of serious punishment for reporting corruption. In 1988–98, procuratorates received nearly 10,000 reports of retribution *(daji baofu)* exacted on corruption complaints (Qin 2000: 100). That is, ordinary citizens reporting corruption faced only a slightly higher chance of reward than penalty. In addition to the risk of informal punishment through retribution, the criminal law stipulates criminal penalties (up to ten years imprisonment) for "false accusations" *(wugao)*.[16] In this light, Qin Xingmin (2000: 103) argues that, "rewarding individuals who contribute through reporting [corruption] not only affirms [their contribution] and provides an incentive [to report], but is also a sort of compensation for risk." He attributes the high proportion of anonymous reports to lack of reward assurances and ineffectiveness in judicial handling of retribution. To be sure, for an official to abuse power to retaliate against complainants for private gain is a crime. The law suggests a sentence of not more than two years imprisonment, unless serious circumstances are involved. From what we know, procuratorates find most cases of retribution do not meet the standard of a criminal offense. Most cases are transferred to party or government agencies with a recommendation for disciplinary action.[17] Liu Sheng (1996: 24) argues this is inadequate protection against retribution and a clear disincentive to reporting corruption.

Overview of Campaigns

Intensified publicity, including mobilization to report or confess corruption, features in all anticorruption campaigns, although most prominently in the 1989 campaign and least prominently in the 1995 campaign. The second defining feature of the campaigns is intensified demands from generalists at the center to produce enforcement results in the form of more cases of criminal corruption. The results sought in the 1980s were quite different from those sought in the 1990s, however. In the 1982, 1986, and especially 1989 campaigns, Chinese leaders sought drastic reductions in the overall high volume of corruption. In 1995 and 1996, leaders were more selective in their demands, focusing on senior officials, big sums, and a few key sectors. The different goals reflect different anticorruption strategies.

Campaign strategy in the 1980s exhibits a logic similar to enforcement swamping, presented by Kleiman (1993) in an analysis of policy measures to combat widespread crime or localized pockets of high crime. It takes as its point of departure the frequency-dependent character of widespread corruption, described in Chapter 1. A high corruption rate not only defines the problem, but also explains its persistence. Bringing the volume of corruption down below a tipping point changes the situation fundamentally, generating momentum toward clean government. The logic of enforcement swamping acknowledges the inadequacy of regular enforcement agencies to achieve a reduction of corruption once it is widespread. Instead, enforcement swamping mobilizes additional enforcement resources to impose higher costs on corrupt activity all at once. It is a huge, sudden, temporary intervention to increase the probability of detection and punishment. In theory, it need not last long. Once a sufficient number of the corrupt have been driven into inactivity, the capacity of regular anticorruption forces becomes a sufficient deterrent. At this point, the momentum has already shifted toward clean government.

Enforcement swamping is essentially an optimistic strategy: the situation is serious, but a massive effort with additional enforcement resources can turn it around quickly and for good. In the campaigns of the 1980s, the Chinese increased resources by promoting the emergence of "voluntary enforcers"—including the corrupt themselves. In 1982 and 1989, the Chinese introduced clemency periods that offered strong incentives to the corrupt to surrender to the authorities. In 1986, the Chinese built similar incentives into an ongoing party rectification campaign. All three campaigns included explicit threats of harsher punishment for those who failed to take the initiative to cooperate voluntarily. Ordinary citizens were also encouraged to act as voluntary enforcers, especially in the 1989 campaign, when regime mobilization to report corrupt officials was greater than in any other recent period. Reports of corruption also put added pressure on the corrupt to turn themselves in, to gain lenient treatment before being discovered.[18]

Voluntary enforcers brought an immense number of corrupt officials to the attention of the authorities, without increasing by the same margin the demands on party and government anticorruption agencies. Enforcement swamping campaigns reduced the number of undiscovered corrupt officials, which allowed anticorruption agencies to concentrate limited resources on the significantly lowered volume of undetected ongoing (and past) corrupt activity. In theory, the contributions of voluntary enforcers swamped corrupt activity during the short campaigns and created conditions for regular agencies to attack corruption with greater proportionate force after the campaigns had produced their dramatic results.

Campaigns in the 1990s reflect a change in strategy to "enforcement targeting." The logic of this strategy takes into account the difficulty of signaling a credible commitment to anticorruption enforcement when corruption is widespread. Enforcement targeting challenges the folklore of corruption, described in Chapter 1. It is a public announcement, along the lines described in that chapter, aimed at changing expectations about corrupt payoffs and players. In the 1993 and 1995 campaigns, the announcement came in the form of demands by top Chinese leaders for more investigation of criminal corruption involving very large sums and high-ranking officials. The investigation of senior officials was especially important to demonstrate to corrupt officials, their accomplices, and ordinary Chinese that the situation had changed and the regime was a reliable anticorruption enforcer.

Table 5.1 presents some enforcement outcomes associated with the different campaign goals in the 1980s and 1990s. The big decreases in 1998 (of all cases and cases involving big sums) are due to new definitions of criminal corruption and big sums, discussed in Chapter 3.

Campaigns in 1982, 1986, and especially 1989 delivered striking results of the sort demanded by top leaders: very significantly higher numbers of investigations of criminal corruption overall, as seen in column 2. By contrast, these numbers barely rose in 1995 and actually declined in 1993. Indeed, even before the change in definition in 1998, the 1990s is generally a period of declining cases overall—although the Chinese acknowledge that corruption grew overall. The impact of the 1989 campaign is particularly notable. Its effects are huge, not only on criminal corruption overall but also in the categories of corruption involving big sums and senior officials.[19] All of these effects also carry over into 1990 and 1991, which is not surprising. In sum, campaign effects are very evident for campaigns of the 1980s, but especially for the 1989 campaign.[20]

The same cannot be claimed for the two campaigns of the 1990s, which focused on cases involving big sums and senior officials. There is no evidence whatsoever of a campaign effect in cases involving big sums in 1993. The rise in these cases anticipates the 1993 campaign by a year and the increase is fairly steady after that year, except for a slight *decline* in 1993. It is more difficult to assess effects in 1995, as the campaign began in July and ended in November. As to cases involving senior officials, the evidence here is not inconsistent with a campaign effect, especially taking into account a carryover effect—but it is also consistent with a simpler view that only sees a strategic shift in 1993.[21] Certainly, the basic shift in strategy, from enforcement swamping in the 1980s to targeting of senior officials in the 1990s, is evident—indeed, at every level. Procuratorates filed somewhat more than 4,000 cases involving officials at the county or division *(xian chu)* level in the 1980s, but more than 15,000 such cases in the 1990s. They filed some 188 cases involving officials at the central bureau *(si ju)* level in the 1980s, but 927 in the 1990s. They filed a mere 6 cases involving provincial or ministerial *(sheng bu)* level officials in the 1980s, but 18 in the 1990s.[22]

Table 5.1 Routine and campaign enforcement: Cases of bribery, embezzlement of public assets, and misuse of public funds filed for investigation by procuratorates, 1979–2000

Year	All cases	Cases involving big sums	Cases involving senior officials
1979	598[a]	—	—
1980	6,941	—	—
1981	9,879	—	—
1982	**22,913**	—	—
1983	16,440	—	—
1984	17,304	—	—
1985	22,301	—	—
1986	**34,382[b]**	—	—
1987	23,581	3,115	263
1988	21,441	2,943	194
1989	**60,494**	**13,057**	875
1990	61,929	13,259	1,344
1991	57,260	13,325	1,004
1992	47,451	18,429	634
1993	**44,540**	**18,191**	990
1994	50,074	23,977	1,713
1995	**51,089**	**29,420**	**2,193**
1996	46,314	31,053	2,361
1997	42,762	33,283	2,156
1998	29,951	9,389	1,654
1999	32,620	12,969	1,985
2000	36,807	16,017	2,502

Sources: I found no figures on criminal corruption for 1979 and none on criminal corruption involving big sums or senior officials for 1979–86. Figures for 1980–85 in column 2 are from He Jiahong with Waltz (1995: 271). Figures for 1987–2000 are from yearbooks published by the procuracy since 1989: *Zhongguo jiancha nianjian 1988* (1989: 351), *1989* (1991: 410), *1990* (1991: 327), *1991* (1992: 342), *1992* (1992: 361), *1993* (1994: 417), *1994* (1995: 550), *1995* (1996: 382), *1996* (1997: 396), *1997* (1998: 486), *1998* (1999: 506), *1999* (2000: 511), *2000* (2001: 646), *2001* (2002: 504). The 1979 figure on economic crime used for the 1979 estimate in column 2 is from Gong (1991: 1).

Notes: Campaign years are in bold.

"Big sums" are defined, until 1998, as money and assets valued at 10,000 yuan or more for bribery and embezzlement of public assets, 50,000 yuan or more for misuse of public funds; beginning in 1998, values are 50,000 yuan and 100,000 yuan, respectively.

Senior officials are those at the county or division *(xian chu)* level and higher, with figures expressed as number of officials, not cases. Senior officials are essentially a subset of individuals investigated in cases involving big sums.

The 1997 Criminal Law no longer considers managers in enterprises that are not state enterprises in defining crimes in these three categories, with the result that cases greatly diminish in number beginning in 1998. See *Zhonghua renmin gongheguo xingfa* (14 March 1997, Arts. 163, 271, 272). I found no statistics to enable me to construct comparable figures for recent years.

a. Estimate, calculated by taking 85 percent of all cases of economic crime filed for

Table 5.1 (continued)

investigation by procuratorates in 1979; we know that bribery, embezzlement of public assets, and misuse of public funds amount to this percentage of all economic crime cases filed for investigation by procuratorates in 1980.

b. Estimate, calculated by subtracting all cases of bribery and embezzlement of public assets filed for investigation by procuratorates in the six-year period 1982–85 and 1987–88, for which data are available, from the figure provided by the Supreme People's Procuratorate, Chief Procurator Liu Fuzhi (29 March 1989) on cases of bribery and embezzlement of public assets filed for investigation by procuratorates in the seven-year period 1982–88; we know that cases of misuse of public funds filed in these years were infinitesimal.

Of course, campaigns are not defined here by their outcomes, but by their features. The rest of the chapter elaborates features of the various campaigns.

The 1982 Campaign

The campaign against economic crime, launched in January 1982, was the first major regime effort to discover and punish economic violations by public officials in thirty years. It was launched as an integral part of an ongoing ideological and political struggle—indeed, in the lexicon of the time, class struggle (see Forster 1985). The appropriate agency to lead this sort of struggle was the communist party, newly purged (at the top, at least) of leaders associated with the leftism of the Cultural Revolution. Top leaders saw official involvement in economic crime as a serious challenge to the reputation of the party. The 1982 campaign was an opportunity to demonstrate that the party was capable of correcting its own mistakes, while carrying out economic reforms.

The campaign unfolded against a backdrop of "structural reform" and "transformation of leading groups," both locally and in party and government agencies in Beijing (see Lee 1983, 1991). Structural reform aimed to reduce staff and departments in party and government. Transformation of leading groups aimed to increase the proportion of younger, better educated, and more professionally competent officials holding positions of leadership at all levels. These efforts accompanied a continued purge of young leftists who had risen to power during the Maoist years as well as a new enforced retirement of older officials, most of whom had been purged during those years and restored to power after 1978 (see Manion 1993). The former activity merged with the 1982 campaign against economic crime in ways that blurred the line between class struggle and criminal punishment. The presentation in the official press of cases uncovered during the campaign often linked exposure of official corruption with accusations of a political nature, designed to discredit leftists (Forster 1985). In this respect, the campaign was more overtly politicized than either the 1986 or 1989 campaigns and much more so than campaigns in the 1990s.

The catalyst for the campaign was a report submitted by the CDIC to the Politburo Standing Committee. It detailed serious smuggling crimes involving officials, including leaders, in Guangdong province, adjacent to Hong Kong. The response to the report was an "urgent notice" (Central Committee 11 Jan. 1982), sent out to provincial and military regional party committees. The notice expressed concern about officials' involvement in smuggling, bribery, and embezzlement of public assets—crimes that were depriving the state of considerable sums and damaging the reputation of the party. The Standing Committee notified lower levels that it was dispatching senior party officials from Beijing to inspect and advise in provinces where smuggling was a serious problem. It instructed provincial party committees and party committees in central ministries to view the problem as a top priority and take appropriate action. Party committees were to discover and punish new ongoing economic crimes, especially those involving officials in positions of responsibility. At the same time, the notice demanded progress on cases of economic crime that had encountered obstacles at the investigation stage or had not been punished (or strictly punished) in the past few years. It placed responsibility with the party committees if such cases were not energetically pursued.

The urgent party notice constitutes the key document of the campaign. It placed the campaign under the leadership of party committees in provinces and central ministries, and it clearly signaled to them that they would be evaluated in terms of their leadership in the investigation of economic crime. The notice exhorted the party committees to take all appropriate measures, but it explicitly prohibited broad mobilization: "[In this campaign] do not launch a movement among the masses generally or among officials to denounce and expose violations. [We wish to] prevent the emergence of false accusations, widespread self-incrimination, and other sorts of confusion and chaos" (Central Committee 11 Jan. 1982: 474).

Two months later, the National People's Congress (NPC) (8 Mar. 1982) passed a companion document, a decision stipulating harsher criminal punishments for various crimes. The decision supplemented and revised some articles of the 1979 Criminal Law. It specifically discussed smuggling, profiteering, trade in narcotics, illegal trade in cultural artifacts, bribery, and illegal protection of criminals.[23] It introduced harsher punishments than stipulated in criminal law for these crimes. In cases involving big sums or particularly serious circumstances, the harshest punishments stipulated in the law became minimum punishments. Officials who abused powers of office to commit any crime specified in the 8 March 1982 decision were to be punished harshly if the crime involved particularly serious circumstances.

The NPC decision introduced a clemency period of one month, beginning in April, when the decision came formally into force. It offered clemency, in the form of punishment according to the standards stipulated in the 1979 Criminal Law, for those involved in crimes committed before 1 April 1982 who confessed to the authorities before 1 May and cooperated by informing on other criminals. The clemency provision included criminals under investigation when the decision was promulgated. In all other circumstances, criminals were threatened with punishment according to the revised harsher standards.

Clemency in the 1982 campaign differed from the clemency offered in 1989, discussed at length in a later section. Most obviously, the 1982 clemency period was shorter. More significantly, clemency in 1982 was more threat than promise. It threatened criminals who failed to give themselves up with harsher punishments according to new standards, to take effect beginning in May. During the clemency period itself, the NPC decision constituted no more than a restatement of the already well established principle in Chinese law of leniency to those who confess and act meritoriously. That is, unlike the 1989 clemency, the new harsher standards raised the expected cost of past offenses, but not immediately. Incentives to surrender to authorities during the clemency period were weaker than in 1989 for another reason too: the likelihood that past offenses would be discovered during or after the clemency period depended mainly on voluntary enforcement by the offenders themselves. Ordinary citizens played a relatively unimportant role as voluntary enforcers in 1982. The threat of higher penalties in the future, if discovered, was the main incentive for officials guilty of economic crimes to give themselves up to authorities in the 1982 clemency period. If other officials did not surrender and confess their crimes in the face of this threat, the dearth of informers meant that there was little incentive for any official to do so.

On its own, the NPC decision offered little incentive. Combined with intensified party enforcement, begun in January 1982, however, the threat of harshness had some bite. This was especially true for those already under investigation for economic violations. Officials could reasonably hope for protection from criminal punishment altogether if they surrendered to party discipline inspection committees and informed on others, especially if they informed on criminals not in the party.

Two weeks into the clemency period, the Central Committee and State Council (13 Apr. 1982) issued a number of cautions that resolved any apparent conflict between the campaign against economic crime and the policies of economic reform—in favor of the latter. Real economic crimes, the notice cautioned, were to be distinguished from mere irregularities such as improper appropriation (for an enterprise or government department) of funds that belonged to the state. This constituted confusion of "big public" and "small public," but not an economic crime. The Central Committee and State Council also emphasized that even those who were in fact guilty of economic crimes were eligible for extraordinary leniency, in the form of exemption from criminal prosecution or criminal punishment, if they confessed and cooperated with the authorities. The notice rejected the argument that the imprecision of reform policy invalidated the effort to punish economic crimes. At the same time, it acknowledged the existence of ill-defined and insufficiently regulated (or unregulated) areas of economic activity—but it advised against criminal punishment for market disruption or damage to state purchase and sale, except in cases that seriously undermined the economy. In this regard, the notice concluded: "Problems that have not been clearly understood should not be handled in haste."

The notice favored errors of caution over zeal. This strengthened incentives for officials to surrender to authorities. The notice disapproved of the campaign as a weapon to oppose economic liberalization, but it was also a resource for perfunctory punishment of economic crimes. Predictably, the result was a diminished campaign. Local procuratorates overused (and misused) exemption from prosecution. In some localities, criminals who had committed crimes involving huge sums and serious circumstances were exempted from prosecution if they confessed and gave themselves up to the authorities (SPP 25 Dec. 1982). Some local party leaders refused to take the campaign seriously and obstructed criminal investigation or criminal punishment of serious cases and cases involving senior officials (SPP Chief Procurator 6 Dec. 1982). A number of government departments and localities substituted fines for criminal punishment in cases of economic crimes, a practice that the CDIC (14

July 1982) criticized as a positive incentive to smugglers, profiteers, and embezzlers. The substitution of fines for criminal punishment undermined deterrence, and it also did not recover revenue for the state, as fines and confiscated assets were usually appropriated by the disciplining agency and not turned over to the government.

The 1982 campaign must be judged fairly successful in achieving the enforcement results sought by top leaders. As shown in Table 5.1, cases of criminal corruption filed for investigation rose from under 10,000 in 1981 to 23,000 in 1982. Cases of all economic crime, including corruption, rose from under 16,000 filed in 1981 to nearly 30,000 in 1982 (Gong 1991: 1). The campaign was only a first response to the revelations of serious economic crime reported by the CDIC, however. Top leaders also sought a longer-term solution to what they determined was the fundamental problem—moral, political, and ideological indiscipline of communist party members, including leading officials in party and government agencies at the center. In this sense, the 1982 campaign against economic crime came to an end with the decision, announced at the Twelfth Party Congress in September 1982, to rectify the party thoroughly, from top to bottom, beginning in 1983 and extending for three years.

The acknowledged failure of party rectification to curb undisciplined conduct, including criminal conduct, of party and government officials and, indeed, the emergence and advance of new forms of corruption in 1984 and 1985, led to a second campaign against economic crime, launched in 1986. This second campaign, prompted by the failure of party rectification, is discussed in the next section.

The 1986 Campaign

Party rectification was formally launched in October 1983, after several months of experimentation. The plan was to implement it in three successive waves: beginning at the center and in provincial party and government agencies, then extending downward to the county level, and finally reaching party members at the grassroots level. The process involved the study of selected political documents, followed by self-examination and investigation, and ending with registration of all qualified party members and rejection of unqualified members. A specially created Central Rectification Guidance Committee supervised the campaign overall, but party discipline inspection committees actually implemented rectification in each workplace (see Ch'i 1991).

In September 1982, party leaders had claimed as their goal a fundamental improvement in party style and social mores *(shehui fengqi)* within five years (Li 1993: 324). Both deteriorated rapidly: 1984 and 1985 were years of "rampant economic crime," according to the chief procurator. Economic reforms, especially the two-track pricing system and encouragement of creative earning for administrative agencies, provided new opportunities to transform official power into private wealth and collective perquisites through official profiteering and other forms of bureaucratic commerce, as described in Chapter 3. The specific policy changes and, more generally, the new climate of economic permissiveness produced confusion about boundaries between illegal and legitimate economic activity. Procurators were cautious, adopting the following informal guideline: "Energetically handle embezzlement cases, wait and see on bribery cases, and [it is] impossible to handle profiteering cases." Enforcement was biased toward "protecting the sense of initiative and enthusiasm of officials." It was relatively easy in 1984 and 1985 to use economic reform as a resource to obstruct anti-corruption enforcement. Many procuratorates did not handle cases of criminal corruption, fearing a reversal of verdicts (see SPP Chief Procurator 3 Apr. 1985, 8 Apr. 1986, 6 Apr. 1987).

In short, the first year and a half of party rectification coincided with an upsurge in official misconduct, including criminal corruption. By early 1985, top leaders were already quite disillusioned with the failure of party rectification to stem indiscipline among officials. The new forms of corruption were especially prominent among officials in party and government agencies at the center, precisely the targets of the first wave of rectification. In late 1985, the Central Committee General Office and State Council General Office (26 Nov. 1985) issued a joint notice that detailed problems evident in the course of party rectification and instructed party and government agencies at the center to show more resolution in eliminating corruption. At the same time, Hu Yaobang, then party general secretary, personally assumed leadership of the effort to transform party style. Beginning in mid-December 1985, the party Secretariat held a series of meetings to hear the Beijing municipal party committee and party committees in central agencies and departments report on progress in party rectification. The result was a decision in late December to require these party committees to take the lead, do more, and achieve obvious results within six months to a year (see Chen 1993: 212).

This new campaign was launched with a meeting of 8,000 officials from central agencies, convened by the Secretariat in early January

1986. Hu Yaobang and Zhao Ziyang, then premier, urged officials at the center and in Beijing to set an example of appropriate conduct for the rest of the country. The new campaign differed from ongoing party rectification in a number of ways. An important difference was the new requirement that party committees, not discipline inspection committees, take responsibility for producing results. Another difference was in the nature of results sought. Rectification involved party members in a process of study and self-examination, the aim of which was essentially educational. By contrast, the 1986 campaign was built on investigation and punishment. The 1986 campaign was not as far-reaching as rectification, however. Top leaders considered that rectification had failed in its initial stage, in central agencies and at the provincial level, and so these were the main focus of the 1986 campaign against economic crime. The campaign was also narrower in focus than the 1982 campaign. Senior officials were designated a special target.

Deng Xiaoping, speaking at a Politburo Standing Committee meeting in mid-January 1986, reflected (and undoubtedly encouraged) the new punitive mood on the issue of economic crime:

> Death penalties cannot be ruled out. There are some crimes that demand the death penalty. Recently, I looked at some material: The number of people who repeatedly commit crimes after repeated education is enormous—reform through labor a few years, commit more crimes a few years after release. The more experience they gain, the better able they are to evade public security and other law enforcement agencies. Why not execute (sha) some of these criminals according to law? . . . Of course, we must be prudent with executions, but in the end some must be executed. If it is a political or ideological matter and there is no crime, then there should be no criminal sentence—here there is no question of the death penalty. But for serious economic crime, ultimately, we must execute some people. The overall tendency now is a weak hand (ruan shou). The death penalty is a necessary educational measure. Now, executions seem reserved for murderers—what about other serious crimes? . . . If an economic crime is very serious, say, a public official causing losses of state assets in the several millions or tens of millions of yuan, why not the death penalty as provided for in criminal law? In 1952, we executed two people, Liu Qingshan and Zhang Zishan [for embezzlement of public assets]—it really had an effect. These days, if we only execute two, it won't have a big effect. We must execute more to really show our resolve. (quoted in Li 1993: 324–325)

The campaign did in fact produce a rise in capital punishments for corruption-related offenses, from almost no death sentences in previous years to about a dozen in 1986 (Wedeman 1996: 70). Other results were also quite significant. As shown in Table 5.1, procuratorates filed more than 34,000 cases of criminal corruption in 1986, an increase of more than 10,000 over 1985 (and 1982). They filed nearly 50,000 cases of all economic crime (including corruption), an increase of more than 20,000 over 1985 (and 1982), and there is also some suggestion that ordinary citizens responded to the campaign by reporting economic crimes in greater numbers—more than 78,000 reports, certainly well above average for this time, before the establishment of special reporting centers and hotlines (SPP Chief Procurator 6 Apr. 1987).[24] It is more difficult to estimate the impact of the campaign on cases involving senior officials, however. The most senior official to fall in the campaign was the governor of Jiangxi province, who was expelled from the party and prosecuted for embezzlement.

Hsi-Sheng Ch'i (1991) writes that, for practical purposes, party rectification ended in late 1986, although it was not formally concluded until May 1987. I date the end of the campaign against economic crime earlier, in late May or June 1986, when the anticorruption effort clearly began to wind down to a much gentler focus on improper (not criminal) conduct. Qiang Xiaochu, a leading CDIC official, provides a good example of the shift in tone at this time: "Cases involving big sums and senior officials are, after all, few in number. Not every department and agency has such cases. But improper conduct *(bu zheng zhi feng)* exists to some degree in every department and agency. So, for those workplaces where there are no cases involving big sums or senior officials, we must conscientiously investigate and handle other problems that seriously damage party style and party discipline" (quoted in Li 1993: 341).[25]

By late June 1986, top leaders began to focus more on the longer-term tasks of strengthening legal institutions and popularizing notions of legality as solutions to the problem of growing corruption. Only three years later, however, the biggest mass protest faced by a communist regime shocked Chinese leaders (and the world) into a new understanding of the threat to regime stability posed by corrupt officials.

The 1989 Campaign

In April 1989, thousands of students marched to Tiananmen Square in Beijing to mourn the death of Hu Yaobang. Hu had been leader of the communist party from 1978 until early 1987, when conservative elders, allied with other leaders, removed him from office for his liberal political views, which condoned (and, for some, promoted) student demonstrations in 1986–87. Hu's death in 1989 precipitated huge mass protests. University students and factory workers formed a loose coalition to demand political reforms. As the movement grew, they were joined by an unusually diverse set of participants that eventually included journalists from the state media, private entrepreneurs, party and government officials, and hundreds of thousands of other Beijing residents, communist party members and ordinary citizens alike. In mid-May, more than a million people assembled on Tiananmen Square to demonstrate their support.

The Western media quickly labeled the protests a "democracy" movement. This characterization is somewhat inaccurate as a description of the content (rather than form) of the protests, however (Manion 1990). As several scholars have argued, the 1989 protests are best characterized by the revulsion against corruption, which unified the protesters (see Ostergaard and Petersen 1991; Sun 1991; Mason 1994). The issue of corruption gave the protests moral force and (for a while, it seemed) immunity from violent repression.

The protests stunned Chinese leaders, bringing to their attention the scope and seriousness of corruption, raising the question of regime legitimacy and survival in a newly urgent way. On 31 May 1989, Deng Xiaoping summed up the link between the mass discontent and regime failure to control corruption: "When we do go after corruption, we are able to discover and solve cases, including cases involving senior officials, but generally we have been indecisive in setting about [this task]. This can cost us mass support, as people infer that we are protecting the corrupt. . . . A cause for the current disorder is the growth of corruption, which has led some people to lose confidence in the party and government. For this reason, we must correct our own mistakes and be forgiving of some mass actions" (quoted in Chen 1993: 245).

As is well known, Chinese leaders reacted to the unprecedented threat to their authority with a brutal suppression of the protests on 4 June 1989. Tanks and guns were a last, and by no means best, defense, however. While unequivocally rejecting the sort of accountability demanded by the protesters, Deng and other top leaders acknowledged the fury about official corruption as well-founded. The suppression of the protests and the crackdown that followed were reactions to the immediate threat to regime survival, but not responses to the evident crisis of regime legitimacy. Chinese leaders did respond, however, in August, when they launched the biggest campaign against corruption since 1952.

In a decision issued in late July (Central Committee and State Council

28 July 1989), the Politburo responded to the mass protests. The decision emphasized the importance of investigating and punishing crimes such as bribery, embezzlement of public assets, and profiteering. It expressed specific concern about nepotism and privileged consumption, especially among highly visible senior officials. It reiterated a number of prohibitions on various practices that fell short of crimes and issued a few new prohibitions.[26] Not least of all, it introduced the key feature of the 1989 campaign against corruption, a clemency period:

> At present, to provide an opportunity for repentance and a fresh start for those who have engaged in embezzlement, bribery, or profiteering, and thereby better enable us to strike out against serious economic crime, it is necessary to stipulate a period of time in which those who surrender, confess, and take the initiative to return illegally obtained [money and] property will be given mild punishment according to law or reduced punishment or will have punishment waived entirely. Otherwise, they will be punished harshly according to law. (Central Committee and State Council 28 July 1989: 56)

The decision instructed the Supreme People's Court (SPC) and SPP to set specific conditions and dates for clemency. Acknowledged precedents for such a clemency period were the 1982 campaign against economic crime and the 1951–52 campaign against corruption, waste, and bureaucratism.

The SPC and SPP issued the key directive of the campaign on 15 August 1989. It announced a clemency period, effective immediately and extending for two and a half months, through 31 October 1989. It was directed mainly at corrupt officials (guilty of bribery, embezzlement of public assets, or profiteering) and corrupt managers (guilty of bribery or profiteering) of enterprises and other organizations.[27] It instructed them to surrender themselves to procuratorates, public security agencies, courts, or other appropriate offices. It offered clemency in return for confessions and cooperation with the authorities, which included informing on others and returning illegally obtained money and property. It offered clemency even if coercive measures, such as detention, had already been adopted in the course of an investigation well underway. It cited Articles 59 and 63 of the 1979 Criminal Law and Article 101 of the 1979 Criminal Procedure Law as the legal basis for clemency.[28]

The directive offered clemency in three forms. At worst, those who confessed their crimes and cooperated with the authorities faced ordinary leniency within the law: mild punishment, but in the range of punishments stipulated by law. Confession and cooperation could also be rewarded with extraordinary leniency, however. One form of extraordinary leniency was reduced punishment: milder punishment than legally stipulated for the particular sum and circumstances of the crime. Another form of extraordinary leniency was exemption from criminal punishment altogether, perhaps including exemption from criminal prosecution too.[29] A second directive, issued by the SPC and SPP on 22 August 1989, clarified the implications of clemency for particular crimes and circumstances. Table 5.2 shows an example of these implications. It summarizes promised clemency for officials who confessed to embezzlement of public assets before the end of the clemency period and cooperated with the authorities. Certainly, procuratorates had some discretion about how much clemency to recommend to the courts (or grant independently, if exempting from prosecution), and much depended on the nature of cooperation with the authorities. Among other things, the example in Table 5.2 illustrates that the conditions for clemency set up strong incentives for officials guilty of crimes involving large sums to combine confessions of their own crimes with "meritorious acts," such as informing the authorities about crimes committed by others. The directive explicitly raised the possibility of exemption from prosecution in all circumstances excepting cases normally punishable by the death penalty.

Consider the situation of an official who has embezzled public assets amounting to more than 50,000 yuan. The law in effect before the clemency period prescribed punishment as harsh as life imprisonment or the death penalty, depending on circumstances. If the same official confessed to the crime and cooperated with the authorities during the clemency period, the directive guaranteed a waiver of the death penalty "no matter how large the sum" embezzled. At all levels of embezzlement, even where circumstances of the crime were "particularly serious" and normally warranted harsh punishment, the authorities promised either leniency within the law or reduced punishment. Assuming circumstances of the crime were not particularly serious, the promise of leniency within the law suggested imprisonment for ten years. The promise of reduced punishment suggested imprisonment for less than ten years. Finally, if cooperation included the return of embezzled money and property or help in investigations (by informing on other criminals, for example), then the authorities could grant an exemption from prosecution and criminal punishment altogether.[30] For embezzle-

Table 5.2 Changing punishments for embezzlement of public assets in the 1989 campaign

Amount and circumstances of crime	Main punishments
Before clemency period	
50,000 yuan or more and particularly serious	Death penalty
50,000 yuan or more	Life imprisonment or 10 years or more imprisonment
10,000–50,000 yuan and particularly serious	Life imprisonment
10,000–50,000 yuan	5 years or more imprisonment
2,000–10,000 yuan and serious	7–10 years imprisonment
2,000–10,000 yuan	1–7 years imprisonment
2,000–5,000 yuan and surrenders, remorseful attitude, restitution of property	Reduced punishment or exemption from criminal punishment
2,000 yuan or less and relatively serious	2 years or less imprisonment or criminal detention
2,000 yuan or less and relatively minor	Administrative disciplinary action
During clemency period: 15 August–31 October 1989	
50,000 yuan or more and particularly serious	Death penalty waived, life imprisonment probable
50,000 yuan or more	Life imprisonment waived, exemption from prosecution or criminal punishment possible
10,000–50,000 yuan and particularly serious	Life imprisonment waived, more than 5 years imprisonment probable
10,000–50,000 yuan	Exemption from prosecution or criminal punishment possible
10,000 yuan or less	Exemption from prosecution or criminal punishment probable
After clemency period	
50,000 yuan or more and particularly serious	Death penalty
50,000 yuan or more	Life imprisonment
10,000–50,000 yuan and particularly serious	Life imprisonment
10,000–50,000 yuan	More than 7 years imprisonment probable

Table 5.2 (continued)

2,000–10,000 yuan and serious	10 years imprisonment probable
2,000–10,000 yuan	5–7 years imprisonment probable
2,000 yuan or less and relatively serious	2 years imprisonment probable
2,000 yuan or less and relatively minor	Harsh administrative disciplinary action

ment involving smaller sums, 10,000 yuan or less, for example, the authorities suggested the strong likelihood of such exemptions. At the same time, the directive threatened harsh punishment to criminals who failed to give themselves up or cooperate with the authorities during the clemency period.

Second, as noted above, directives appealed to ordinary citizens to participate in the campaign. In an interview with the press (SPC and SPP 18 Aug. 1989), the authorities explained that the lengthy clemency period was not only to give corrupt officials and managers sufficient opportunity to consider terms and consequences, but also to publicize the campaign widely and mobilize the mass public to report corruption. The 15 August directive instructed those with knowledge of corrupt acts to report them to the authorities immediately.[31] It offered informants protection from vengeful retribution. It promised rewards for particularly helpful contributions. The authorities appealed to family and friends of corrupt officials and managers to persuade these criminals to give themselves up. They also threatened harsh punishment to those who protected the corrupt from the law.

For Chinese leaders, the appeal to the mass public to take up a role as voluntary enforcers was a delicate maneuver. On the one hand, to regain the public trust, leaders had to convince ordinary citizens that the campaign signified real change in enforcement practices. A commitment to clean government had been part of standard official rhetoric since the early 1980s, but that had not prevented the explosion of public anger in spring 1989. On the other hand, Chinese leaders wanted to tap, but also to contain, these forces in the 1989 campaign. They had already witnessed large-scale mass protests in which ordinary citizens had expressed openly their critical views about regime corruption. In 1989, Chinese leaders wanted ordinary citizens to make their contributions to clean government singly, through official channels, by providing specific information to help the authorities in criminal investigations of corruption.

The Central Committee and State Council decision of 28 July had put local party committees on notice that they would be evaluated in terms of cases of criminal corruption discovered and investigated. The Politburo reiterated this warning early in the campaign, instructing party committees to step up their leadership and support anticorruption agencies in "boldly exercising the authority of their offices" in the investigation and punishment of corruption (see Chen 1993: 250). At the same time, the key clemency notice of the campaign was issued by the SPC and SPP: clemency was clemency for crimes, including quite serious crimes, and this gave procuratorates a very important role in the campaign.[32] Similarly, ordinary citizens were to report criminal acts of corruption and to take advantage of crime reporting centers and hotlines opened by procuratorates in 1988. In effect, the clemency notice and other campaign appeals emphasized the role of procuratorates at the expense of party agencies. For corrupt officials, clemency for crimes was possible through the criminal justice agencies they could avoid or frustrate in usual times. For ordinary Chinese, the publicity drew particular attention to the procuratorates, especially as it was accompanied by a promise to use the criminal justice system to punish corrupt officials who failed to give themselves up.

The 1989 campaign provided two categories of incentives for corrupt officials to surrender, confess their crimes, and cooperate with the authorities during the clemency period: changes in expected costs of corruption and changes in the probability of detection and punishment.

First, the promise of clemency suddenly reduced the expected cost of past corrupt activity for officials who confessed and cooperated with the authorities, just as the threat of harshness after the clemency period suddenly raised this expected cost for officials who failed to give themselves up. Past corrupt activity could be discovered at any time. Once discovered, corrupt officials might be subjected to criminal punishment, particularly if the crime was serious or involved big sums. The promise of clemency allowed officials to pay less for past corrupt actions, so long as they chose to pay immediately and with certainty. It allowed officials to start anew. As it brought corrupt officials to the attention of the authorities, however, it probably also cramped their venality for a time. The threat of harshness for officials who failed to give themselves up to the authorities was the other side of this coin: Punishment was not a certainty, but it would be more costly to corrupt officials than before if the authorities discovered the crimes through means other than a confession. Considering the episodic attention to corruption control in the 1980s, the promise of immediate clemency may have been more credible to the corrupt than the threat of harshness to follow.

Second, the 1989 campaign increased the probability of detection and punishment for corrupt acts. To the extent that ordinary citizens responded by reporting corruption to the authorities and corrupt officials responded by informing on others, the campaign suddenly increased the probability that past corrupt activity would be discovered by the authorities. Many corrupt acts involve more than one individual, and corrupt officials acting as informants were promised extraordinary leniency for this sort of cooperation. More than likely, evidence from any participant in corruption who informed on others was sufficiently specific to provide grounds for a criminal investigation (and probably prosecution) of other participants. As to reports from the mass public, the protests in the spring had already warned corrupt officials of public sentiments.

The campaign increased the probability of detection and punishment in other ways too. If the campaign yielded massive voluntary enforcement by corrupt officials and ordinary citizens, as expected, then the volume of ongoing corrupt activity would decrease by some significant fraction as more and more corrupt officials either surrendered or were brought to the attention of the authorities by others. This sudden decrease in corrupt activity would produce less competition for attention by regular enforcement agencies. Put another way, corrupt officials who survived the clemency period undiscovered would face a higher probability of detection after the clemency period than before.

Finally, the intensification in party committee responsiveness, demanded by the Politburo during the campaign, increased the probability of criminal punishment for corrupt activity if discovered by the authorities. This increased probability certainly applied to corrupt officials discovered during the clemency period. To the extent that top leaders continued to evaluate local party committees in these terms, the increased probability applied after the clemency period too—although, as we know, this did not happen.

By any measure, the 1989 campaign yielded impressive results. A staggering number of officials and managers took advantage of the opportunity to surrender, confess, and cooperate with authorities in exchange for promised clemency. More than 36,000 people surrendered to procuratorates during the clemency period.[33] There is nothing remotely comparable to this. Indeed, it exceeds by an order of magnitude the highest numbers reported for other years.[34] More than 25,000 of those who surrendered confessed to crimes of bribery or embezzlement of public assets; more than 10,000 confessed to other sorts of economic crimes. Additionally, more than 9,000 people already in prison confessed to new economic crimes. About one-half of the number who surrendered did so in the last ten days of the clemency period. In Shanghai, 400 people surrendered to procuratorates on the last day of the clemency period, ten of them in the last minute. To be sure, clemency period results were uneven. More than 100 (of nearly 3,000) county-level procuratorates handled not a single case of bribery or embezzlement during the clemency period, and more than 700 saw not a single person surrender (SPP Chief Procurator 25 Oct. 1989, 29 Mar. 1990).

Nearly 4,000 of those who gave themselves up during the clemency period confessed to bribery or embezzlement involving sums of 10,000 yuan or more, more than 300 involving sums of 50,000 yuan or more. Three involved sums of more than one million yuan. Nearly 800 of those who gave themselves up were senior officials, holding offices at the county level or higher. This included two very high-ranking officials: the deputy head of government in the Xinjiang autonomous region and the deputy minister of railways, each confessing to accepting bribes worth thousands of yuan. Cooperation by those who surrendered during the clemency period allowed procuratorates to recover more than 200 million yuan worth of money and property (SPP Chief Procurator 25 Oct. 1989, 29 Mar. 1990)

These results account in large part for the unprecedented (and as yet unmatched) enforcement peak in 1989. As most of the clemency period figures are measured in number of officials, not cases, figures on cases filed and investigated by procuratorates in 1989 or other years are not strictly comparable, except for cases involving senior officials. A rough comparison is possible, however. Assuming that procuratorates filed cases on those who surrendered to the authorities, which is a reasonable assumption, clemency period figures account for about 38 percent of all officials whose cases of bribery and embezzlement were filed and investigated in 1989, about 27 percent of all such cases involving sums of 10,000 or more, about 45 percent of all such cases involving 50,000 yuan or more, and about 89 percent of all such cases involving senior officials.[35] These proportions seem to confirm that clemency period incentives appealed most to senior officials and others guilty of crimes involving big sums.

In a report on the campaign, the chief procurator came to the same conclusion and offered some additional interesting observations based on results achieved by late October 1989 (SPP Chief Procurator 25 Oct. 1989). By then, about 18,000 people had taken advantage of clemency promises. One-fourth of them were senior officials or individuals involved in economic crimes involving big sums. Furthermore, about 40 percent of criminals who gave themselves up in the clemency period had either engaged in criminal activity with someone who had already surrendered to the authorities or worked in the same workplace as someone who had surrendered. In many cases, soon after one participant in a crime surrendered, other participants or others in the same workplace did the same. In many cases, criminals who gave themselves up had been actively persuaded to do so by their family or had been brought to the authorities by family members. Many who had committed crimes of corruption apparently surrendered because of the high volume of public reports in their localities. Finally, most of those who gave themselves up also returned much of the money and property obtained illegally and promised to return the remainder. These results are consistent with the incentive structure established by the authorities. Clemency promises were quite successful in encouraging the corrupt to surrender, confess, and cooperate—in short, to contribute as voluntary enforcers to swamp corruption in 1989.

The overall clemency period yield, as a proportion of 1989 figures, highlights the importance of other features of the campaign. Consider, for example, figures on bribery and embezzlement of public assets involving neither big sums nor senior officials. The clemency period yield accounts for about 40 percent of 1989 results.[36] Put another way, about 30,000 of such officials whose cases were filed and investigated in 1989 did *not* give themselves up to authorities. This figure is much higher than the approximately 21,000 such cases filed and investigated in 1988 or any previous year. Conceivably, procuratorates discovered enough about the corrupt activities of these people to file and investigate the cases in the seven months of routine enforcement before the campaign. It is more likely, however, that public reports, criminal informants, party committee attention, and other features of intensified enforcement in the campaign contributed a great deal. Similarly, more than 10,000 people, about three-fourths of all those involved in bribery and embezzlement of big sums whose cases were filed and investigated in 1989, did not give themselves up to authorities. Considering that these sorts of cases typically involve more participants and face more obstruction than routine cases, procuratorates undoubtedly achieved these results (also higher than comparable figures for any previous year) in large part because of the campaign features noted above.

As described in Chapter 3, after a case is filed and investigated by procuratorates, it is concluded in one of three ways. It is usually prosecuted, but sometimes it is dropped for lack of sufficient grounds. Alternatively, procuratorates may exempt the subject of the investigation from prosecution entirely. Campaign directives in 1989 promised greater use of such exemptions to those who confessed and cooperated with the authorities during the clemency period. Procuratorates did not break this promise. Of bribery and embezzlement cases completed by the end of 1989, 85 percent of those who confessed and gave themselves up to procuratorates during the clemency period were granted an exemption from prosecution (SPP Chief Procurator 29 Mar. 1990). Twenty percent of those granted such an exemption had committed a crime involving sums of more than 10,000 yuan. This extraordinary leniency helps explain the high rate of such exemptions in all of 1989, examined in Chapter 4. It undoubtedly also explains the high rate of exemptions in 1990: By the end of 1989, procuratorates had concluded only about one-fourth of cases of criminals who had surrendered during the clemency period and confessed to bribery or embezzlement.[37]

The achievements of 1989 carried over into 1990, as shown in Table 5.1. Procuratorates filed and investigated more cases in 1990 than in 1989, even though the number of people surrendering was less than one-tenth of the 1989 figure (SPP Chief Procurator 3 Apr. 1991). Enforcement swamping in 1989 created the possibility of continued success after the end of the campaign. Corrupt activity did not diminish, however. It grew. The biggest campaign in the post-Mao period did not effectively deter corruption, even in the very short term. About half of the cases of bribery and embezzlement filed and investigated in 1990 were crimes committed *after* the clemency period had been declared (SPP Chief Procurator 6 Nov. 1990).

The 1993 Campaign

The catalyst for a new campaign against corruption in 1993 came in the form of waves of large-scale, often violent uprisings in late 1992 and early 1993—not in the cities, but in the countryside. The rural disturbances were not on the same scale as the 1989 protest movement, and, for the most part, they did not openly (or directly, at least) question the legitimacy to rule of leaders in far-off Beijing. Nonetheless, top Chinese leaders, undoubtedly sensitized to the dangers of escalating popular disorder by the 1989 urban protests, feared the rural uprisings were gaining momentum. Disgruntled peasants had legitimate serious grievances, especially the extraordinary number of arbitrary and excessive fees levied by local governments, described in Chapter 3 as predatory exactions. For Jiang Zemin, catapulted to the position of party leader after the dismissal of Zhao Ziyang in 1989, the 1993 campaign was an opportunity to promote an issue of real importance to him (see Gilley 1998) and boost his national image at the same time. The anticorruption campaign also complemented an austerity campaign, initiated in mid-1993 to tighten macroeconomic control after a nationwide boom set off by Deng Xiaoping in spring 1992.

As reported by CDIC First Secretary Wei Jianxing, the Central Committee decided to launch a new anticorruption campaign sometime before mid-August 1993 (see Li 1993: 745–746). Jiang Zemin launched the campaign in his speech at the CDIC Second Plenary Session on 21 August, and it was reproduced in the *Renmin ribao* on 15 September. He called on party committees and local governments to grasp the anticorruption struggle "as a major political duty." The Central Committee and State Council (5 Oct. 1993) issued the key document of the campaign in October. It reiterated the three tasks set out in Jiang's speech and established them as concrete work priorities for the current period.

The first of the three tasks set out by Jiang in his talk and elaborated in the Central Committee and State Council document was not, as the term is used here, a campaign initiative. Rather, it was part of a shift in anticorruption strategy that was continually refined throughout the 1990s. The new strategy focused mostly on corruption among senior officials. The first task required leading officials in party and government agencies to exercise strict self-discipline in meeting specified standards of probity *(lianjie zilü)*. A five-point set of prohibitions was elaborated for senior officials: (1) no engaging in commerce or setting up enterprises; (2) no holding concurrent positions in any form of economic entity; (3) no buying or selling stocks; (4) no accepting gifts, money, or valuable negotiable securities in the course of official business; and (5) no using public funds to pay for club memberships or to take part in extravagant recreation.[38] The CDIC, Central Organization Department, and Ministry of Supervision (8 Oct. 1993) set out these prohibitions in more detail. The prohibitions reflected a new emphasis on stricter demands for leading officials than for ordinary party members. They also made the standards more salient and revived, from the party rectification in the mid-1980s, the method of implementation through self-examination, beginning in 1993–94 with officials at and above the provincial or ministerial level and moving down, level by level. In terms of content, however, nothing in the prohibitions was really new. More to the point, nothing about this first task suggests an anticorruption campaign.

In contrast, the second and third tasks set out by Jiang in August 1993 and by the Central Committee and State Council in October 1993 does signal the launching of a campaign. The second task required intensified investigation and handling of criminal corruption involving big sums and senior officials. The campaign also had a sectoral focus, but not a very selective one, on party and government executive agencies, judicial agencies, administrative law enforcement agencies, and agencies involved in management of the economy. The Central Committee and State Council (5 Oct. 1993) described this focus as an urgent matter. They instructed subordinate agencies to "combine mass mobilization and reliance on public reports with handling of cases by specialized agencies according to law." They required achievement of "obvious results in a very short time."

The third task demonstrated concern about public opinion and social disorder, especially in rural China. It demanded the termination, by the end of 1993, of some inappropriate practices that had aroused particularly strong reactions from ordinary citizens. It specified the practice of arbitrary fees—noting that some government agencies and departments had transformed their work into fee collection without provision of services, had transferred their duties to an affiliated economic entity to offer services for fees, or had used their official authority and monopoly power to offer new services in exchange for high fees.

Top leaders charged party committees and local governments at the county level and higher with producing concrete measures to achieve quick results. They required them to report in a timely way to agencies one level higher on measures adopted. They presented, as the model for campaign implementation, a formula that combined leadership by the party committee, coordinated action by the party committee and government, and personal responsibility for the work by the number one leaders in the party committee and government. Within this framework, party committees and local governments were responsible for implementation at their own level and one level lower.

Wang Hongguang (1994) describes this combination of leadership, coordination, and individual responsibility in practice in a municipality in the Guangdong province. Not surprisingly, the role of the party committee was pivotal to the action. The municipal party committee convened meetings of subordinate party committees to inform them of the new priority of the anticorruption effort and dispel notions that the effort was detrimental to economic growth. It set up a Leading Small Group for Investigation and Punishment in Cases Involving Big Sums and Senior Officials, to coordinate work among various agencies. For example, in cases that involved criminal violations, the leading small group ensured a quick transfer of the case to procurators for investigation. The party committee worked through its political-legal committee to exercise leadership over investigation of cases involving big sums or senior officials. In order to eliminate obstacles in investigating these sorts of cases, it established a responsibility system. The party committee secretary, deputy secretaries, party committee members, and the mayor each took individual responsibility for particular cases. This involved maintaining a close watch on progress, working to eliminate difficulties, and urging timely completion.

As shown in Table 5.1, the campaign did not coincide with a rise in the discovery and investigation of criminal corruption involving big sums: the rise anticipates the campaign by a year. The campaign was more successful in its focus on senior officials. In September through December 1993, procuratorates filed 715 cases of corruption involving senior officials, more than six times the number filed over the same period in 1992. Reports of corruption, strongly encouraged during the campaign, also increased. Procuratorates received some 120,000 reports in this period, 65 percent of reports received in all of 1993. According to the chief procurator, the increased risk of discovery due to the rise in corruption reports and the intensification of enforcement also led greater numbers of the corrupt to turn themselves in to seek leniency. More than 670 did so in the September through December period (SPP Chief Procurator 15 Mar. 1994).

Authorities also made progress on reducing arbitrary fees, although reports on the extent of progress are perhaps most impressive for what they reveal about the scope of the problem. The Ministry of Finance and State Planning Commission (with State Council approval) eliminated a total of 192 fee items, central departments and agencies eliminated or stopped implementation of more than 2,800 fee items, and provincial governments eliminated more than 48,000 fee items (Wei 20 Jan. 1995). Elimination of fee items is, of course, merely the formal step. The work of ensuring that these fees and others were not collected on the ground remained a work priority a decade later.

The period from 21 August through December 1993 was the most intense of the campaign. It is certainly plausible to date the end of the campaign with the end of the year, but probably more reasonable to date its conclusion in late February or March 1994, or even as late as mid-June 1994. A notable change in emphasis, from the fight against corruption to stability and economic reform, appeared in March. In June, the Central Committee sent out 20 high-level teams to investigate and report back on results of the campaign.

The 1995 Campaign

In February 1994, as the 1993 campaign was winding down, Jiang Zemin alluded to the legitimation goal of anticorruption campaigns: "In the end, the point of launching an anticorruption struggle is to consolidate and strengthen the relationship between the [communist] party and the ordinary masses in this new situation—to consolidate the party's status as a ruling party" (quoted in Huang and Liu 1997: 429). The response of ordinary citizens to the regime's anticorruption effort was crucial to the decision to intensify the effort with a new campaign in 1995. At the same time, leaders were concerned about possible counterproductive effects of anticorruption publicity. The reason for their concern was a case of criminal corruption uncovered in 1995 that reached to the highest level of communist party leadership.

The 1995 campaign cannot be separated from the case of Chen Xitong (see Wedeman 1996; Gilley 1998; Bo 2000), the highest-ranking official prosecuted for criminal corruption in China.[39] Chen had been appointed deputy mayor of Beijing in 1979, had risen to positions of mayor and deputy party secretary in the early 1980s, and had been promoted to party secretary in 1992. This last position had brought with it membership on the powerful Politburo. In his years of party and government leadership in Beijing, Chen had built up a tightly controlled network of informal ties that facilitated a profitable exchange of favors. In Chinese, the web of Beijing insiders was characterized as the "Chen system," from the homonym *xitong* (which means system). The Chen system was permeated with official misconduct, ranging from cronyist protection to major financial crimes. Chen's own corrupt activities mainly involved corrupt exchanges of advantage for material benefits. Many of the exchanges involved approval for construction projects: As mayor, Chen had been head of the capital construction program commission.[40] Both Chen and longtime close associate Deputy Mayor Wang Baosen had also diverted $4 million of public funds to build and furnish luxury villas for private use in assignations with their mistresses.[41] The exposure of Chen and Wang grew, in mid-1994, out of an investigation of large-scale illegal fundraising, involving bribery of officials across 12 provinces to invest public funds, by the Wuxi Xinxing Company in Jiangsu province.[42] Xinxing promised investors monthly returns of up to 5–10 percent, but collapsed when the company president ceased paying dividends and failed to return invested capital—which led some investors to report to the authorities. Wang had invested $12 million of Beijing municipal government funds in Xinxing. On 4 April 1995, with the prospect of an interview with CDIC investigators before him, he committed suicide.

Wang's suicide created a sensitive political situation for top leaders, because of his close association with Politburo member Chen Xitong. The initial response came in a form that, as Yang Shuang (1996: 78) notes, China had not seen in many years. On 7 April, the same day that leaders in the provinces and central departments were formally notified of the suicide, the *Renmin ribao* printed an article extolling the moral uprightness of an exemplary official, Kong Fanlin. The article was accompanied by an editorial and exhortations by Jiang Zemin and other top leaders, urging communist party members to emulate the example of Kong. This was soon followed by reports and meetings convened to study his example.

As the preliminary CDIC investigation progressed, leaders further considered public relations strategy. Should they minimize publicity of the Chen Xitong–Wang Baosen situation to avoid undue attention to criminality at the highest level of communist party leadership? Or should they take the initiative to preempt (and channel) a feared explosion of public outrage at this latest scandal? Jiang Zemin (1995) and Premier Li Peng (1995) showed great concern about public order in the capital when they announced approval of Chen's resignation from all positions on the Beijing party committee and promotion of CDIC First Secretary Wei Jianxing to the concurrent position of Beijing party committee secretary. At the same time, Jiang urged his colleagues to "persist unwaveringly" in developing the anticorruption struggle.

A CDIC formal investigation of Chen Xitong was approved on 7 July 1995. Wei Jianxing (9 Aug. 1995: 576–577) describes the investigation as a high-stakes test of the party's ability to show doubters its ability to correct its own mistakes:

> Some comrades believe that the timely investigation into the case of Wang Baosen and others has greatly enhanced the party's prestige, so that every-

one senses the Central Committee is resolute and able to solve its own problems of corruption. . . . Another view is that the grave actions of Wang Baosen truly damaged our party's prestige. . . . The crux of the matter is to consider our work. . . . For the CDIC, the key is to do a good job in handling the case of Chen Xitong. If this work is done well, then its influence will be far greater than the effect of the recent Wang Baosen matter. It will enhance everyone's confidence. . . . We need to show that our party is able to use its own mechanisms *(jizhi)* to handle its own problems. We need to use this sort of experience to demonstrate that the people who think it necessary to practice multipartism and western-style parliamentarism to avoid Wang Baosen-type incidents are wrong in their views.

The August 1995 speech quoted here is the same one quoted at the beginning of this chapter, in which Wei calls on "every locality, every workplace" to handle several influential cases. The July 1995 Central Committee decision to investigate Chen Xitong and other signs of support at the top for the anticorruption effort, such as the appointment of Wei Jianxing to head the Beijing party committee, did apparently serve as a "model and stimulus," boosting investigations at lower levels. Top leaders asked local party committees and governments to pay more attention to cases involving big sums and senior officials, to convene special meetings to hear reports on the status of investigations of these cases, and to eliminate obstacles to create the conditions for progress (see Wei 24 Jan. 1996).

From this perspective, the beginning of the campaign can be dated as July or August 1995. In these months too, top leaders sent out investigation teams to check on compliance with prohibitions on various forms of improper conduct in central party and government departments and agencies. Of particular concern were abuses relating to conspicuous consumption, such as the purchase of luxury vehicles and extravagant banqueting at public expense. Yet, it is also true that the stance of top leaders on corruption began to harden earlier than July, perhaps as early as March 1995. In that month, for example, CDIC leading official Wang Guang (1995) adopted the language of Deng Xiaoping in 1986, pointing out the need to "execute a few." Wang described current anticorruption work as a long way from the standards enunciated by Deng. Indeed, according to him, top leaders found the recent effort insufficiently intense and punishments insufficiently harsh. Wang indicates that the Politburo Standing Committee recommended harsher punishments in a number of cases recently reported to them by the CDIC. It would not be unreasonable to date the 1995 campaign as late as September, however, when the Central Committee removed Chen

Xitong from the Politburo and Central Committee, and Jiang Zemin spoke of the problem of public order in a number of localities, linking it to the reappearance and growth of corruption. Jiang called for a deepening of the anticorruption struggle, with more investigations and punishment.[43]

Although there was an intensification of the anticorruption effort in March, July, August, and September, the 1995 campaign differs from other campaigns in its more muted emphasis on the role of the mass public and less clear statement of deadlines for achievement of goals. The weaker attention to mass mobilization is probably due to the ambivalence of leaders about more anticorruption publicity. On the one hand, it was an achievement that the CDIC had discovered on its own the high-level corruption in Beijing and was investigating it, but Chen Xitong was a Politburo member after all—there was no denying that corruption reached to the highest levels of communist party leadership. As to deadlines, top leaders called in late November for the completion of more cases involving big sums and senior officials before the end of the year (see Huang and Liu 1997: 454–455), but the campaign also appears to have been winding down by about that time.

In terms of results, as shown in Table 5.1, much was achieved in 1995. Compared to 1994, cases involving big sums rose by 23 percent to more than 29,000 in 1995, and cases involving senior officials rose by 28 percent to nearly 2,200—and these 1995 figures are higher than in any previous year. How much of this was achieved in the period from July through November 1995 is unclear, however. Various CDIC and other law enforcement meetings in early 1996 do not isolate figures for the last half of 1995, essentially because the Chinese present it as part of the current, ongoing anticorruption struggle rather than an intensification of that struggle.[44]

Conclusion

Anticorruption campaigns in the 1980s and 1990s were short periods of intensified enforcement during which corrupt officials could no longer count on the routine substitution of party disciplinary action for criminal punishment—because party committees were under pressure to produce higher numbers of criminal cases filed and investigated. In the 1990s, the pressure was to discover and investigate more criminal corruption among senior officials or involving big sums. At the same time, increased anticorruption publicity and mass mobilization during campaigns raises the number of reports of corruption. This increases the likelihood that corrupt officials will in fact be discovered. Corrupt officials do have a possibility to reduce their punishment, however, if they take the initiative to give themselves up to the authorities, confess their crimes, and report on others. Of course, the structure of leniency built into Chinese law offers this possibility to criminals at any time, not only during campaigns, but the incentives to take advantage of it are more attractive during campaigns. In 1982 and especially 1989, these incentives included very generous rules for clemency. For these reasons, campaigns are generally observable as an integrally related set of enforcement peaks, report peaks, and confession peaks. From this perspective, campaigns in the 1980s and 1990s achieved some fairly spectacular results not realized during routine anticorruption enforcement.

From what we know, corruption in China continued to grow in the 1980s and 1990s, and it involved a greater number of officials, more sectors of government and the economy, bigger sums, and probably more officials at higher levels. We can surely find plausible the counterfactual that corruption might have grown even more without the regime anticorruption enforcement effort, both routine and in campaigns. It is not, however, inconsistent to acknowledge campaign results and at the same time question the contribution of campaigns in the longer term.

First, it does not seem that campaigns (or, for that matter, routine enforcement) have effectively deterred corruption. This conclusion need not rest simply on an assertion about the continued overall growth of corruption. As noted by SPP Chief Procurator Liu Fuzhi (6 Nov. 1990), one-half of the cases filed and investigated in 1990 were crimes committed *after* the clemency period associated with the biggest anticorruption campaign in the post-Mao era. This did not seem to change in the 1990s. Li Xueqin (1997: 21–22), a senior researcher at the CDIC, points to a continued growth of criminal corruption and indicates that more than 50 percent of cases investigated in a year are crimes committed in that year. Is it possible that campaigns, while delivering short-term results, weakened deterrence? In times of routine enforcement, corrupt officials could anticipate mild party punishments; during campaigns, they could anticipate leniency, sometimes extraordinary leniency. Indeed, extraordinary leniency was made so attractive that campaign enforcement was not necessarily more stringent than routine enforcement.

Second and relatedly, if punishment according to law was often avoidable in routine times, it was highly distorted by (and during) campaigns. The most important point here is that the legal process was most emphasized in highly politicized campaign periods. Political disruptions were required to make the law work. During campaigns, party committees were urged to reduce obstacles standing in the way of investigating corrupt officials for crimes. Top leaders set short deadlines, and a small number of cases was interpreted politically as weak commitment by generalist leaders to the anticorruption effort. That the legal process worked best during campaign periods when party committees were impelled to support it is not surprising, but it has not promoted expectations of routine legality. That is, while boosting cases of criminal investigation, the campaign context and methods have undoubtedly undermined beliefs that the law operates routinely and impartially to punish those who flagrantly violate it, no matter how powerful. Put another way, campaigns have frustrated the institutionalization of rule of law.

Rule of law was not only distorted by campaigns, but also during campaigns. Campaign periods were not in fact times of punishment according to law, but rather times of leniency. This is not surprising. More criminals give themselves up and are thereby eligible for leniency. On the one hand, it must be said that the sorts of clemency periods established in 1982 and 1986 are highly arbitrary. On the other hand, as shown in Chapter 4, when the number of cases filed and investigated is high, exemptions from prosecution are high. Procuratorates are overwhelmed with cases during campaigns, and these cases must be completed one way or another. Exemptions from prosecution are the fastest way to complete cases. Campaigns put procuratorates under pressure to complete cases, and this contributed to a distortion of punishment according to law.

Finally, the campaigns were intended to boost regime legitimacy. Indeed, in the opinion of Leslie Holmes (1993), this is the real purpose of anticorruption campaigns in communist systems. Since the mid-1980s, Chinese communist leaders have been acutely aware of strongly negative mass public opinion about corruption and regime anticorruption efforts. Indeed, the 1989 campaign was triggered by the show of anticorruption sentiment on the streets of Beijing and other major cities, the 1993 campaign by the show of this sentiment in the countryside, and the 1995 campaign by fearful anticipation of a repeat of 1989 mass protests. Post-Mao campaigns sought to involve ordinary Chinese in the anticorruption effort by channeling involvement into reports. Yet, the campaigns could boost legitimacy only if ordinary citizens viewed them as credible and effective anticorruption efforts. That the mass public viewed campaigns as better than usual opportunities to get enforcement results is suggested by the campaign pattern of reported corruption. At the same time, the enforcement results during campaigns and continued corruption between campaigns could not disguise the failure of routine anticorruption enforcement.

Kevin O'Brien and Lianjiang Li (1999) find signs of nostalgia for Maoist-style campaigns in the Chinese press and among villagers interviewed in the mid-1990s. Li (2001) examines this apparent nostalgia for campaigns more systematically in a survey conducted in the late 1990s. Support for Maoist-style campaigns against corruption is not a widely prevailing view, but its correlates are important for the discussion here. Support for "mass movements" against corruption varies inversely with evaluations of the extent to which local officials govern according to law, beliefs about how impartially law is enforced, and confidence in the effectiveness of legal channels to bring corrupt officials to justice. Li concludes that public support for Maoist-style campaigns against corruption is not rooted in simple "campaign nostalgia," but rather in "profound frustration with widespread corruption . . . and lack of confidence in existing ways to handle these problems." He quotes the praise of one Hebei villager for the instantaneous and gratifying results of Maoist-style campaigns against corruption: like "setting up a pole and immediately seeing the shadow" (Li 2001: 584).

Maoist-style campaigns are antithetical to the order and stability that Chinese leaders see as requisite to economic growth. Anticorruption campaigns in the 1980s and 1990s are constrained by the new priority of economic growth and also by the regime's fear of a mass public truly mobilized against corruption, as it was in 1989, and perhaps ultimately mobilized against the regime itself.

CHAPTER SIX

Institutional Designs
for Clean Government

The title of this book answers questions posed in Chapter 1 about prospects and prescriptions for reform in a setting where corruption is so widespread as to constitute its own informal political system. "Corruption by design" summarizes a view that some institutional designs promote clean government, while others generate and sustain corruption. Explicit choices of institutional design explain much of Hong Kong's successful transformation from widespread corruption to clean government. Different choices, in different contexts, explain the emergence and tenacity of mainland Chinese corruption—and suggest the country may not be poised to advance quickly from its corrupt or barely (and theoretically unstable) intermediate status toward the superior stability of clean government.

As described in Chapter 1, the central conundrum posed by widespread corruption is its sheer volume and the accompanying expectations that sustain it. Escaping this inferior frequency-dependent equilibrium requires reducing corrupt payoffs and changing the beliefs that comprise a folklore of corruption. These anticorruption tasks are formidable, in no small part *because* corruption is widespread. What solutions to this conundrum are reflected in Hong Kong's institutional designs for clean government? What generalizable lessons, if any, do they offer to mainland China and other countries mired in corruption?

This chapter addresses these questions by focusing on three notions of institutional design that unfold in the empirical story in Chapters 2 through 5. Each notion highlights basic differences between the Hong

Kong and mainland Chinese experiences. The first points to the obvious contrast between *anticorruption agencies:* in Hong Kong, a powerful, well-financed, independent agency is answerable solely to the chief executive; in mainland China, a tangle of party and government agencies with ill-defined intersecting jurisdictions are dominated by communist party committee generalists at each level. The second notion is the main sense in which institutional design is used in this book: It connotes the *incentive structures* that facilitate (or obstruct) corrupt practices. In Hong Kong, corruption prevention through institutional design is one of three essential methods of anticorruption reform; in mainland China, not only have certain economic reform policies actually encouraged corruption, but leaders have only recently shown substantial interest in reorganization of procedures to lessen incentives for corrupt transactions. Finally, this chapter returns to the underlying issues of *constitutional design,* in particular, important contextual differences between anticorruption reform created by a functioning rule of law regime and real civil liberties in Hong Kong (even today) and that created by a fundamental misconstruction of rule of law and trivialization of civil liberties in mainland China.

Anticorruption Agencies

Anticorruption reformers often create new agencies to reduce the massive volume of corruption. Yet, in a setting of widespread corruption, corrupt enforcers and a shortage of enforcement resources, relative to the scope of the problem, pose significant obstacles. Cooperation from the interested mass public offers a possibility of boosting the ranks of clean enforcers, but ordinary citizens are generally reluctant to assist unless convinced that the authorities are reliable anticorruption allies. The Independent Commission Against Corruption (ICAC) in Hong Kong is an example of an agency design that solved these problems, thereby opening the way to reducing widespread corruption rather quickly.

Policy analysts tout ICAC independence as the key component of agency design that reformers should emulate. This refers to the exclusive anticorruption mission of the agency: The ICAC is not embedded in the civil service or any other larger organization with multiple goals. Most important of all is ICAC's independence of the police force, especially in the 1973 context of a public perception of that department as the most corrupt of all and certainly after the Godber incident. Agency independence worked in Hong Kong primarily because this agency design worked as a signal, a public announcement of an "equilibrium switch"—but it worked especially well in a particular context. The key feature of this context was the extraordinarily high popular salience of police corruption, with its many victims of "squeeze" available for mobilization. With corruption structured this way, the creation of an agency that effectively rejected the police as anticorruption agents helped legitimate the government effort and enlisted ordinary citizens as voluntary enforcers. Independence was complemented by power, also an element of agency design: the ICAC was given strong investigative powers and considerable financial resources.

Yet agency design offers only the possibility of success. Ultimately and continuously, the ICAC earned its credibility and popular support via its enforcement performance. In this regard, it is worth noting that there is nothing inherently credible about an independent agency design. Indeed, as 1997 approached, panic developed among Hong Kong democrats contemplating an independent ICAC under a chief executive selected in Beijing. The credibility of the Hong Kong governor's commitment to anticorruption reform in 1973 was a condition of ICAC agency design as a credible signal of equilibrium shift. A sizeable literature in political science (see, for example, Schelling 1960; Root 1989; North and Weingast 1989) elaborates how credibility inheres in self-enforcing mechanisms that bind the sovereign to her commitment by structuring incentives to make adherence preferable to reneging, thereby effectively ruling out the latter option. The governor publicly staked his reputation on the ICAC, but he did not strictly "tie his hands" with agency design. Rather, the constraints to respond effectively with publicly acceptable solutions of "good government" inhered in other contextual features. These are taken up in the discussion of constitutional design later in this chapter.

It follows that an independent anticorruption agency answerable to the communist party chief is not a clear blueprint for agency credibility, setting aside, for the sake of argument, the patent incompatibility of agency independence with the overarching Leninist political design of mainland China. If self-enforcing constraints to respond responsibly are the crucial feature of context, the chief executive in mainland China today is unquestionably less constrained than was the governor of Hong Kong in the 1970s.

Quite apart from this broader issue of context, agency design undermined anticorruption effectiveness in mainland China. Two agencies, party discipline inspection committees and government procuratorates, with overlapping jurisdictions and an unclear division of labor, investigate corrupt officials. The privileged organizational position of discipline inspection committees ensures that problems of coordination, such as joint investigations or transfer of criminal cases to procuratorates, depend on party initiative. One result is the routine delay in transferring cases, botching criminal investigations for procuratorates. Another result is appropriation of cases and substitution of mild party disciplinary actions for harsh criminal punishments. Party agency aggrandizement explains some delays in transferring cases. A different problem of agency design better explains appropriation of cases: leadership by generalist party committees. Despite a dual leadership structure introduced in 1982 and the strengthening of vertical integration in 1992, party committees exercise leadership over discipline inspection committees in many specific ways. These include the *nomenklatura* system, party groups, and party member discipline. Generalist party committees are executive agencies with multiple goals; their leadership creates friction with specialist discipline inspection committees. This may be clearly contrasted with the advantage of exclusive mission in independent agency design.

A simple fact of timing handicapped Chinese anticorruption agencies as organizational responses to corruption: like the ICAC, both discipline inspection committees and procuratorates were new (or renewed) agencies, but both were reinstated a few years before corruption grew noticeably and rapidly. Perhaps more to the point, to the extent that Chinese leaders have used organizations to signal anything, agency design signals commitment to communist party leadership. Finally, although the locus of corruption in mainland China is broader and does not advantage anticorruption agencies as it did in Hong Kong, top leaders in Beijing have neglected the political for the economic problem, thereby squandering the opportunity to use the salience of corruption to their advantage in mobilizing ordinary Chinese to cooperate as voluntary enforcers. For predatory exactions and bureaucratic commerce, outgrowths of policy that inspire great popular resentment, officials have been reprimanded for "irregularities" as authorities focus enforcement attention on activities that cost the state higher losses of revenue but affect ordinary citizens less directly and visibly.

In the past few years, however, this focus has begun to change, as Chinese leaders begin to examine the sources of corruption to find a "fundamental solution." They have shown a new interest in redesigning institutions to prevent corruption.

Incentive Structures

Nowhere in the world has the institutional design strategy of anti-corruption reform been articulated and developed as thoroughly as in Hong Kong. It is standard practice for the ICAC's Corruption Prevention Department to study the organization of work in government departments to identify opportunities for corruption inherent in work procedures and suggest ways to redesign procedures in order to minimize such opportunities. After recommended measures are implemented, corruption prevention analysts return to the client department to assess effectiveness and to check that changes have not produced new opportunities for corruption. Most remarkable of all is the role of the Corruption Prevention Department as consultant at the stage of policy formulation or legislative drafting. This involvement ensures that corruption prevention considerations are taken into account before new laws or regulations are introduced.

In contrast, Chinese leaders have mostly neglected institutional design in favor of an enforcement strategy. Yet, as described in Chapter 3, the policy roots of the most common forms of corruption strongly recommend attention to incentive structures as an important component of anticorruption reform in China's changing political economy. Without abandoning enforcement as the main component of corruption control, Chinese leaders have begun in recent years to complement blunt prohibitions with redesigned incentive structures to reduce corruption. Examples of changes in institutional design in the late 1990s or more recently are many: reduction in the number of required permits and licenses, a judicial recusal system, salary increases for judges, competitive bidding in government procurement, a requirement that village party branch secretaries stand for election to village committees, rotation of posts in the civil service, and divestiture of interests in commercial enterprises by the military, public security agencies, procuratorates, courts, and government departments at the center and in the localities. An institutional design approach is evident in local innovations too, such as the response of Hainan provincial authorities to the personal approval by a former president of the Hainan Provincial Construction Bank of easy loans to enterprises in return for massive bribes. The province replaced this independent design featuring monopoly power with a sequential one that distributes functions of loan approval, processing, and investigation among three different agencies. With no other changes, this reorganization of work procedures can be expected to reduce loans to unqualified applicants who pay bribes (see Rose-Ackerman 1978: 167–188).

Another good example of the shift from prohibitions to incentives is the "taxes-for-fees" reform that began as an experiment in Anhui province in 2000 and was adopted as nationwide policy in 2003 to address the problem of predatory exactions in the countryside. Unlike the many regulations issued against excessive taxes and illegal fees since the early 1990s, the taxes-for-fees reform transforms the basic collection system to reduce opportunities for predatory exactions. The reform frees officials at the rural grassroots level from fee collection and makes corruption at the township and village levels more difficult. It substitutes a single agricultural tax (or agricultural specialty product tax), capped at about 7 percent of income and collected by higher-level governments, for the various fees and charges levied by township and village administrations. Based on the experience in Anhui province, the reform is expected to reduce the peasant burden by about a third. Anticipated shortfalls in township revenues are to be partly made up by central transfers, but central authorities are also encouraging administrative streamlining to reduce expenditures at lower levels of government. Indeed, a bold proposal to eliminate the township level of government entirely was discussed in 2003.

Constitutional Design

Tinkering with organizational charts and work procedures to create incentive structures that guard against corruption is small-scale institutional design, a characterization that by no means trivializes its evident results. This section considers grander contextual issues of constitutional design in anticorruption reform. In particular, it discusses how different roles of law set different expectations in Hong Kong and mainland China, generally supporting anticorruption efforts in the former and frustrating them in the latter. These differences are partly the result of policy choices that reflect different experiences and different views about what works. To a much greater degree, however, they reflect fundamental differences in views about constraints on power.

Hong Kong began its anticorruption reform with a strong legal base. A single law, the Prevention of Bribery Ordinance, strengthened in 1971 with the inclusion of "unexplained income or property" as evidence of corrupt practices, offered a clear and tractable definition. The only new law, passed in 1974, established the ICAC and its authority to investigate corruption.

A main thrust of the early anticorruption effort was popular education about the connotation of corruption and the powers of the ICAC to investigate it. Judicial corruption was rare, which meant that legal standards upheld by the ICAC in enforcement were upheld in the courts. In short, legal clarity, breadth, stability, and ease of application all contributed to a situation where corrupt officials were routinely punished according to law. That the law is harsh, violating notions of presumption of innocence, probably enhanced public confidence in the reliability of anticorruption enforcers as it augmented the predictability of punishment.

In mainland China, by contrast, anticorruption campaigns were interspersed with routine enforcement, a strategy affirmed by the Central Discipline Inspection Commission (CDIC) as necessary while the legal system remains weak:

> From relying on mass movements to fight corruption [in the Maoist period] to relying completely on institutions and the legal system as the norm, there is a transitional period. We are currently in this transitional period. The anticorruption effort at this stage cannot rely on mass movements. Yet, as the new anticorruption institutions are not yet fully established, [the effort] cannot completely rely on the legal system. The fundamental characteristic of appropriate anticorruption measures in the transitional period is the combination of routine work and focused "clean ups." (quoted in Li 1993: 688)

This strategy has in fact undermined the emergence of a norm of law insofar as official misconduct is concerned.

To be sure, anticorruption reform in mainland China did not begin with an especially propitious base: the first criminal code was passed only in 1979, in a legal vacuum. Moreover, a rapidly changing political economy in the 1980s presented law makers with new activities to take into account as they developed a definition of criminal corruption. These problems were compounded, however, by policy choices. As noted above, party anticorruption agencies routinely usurp the function of procuratorates in investigating corrupt officials, delaying the transfer of cases and thereby bungling prospects for criminal prosecution. They keep investigation and punishment of other cases entirely within the party system. This problem of agency design, with its clear bias toward handling official abuses outside the criminal justice system, has sapped the development of law and legal institutional authority.

Chinese leaders have tried to "solve" the problems of routine enforcement with irregular campaigns that raised demands for more cases of criminal corruption. "Punishment according to law" during campaigns has frustrated an emerging role of law in even more serious ways, however. The emphasis on legal standards, procedures, and institutions has been irregular and essentially the result of pressure from leaders at the top producing greater attention to the problem from party generalists below. As intense politicization is required to put the law to work, politics, not law, was effectively at work during the campaigns—politics that undermined law with its ostensible support. Campaigns have obstructed the expectation of routine legality in other ways too. They overloaded procuratorates with cases. Procurators responded with higher than usual proportions of exemptions from prosecution to complete cases expeditiously. Campaigns were effectively peaks of leniency, not punishment.

Choices about the roles of law and legal institutions, reflected in anticorruption agency design and the politicization of the authority of law in campaigns, reflect (at best) a fundamental ambivalence about the rule of law in mainland China—which hobbles law as a meaningful constraint on the abuse of official power.

For anticorruption reform to succeed, the government's commitment to it must be credible to ordinary citizens and corrupt officials. The only guarantee of this is the operation of self-enforcing mechanisms that raise the costs of reneging on promises—to prohibitively high levels. Incentive structures can operate in this way as commitment devices, promoting clean government through the reorganization of responsibilities and procedures. Anticorruption agencies can also signal commitment to clean government, but the signal may or may not be credible. This is true too of laws, legal institutions, and the roles assigned to both in constraining official abuses.

In Hong Kong, the governor's signals of commitment to anticorruption reform were viewed as credible, a view that makes sense only within a context of shared understanding of government responsibility toward the governed. Usually, this derives from a contextual bundle of grand constitutional design that constrains public power with liberal democratic devices, such as meaningful elections. Electoral constraints were absent from the Hong Kong context in 1973—although not, of course, from the British context, the ostensible source of "good government" for Hong Kong. Civil liberties were not absent, however. Furthermore, corruption did not extend to the highest levels of government or to the judicial branch. When the governor staked his reputation on ensuring that rule of law extended to law enforcers from top to bottom, it was within this context.

By contrast, although mainland Chinese leaders have recently acknowledged the importance of appropriate incentive structures to promote good government, they have not signaled commitment to clean government with agency design or the role assigned to laws and legal institutions. Instead, they have signaled the dominance of party and politics. This failure to signal commitment to anticorruption reform raises questions of possibility and willingness.

Is it possible to commit credibly to institutional designs for clean government in the context of a Leninist constitutional design? Of course not. Yet, considering the ideological flexibility of a "socialist market economy" designed to promote economic growth, there is no reason to believe that the Chinese cannot similarly adopt changes in political design that may be incompatible with Leninism.

Assuming Chinese leaders are sincere anticorruption reformers, why *not* choose a constitutional design for clean government? A cynical observer would reject the assumption of sincerity in the premise, yielding a clear answer. Many ordinary Chinese do in fact reject the premise. Should an observer outside the setting be more sanguine about prospects for anticorruption reform? Perhaps. Top Chinese leaders have tied their claims of political legitimacy to the sustained health and growth of the Chinese economy. Institutional designs that constrain abuse of public power also promote these objectives. A bet on corruption by design is not a winning bet. In recent years, Chinese anticorruption reformers appear to have endorsed institutional design to prevent corruption. In the space of the next decade, the continued growth of corruption surely poses a greater challenge to the stability of political rule than the extension of small-scale institutional design to grand constitutional design.

Notes
Works Cited
Author Index
Subject Index

Notes

1. Anticorruption Reform in a Setting of Widespread Corruption

1. On Transparency International's "corruption perceptions index," scores for Hong Kong range from 7.0 in 1996 to 8.2 in 2002 and average 7.6 for the 1995–2003 period. Compare these to scores for the United States, which also average 7.6 for this period and range from 7.5 in 1998 and 1999 to 7.8 in 1995. Scores for China range from 2.16 in 1995 to 3.5 in 1998, 2001, and 2002, and average 3.1 for the 1995–2003 period. To be sure, China ranks as less corrupt than many other developing countries, other Asian countries, and other countries that have recently made the transition to a market economy.

2. Rules must be considered as a bundle, rather than singly, for when corruption in government is widespread, there is no reason to suppose that corrupt officials choose their violations only so as to bring about Pareto improvements. This issue is elaborated in connection with property rights in Barzel (1989).

3. Of course, that the formal-legal standard does not measure up to a more stringent moral code may be (and has been) a stimulus to legal reform.

4. The literature considering issues in the definition of corruption is huge. Also, practically every study of corruption includes a lengthy dissertation on this problem. The choice of definition appears to be largely a matter of taste and objectives. This book has little to add to the already exhaustive treatment of definition elsewhere. See selections in Heidenheimer (1970), Heidenheimer, Johnston, and LeVine (1989), Fiorentini and Zamagni (1999), and Heidenheimer and Johnston (2002).

5. The score is an average of standardized scores from the surveys. In recent years most scores are calculated from considerably more than three surveys. While different sources measure corruption in different ways and there is a

212 Notes to Pages 6–10

selection bias in sources toward business, especially multinational businesses, correlations across sources are generally quite high (about 0.8 or higher). A bigger problem than the measurement of corruption in included countries may be that source selection bias results in inclusion of almost all large countries but only those small countries that are relatively well-governed—and this has implications for analytical findings (see Knack and Azfar 2001). The CPI and related material can be accessed at the Internet Center for Corruption Research at http://www.gwdg.de/~uwvw/icr.htm. This Web site includes background papers and framework documents that discuss data sources, aggregation methodology, and measurement precision. For statistical studies of corruption that make use of the index, see Goldsmith (1999), Treisman (2000), Sandholtz and Koetzle (2000), and Anderson and Tverdova (2003).

6. A number of studies make use of one or more of the surveys that are sources for the CPI, usually scores from risk agencies. One advantage of using these sources is potentially larger country coverage. For example, the International Country Risk Guide rates 129 countries in 1995 on "corruption in government," but the 1995 CPI includes only 41 countries because CPI scores are based on at least three surveys. Daniel Kaufmann, Aart Kraay, and Pablo Zoido-Lobatón (1999a, 1999b) have produced a "graft" index, using essentially the same sources as the 1999 CPI, but relaxing source requirements to include countries with only two surveys and weighting more heavily those indicators that are more highly correlated with one another. Their index coverage is 155 countries, compared to 99 countries for the 1999 CPI. An updated index (Kaufmann, Kraay, and Zoido-Lobatón 2002) has a coverage of 175 countries.

7. See Knack and Keefer (1995), Mauro (1995, 1997), Kaufmann, Kraay, and Zoido-Lobatón (1999b), Li, Xu, and Zou (2000), Broadman and Recanatini (2002), Anderson and Tverdova (2003). The pioneering study on consequences of corruption is by Mauro (1995). For arguments about generally harmful consequences, see Myrdal (1968), Kurer (1993), Shleifer and Vishny (1993), Murphy, Shleifer, and Vishny (1993), and Rose-Ackerman (1978, 1999). For more nuanced views, see Khan (1996) and Wedeman (1997a). Arguments about beneficial consequences of corruption are found in Leff (1964), Bayley (1966), and Huntington (1968). Recent work about corruption, mainly theoretical and mainly in economics (including work on the consequences of corruption), is reproduced in Fiorentini and Zamagni (1999).

8. Ades and Di Tella (1997, 1999), Goldsmith (1999), Treisman (1999, 2000), Fisman and Gatti (2000), Sandholtz and Koetzle (2000), Wei (2000), Knack and Azfar (2001), Lederman, Loayza, and Soares (2001). Knack and Azfar (2001) demonstrate that effects of trade openness and country size are artifacts of the CPI sample selection bias against small countries; these effects disappear when the "graft" index (see note 6 above) is substituted. They also find an inverse relationship between corruption and political freedoms, without a threshold effect. A variety of causal mechanisms are proposed for the

various relationships summarized above. For economic causes of corruption, the major theoretical studies are reproduced in Fiorentini and Zamagni (1999).

9. Recent alternatives to these subjective measures include firm-level survey data on actual bribery transactions in 22 transition economies (Clarke and Xu 2002; Hellman, Jones, and Kaufmann 2000), individual-level survey data on specific experiences with corruption in four Latin American countries in the late 1990s (Seligson 2002), and, most novel of all, differences between physical quantities of public infrastructure and the value of public capital stocks in 20 Italian regions in the mid-1990s (Golden and Picci 2002). The International Crime Victim Survey is also noteworthy: In 1996–97, it asked about solicitations of bribes by government officials. Transparency International included this source in compiling the CPI for 1998–2000.

10. See Heidenheimer (1970), Heidenheimer, Johnston, and LeVine (1989), and Heidenheimer and Johnston (2002) for selections from early studies. See Table 1.1 for the 2003 CPI. The striking exceptions to this generalization are Singapore and Hong Kong in Asia and Botswana in Africa. On Singapore, see Quah (1989, 1995, 1999) and Leak (1999). On Botswana, see Good (1994), Fombad (1999), Holm (2000), and Theobald and Williams (2000). Many Central and South American countries are also low scoring in corruption rankings, but corruption in these countries (which is not a new phenomenon) appears to have been subjected to less scrutiny in traditional studies by Western scholars writing in the English language. Some examples of more recent work that discusses long-standing problems of corruption in Latin America are Whitehead (1983), Little and Posada-Carbó (1996), Geddes and Neto (1999), and Manzetti (2000).

11. As the CPI is calculated using surveys for up to the past three years, sources often overlap from one year to the next. Thus consistency of scores in different (especially adjacent) years can result simply from use of the same sources and surveys. I looked at five rankings that cover the 1980–2003 period, but overlap little: the 1980–85 CPI (based on four surveys, from 1982 and 1984–85), the 1988–92 CPI (based on four surveys, from 1988 and 1992), the 1996 CPI (based on ten surveys, from 1993–96), the 1999 CPI (based on 17 surveys from 1996–99, of which 16 are from 1997–99), and the 2003 CPI (based on 17 surveys from 2000–2003).

12. Of the 48 countries I characterize as "basically consistent" across the period, 34 retain high, low, or intermediate scores in all five rankings, and 14 have one score outside their category. This discrepant score is usually different by very little and usually is from the 1980s rankings, many of which were based on fewer than three surveys.

13. China is one of the five; the others are Argentina, Portugal, South Africa, and Spain.

14. Of course, a number of seriously corrupt countries show up in few or none of the rankings because of an insufficient number of surveys. See note 6 above on sample selection bias in the CPI.

15. In game theoretic terms, this is a Nash equilibrium.

16. For relatively more sophisticated models with insights relevant to the discussion below, see Lui (1985), Cadot (1987), Andvig and Moene (1990), Andvig (1991), Shleifer and Vishny (1993), Huang and Wu (1994), Bicchieri and Rovelli (1995), Manion (1996), and Tirole (1996).

17. The discussion above, of mechanisms sustaining the equilibria, does not address two issues implied by the curves as drawn in Figure 1.1: the decreasing profitability of corrupt transactions (although not relative to clean transactions) at some point to the right of B and the negative payoffs from a clean transaction once all other players choose corruption. That the corrupt payoffs curve turns downward reflects two trends. First, as corruption becomes more common, competition among corrupt officials drives bribe payments down. Second, as corrupt officials must also transact with other officials, bribe payments to other officials must be deducted from corrupt earnings. It follows, then, that when all other players act corruptly, acting otherwise yields a negative return: A clean official must pay bribes as an ordinary citizen, but she has no corrupt earnings as an official to offset them. On these issues, see Andvig (1991).

18. This raises an interesting issue. In principle, anticorruption interventions can aim to shift corrupt payoffs abruptly or gradually, but gradualism may be less promising than a strategy of "big moves," especially in contexts close to C. Policy measures that shift the corrupt payoffs curve in increments toward (but not initially to or beyond) the tipping point may have no immediate impact on the corruption rate and carry no momentum. Further, their impact (i.e., once incremental changes add up to a shift beyond the tipping point) may be mitigated because of the information problem presented by the illegality of corruption. That is, gradualism may prolong corruption not only because its initial effects may have no impact on the corruption rate, but also because incremental changes may delay the updating of information even when cumulative change is actually enough to generate momentum.

19. Another effect is theoretically possible. Gary Cox and Morgan Kousser (1981) analyze the impact of the secret ballot on voting in upstate New York at the turn of the century and find that it changed the nature of electoral corruption, but not necessarily the scope. Instead of paying voters for votes, parties paid voters to abstain from voting. For some time after the introduction of the secret ballot in 1890, this "deflationary" corruption appears to have significantly replaced "inflationary" vote buying.

20. The researchers think it unlikely that the gap is mainly explained by greater unwillingness to admit bribery experiences. Interviews with officials largely corroborate the smaller scope of actual bribery, and ordinary citizens in focus groups describe experiences of petty corruption openly.

21. The discussion by Randall Calvert (1995) is the most relevant reference point here. He analyzes institutions as game-theoretic equilibria that solve a number of problems, one of which is the achievement of coordination in complex settings.

22. Indeed, whether the campaigns were better than nothing is not obvious; at best, the evidence in Chapter 5 is equivocal about their net value in reducing and deterring corruption.

2. Corruption and Anticorruption Reform in Hong Kong

1. Reports and data books for surveys conducted before 1994 are restricted or confidential documents of the ICAC. I was granted permission to study all of these documents at the offices of the Community Relations Department, but did not have access to any raw survey data for analysis. To my knowledge, the only study in the public domain that draws on the surveys is Clark (1987), which makes limited use of some findings from the first six surveys.

2. From 1978 through 1992, surveys were conducted biannually. Beginning in 1992, surveys have been conducted annually. For 1977, 1978, and 1980, samples are representative samples of the Hong Kong population aged 15–64 years, excluding the marine population. Proportions of non-Chinese in the samples are small: 1.6 percent in 1978, 0.7 percent in 1980. From 1982 through 1995, non-Chinese speakers were excluded at the interviewing stage. Samples for 1982–95 are representative samples of the Chinese-speaking population of Hong Kong, aged 15–64 years, excluding the marine population. Beginning in 1996, surveys were conducted in Chinese (Cantonese and Mandarin) and English, and samples for 1996–2002 are representative samples of the Hong Kong population aged 15–64 years, excluding the marine population. Sampling error in the surveys varies from about 3 to 4 percent.

   Surveys for 1977 through 1990 were conducted via face-to-face interviews. The sampling frames for these surveys are random samples of living quarter addresses, including permanent and temporary structures, compiled and maintained by the Hong Kong Government Census and Statistics Department. The number of eligible respondents varied from residence to residence, but at the interviewing stage one respondent was selected at random from each living quarter. Beginning in 1992, surveys have been conducted by telephone, with respondents at randomly sampled telephone numbers drawn from current telephone directories. At the interviewing stage, one respondent is selected at random from eligible respondents at the number. Both methods of selection at the interviewing stage resulted in unequal probabilities of selection for eligible respondents at different residences. To adjust for this, beginning in 1984, observations were weighted by the number of eligible respondents at their respective residences to permit strictly valid generalizations to the population of interest. Before 1984, the survey data were analyzed and presented without weighting of observations. Analysis of the 1984 data reportedly revealed no major differences between weighted and unweighted results. Analysis of the 1992 data reportedly revealed only very small differences with weighting. For this reason, beginning in 1993, the survey data have been analyzed and presented in unweighted form.

   Fieldwork for the samples was conducted in the following months: August and September 1977, November and December 1978, November and December 1980, November 1982 through January 1983, November and December 1984, April through June 1986, March and April 1990, June 1992, April 1993, August 1994, June 1995, June 1996, July 1997, July 1998, March 1999, March and April 2000, March 2001, and November 2002.

3. See also Elliott (1971) for a vivid account of corruption, especially police corruption, presented by an early anticorruption activist in the expatriate community.

4. In 1977 the ICAC commissioner defined a corruption syndicate as "a group of Government servants of virtually any number—ten, fifty, sometimes many more—who combine to extort money for forbearing to carry out the duties imposed on them by their office or by the law" (ICAC 1977: 2).

5. Measures are not consistent from year to year, and there are four years for which reports are not disaggregated by sector, but these inconsistencies do not affect the conclusion noted above. See note 11 for a discussion of available measures.

6. It is useful to point out here that laws governing Hong Kong were not routinely translated into Chinese.

7. Section 10 was controversial in the legal community (and remains so) for this reason (see Downey 1976; Ma 1991). In 1994, a Hong Kong District Court judge ruled that Section 10 contradicted Hong Kong's Bill of Rights, passed in 1991. The ruling was overturned on appeal in 1995. The ICAC commissioner stated in 1996 that Section 10 had been the basis of only about 50 prosecutions over 21 years (ICAC 1996: 13). By my count, this amounts to 0.65 percent of cases prosecuted as a result of ICAC investigations in that time period.

8. The incident is described in detail in the first of two reports by Blair-Kerr (July 1973), commissioned by the government. See also Lethbridge (1985: 93–97, 110–115).

9. As late as 1972 (the year before the Godber scandal erupted), the governor had informed the media at a press conference that corruption was not a problem in Hong Kong. In making that statement, he had ignored advice that he acknowledge the problem if asked and indicate his intention to take action (Cater 1995).

10. Public confidence in the new organization may also be reflected in the high volume of reports to the ICAC on problems, such as family disputes, completely unrelated to corruption: 2,769 in 1974. The volume of such reports has remained fairly high, which suggests that the public views the ICAC as an ombudsman organization as well as an anticorruption force. See below on reported corruption.

11. While Hong Kong's annual police reports do not use obviously consistent or comparable indicators to report on anticorruption work from year to year, reported corruption appears to be lower in the years before 1970. Beginning in 1952–53, police reports provide figures on reported corruption for the financial year. The figure of 1,457 reports of corruption to the ACO in 1973

was provided by the ICAC; the last year for which figures are reported by the police is 1972–73, a period ending 31 March 1973. Police figures on reported corruption in previous years vary as follows. From 1952–53 through 1959–60, police reports provide figures on only those reports of corruption that resulted in investigations and also disaggregate these reports by sector (for example, police corruption, corruption in all other government departments) or at least indicate figures on police corruption. The method of counting investigations changed in 1956–57, when independent reports referring to the same or closely related circumstances began to be recorded as one case. The police report for 1960–61 provides only one figure, reports of police corruption. It is unclear whether the figure refers to all such reports or only investigated reports. Because of structural changes at the end of 1960, which affected the consideration of reports of corruption and the delegation to the Anti-Corruption Branch (an earlier version of the ACO) of reports for investigation, it is not clarified by comparing the figure with that for 1959–60 or 1961–62. The police report for 1961–62 disaggegates by sector figures on all reports of corruption, and the report for 1962–63 does this for all reports and investigated reports. The police reports for 1963–64 through 1971–72 provide figures on all reports of corruption, non-anonymous reports of corruption, and disaggregated (by sector) figures on investigated reports of corruption. The police report for 1972–73 provides figures on all reports of corruption, non-anonymous reports of corruption, and disaggregates figures on all reports of corruption. See Royal Hong Kong Police Force (1953–73).

12. Cases are normally prosecuted not by ICAC officers, but by public prosecutors in the Attorney General's Office.

13. Associated with each of the three departments is an advisory committee, which includes members external to the ICAC. A fourth advisory committee monitors and advises the ICAC organization on its work and policies more generally. A fifth committee (an external committee) monitors and reviews all noncriminal complaints against the ICAC or its officers. Advisory committee membership is based on expertise in specialized fields and is quite widely representative of the Hong Kong community. Heads of a few relevant government departments are often members of advisory committees too. Beginning in 1996, following recommendations of an independent review committee, nonofficials were appointed to head the advisory committees, and the heads of the advisory committees associated with each of the three departments were made ex officio members of the general advisory committee on corruption. Complaints of corruption against the ICAC are investigated by an internal monitoring group under the immediate command of the Director of Intelligence and Support (and since August 1996, the Director of Investigations, Private Sector) in the Operations Department; complaints of noncorruption related criminal offenses are investigated by the police. Reports on completed investigations are reviewed by the advisory committee associated with the Operations Department, which submits recommendations for action as necessary to the commissioner. Over the years, corruption complaints against

ICAC officers have been rare, complaints about other criminal offenses (assault, deception, et cetera) have been slightly more numerous (less than a half-dozen a year), and noncriminal complaints (improper treatment of detainees, mishandling of witnesses, et cetera) have been much more common. Many complaints, criminal and noncriminal, have been judged unsubstantiated upon investigation. Obviously, it is difficult to evaluate this process and its results.

14. These figures and others in this and the next three paragraphs are from ICAC annual reports (ICAC 1975–2001), unless otherwise indicated. The 2000 figure is about one-fourth that of the Immigration Department, about one-tenth that of the Housing Department, and well under 1 percent of officials in all other Hong Kong government departments. Considering its functions, however, comparison of the ICAC with some other government departments may be misleading. Figures on the size of government departments are available from the Hong Kong Civil Service Bureau at http://www.csb.gov.hk.hkgcsb.

15. In expressing size of departments as a proportion of ICAC officers, I exclude those in the Administration Department.

16. This is reflected in absolute as well as relative department size in the 1970s. In 1975, after one year of operation, the ICAC had 434 officers working in the Operations Department, 64 in the Corruption Prevention Department, and 28 in the Community Relations Department. Obviously, it is important to put this in perspective by recalling that institutional design and public education had no precedents organizationally, while the function of the Operations Department was not different from that of the ACO.

17. Reports, investigations, and prosecutions of activities under the purview of the Corrupt and Illegal Practices Ordinance have accounted for a much smaller proportion of the ICAC caseload, however, even with the increased number and importance of electoral offices in the 1990s. For example, for the various 1995 elections, legislative council elections generated 95 reports of corruption, urban council elections 62 reports, regional council elections 59 reports, and rural committee elections 7 reports—and these figures include election-related reports of corruption received in the two years after the elections (ICAC 1998: 26). To put these figures in perspective, the ICAC received a total of 2,987 reports of corruption in 1995 alone. While the 1994 district board elections generated significantly more reports (345 by the end of 1997), they were nonetheless a small proportion of reported corruption in 1994–97 (see discussion in this chapter's section on reported corruption).

18. In 1980 the law was amended to include offering (accepting) an advantage *overseas* to (by) a Hong Kong public servant in connection with her official duties.

19. It excludes, for example, "entertainment," which is defined as "the provision of food or drink, for consumption on the occasion when it is provided, and of any other entertainment connected with, or provided at the same time as, such provisions" (Prevention of Bribery Ordinance 14 May 1971, Sec. 2).

20. Tsui had been the Operations Department's deputy director until November

1993, when the commissioner exercised his right to dismiss without explanation any ICAC officer in whom he had lost confidence. In public hearings at the Legislative Council, Tsui, a local Chinese, accused the ICAC of racism. He also alleged that the ICAC director of operations was preparing a list of "political targets" (and collecting information about them) for use after the transfer of sovereignty, that the ICAC carried out political vetting (a police force responsibility) involving wiretaps and other monitoring activities, and that the ICAC inflated corruption figures to win more resources from the government. The governor maintained in a public response that the ICAC did not have any "target lists." The ICAC commissioner also denied Tsui's allegations. He agreed that the ICAC did conduct "integrity checks" on behalf of the government, but stated that political vetting had never been (and would never be) conducted by the ICAC. A Legislative Council inquiry into the circumstances surrounding Tsui's dismissal concluded that the dismissal was "proper and reasonable." The allegations nonetheless damaged the reputation of the ICAC, as they called into question its political neutrality and organizational integrity. Tsui was the highest ranking local Chinese in the organization, and the allegations of racism, although not substantiated, generated unwelcome publicity. Looking ahead to the transfer of sovereignty, many legislators began to reconsider the draconian powers of the ICAC as an agency accountable only to the chief executive (see Lo 1994).

21. The ICAC commissioner in the early 1980s noted the importance of prosecuting the "big tigers" as swiftly as possible: "Nothing will kill public confidence quicker than the belief that the anticorruption effort is directed only at those below a certain level in society" (quoted in Klitgaard 1988: 118–119).

22. For a description of the "police mutiny" and subsequent events, see Lethbridge (1985: 126–158).

23. To put the governor's decision in context, it is useful to recall that the importance of police loyalty to the Hong Kong government had been well established in the explosive political riots in the 1960s. The partial amnesty not only avoided a police strike, but returned some of the prestige that the police had lost in the anticorruption battle. It is also relevant to point out that the governor did not give in fully. The militant police response to the announcement of partial amnesty was to demand more—including an amnesty of all past acts of corruption—backed with a threat to march on Government House if their demands went unmet. The governor met this threat more resolutely: After meeting throughout the day with advisors and top aides, he called an emergency meeting of the Legislative Council and in 20 minutes passed an amendment to the Police Force Ordinance, granting powers of summary dismissal to the police commissioner. With the amendment, the police associations obtained pledges of loyalty to their commissioner and agreement that grievances would be aired through established organizational channels in the future. On this issue, see Lethbridge (1985: 143–145).

24. The 1977 survey commissioned by the ICAC asked respondents the follow-

ing question: "Some people say that a general amnesty should be granted to those who committed corruption offenses before the establishment of the ICAC. Do you agree or not?" Of the 89 percent who responded, 79 percent disagreed.

25. Reports of police corruption dropped from 74 in October 1977 to 31 in November 1977 (unpublished monthly figures provided by ICAC Operations Department).

26. Of 286 investigations in progress at the time of the amnesty, 83 had to be immediately terminated (ICAC 1978: 9).

27. Recall (from the discussion above) that the law permits the ICAC to investigate other crimes revealed in the course of investigating offenses under the Prevention of Bribery Ordinance if the other crimes are reasonably suspected of being connected with the bribery offense.

28. Indeed, the ICAC made slow progress in recruitment in community relations in the first few years because specialists with these qualities were not easily found.

29. It was not standard practice to produce a Chinese version of laws in Hong Kong until 1986.

30. The interesting problem here was the contradiction between law and policy. Standard practice in the Labor Department was for officials to look the other way regarding factories in buildings not designed for industrial activities (and thereby not registered as legal factories). Since the department tolerated these factories, corruption prevention analysts recommended granting them legal status: "A situation which placed Government officers in a position where they are aware of unlawful activities which, nevertheless, are being tolerated provides obvious opportunities for corruption" (ICAC 1976: 29).

31. Some information about the surveys is summarized in note 2. Question wording often varies from survey to survey, with variations ranging from minor to very major. While acknowledging the well-established evidence that question effects can defeat comparability (see, for example, Schuman and Presser 1981), I have tried to strike a sensible balance between rejecting as noncomparable every question that is not exactly the same and treating as comparable all questions on the same or related issues.

32. Obviously, the 1977 partial amnesty is a salient event directly relevant to mass beliefs about the credibility of the government anticorruption commitment. Public opinion was strongly against the amnesty (see note 24), but any potentially big impact on response in the 1978 survey was probably attenuated by a separation in time of about a year between amnesty and survey.

33. For all nine surveys conducted in 1993–2002, of those respondents who stated they had personally encountered corruption, most (72 percent on average) indicated the encounter was in the private sector only, a small proportion (14 percent on average) indicated the encounter was in government only, and an even smaller proportion (9 percent on average) indicated they had encountered corruption in both the private sector and government.

34. They can be the basis for estimates of corrupt encounters in government.

This is of no small intrinsic interest, but these figures are not comparable to estimates from the seven surveys conducted in 1993–2002. Nothing is revealed about change over time.

35. The lower of these percentages is based only on combined responses about encounters of corruption in the police department, which is the most frequently cited department, named by more than half of respondents who name a department in these years. This involves no double-counting, but also fails to consider corrupt encounters in other government departments. The higher of the percentages is calculated from combined responses about encounters of corruption in any government department mentioned by at least 2 percent of respondents who name a department. Other methods of calculating the higher percentages do not yield very different results.

36. Considering sampling error, this might be ignored except that the pattern is similar to that revealed by other evidence, discussed below.

37. The two rankings of "historical scores" (prior to 1995) suggest corruption was most widespread in 1988–92. They are compiled mainly from assessments by risk analysts and foreign businesses. The scores are not strictly comparable across years for a number of reasons, and comparisons using the 1995 data are particularly problematic. Although Transparency International appropriately labels the scores as "corruption perception" scores, I do not treat them here as comparable to the ICAC survey data on beliefs about corruption because only one survey of ordinary citizens (a 1997 Gallup poll) is used in compiling the scores for Hong Kong. See Chapter 1 for a discussion of the corruption perceptions index. Scores may be accessed at the Internet Center for Corruption Research at www.gwdg.de/~uwvw/icr.htm.

38. For example, in 1988, the commissioner made these distinctions for corruption in the private and public sectors as follows: "There is no absolute yardstick by which corruption can be measured. We can record with certainty the number of corruption reports received, and we can report the public's perception of the levels of corruption in the community by means of independent, and statistically valid, surveys of public opinion. But whether fewer reports mean less corruption, and more reports mean increased corruption, cannot be assumed automatically. The greater number of allegations in the private sector could, for example, mean increased corruption, or more reports of the same level of corruption as a result of a better understanding and less tolerance of it, or a combination of the two. I suspect the latter is nearest the truth; although to apply the reverse arguments to public sector reports would seem to miss the mark. For many years after its establishment the thrust of the Commission's efforts was directed mainly, but by no means exclusively, at public sector corruption. The results of these efforts are now being seen. Based on public opinion surveys, corruption prevention measures taken (and interest shown) and assessments provided by our liaison staff, I believe the situation in the Government sector is simply as the reports indicate: that in recent years there has been a genuine reduction of corruption in the public service" (ICAC 1988: 7).

39. Of direct relevance to this issue is the insight into sources of beliefs about the scope of corruption suggested by responses to questions asked in six ICAC surveys. As noted in Table 2.1, in 1986, 1988, and 1990, respondents who named departments in which corruption existed were asked: "How do you know?" On average, 10 percent of respondents stated the source of their beliefs was personal experience, 31 percent reported it was stories told by others, 37 percent indicated it was the media, and 29 percent responded they were guessing. Of course, these are responses about specific departments, not about the overall volume of corruption in government. In 1998–2002, however, respondents who expressed beliefs that corruption existed in most or a number of government departments were asked the same follow-up question. On average, 3 percent reported the source of their beliefs was personal experience, 7 percent indicated it was stories told by others, 9 percent responded they were guessing, and 70 percent said it was media reports of corruption cases. Multiple responses were permitted in all surveys. Presumably, the intensity and number of media reports reflect something about actual corruption. Nonetheless, the high reliance on guesses in earlier surveys and on the media as a source (especially recently) highlights the importance of examining other sorts of evidence on actual corruption and also focuses attention on these beliefs as corruption and anticorruption inputs.

40. This is the same pattern for responses indicating there is corruption "in most government departments." See column 2 of Table 2.2.

41. In addition to clarifying the pattern of changing beliefs about corruption in government, Figure 2.1 also illustrates considerable differences in patterns and proportions. First, for the entire 1977–2002 period, the proportions responding that illegal commissions in business are common are much higher than for corruption in government. At the 1994 peak, nearly 70 percent of respondents state illegal commissions are common in business. At the lowest point, more than 40 percent indicate they are common. Compare this latter percentage to the proportions stating corruption is common in government departments: the private sector's "best" years are about the same as government's "worst" years, and more than twice as high as government's "best" years. Measured by beliefs in the scope of corruption, the ICAC has been quite successful in the government sector but not in the private sector. Second, while beliefs about corruption in government as common begin to rise in the early 1990s (especially in 1993 and 1994) and beliefs about illegal commissions in business begin to rise somewhat earlier (in 1988 and 1990), 1994 is the peak for both: a higher proportion of respondents believe corruption is common than recorded in any other survey.

42. I examined the surveys conducted by the Hong Kong Policy Research Institute on changing "confidence" of ordinary citizens along a number of dimensions beginning in 1996. Although one dimension is corruption in the civil service, the question taps confidence in future improvements rather than assessments of the volume of corruption. Confidence indexes can be found at www.hkpri.org.hk/hkci.

43. In the July 1996 survey, the proportion is 32 percent; in the February and June 1997 surveys, it is 38 and 37 percent respectively. The comparison is not straightforward, however: The ICAC 1997 survey was conducted in July, only a month after the Hong Kong Transitions Project survey. Results of the two surveys can be considered comparable only if the transfer of sovereignty on 30 June 1997 is taken as the pertinent distinction between time periods, that is, the Hong Kong Transitions Project results for June 1997 are incomparable to ICAC results for July 1997 because the former survey was conducted before the transfer of sovereignty. Survey results for this project can be found at http://www.hkbu.edu.hk/~hktp.

44. Note that only in 1986 do these survey questions distinguish between corruption in government and corruption in the private sector.

45. The next largest category (11 percent) refers to economic and social instability. After this, the next largest category (6 percent) refers to the importation of corruption from mainland China.

46. Exact figures and related questions are found at http://www.hkbu.edu.hk/~hktp. See also the survey of local entrepreneurs by Weder and Brunetti (1998) for another example of fears about a rise of corruption in government after the transfer of sovereignty.

47. This follow-up question was asked only in 1994–96. For the first question, respondents reporting weakened confidence in 1990–96 surveys are: 27 percent, 32 percent, 29 percent, 36 percent, 42 percent, and 36 percent.

48. For example, in six surveys conducted in 1998–2000 by the Chinese University of Hong Kong, Hong Kong Institute of Asia-Pacific Studies, public satisfaction with the ICAC averaged 71 percent (and is never lower than 68 percent). By contrast, average public satisfaction with the civil service is 30 percent, with the Hong Kong government at 26 percent, with the chief executive at 23 percent, with the Legislative Council at 20 percent, and with the Executive Council at 15 percent (Kuan 2001).

49. In 1983, the ICAC commissioner noted that an analysis of reported corruption suggested that reports frequently reflect media trends: When corruption in social services was the subject of media attention, reports in these departments increased, et cetera (ICAC 1983, 26).

50. The ICAC commissioner concluded that increases in reported corruption in the private sector in 1988 reflected greater willingness to report, not only increased corruption in this sector (ICAC 1989: 7). Election-related corruption reports do not appear to explain the rise—the number of cases is too small. See note 17 above.

51. Non-anonymous reports are crucial to success in the anticorruption effort, as complainants who fail to identify themselves often supply insufficient information for the ICAC to pursue an investigation. The percentage of pursuable corruption reports is fairly highly correlated with the percentage of nonanonymous corruption reports (Pearson's r is 0.61).

52. Of course, even before the 1990s, the public reported cases of official malpractice that did not amount legally to corruption. The ICAC commissioner

noted: "Many of these reports, which cover a multitude of matters, are accompanied by requests that they be passed on to the government department or other body concerned. Rightly or wrongly, there exists the belief that if the matter is channelled through the ICAC, it will receive more detailed or more prompt consideration" (ICAC 1981: 21).

53. This conclusion is based on a size-adjusted examination of corruption in the Housing Department, Urban Services Department, and Lands Department. These are the departments where reported corruption has been high over the years.

54. This also appears to be the prevalent view of ordinary citizens in Hong Kong. In 1998–2000 surveys, respondents were asked their opinion about the effect on corruption of the economic downturn that began in 1998 as part of the Asian financial crisis. About three-quarters of respondents stated they believed it had increased the level of corruption, while only about 5 percent responded it had decreased the level of corruption. These proportions varied little in the three surveys.

55. I looked mainly at growth rate of per capita GDP (in constant U.S. dollars) in the 1980s and 1990s. Hong Kong's economy grew on average by about 6 percent annually in the 1980s, which includes growth rates averaging just over 1 percent in 1982, 1985, and 1989. Growth rates in the 1990s were much lower, averaging just over 2 percent annually.

56. The bivariate correlation of per capita GDP growth rates and proportion of respondents believing corruption in government is common is −.058 (and statistically insignificant). Given the thinness of the theory and the limited number of observations on the dependent variable, I have not constructed a multivariate model. Of course, the cross-national empirical literature on the relationship between growth and corruption mostly develops theories and tests that analyze the effect of corruption on growth, not the opposite relationship discussed above.

57. This is a fairly large proportion compared, for example, to bribes offered by businesses operating in Central and Eastern Europe (which averaged 2 percent in 2000) and even the former Soviet Union (which averaged 3.7 percent). See Hellman, Jones, and Kaufmann (2000: 7). Of course, the results for the post-communist countries are for domestic businesses. It is not obvious to me, however, that we should expect *proportions* to be bigger for foreign businesses.

58. The figure of US $20 billion comes from the Hong Kong Association of Chinese Enterprises, an organization set up by the Chinese government to monitor Chinese investment in Hong Kong. There are no official data on the size of Chinese investment in Hong Kong. Figures for 1989 and 1993 are from *Gang ao jingji* (1993, no. 2: 64) and *Gang ao jingji* (1994, no. 8: 61). Hing Lin Chan (1995) estimates Chinese investment in Hong Kong in 1993 as about US $7.4 billion in banking, US $7.9 billion in listed companies, and somewhat less than US $7.4 billion in unlisted companies, that is, a total investment figure in excess of US $22 billion. Kevin Cai (1999) looks at Chi-

nese outward foreign *direct* investment (the largest proportion of which is investment in Hong Kong) and finds the same pattern for this subset: From about US $900 million in 1991, it rises to more than US $4 billion in 1992 and 1993. It then drops to about half those amounts in 1995.

59. See the discussion and specific examples in Chan (1995). Chan also argues that the level playing field of market competition for investment in mainland China was threatened, as Hong Kong companies in which these mainland investors acquired controlling shares (or simply significant financial interests) could expect "conveniences" in their dealings with the mainland. Chinese companies in Hong Kong engaging in "reverse investment" claimed better connections to mainland authorities as an advantage over other companies, according to a survey by Danming Lin (1996).

60. For example, Lu Ping, director of mainland China's Hong Kong and Macau Affairs Office, publicly criticized mainland Chinese investors for property speculation. See *South China Morning Post* (19 Mar. 1994).

61. This does not include mainland Chinese entering Hong Kong on labor importation schemes (such as labor imported specifically for the new airport project at Chek Lap Kok) begun in 1989.

62. In the ICAC annual reports, beginning with the 1980 report, there are a number of descriptions of cases of corruption involving illegal Chinese immigrants—police solicitation of bribes for not arresting illegal immigrants, forged passports obtained with the collaboration of immigration officials, and sales of fake identity cards by a small syndicate associated with immigration officers.

63. Yat-ming Siu (1999) offers estimates of returnees, but cannot actually distinguish between returning emigrants who entered as Hong Kong residents and returning students or other residents who did not depart as emigrants. Moreover, those returnees who do enter under a foreign passport cannot be distinguished from other foreign nationals.

64. Emigration statistics do not indicate how many left (or when) before 1997, as they did not need to apply to emigrate.

65. A controversy on this issue arose in 1994 when a police commissioner took up employment with a local construction company during his preretirement leave. One outcome was a change in regulations about employment outside the public sector after retirement. New guidelines required the governor's approval for a position in any company based in Hong Kong (Lee 1997).

3. An Explosion of Corruption in Mainland China

1. He Qinglian (1997: 257) reports survey results that put the Gini coefficient at 0.434 as early as 1994. She also reports the real figure in 2001 as closer to 0.6, because official figures do not take into account illegal or undeclared earnings that contribute a substantial amount of income for the wealthy.

2. See survey findings reported in Xu and Nie (1994), Yang (1996), Yuan (1997), and *South China Morning Post* (8 Dec. 2000). Generalizations based

on findings from Chinese public opinion polls must be viewed with caution (see Manion 1994), but the survey evidence that corruption is a problem of high salience for ordinary citizens is very consistent. It is also consistent with other sorts of evidence, not least of all urban protests and peasant riots.

3. Approval of annual reports of the chief procurator is part of the monitoring role of the NPC. In 1998, of the nearly 3,000 delegates, 55 percent voted approval, 29 percent voted against it, and 16 percent abstained. In 1997, the report passed with 60 percent approval (see Rowen 2001: 15). In February 2001, the Shenyang Municipal People's Congress failed to pass the report of the Shenyang municipal court justice—the first time such a report has failed to pass at any level of the people's congress. The main cause of dissatisfaction with the court was the handling of several major corruption cases in 2000.

4. In corruption cases that mainly or exclusively involve ordinary citizens, public security agencies conduct their own criminal investigations, and procurators review the completed investigation. Public security agencies generally transfer to the procuracy, for independent investigation, cases in which criminal suspects are public officials (Sun 1990; Dong and Ding 1993). Also, the 1979 Criminal Procedure Law and subsequent regulations assigned investigation of certain crimes exclusively to the procuracy. These include all crimes involving abuse of public office, an arrangement confirmed in the 1996 Criminal Procedure Law. See *Zhonghua renmin gongheguo xingshi susong fa* (1 July 1979, Art. 13 and 17 Mar. 1996, Art. 18). The actual authority of procurators in investigations of criminal corruption (and especially their working relationship with communist party agencies) is explored in Chapter 4.

5. Tax evasion and tax resistance are the next biggest category, accounting for about 12 percent of all economic crime investigated by the procuracy in 1987–96 (earlier and later figures are unavailable) and about 11 percent of economic crime involving big sums or senior officials.

6. When procurators receive information about a crime, they conduct a preliminary review to verify basic facts and consider the likelihood that the matter is indeed in the nature of a crime. In principle, a case is filed for investigation if the review indicates that the facts of a crime are reasonably clear and that the matter concerns a violation of law. That is, the decision to investigate a case presumably signifies that a report or accusation has sufficient merit to pursue a more specialized investigation of a crime, with some possibility of criminal prosecution. My calculations based on available procuratorial yearbook figures indicate that only about 50 percent of corruption cases reviewed preliminarily were actually filed for investigation in 1988–2000; this proportion has decreased quite significantly in recent years.

7. The relatively low figure for misuse of public funds is partly due to the legal categorization of this crime as a subset of the crime of embezzlement of public assets until 1988 (see Chapter 4).

8. The 3 percent is from figures on total number of officials investigated in 1990–2000, available in procuratorial yearbooks noted as sources in Table

3.1. The yearbooks present figures on officials investigated only beginning in 1990; in 1990–2000, the ratio of cases to individuals investigated by the procuracy is 0.89:1. Bribery dominates in corruption involving senior officials: It accounts for 65 percent of officials investigated, compared to 25 percent for embezzlement of public assets and 10 percent for misuse of public funds.

9. Embezzlement of public assets dominates in corruption involving big sums: It accounts for 48 percent of such cases in the 1990s, compared to 29 percent for misuse of public funds and 28 percent for bribery. Figures are calculated from procuratorial yearbooks noted as sources in Table 3.1.

10. CDIC (11 Sept. 1982, 30 Oct. 1987, 9 Oct. 1992, 9 Sept. 1997), Wei (12 Jan. 2000, 25 Dec. 2000), *Nanfang ribao* (27 Oct. 2000).

11. Data to adjust later (or earlier) figures are unavailable.

12. The trend line in Figure 3.1 plots predicted values from regressing number of cases on year, excluding 1982, 1986, and 1989–90 (because of upward enforcement bias) and 1998–2000 (because of incomparable measurement). This is fairly conservative in its exclusion of 1990 (not strictly a campaign year, but with an identifiable enforcement boost resulting from 1989 campaign strategy, described in Chapter 5) and inclusion of 1993–97.

13. Available figures on economic crime involving big sums and senior officials are combined for the 1980s. As the latter tend to be a tiny proportion of these sorts of cases, it is reasonable to consider the increases in the 1980s as evidence of increases in corruption involving big sums, but I do not draw from these data the same inference for corruption involving senior officials.

14. SPP, Chief Procurator (8 Apr. 1986, 3 Apr. 1991, 12 Mar. 1996, 10 Mar. 2001).

15. SPP, Chief Procurator (29 Mar. 1989, 29 Mar. 1990, 3 Apr. 1991, 28 Mar. 1993, 10 Mar. 1998). In detailing cases involving big sums for 1988, the chief procurator noted no cases involving sums of these magnitudes and only 15 cases involving sums of over 100,000 yuan. Only in the report on 1989 do sums of over 500,000 yuan begin to be noted, and only in 1990 do sums of over one million yuan begin to be noted. In real terms, the comparison between 1988–82 and 1993–97 is less striking: a million-yuan case in 1997 is roughly comparable to a 400,000-yuan case in 1988. These two periods include several years of unusually high inflation in China: Increases in consumer prices averaged 23 percent per year in 1988–89 and 36 percent per year in 1993–96.

16. This is how Deng Xiaoping explained economic reform to American journalists in 1985. See *Time* magazine's "An Interview with Deng Xiaoping" (1985: 35).

17. Brewer Stone (1993) suggests that the greater reliance on currency in the post-Mao economy may have created an exaggerated Chinese perception of corruption in the 1980s. Lack of easy currency prior to the reforms meant that bribes mostly took the form of commodities—and these could be more easily construed as "gifts" (see also Mulvenon 1998). In this sense, the

marketization of the Chinese economy may have contributed to the development of the folklore of corruption.

18. There are a number of recent publications that offer excellent discussions of definitions of corruption in the Chinese mainland context. See especially Levy (1995), White (1996), Kwong (1997), and Lu (2000b).

19. I do not examine here the business activities of the People's Liberation Army, which also engaged in bureaucratic commerce. Military bureaucratic commerce and corruption, as well as anticorruption measures directed at these activities, are described and analyzed well by James Mulvenon (1998, 2001).

20. Yi-Min Lin and Zhanxin Zhang (1999: 205) cite State Administration of Industry and Commerce statistics indicating that of 27,000 bureaucratic companies investigated in 1984–85, 23 percent were registered under state ownership, 67 percent under collective ownership, and 10 percent as jointly owned by the state and a collective; of approximately 24,000 such companies investigated in 1988–89, 43 percent were registered under state ownership and 53 percent under collective ownership.

21. The central authorities have issued scores of documents attempting to constrain and regulate bureaucratic businesses over the years. Two especially good collections that include many such documents issued by party and government agencies are Ministry of Supervision, Bureau of Policy, Regulation, and Law (1991) and Central Committee, General Office, Office of Laws and Regulations, Central Discipline Inspection Commission, Office of Laws and Regulations, and Central Organization Department, General Office (1996).

22. Whether these rents were higher or lower in value than those generated by central planning is another matter. See Liew (1993) for a consideration of this issue.

23. See Chapter 4 for further discussion. The crime, *tanwu zui* in Chinese, is translated variously as "graft," "embezzlement," and "corruption" by Chinese and Western scholars. Strictly, "corruption" best conforms with the standard usage given in *Black's Law Dictionary*. "Graft" is more popular than legal, and its connotation is less close (Black 1990: 345, 698). I use "embezzlement" to refer to this crime because the strictly best translation risks confusion with "corruption" in the broader sense.

24. Some of these activities were identified as crimes separate from embezzlement of public assets in the 1997 Criminal Law. See Chapter 4.

25. The law does not use the term "organizational corruption" or any general term. Instead, it refers to particular crimes that seek benefits for the workplace and its staff collectively. See *Zhonghua renmin gongheguo xingfa* (14 Mar. 1997, Arts. 387, 391, 393, 396). Chapter 4 surveys the specific crimes under the rubric of "organizational corruption," in the sense discussed here.

26. This considers only the single category of corruption in public investment and expenditure. This category includes losses due to: corruption in government procurement, embezzlement of public assets, misuse of public funds, illegal construction and expansion of public buildings, and excessive banqueting and illegal gift giving with public funds. It also includes state revenue

losses due to predatory exactions, although these must be relatively small; for the most part, this is theft from the citizenry directly, not the state.

27. It is worth noting too that official growth rates have been called into question recently by Western scholars with expertise on the Chinese economy (see Rawski 2002). Yet, while questions about increased growth in the context of decreased energy consumption, for example, appear warranted, even fairly cautious assessments characterize the past two decades as a period of relatively fast economic growth in China, relative to its past and to other countries.

28. The major caveat here is that some considerable proportion of corrupt gains is invested in Hong Kong. Even with capital flight, however, some capital returns to China as reinvestment.

29. I hesitate to make too much of this survey. Apart from my usual caution about generalizations from Chinese surveys (see Manion 1994), this particular survey is so big (20,000 respondents) and the response rate so high (99 percent) that it must give rise to suspicions about appropriate field management, response incentives, and reliability of response. In addition, considering the sponsoring State Council agency, my guess is that responses about abuses were biased toward less serious irregularities and not criminal corruption—and indeed this bias may have been prompted by wording of the question items. Without seeing the items, it is impossible to know.

4. Problems of Routine Anticorruption Enforcement

1. The earliest and clearest expression of this commitment to problem solving through system building is in Deng Xiaoping (1980).

2. A third agency, the Ministry of Supervision, was reinstated in 1986, but was merged with the party discipline inspection system in early 1993. An examination of the supervisory network is not essential to an understanding of anticorruption enforcement, but my readings do suggest that the ministry and its subordinate departments played a nontrivial role from 1987 through 1992, especially in Beijing. Their revival was part of a policy to "separate party and government," promoted by then party leader Zhao Ziyang. As the function of government supervisory departments overlapped nearly completely with party discipline inspection groups, much work handled by discipline inspection groups inside government departments at the center and in local governments was apparently transferred to the supervisory departments in the late 1980s. Zhao's open sympathies with the protesters in Tiananmen Square in 1989 led to his removal from all party offices and the reversal of his policy. In January 1993, the Ministry of Supervision and its subordinate supervisory departments "combined operations" with the Central Committee's Discipline Inspection Commission (CDIC) and party discipline inspection committees to form a "single work structure with two names." The merger reduced duplication of work in favor of strengthened party leadership. Wei Jianxing, concurrently minister of supervision and CDIC first sec-

retary, explained that the Ministry of Supervision would continue to exist under the State Council, but the CDIC would carry out both party discipline and administrative supervision functions under the leadership of the Central Committee. Merged agencies in the localities would work under the dual leadership of local governments and merged discipline inspection and administrative supervisory agencies one level higher. For a description of the supervisory structure and its functions, see State Council (15 July 1987), Commission on State Organ Establishment (4 Nov. 1988), *Zhongguo jiancha nianjian 1987–1991* (1993: 501–503, 510–511), Ministry of Supervision Bureau of Policy, Regulation, and Law (1991: 1–97), and Liang, Ye, and Hu (1994: 396–405). For a study of the relationship between the party discipline inspection system and the government supervisory system, see Chang (1998).

3. Qiao Shi became first secretary in 1987, and Wei Jianxing replaced him in 1992.

4. Zhao 1995: 175; *Zhongguo jiancha nianjian 1996* 1997: 395. The figure for procurators includes assistant procurators.

5. There are also "special procuratorates" in the Chinese armed forces and the railway transportation system.

6. The procuratorial committees are not large. The SPP has a committee of 13–19 members, provincial committees have 9–15 members, municipal committees have 7–11 members, and county committees have 5–9 members.

7. The Criminal Procedure Law gave exclusive investigative authority to procuratorates for three categories of crimes when they involve state functionaries: corruption, dereliction of duty, and violation of the personal and democratic rights of citizens. The specific crimes in these categories are described in the 1979 Criminal Law (*Zhonghua renmin gongheguo xingfa* 1 July 1979, Arts. 155, 131–149, 185–192) and the 1997 Criminal Law (*Zhonghua renmin gongheguo xingfa* 14 Mar. 1997, Arts. 232–262, 382–419). In the 1979 Criminal Law, specific crimes in these categories were fewer than in the 1997 version, but the 1979 Criminal Procedure Law gave procuratorates authority to investigate other cases as they considered necessary. The 1996 Criminal Procedure Law requires procuratorates to obtain permission from procuratorates at the provincial level or higher to investigate other cases (cf. *Zhonghua renmin gongheguo xingshi susongfa* 1 July 1979, Art. 13; *Zhonghua renmin gongheguo xingshi susongfa* 17 Mar. 1996, Art. 18).

8. See the figures in Table 3.2. Bribery, embezzlement of public assets, and misuse of public funds amount to 75 percent of all cases of economic crime filed for investigation by the procuracy in 1980–85.

9. For the changes in the 1982 Party Constitution see *Zhongguo gongchandang dangzhang* (11 Sept. 1982, Arts. 6, 43, 44, 45).

10. According to Young (1984), similar measures to strengthen discipline inspection as a vertical system were proposed in 1955, but were quickly abandoned.

11. At the grassroots level, the party congress or party members meeting elects the discipline inspection committee, and its membership is approved by the party committee one level up. Grassroots discipline inspection committees can only be established where there are primary party committees. Where the party organization at the grassroots is a party general branch or party branch, the position of discipline inspector is established. The decision to establish a discipline inspection committee or appoint a discipline inspector where there is a primary party committee is at the discretion of the party committee one level higher.

12. For more discussion of party committee approval, see the later discussion of the *nomenklatura* system. Normally, the local discipline inspection committee secretary is a member of the party committee standing committee at that level. The 1982 Party Constitution stipulated that the CDIC first secretary must be a member of the Politburo Standing Committee, but this stipulation was removed in 1987.

13. Specifically, organization departments must involve discipline inspection committees before they pass the vetting materials they have assembled on to the party committee for discussion and decision (Wei 24 Jan. 1996).

14. The CDIC and the Central Organization Department sent out notices in March and April 1979, instructing party organizations to establish discipline inspection committees or discipline inspectors. By August 1979, most localities and grassroots organizations had apparently accomplished this. See Chen (1993: 160) and Huang and Liu (1997: 232–233).

15. The Central Committee (29 Feb. 1980) approved the document in 1980.

16. As part of the short-lived effort to separate party and government, political-legal committees were abolished in 1987 on the instructions of Zhao Ziyang. Writing in the *South China Morning Post* (10 Jan. 1990), Willy Lam reports that most had been dismantled by the beginning of 1989, but were restored by late 1989 (and indeed given more staff and powers). See also Cohen (1990) and Tanner (1994).

17. CDIC first secretaries are typically members of the Politburo Standing Committee, the half-dozen top policy makers in China. As such, they have responsibility for shaping policy and major decisions in political-legal matters. Wei Jianxing assumed the CDIC first secretary position in 1992; however, he did not join the Politburo Standing Committee until 1997.

18. A measure, adopted in 1996 to strengthen the discipline inspection system, requires party organization departments to obtain the agreement of discipline inspection committees one level higher as part of the process of vetting officials for appointments, promotions, transfers, or removals in discipline inspection committees (Wei 24 Jan. 1996).

19. Officials in positions of any consequence are party members, and it would be highly unusual for even an assistant procurator, who is empowered by law to investigate and prosecute senior officials, to be a noncommunist. In 1990, communist party members constituted 70 percent of the work force in procuratorates (Wang 25 Nov. 1989). Procurators, including assistant procu-

rators, accounted for 72 percent of the work force in 1990 (*Zhongguo jiancha nianjian 1991* 1992: 341).

20. Figures for 1979–87 are from reports to party congresses (CDIC 11 Sept. 1982, 30 Oct. 1987, 9 Oct. 1992, 9 Sept. 1997), except for 1987, which is reported in the *Renmin ribao* (12 Oct. 1988). The 1998 figure is from the *Nanfang ribao* (27 Oct. 2000). Figures for 1999 and 2000 are from reports by CDIC First Secretary Wei Jianxing (12 Jan. 2000, 25 Dec. 2000) to CDIC plenary sessions.

21. Figures for the early 1980s and 1987–97 indicate that well over 80 percent of party members investigated were punished with some form of disciplinary action.

22. The number refers to individuals in cases filed after preliminary investigation. Sources are those listed in Table 3.1, but for comparability, here I use figures on individuals, not cases. Before 1990, only figures on cases are reported. To convert these, I used the ratio of cases to individuals for 1990. On the intersection of those investigated by discipline inspection committees and procuratorates, while not all individuals investigated in criminal corruption cases are communist party members, I assume that party members make up a very high proportion because most officials are party members and crimes of corruption are defined in ways that necessarily involve officials.

23. Hou reports on surveys of work from a number of unspecified provinces and cities.

24. Theft and embezzlement of public assets accounted for 55 percent of economic violations, bribery for 15 percent. Other offenses accounting for significant numbers of party members disciplined in these years are sexual misconduct (12 percent), violations of the one-child family policy (12 percent), and gambling (5 percent). Violations of the one-child family policy seem to be a common problem. Wu Baoliang (1998: 6) notes that the rate of punishment of party members decreased in the mid-1990s due to a lower incidence of this sort of misconduct.

25. Among those expelled for economic violations, embezzlement of public assets accounted for 55 percent, bribery for 18 percent, and theft for 15 percent.

26. Song suggests that many leading officials are prompted to engage in corruption by their impending retirement. He notes that more than half of officials disciplined were approaching retirement age. This may, of course, be related more to rank, as rank and age are strongly correlated.

27. This is true of procuratorial investigations of corruption too, of course, but this point does no harm to the argument here.

28. The Party Constitution states that party members who commit serious violations of criminal law are to be punished with expulsion from the party (*Zhongguo gongchandang dangzhang* 11 Sept. 1982, Art. 38; *Zhongguo gongchandang dangzhang* 18 Oct. 1992, Art. 38). See also the discussion of punishments below.

29. Dismissal from party positions also used to include "recommendation to nonparty organizations of dismissal from nonparty positions," but this

phrase was removed in the 1992 Party Constitution and is not in party regulations issued after 1992. In revising the constitution, party officials concluded that such a recommendation had nothing to do with party disciplinary actions. See Small Group on Revision of the Party Constitution (12 Oct. 1992).

30. Control may be for terms of three months to two years. Individuals sentenced to control continue to work as usual, receiving normal wages, but are subject to supervision by the community and public security agencies and are required to report periodically to public security agencies. Criminal detention consists of confinement to a detention center managed by the local public security agency. Detention terms stipulated in the 1979 Criminal Law are 15 days to six months. In the 1997 Criminal Law, they are one to six months. Individuals sentenced to criminal detention are permitted to go home for one or two days per month and may be paid for work if work is performed.

31. None of the legal provisions refers to communist party discipline inspection committees. Government supervisory departments also take disciplinary actions. The 1982 and 1985 provisions predate the establishment of the Ministry of Supervision and its subordinate departments, however. The 1997 Criminal Law notes that administrative actions are to be taken by the workplace or "superior managing agency" *(shangji zhuguan jiguan)*, that is, the bureaucratic unit in charge of the workplace. Interestingly, the distinction between crimes punishable by criminal punishment and those for which disciplinary action constitutes sufficient punishment is made initially in a party document. For example, the party document specifies that embezzlement of public assets valued at 2,000 yuan or less may be punished with disciplinary actions if the circumstances of the crime are "minor" (Central Committee General Office 13 Aug. 1982).

32. The 1997 regulations specify that criminal punishment here implies a main criminal punishment. More substantial exceptions have been noted too. For example, when criminal punishment is a sentence of imprisonment for three years or less; is reduced to a reprieve, surveillance, or detention and labor; and does not deprive the individual of political rights, then expulsion is not necessarily required. It depends on the circumstances of the crime and the attitude of the criminal (Fei 1991: 142).

33. On government supervisory departments, see note 2.

34. For reports after 2000, categories are not strictly comparable to previous years.

35. The language stands in contrast to that in other articles of the regulations. For example, if an investigation reveals an accuser has knowingly produced false evidence, then discipline inspection committees should *(ying)* recommend that the relevant agency pursue the matter.

36. A main point of the document is to set up a system of regular and ad hoc meetings of the party and government anticorruption agencies. Among other things, these meetings would exchange information in cases of party disciplinary violations that also involve crimes.

37. A second document clarifies that discipline inspection committees may post-

pone the talk to a more appropriate time, if they believe early notification will harm the investigation (CDIC 25 Mar. 1994).

38. The failure to transfer cases of criminal corruption to government procurators is not unique to the party organization. In the early 1980s, a number of customs departments, public security agencies, and offices that regulate industry and commerce punished economic crimes by issuing fines or confiscating property—which reportedly led some smugglers and speculators to boast, "Fined for five crimes in ten, I cover my capital investment, [fined] for three crimes in ten, I turn a profit" (CDIC 14 July 1982).

39. Exemption from criminal prosecution is different from exemption from criminal punishment *(mianyu chufen)*. The latter is a decision taken by the court, which occurs after a procuratorial decision to prosecute.

40. He Jiahong (with Waltz 1995: 23) states that party appropriation of criminal cases applies only to party members who are fairly high-ranking officials, not ordinary party members or ordinary officials.

41. A total of 1.6 million party members were investigated in this period. Of this number, 1.4 million were subjected to some party disciplinary action, 276,000 to expulsion from the party. See CDIC (9 Oct. 1992, 9 Sept. 1997).

42. It seems low even taking into account the high rate of exemptions from prosecution (discussed later) after cases are transferred to procuratorates. That is, even if we assume only 58 percent of cases transferred were prosecuted, which is the average rate for this period (see Table 4.2), the estimated number of party members whose cases were transferred is less than 10 percent of the 1.4 million party members disciplined by the party in 1988–97.

43. Here I apply the rate of prosecutions (58 percent) to the number of officials in cases filed and investigated by procurators in 1988–97 (545,000).

44. Two other figures, both provided by SPP Chief Procurator Zhang Siqing (28 Oct. 1993) suggest even lower proportions, in the range of 8–10 percent for 1993 and 1988–93.

45. Approval authority to file a case for investigation is organized along the following lines. Investigation of Central Committee members and Central Discipline Inspection Committee members requires authorization by the Central Committee. At lower levels, investigations of party committee standing committee members and discipline inspection committee standing committee members are authorized by the discipline inspection committee one level higher. Before authorization, this discipline inspection committee is supposed to solicit opinions from its leading party committee. The same arrangement applies to investigations of workplace party committee members and workplace discipline inspection committee secretaries and deputy secretaries. Local party committees authorize investigation of their own party committee members who hold no party committee leadership positions. Investigations of all other party member officials are authorized by the discipline inspection committee at the level where *nomenklatura* authority resides, but it is supposed to solicit opinions from its leading party committee (CDIC 12 May 1988, 25 Mar. 1994; Fei 1991: 110–112).

46. Chief Procurator Yang Yichen noted in his 1986 report to the legislature that leaders in some localities and workplaces promoted a view of economic criminals as "pathbreakers" and "vanguards of reform," requested an open discussion of the issue and obstructed criminal investigations of bribery and swindling. In a number of localities, procurators apparently did not prosecute these sorts of crimes, fearing a "reversal of verdicts." In 1987, Yang pointed to further obstruction of investigations and prosecutions by officials who viewed the anticorruption effort as a constraint on economic reform and opening. See SPP Chief Procurator Yang Yichen (8 Apr. 1986, 6 Apr. 1987).

47. This was due to a lack of a statutory codification system by which new laws could be codified in the appropriate section of an existing statute.

48. Public officials were defined as functionaries working in state organs, enterprises, schools, or agencies affiliated with any of these units.

49. Profiteering *(touji daoba)* and "official profiteering" *(guandao)* are examples of crimes that disappeared or were redefined in the 1997 Criminal Law. For a preliminary examination of these crimes, see "Commentary: Official Speculation and Profiteering" (1989). For a more detailed and recent review of legal changes in the treatment of profiteering, see Sheng (1996: 142–181).

50. The discussion in this section summarizes relevant content from *Zhonghua renmin gongheguo xingfa* (1 July 1979, Art. 155), *Zhonghua renmin gongheguo xingfa* (14 Mar. 1997, Art. 382), NPC Standing Committee (8 Mar. 1982); SPC and SPP (8 July 1985, 6 Nov. 1989), NPC Standing Committee Working Committee on the Legal System, Office on the Criminal Law (1997: 546–547). Luo (1996: 16–50) presents a useful discussion of the crime from a legal standpoint.

51. This includes managers of state-owned enterprises and authorities in public institutions such as hospitals and schools, for example. However, the 1997 Criminal Law discusses crimes by managers of state-owned enterprises in a separate chapter on crimes of disrupting the socialist market economy. See later discussion and note 54.

52. Illegal appropriation of collective assets by individuals entrusted to manage them became an "ordinary crime," not a crime of corruption (*Zhonghua renmin gongheguo xingfa* 14 Mar. 1997, Art. 271).

53. This can be a position of general leadership (of a locality, department, or workplace) or specific authority to manage particular public assets.

54. The article is Article 165 in Chapter 3 on crimes of disrupting the socialist market economy. Articles 166, 168, and 169 in the same chapter fit somewhat less well here, but I consider them as crimes of corruption, not unlike some aspects of criminal dereliction of duty described in Chapter 9 of the law. Article 166 makes it a crime for an employee of a state-owned company, enterprise, or organization *(shiye)* to cause the state to incur losses by transferring management of the profit-making business of the workplace to friends or relatives, purchasing goods at obviously higher than market prices from a business operated by friends or relatives, selling goods at obviously lower than market prices to a business operated by friends or relatives, or

purchasing substandard merchandise from a business operated by friends or relatives. Article 168 makes it a crime for the manager of a state-owned company or enterprise to cause the organization to incur bankruptcy or heavy financial losses due to malfeasance involving personal favoritism toward friends or relatives. Article 169 makes it a crime for the manager of a state-owned company or enterprise or the department supervising them to practice favoritism toward friends or relatives by converting state-owned assets into low-value stocks or selling the stocks at very low prices.

55. This notion was introduced in SPC and SPP (8 July 1985). Chinese documents do not use the term "organizational corruption," but refer to various forms of corruption that seek benefits for the workplace and its staff collectively.

56. Relevant regulations issued before 1988 were vague or weak. The SPC and SPP (8 July 1985) described the following circumstances in which misuse of public funds is criminal embezzlement of public assets. If the funds are returned within a "reasonable" period of time, then the misuse of public funds is a violation of financial discipline, not a crime, and is punished by administrative action. If the funds are not returned, the misuse is criminal embezzlement of public assets, but only if considerable time has elapsed and the sums involved are significant. The 1985 document then offers greater specificity, summarizing legal experience over the past few years. If a state functionary misappropriates public funds for private use and does not return them within six months or if the funds are used for illegal activities, then it is criminal embezzlement of public assets, to be punished accordingly. If the sums involved are huge and the funds are invested to earn private profits, the misappropriation can be prosecuted as embezzlement of public assets even if six months have not elapsed and the investment activity per se is not illegal. But if the funds are not used for illegal activities, mitigating circumstances should be considered even if the funds were not returned within six months. Examples are misappropriation of public funds due to family illness or financial difficulties; in such cases, the misappropriation could be punished with administrative action. Two years later, the SPC and SPP (14 Mar. 1987) went further, introducing more circumstances under which misuse of public funds could be handled as a violation of financial discipline, punished with administrative action only. Misuse of public funds is not a crime when the sums are relatively large (5,000–10,000 yuan or more) and the funds have not been returned within six months, so long as the funds are returned before the case is discovered. Further, misuse of public funds is not a crime when the losses to the state or collective are not large, even if the sums of the public funds misappropriated are huge (50,000 yuan or more). Seen against this background, the 1988 provision and its affirmation in the 1997 Criminal Law are considerably stronger. See Ye and Yu (1996).

57. In a 1982 Central Committee General Office provision (13 Aug. 1982), unexplained assets are declared equivalent to illegally obtained income for any public official. In a 1990 CDIC provision (1 July 1990), unexplained assets

are declared a violation of party discipline, punishable by expulsion from the party in serious cases.

58. The principle is nowhere presented explicitly or generally as such in the 1979 Criminal Law, although Article 119 on smuggling and profiteering states that officials who exploit public office to commit these crimes are to be punished more harshly. See *Zhonghua renmin gongheguo xingfa* (1 July 1979).

59. Criminal detention is considerable harsher than control, as it constitutes a deprivation of freedom. See note 30 above.

60. Other crimes for which the 1997 Criminal Law states monetary values are bribery, smuggling, tax evasion, resistance of tax payment, manufacture or sale of fake or shoddy goods, and certain crimes involving illegal drugs. See *Zhonghua renmin gongheguo xingfa* (14 Mar. 1997).

61. There is also an organizational incentive that may have led procuratorates to prosecute crimes of embezzlement or bribery as ordinary theft or swindling. Under the 1979 Criminal Procedure Law (Art. 13), the former sorts of cases are investigated exclusively by procurators, but the latter are normally investigated by public security agencies. When a case involves an official rather than an ordinary citizen, the procuratorate can take it up, as the Criminal Procedure Law permits investigation by procuratorates of any cases "considered necessary." Nonetheless, the distinction in the law itself, which assigns some sorts of cases more routinely to one agency than another, may have contributed to the purposeful categorization of cases of ordinary theft or swindling as cases of corruption or bribery. This basic division of labor was not altered in the 1996 Criminal Procedure Law (Art. 18), although procurators now require approval by a procuratorate at or above the provincial level to investigate cases outside the categories specified in the law. See *Zhonghua renmin gongheguo xingshi susong fa* (1 July 1979) and *Zhonghua renmin gongheguo xingshi susong fa* (17 Mar. 1996).

62. That is, by law, procurators are obligated to prosecute all criminal cases except where there is insufficient evidence to convict. On this issue, He Jiahong (with Waltz 1995: 324) remarks: "The only factor—and it is a significant one—that makes a prosecutor drop a prosecutable case is political influence."

63. *Zhonghua renmin gongheguo xingshi susong fa* (1 July 1979, Art. 1), *Zhonghua renmin gongheguo xingshi susong fa* (17 Mar. 1996, Art. 15).

64. Exceptions are cases of political dissidents, who are not infrequently subjected to re-education through labor, an administrative sanction distinguished from reform through labor (a criminal punishment) almost solely by the principle that individuals undergoing re-education are to be paid for their labor. See Lawyers Committee for Human Rights (1993: 66–76).

65. These are the years for which such figures are available; procuratorial yearbooks ceased to present these sorts of figures in later years.

66. The proportion of cases that government procurators dropped in the course of investigation (that is, after filing for investigation) can be roughly estimated by comparing figures in column 5 in Table 4.2 with figures on all cases

of embezzlement of public assets filed and investigated in the same years (presented in Table 3.1). Obviously, imprecision is introduced as the differences between the two sets of figures include cases filed for investigation and dropped in the same year and cases carried over from the previous year (that is, filed for investigation in one year, but prosecuted or exempted from prosecution in a later year). The latter sort of situation is probably not uncommon, but if we sum the differences over the ten-year period, the year-to-year variation probably averages out. By this calculation, procurators dropped about 9 percent of cases of embezzlement of public assets after filing them for investigation.

67. In general, public security agents conduct initial investigations of cases in the former category and transfer them to procuratorates with recommendations to prosecute or exempt from prosecution. After reviewing the investigations, procurators may decide to transfer the case back to public security agencies for further investigation or conduct their own further investigation. Typically, however, cases are not investigated further but are prosecuted or exempted from prosecution. Occasionally, procurators decide to drop cases transferred to them by public security agencies.

68. Exemptions from prosecution in cases of bribery (which, by legal definition, involves public officials) is similarly high and exhibits similar volatility.

69. Even before passage of the 1997 Criminal Law, exemption from prosecution could also be granted in cases of corruption involving more than 2,000, even in noncampaign periods. The SPP (25 Dec. 1982) introduced measures permitting exemption from prosecution in cases of embezzlement or bribery involving amounts of up to 5,000 yuan if officials guilty of the violation turned themselves in, offered assistance to the authorities or otherwise demonstrated remorse, and took the initiative to return the illegally obtained property. Normally, however, cases involving more than 2,000 yuan were to be prosecuted.

70. This is so whether 1989, 1993, and 1995 are all categorized as campaign years or whether 1989 alone is treated as a campaign year (as it could be, considering the features of campaigns in the 1980s, an issue elaborated in Chapter 5). The conclusions summarized are the results of simple bivariate or multivariate regression analyses, with number or percentage exempted from prosecution as dependent variables. Statistical significance for the first set of conclusions is at the .001 and .05 levels, respectively.

71. For example, although exemption from prosecution is normally supposed to be granted only when the circumstances of the crime are minor, it was permissible in a much wider range of circumstances during the clemency period of the 1989 anticorruption campaign. See Chapter 5.

5. Anticorruption Campaigns as Enforcement Mechanisms

1. Secondary sources on the campaign are few. Frederick Teiwes (1978), Xiaobo Lu (2000b), and Lynn White (1988) discuss it in some detail.

2. The definition that was offered in April 1952 was quite inclusive: only those working in some sort of state agency (enterprises and schools, for example) could commit the crime of corruption (*tanwu,* embezzlement), but abuse of public office was not a defining feature (Central People's Government Council 18 Apr. 1952).

3. All sums in this section are converted here from "old currency" denominations to "new currency," a reduction by an order of 10,000.

4. This number excludes 184,170 officials initially accused as tigers in the campaign, but later reclassified as having committed less serious acts of corruption (Lu 2000b: 55, 56).

5. I found no statistics on confessions in the campaign.

6. For example, a party document issued early in the campaign estimated that among officials involved in corruption, 95 to 97 percent were involved in only small corruption, in amounts of 1,000 yuan or less. It suggested that most could be exempted from criminal prosecution (Central Committee Feb. 1952).

7. This is not simply my estimate, of course. In addition to my own survey of Chinese-language and English-language materials for this purpose, I assigned a research assistant the task of reading three anticorruption chronologies (Chen 1993; Li 1993; Huang and Liu 1997) and coming up with plausible candidates for the beginning and end of anticorruption campaigns, based on anticorruption publicity, nuance in language, initiatives by top generalist leaders, and documents issued by central party and government executive organs. I also reviewed newspaper materials from the period to the end of the 1990s. For most campaigns, the beginning is obvious and indeed is acknowledged in numerous Chinese sources. An exception is the 1995 campaign, about which I am least confident. Determining when a campaign has ended is decidedly more arbitrary. Readers can judge my choices for themselves in the description of campaigns that comprises most of this chapter.

8. Liu Sheng (1996: 22) writes that about 80 percent of cases of bribery and embezzlement of public assets filed for investigation by procurators in the mid-1990s are based on reports from the mass public. Qin Xingmin (2000: 98, 102) writes that reports from the mass public, offices, and organizations were the source of *more than* 80 percent of bribery and embezzlement cases filed for investigation by procurators in 1988–98, but this seems high, considering earlier figures. The inclusion of reports from "offices and organizations" *(jiguan tuanti)* probably inflates the percentage.

9. Obviously, I am not strictly interested in only these two crimes, although they do account for most criminal corruption (see Chapter 3) and a high proportion of reports (e.g., only 46 percent in 1989 but 87 percent in 2000). See *Zhongguo falü nianjian 1990* (1990: 44) and *Zhongguo falü nianjian 2001* (2001: 184). My purpose is simply to find a consistent series relating plausibly to corruption. I rejected figures on "letters and visits" as too broad a category and figures on economic crimes because of incomplete data.

10. The increase from 1999 to 2000 is trivial (under 2 percent).

11. Willingness to report non-anonymously is another behavioral indicator of public confidence in the regime as anticorruption enforcer, but these sorts of figures are notably unavailable in the Chinese case. SPP Chief Procurator Liu Fuzhi (28 Mar. 1992) stated that more than 60 percent of reports on corruption and bribery to procuratorates in 1991 were non-anonymous, but my research has turned up no figures for other years. Sixty percent is impressively high, especially in the mainland context where fear of retribution is presumably stronger than in Hong Kong, for example. The lack of figures for other years or other sources confirming this figure may indicate it is incorrect. Qin Xingmin (2000: 101, 103) decries a continuing high proportion of *anonymous* reports, but does not provide figures. According to CDIC First Secretary Wei Jianxing (24 Jan. 1996), only 21 percent of reports to discipline inspection committees on violations by senior officials were non-anonymous in 1994, and 27 percent of such reports were non-anonymous in 1995. This is not really a comparable figure, of course: we might expect a lower proportion of reports about senior officials to be non-anonymous.

12. An early formulation by the Ministry of Finance (30 Dec. 1986) indicates that rewards to complainants whose reports help solve cases should not exceed 10 percent of sums confiscated and generally should be less than 1,000 yuan for individual complainants or 10,000 yuan for workplaces. Draft regulations issued in 1988 (SPP 25 Nov. 1988) state that complainants whose reports result in punishment for criminals may be rewarded, and that those with major contributions should be given big rewards. The provisions leave to provincial authorities the details of methods, sums, and funding of such rewards. Regulations issued in 1996 (SPP 18 July 1996) state that individuals should be rewarded materially if they contribute, through their reporting, to the eventual prosecution of economic crimes, including corruption, that involve big sums or senior officials, and that individuals with major contributions should receive big rewards.

13. Size of average rewards is not constant, of course. Moreover, in any given year, rewards were not doled out equally to all who received them. For example, 821 people were rewarded in 1994, of whom 13 received rewards that averaged more than 1,000 yuan, although others received rewards averaging about 200 yuan (*Zhongguo falü nianjian 1995* 1995: 115).

14. This is based on a comparison of 1993, 1994, and 1996 figures. Ideally, we might like to compare campaign years with adjacent years, but most available figures combine several years or are incomplete. In the campaign year 1993, the likelihood of being rewarded was 0.26, but it was 0.61 in 1994 and even higher in 1996. See *Zhongguo falü nianjian 1994* (1994: 122), *1995* (1995: 122), and *1997* (1997: 182–183).

15. In the campaign year 1993, the average reward was 461 yuan, in 1994 it was 353 yuan, and in 1996 it was 3,292 yuan. Also, the expected value of each report is lower in campaign years because reports rise during campaigns. For example, in 1993 it was 121 yuan, while in 1994 it was 214 yuan (despite the smaller average reward). In 1998, with more reports than in 1993 but bigger rewards, the expected value of a report was 936 yuan. In 1996, with fewer

reports and much bigger rewards, it was 2,436 yuan. See *Zhongguo falü nianjian 1994* (1994: 122), *1995* (1995: 122), *1997* (1997: 182–183), and *1999* (1999: 143).

16. See *Zhonghua renmin gongheguo xingfa* (1 July 1979, Art. 138; 14 Mar. 1997, Art. 243). For "false accusations," the 1997 Criminal Law specifies criminal penalties of up to ten years imprisonment for serious circumstances and up to three years imprisonment otherwise. The law cautions procurators to distinguish these from "mistaken accusations" *(cuo gao)* and "accusations inconsistent with the facts" *(jianju shishi)*, but it is easy to understand how fear of being accused might discourage potential accusers.

17. On guidelines for sentences, see *Zhonghua renmin gongheguo xingfa* (1 July 1979, Art. 146; 14 Mar. 1997, Art. 254). SPP Chief Procurator Liu Fuzhi (28 Mar. 1992) reports the following for 1991: 39 of the 1,835 cases of retribution reported resulted in criminal punishment, 530 resulted in party disciplinary action, and the rest were transferred to government departments for disciplinary action.

18. Qin Xingmin (2000: 99–100) writes that 61,000 criminals turned themselves in to procuratorates in 1988–98, and he attributes this figure to pressure from reporting.

19. Campaigns in 1982 and 1986 probably also produced significantly higher numbers of cases involving big sums (and perhaps senior officials too). Cases of economic crime involving big sums or senior officials filed and investigated by procuratorates in 1979–85 increase significantly in both those years (but also in 1985). See Table 3.2 in Chapter 3.

20. Wu Baoliang (1998: 6) notes that 1982, 1986, and 1989 are peak years for communist party disciplinary action too.

21. I reach the same conclusion looking only at cases involving very senior officials, at the central bureau *(si ju)* level and higher. Figures on these cases are presented in most annual reports by the chief procurator to the legislature; they are also available in some law yearbooks. See note 22.

22. The figures for the 1980s are extrapolated from figures for 1982–92 presented in the *Renmin ribao* (12 May 1994). I made a reasonable simplifying assumption that procuratorates filed no criminal corruption cases involving senior officials in 1980 and 1981. For the 1990s, the figures are from annual reports to the legislature (SPP Chief Procurator 28 Mar. 1992, 15 Mar. 1994, 13 Mar. 1995, 12 Mar. 1996, 11 Mar. 1997, 10 Mar. 2000) or, if relevant figures are not reported, from law yearbooks (*Zhongguo falü nianjian 1991* 1991: 24; *Zhongguo falü nianjian 1993* 1993: 95; *Zhongguo falü nianjian 1998* 1998: 148).

23. The notice discussed Article 185 on bribery, but did not revise Article 155 on embezzlement of public assets. It did revise punishments in other articles on appropriation of "huge" amounts of public or private property through theft, swindling, or forcible seizure. Obviously, if public officials abused powers of office to steal, swindle, or forcibly seize huge amounts of public property, it met the definition of embezzlement of public assets.

24. Of course, the figure of 78,000 reports is for all economic crimes (not only

bribery and embezzlement of public assets), but it is nonetheless a great deal higher than the average of 30,000 per year in 1983–87, shown in Figure 5.1. Also, as noted earlier, these two crimes account for a very high preponderance of reports.

25. The contrast with the comments of CDIC First Secretary Wei Jianxing in August 1995, cited at the beginning of this chapter, is a good example of language markers for campaign beginnings and endings.

26. New measures included ending the practice of sons and daughters of senior officials engaging in commerce, eliminating the special food supply enjoyed by some senior leaders, strictly applying rules about allocation of vehicles, prohibiting vehicle imports, prohibiting gift giving and entertaining at banquets, and restricting trips abroad by leading officials. These prohibitions were to start with Central Committee and State Council leaders.

27. Near the end of the directive was a promise of clemency to those who confessed to other economic crimes as well, if they surrendered to the authorities before 31 October 1989 and informed on others.

28. Article 59 of the 1979 Criminal Law states that a punishment milder than stipulated for the particular crime is appropriate if the circumstances of the criminal are mitigating. These circumstances are identified in Articles 14, 16, 17, and 18. Examples are crimes by youth and acts of self-defense. Article 63 states that criminals who surrender to the authorities may be granted clemency. For relatively minor crimes, punishment may be milder than stipulated for the particular crime, or the criminal may be exempted from punishment altogether. For relatively serious crimes, punishment may be milder than stipulated for the particular crime if the criminal renders "meritorious services." Article 101 of the 1979 Criminal Procedure Law states that procuratorates may grant exemption from prosecution in circumstances where the Criminal Law stipulates that criminal punishment is unwarranted or may be waived. See *Zhonghua renmin gongheguo xingfa* (1 July 1979) and *Zhonghua renmin gongheguo xingshi susong fa* (1 July 1979).

29. As discussed in Chapter 4, exemption from prosecution differs from exemption from criminal punishment. The former decision is made entirely within the procuratorial system, while the latter decision is made by the courts.

30. A directive issued by the SPC and SPP on 14 September 1989 clarified that exemption from criminal prosecution or exemption from criminal punishment for criminals guilty of embezzlement of public assets in amounts of 50,000 yuan or more should not automatically be granted to those who had surrendered during the clemency period. In deciding on exemption from prosecution, procuratorates were instructed to take into account whether or not the criminal had surrendered and confessed within the clemency period, returned all embezzled money and property, caused no great losses to the state or collective interest, and acted meritoriously. Furthermore, decisions to exempt from prosecution in all cases of embezzlement involving sums of 50,000 yuan or more were to be reported to the procuratorate at the next level up (and ultimately be examined by the Supreme People's Court). SPP

Chief Procurator Liu Fuzhi (25 Oct. 1989) reiterated these guidelines as procuratorates worked in late 1989 and into 1990 to process the cases of those who had surrendered during the clemency period. Even under these guidelines, the only sorts of cases of corruption explicitly ruled out for exemption from prosecution were cases involving sums of 100,000 yuan or more, cases involving particularly serious circumstances, and cases involving sums of 50,000 yuan or more and serious circumstances. The 22 August 1989 directive was somewhat less stringent, however, as it made no mention of losses to the state or collective and did not require the authorities to report to higher levels. Officials guilty of embezzlement of public assets in amounts of 50,000 yuan or more could be granted exemptions if they confessed to the authorities within the clemency period and returned embezzled money and property (or acted meritoriously). Of course, by mid-September, when conditions for exemption from prosecution were clarified, the clemency period had been in force for a month already. Many officials had already surrendered to the authorities, based on the incentive structure outlined in the August directives, and their expectations of exemption from prosecution were probably quite high. These expectations were apparently met. See the later discussion on results of the 1989 campaign.

31. It also threatened harsh punishment to anyone who intentionally provided false information.

32. To be sure, not long after the SPC and SPP issued the key clemency notice on 15 August, the Ministry of Supervision issued its own clemency notice. It encouraged corrupt officials to give themselves up to government supervisory departments (or other relevant agencies) and promised leniency to those who complied. The Ministry of Supervision could promise clemency only for minor misconduct, however, not for crimes.

33. An additional 17,600 officials took advantage of the clemency for minor violations offered by the Ministry of Supervision during the clemency period (Huang and Liu 1997: 367).

34. Figures began to be reported after the establishment of reporting centers in 1988, but are not systematically reported in yearbooks or publicized at meetings. In 1988, 650 gave themselves up to procuratorates and confessed their crimes, 3,500 gave themselves up in 1990, 2,389 in 1991, 1,307 in 1994, and more than 2,121 in 1996. See SPP Chief Procurator (3 Apr. 1991, 28 Mar. 1992), *Zhongguo falü nianjian 1989* (1990: 13), *Zhongguo falü nianjian 1995* (1995: 115), Wen (1997).

35. Figures are available on numbers of people as well as cases only after 1990, and the ratio of cases to people ranges from 1:1.11 to 1:1.14, with 1:1.13 as the mean. I found no figures that separate cases involving big sums from other cases, however. To obtain the percentages above, I increased cases filed and investigated by 13 percent (except for cases involving senior officials, which are always expressed as number of officials).

36. This adjusts for the cases to people ratio, as above.

37. Here, I am making the reasonable assumption that few cases initiated by such

confessions were dropped for lack of grounds to prosecute. Cases concluded as a percentage of cases filed and investigated is lower in 1989 (75 percent) and higher in 1990 (105 percent) than in any other year for which data are available in procuratorial yearbooks (which is 1987–2000). See *Zhongguo jiancha nianjian 1988* (1989: 351), *1989* (1991: 410), *1990* (1991: 327), *1991* (1992: 342), *1992* (1992: 361), *1993* (1994: 417), *1994* (1995: 550), *1995* (1996: 382), *1996* (1997: 396), *1997* (1998: 486), *1998* (1999: 506), *1999* (2000: 511), and *2000* (2001: 646).

38. The elaboration of these first "five points" produced a set of 12 prohibitions *(bu zhun)*. A "second five points" issued in 1994 raised 13 prohibitions, and a "supplementary four points" issued in 1995 raised to 31 the number of prohibitions. These were the foundation for the Standards of Integrity for Communist Party Member Leading Officials, issued in 1997 (see Xu 1997).

39. There is also a popular fictionalized account of the case (Fang 1996), which details the investigation. The account was officially banned after publication.

40. In the end, Chen was charged not with accepting bribes but with embezzlement of state assets in the form of gifts, valued at about $67,000 altogether and received over a period of three years, which Chen was required to report and surrender to the state. Zhiyue Bo (2000) suggests the charge of embezzlement may have been politically prudent: bribery would implicate whoever gave the gifts, thereby straining the relationship between Chinese authorities and foreign investors. For example, one vexing issue was a $2 billion Hong Kong-financed real estate project, approved despite its serious violation of municipal building height restrictions. Deputy Mayor Wang Baosen and Chen Xiaotong (son of Chen Xitong, but without an official position) apparently both accepted bribes for facilitating the approval. The approval also raised serious concerns among foreign investors about the security of contracts in China because the project site was the (highly desirable) location of a McDonald's, for which a 20-year lease had recently been signed. McDonald's initiated a lawsuit against the Beijing government, but lost. The huge Oriental Plaza project was built despite intense criticism.

41. This was characterized legally not as misuse of public funds but as dereliction of duty.

42. According to Huang Xiurong and Liu Rongbing (1997: 455), some 1,500 people worked on the investigation.

43. Andrew Wedeman (1996) dates the beginning of the 1995 campaign in March. It is worth noting that Bruce Gilley (1998) finds no evidence to sustain an argument that the investigation of Chen was a politically-motivated purge by Jiang Zemin to consolidate his power.

44. Yang Shuang (1996) refers to 1995 as a peak year for the anticorruption effort.

Works Cited

Works in English

Ades, Alberto, and Rafael Di Tella. 1997. "National Champions and Corruption: Some Unpleasant Interventionist Arithmetic." *Economic Journal,* 107, no. 443: 1023–1042.

———. 1999. "Rents, Competition, and Corruption." *American Economic Review,* 89, no. 4: 982–993.

Advisory Committee on Corruption. 1961. Sixth Report. In Reports of the Standing Committee and the Advisory Committee on Corruption, 43–67. Hong Kong: Government Printer, 29 Dec.

Anderson, Christopher J., and Yuliya V. Tverdova. 2003. "Corruption, Political Allegiances, and Attitudes toward Government in Contemporary Democracies." *American Journal of Political Science,* 47, no. 1: 91–109.

Andreski, Stanislav. 1968. "Kleptocracy or Corruption as a System of Government." In *The African Predicament: A Study in the Pathology of Modernization,* 92–109. London: Michael Joseph.

Andvig, Jeans Christopher. 1991. "The Economics of Corruption: A Survey." *Studi economici,* 43, no. 1: 57–94.

Andvig, Jeans Christopher, and Karl Ove Moene. 1990. "How Corruption May Corrupt." *Journal of Economic Behavior and Organization,* 13, no. 1: 63–76.

Anechiarico, Frank, and James B. Jacobs. 1996. *The Pursuit of Absolute Integrity: How Corruption Control Makes Government Ineffective.* Chicago: University of Chicago Press.

Baird, David. 1970. "On the Cheap." *Far Eastern Economic Review,* 19 Dec., 20.

Bardhan, Pranab. 1997. "Corruption and Development: A Review of Issues." *Journal of Economic Literature,* 35, no. 3: 1320–1346.

Barzel, Yoram. 1989. *Economic Analysis of Property Rights*. Cambridge: Cambridge University Press.

Bates, Robert H. 1981. *Markets and States in Tropical Africa: The Political Basis of Agricultural Policies*. Berkeley: University of California Press.

Baum, Richard, and Alexei Shevchenko. 1999. "The 'State of the State'." In *The Paradox of China's Post-Mao Reforms*, ed. Merle Goldman and Roderick MacFarquhar, 333–360. Cambridge: Harvard University Press.

Bayley, David H. 1966. "The Effects of Corruption in a Developing Nation." *Western Political Quarterly,* 19, no. 4: 719–732.

Bennett, Gordon. 1976. *Yundong*. Berkeley: University of California, Institute of East Asian Studies, Center for Chinese Studies.

Bernstein, Thomas P., and Xiaobo Lu. 2000. "Taxation without Representation: Peasants, the Central and Local States in Reform China." *China Quarterly,* no. 163: 742–763.

———. 2003. *Taxation without Representation in Contemporary Rural China*. Cambridge: Cambridge University Press.

Bicchieri, Cristina, and Carlo Rovelli. 1995. "Evolution and Revolution: The Dynamics of Corruption." *Rationality and Society,* 7, no. 2: 201–224.

Black, Henry Campbell. 1990. *Black's Law Dictionary*. 6th ed. St. Paul, Minn.: West Group.

Blair-Kerr, Alastair. 1973a. First Report of the Commission of Inquiry under Sir Alastair Blair-Kerr. Hong Kong: Government Printer. July.

———. 1973b. Second Report of the Commission of Inquiry under Sir Alastair Blair-Kerr. Hong Kong: Government Printer. Sept.

Bo, Zhiyue. 2000. "Economic Development and Corruption: Beijing beyond 'Beijing'." *Journal of Contemporary China,* 9, no. 25: 467–487.

Broadman, Harry G., and Francesca Recanatini. 2002. "Corruption and Policy: Back to the Roots." *Journal of Policy Reform,* 5, no. 1: 37–49.

Burns, John P. 1989. *The Chinese Communist Party's Nomenklatura System*. Armonk, N.Y.: M.E. Sharpe.

———. 1994. "Strengthening Central CCP Control of Leadership Selection: The 1990 *Nomenklatura*." *China Quarterly,* no. 138: 458–491.

———. 2003. "Rewarding Comrades at the Top in China." In *Reward for High Public Office: Asian and Pacific-Rim States*, ed. Christopher Hood and B. Guy Peters, with Grace O. M. Lee, 49–69. London: Routledge.

Cadot, Olivier. 1987. "Corruption as a Gamble." *Journal of Public Economics,* 33, no. 2: 223–244.

Cai, Kevin G. 1999. "Outward Foreign Direct Investment: A Novel Dimension of China's Integration into the Regional and Global Economy." *China Quarterly,* no. 160: 856–880.

Callick, Rowan. 2001. "East Asia and the Pacific." In *Global Corruption Report 2001*, ed. Robin Hodess, Jessie Banfield, and Toby Wolfe, 10–21. Berlin: Transparency International.

Calvert, Randall L. 1995. "The Rational Choice Theory of Social Institutions: Cooperation, Coordination, and Communication." In *Modern Political*

Economy: Old Topics, New Directions, ed. Jeffrey S. Banks and Eric A. Hanushek, 216–267. Cambridge: Cambridge University Press.

Cater, Jack. 1977. Speech to the Rotary Club of Hong Kong. Independent Commission against Corruption. Hong Kong. 15 Feb.

———. 1995. Interview with author. Hong Kong. 3 May.

Cell, Charles. 1977. *Revolution at Work.* New York: Academic Press.

Chan, Anita, and Jonathan Unger. 1982. "Grey and Black: The Hidden Economy of Rural China." *Pacific Affairs,* 55, no. 3: 452–471.

Chan, Hing Lin. 1995. "Chinese Investment in Hong Kong: Issues and Problems." *Asian Survey,* 35, no. 10: 941–954.

Chang, I-Huai. 1998. "An Analysis of the CCP's Role in Mainland China's State Supervisory Systems." *Issues and Studies,* 34, no. 1: 38–78.

Cheung, Tak-sing, and Chong-chor Lau. 1981. "A Profile of Syndicate Corruption in the Police Force." In *Corruption and Its Control in Hong Kong,* ed. Rance P. L. Lee, 199–221. Hong Kong: Chinese University Press.

Ch'i, Hsi-Sheng. 1991. *Politics of Disillusionment: The Chinese Communist Party under Deng Xiaoping, 1978–1989.* Armonk, N.Y.: M. E. Sharpe.

Clark, David. 1987. "A Community Relations Approach to Corruption: The Case of Hong Kong." *Corruption and Reform,* 2, no. 3: 235–257.

Clarke, Donald C., and James V. Feinerman. 1995. "Antagonistic Contradictions: Criminal Law and Human Rights in China." *China Quarterly,* no. 141: 135–154.

Clarke, George R. G., and Lixin Colin Xu. 2002. "Ownership, Competition, and Corruption: Bribe Takers versus Bribe Payers." World Bank Working Paper no. 2783. 15 February. Washington, D.C.

Cohen, Jerome Alan. 1990. "Tiananmen and the Rule of Law." In *The Broken Mirror: China after Tiananmen,* ed. George Hicks, 323–344. Essex: Longman.

"Commentary: Official Speculation and Profiteering." 1989. *Hong Kong Law Journal,* 19, no. 3: 354–366.

"Concepts of Law in the Chinese Anti-Crime Campaign." 1985. *Harvard Law Review,* 98, no. 8: 1890–1908.

Corrupt and Illegal Practices Ordinance (Chapter 288). 1955. Hong Kong. 10 June.

Cox, Gary W. 1987. *The Efficient Secret: The Cabinet and the Development of Political Parties in Victorian England.* Cambridge: Cambridge University Press.

Cox, Gary W., and J. Morgan Kousser. 1981. "Turnout and Rural Corruption: New York as a Test Case." *American Journal of Political Science,* 25, no. 4: 646–663.

"Dang Jian Cites Statistics." 1989. Beijing *Xinhua,* in Foreign Broadcast Information Service, *Daily Report.* 21 Aug.

Davies, Derek. 1973. "Inherent Dangers." *Far Eastern Economic Review,* 29 Oct., 28.

Deng Xiaoping. 1980. "On the Reform of the System of Party and State Leadership." In *Selected Works of Deng Xiaoping, 1975–1982,* 302–325. Beijing: Foreign Languages Press. 18 Aug.

Ding, X. L. 1999. "Who Gets What, How? When Chinese State-Owned Enterprises Become Shareholding Companies." *Problems of Post-Communism,* 46, no. 3: 32–41.

———. 2000a. "The Illicit Asset Stripping of Chinese State Firms." *China Journal,* no. 43: 1–28.

———. 2000b. "Informal Privatization through Internationalization: The Rise of *Nomenklatura* Capitalism in China's Offshore Businesses." *British Journal of Political Science,* 30, no. 1: 121–146.

———. 2000c. "Systemic Irregularity and Spontaneous Property Transformation in the Chinese Financial System." *China Quarterly,* no. 163: 655–676.

Downey, Bernard. 1976. "Combatting Corruption: The Hong Kong Solution." *Hong Kong Law Journal,* 6, no. 1: 27–66.

Duckett, Jane. 2001. "Between Developmentalism and Corruption: Understanding China's New State Business." Paper presented at the Annual Meeting of the Association for Asian Studies, Chicago, Mar. 22–25.

Einwalter, Dawn. 1998. "Selflessness and Self-Interest: Public Morality and the Xu Honggang Campaign." *Journal of Contemporary China,* 7, no. 18: 257–269.

Eitel, E. J. 1983 [1895]. *Europe in China.* Hong Kong: Oxford University Press.

Ekpo, Monday U. 1979. "Gift-Giving and Bureaucratic Corruption in Nigeria." In *Bureaucratic Corruption in Sub-Saharan Africa: Toward a Search for Causes and Consequences,* 161–188. Washington, D.C.: University Press of America.

Elections (Corrupt and Illegal Conduct) Ordinance (Ordinance 10). 2000. Hong Kong. 24 Feb.

Ellenberg, Adrien, Personnel Director, City of New York Department of Investigation. 2000. Letter to author. 2 Nov.

Elliott, Elsie. 1971. *The Avarice, Bureaucracy and Corruption of Hong Kong.* Hong Kong: Friends Commercial Printing.

Endacott, G. B. 1978. *Hong Kong Eclipse.* Hong Kong: Oxford University Press.

Etzioni, Amitai. 1984. *Capital Corruption: The New Attack on American Democracy.* San Diego: Harcourt Brace Jovanovich.

Fan, Chengze Simon, and Herschel I. Grossman. 2000. "Incentives and Corruption in Chinese Economic Reform." Lingnan University, Centre for Public Policy Studies, Working Paper no. 103. June. Hong Kong.

Faure, David. 1981. "Paying for Convenience: An Aspect of Corruption That Arises from Revenue Spending." In *Corruption and Its Control in Hong Kong,* ed. Rance P. L. Lee, 133–165. Hong Kong: Chinese University Press.

Fiorentini, Gianluca, and Stefano Zamagni, eds. 1999. *The Economics of Corruption and Illegal Markets.* Vol. 1, *The Economics of Corruption.* Cheltenham: Edward Elgar.

Fisman, Ray, and Roberta Gatti. 2000. "Decentralization and Corruption: Evidence across Countries." World Bank Policy Research Working Paper no. 2290. Washington, D.C.

Fombad, Charles Manga. 1999. "Curbing Corruption in Africa: Some Lessons from Botswana's Experience." *International Social Science Journal,* 51, no. 2: 241–254.

Forster, Keith. 1985. "The 1982 Campaign against Economic Crime in China." *Australian Journal of Chinese Affairs,* no. 14: 1–19.

Francis, Corinna-Barbara. 1999. "Bargained Property Rights: The Case of China's High-Technology Sector." In *Property Rights and Economic Reform in China,* ed. Jean C. Oi and Andrew G. Walder, 226–247. Stanford, Calif.: Stanford University Press.

Gardiner, John A. 1993. "Defining Corruption." *Corruption and Reform,* 7, no. 2: 111–124.

Geddes, Barbara, and Artur Ribeiro Neto. 1999. "Institutional Sources of Corruption in Brazil." In *Corruption and Political Reform in Brazil: The Impact of Collor's Impeachment,* ed. Keith S. Rosen and Richard Downes, 21–48. Coral Gables, Fla.: North-South Center Press, University of Miami.

Gillespie, Kate, and Gwenn Okruhlik. 1991. "The Political Dimensions of Corruption Cleanups: A Framework for Analysis." *Comparative Politics,* 24, no. 1: 77–95.

Gilley, Bruce. 1998. *Tiger on the Brink: Jiang Zemin and China's New Elite.* Berkeley: University of California Press.

———. 2001. *Model Rebels: The Rise and Fall of China's Richest Village.* Berkeley: University of California Press.

"Godber" (editorial). 1973. *Hong Kong Law Journal,* 3, no. 3: 249–252. Sept.

Golden, Miriam A., and Lucio Picci. 2002. "Proposal for a New Measure of Corruption and Tests Using Italian Data." University of California at Los Angeles, Department of Political Science.

Goldsmith, Arthur A. 1999. "Slapping the Grasping Hand: Correlates of Political Corruption in Emerging Markets." *American Journal of Economics and Sociology,* 58, no. 4: 865–883.

Gong, Ting. 1994. *The Politics of Corruption in Contemporary China: An Analysis of Policy Outcomes.* Westport, Conn.: Praeger.

———. 1996. "Jumping into the Sea: Cadre Entrepreneurs in China." *Problems of Post-Communism,* 43, no. 4: 26–34.

———. 1997. "Forms and Characteristics of China's Corruption in the 1990s: Change with Continuity." *Communist and Post-Communist Studies,* 30, no. 3: 277–288.

Good, Kenneth. 1994. "Corruption and Mismanagement in Botswana: A Best-Case Example?" *Journal of Modern African Studies,* 32, no. 3: 499–521.

Goodstadt, Leo. 1970a. "The Fixers." *Far Eastern Economic Review,* 30 July, 21–23.

———. 1970b. "Squeeze Me Please." *Far Eastern Economic Review,* 25 June, 7–8.

———. 1973. "Rude Awakening." *Far Eastern Economic Review,* 22 Oct., 19–20.

Grantham, Alexander. 1965. *Via Ports, From Hong Kong to Hong Kong.* Hong Kong: Hong Kong University Press.

Gwyn, William B. 1962. *Democracy and the Cost of Politics in Britain.* London: University of London, Athlone Press.

———. 1970. "The Nature and Decline of Corrupt Election Expenditures in Nineteenth-Century Britain." In *Political Corruption: Readings in Compara-*

tive Analysis, ed. Arnold J. Heidenheimer, 391–403. New York: Holt, Rinehart, and Winston.

Han Minzhu, ed. 1990. *Cries for Democracy: Writings and Speeches from the 1989 Chinese Democracy Movement.* Princeton, N.J.: Princeton University Press.

He, Jiahong, with Jon R. Waltz. 1995. *Criminal Prosecution in the People's Republic of China and the United States of America: A Comparative Study.* Beijing: China Procuratorial Press.

He, Zengke. 2000. "Corruption and Anti-Corruption in Reform China." *Communist and Post-Communist Studies,* 33, no. 2: 243–270.

Heidenheimer, Arnold J., ed. 1970. *Political Corruption: Readings in Comparative Analysis.* New York: Holt, Rinehart, and Winston.

Heidenheimer, Arnold J., and Michael Johnston, eds. 2002. *Political Corruption: Concepts and Contexts.* 3rd ed. New Brunswick, N.J.: Transaction Publishers.

Heidenheimer, Arnold J., Michael Johnston, and Victor T. LeVine, eds. 1989. *Political Corruption: A Handbook.* 2nd ed. New Brunswick, N.J.: Transaction Publishers.

Hellman, Joel S., Geraint Jones, and Daniel Kaufmann. 2000. "'Seize the State, Seize the Day': State Capture, Corruption, and Influence in Transition." World Bank Policy Research Working Paper no. 2444. Washington, D.C.

Holm, John D. 2000. "Curbing Corruption through Democratic Accountability: Lessons from Botswana." In *Corruption and Development in Africa: Lessons from Country Case-Studies,* ed. Kempe Ronald Hope, Sr. and Bornwell C. Chikulo, 288–304. New York: St. Martin's Press.

Holmes, Leslie. 1993. *The End of Communist Power: Anti-Corruption Campaigns and Legitimation Crisis.* New York: Oxford University Press.

Hong Kong Civil Service Bureau. 2002. At http://www.csb.gov.hk/hkgcsb. Last retrieved Aug. 2002.

Hong Kong Policy Research Institute. 2002. At http://www.hkpri.org.hk/hkci. Last retrieved Aug. 2002.

Hong Kong Transitions Project. 1982–2007. At http://www.hkbu.edu.hk/~hktp. Last retrieved Aug. 2002.

Hsueh, T. T., and T. O. Woo. 1994. "The Development of Hong Kong-China Relationship." In *25 Years of Social and Economic Development in Hong Kong,* ed. Benjamin K. P. Leung and Teresa Y. C. Wong, 689–727. Hong Kong: University of Hong Kong Press.

Huntington, Samuel P. 1968. *Political Order in Changing Societies.* New Haven, Conn.: Yale University Press.

Huang, Peter H., and Ho-Mou Wu. 1994. "More Order without More Law: A Theory of Social Norms and Organizational Cultures." *Journal of Law, Economics, and Organization,* 10, no. 2: 390–406.

Independent Commission against Corruption. 1975–2002. *Annual Report by the Commissioner of the Independent Commission Against Corruption.* Hong Kong: Government Printer.

Independent Commission against Corruption. 1993. Main Findings of Research

Report on Hong Kong Companies with a Production Base in China (official press release). Hong Kong. 24 July

Independent Commission against Corruption Operations Department. 5 July 1995, 21 July 1995, 11 June 1998. Intelligence officials' interviews with author. Hong Kong.

Independent Commission against Corruption Ordinance (Chapter 204). 1974. Hong Kong. 15 Feb.

"Interview with Deng Xiaoping." 1985. *Time,* 4 Nov., 35.

Kaufmann, Daniel, Aart Kraay, and Pablo Zoido-Lobatón. 1999a. "Aggregating Governance Indicators." World Bank Policy Research Working Paper no. 2195. Washington, D.C.

————. 1999b. "Governance Matters." World Bank Policy Research Working Paper no. 2196. Washington, D.C.

————. 2002. "Governance Matters II: Updated Indicators for 2000/01." World Bank Policy Research Working Paper no. 2772. Washington, D.C.

Khan, Mushtaq H. 1996. "The Efficiency Implications of Corruption." *Journal of International Development,* 8, no. 5: 683–696.

King, Ambrose Yeo-chi. 1980. "An Institutional Response to Corruption: The ICAC of Hong Kong." In *Hong Kong: Dilemmas of Growth,* ed. Chi-keung Leung, J. W. Cushman, and Wang Gungwu, 115–142. Canberra and Hong Kong: Australian National University, Research School of Pacific Studies, and University of Hong Kong, Centre of Asian Studies.

King, John P. 1970. "Socioeconomic Development and the Incidence of English Corrupt Campaign Practices." In *Political Corruption: Readings in Comparative Analysis,* ed. Arnold J. Heidenheimer, 379–390. New York: Holt, Rinehart, and Winston.

Kleiman, Mark A. R. 1993. "Enforcement Swamping: A Positive-Feedback Mechanism in Rates of Illicit Activity." *Mathematical Computational Modelling,* 17, no. 2: 65–75.

Klitgaard, Robert. 1988. *Controlling Corruption.* Berkeley: University of California Press.

Knack, Stephen, and Omar Azfar. 2001. "Trade Intensity, Country Size, and Corruption." University of Maryland, College Park, IRIS Center Working Paper.

Knack, Stephen, and Philip Keefer. 1995. "Institutions and Economic Performance: Cross-Country Tests Using Alternative Institutional Measures." *Economics and Politics,* 7, no. 3: 207–227.

Kolenda, Helena. 1990. "One Party, Two Systems: Corruption in the People's Republic of China and Attempts to Control It." *Journal of Chinese Law,* 4, no. 2: 187–232.

Kuan, Hsin-chi. 1981. "Anti-Corruption Legislation in Hong Kong: A History." In *Corruption and Its Control in Hong Kong,* ed. Rance P. L. Lee, 15–43. Hong Kong: Chinese University Press.

————. 2001. Fax to author. 2 Mar.

Kurer, Oskar. 1993. "Clientelism, Corruption, and the Allocation of Resources." *Public Choice,* 77, no. 2: 259–273.

Kwong, Julia. 1997. *The Political Economy of Corruption in China.* Armonk, N.Y.: M.E. Sharpe.

Kwong, Paul C. K. 1993. "Internationalization of Population and Globalization of Families." In *The Other Hong Kong Report 1993,* ed. Choi Po-king and Ho Lok-sang, 147–174. Hong Kong: Chinese University Press.

Langseth, Peter, Rick Stapenhurst, and Jeremy Pope. 1999. "National Integrity Systems." In *Curbing Corruption: Toward a Model for Building National Integrity,* ed. Rick Stapenhurst and Sahr J. Kpundeh, 127–148. Washington: World Bank, Economic Development Institute.

Lawyers Committee for Human Rights. 1993. *Criminal Justice with Chinese Characteristics: China's Criminal Process and Violations of Human Rights.* New York: Lawyers Committee for Human Rights.

Leak, Tan Ah. 1999. "The Experience of Singapore in Combatting Corruption." In *Curbing Corruption: Toward a Model for Building National Integrity,* ed. Rick Stapenhurst and Sahr J. Kpundeh, 59–66. Washington, D.C.: World Bank, Economic Development Institute.

Lederman, Daniel, Norman Loayza, and Rodrigo Reis Soares. 2001. "Accountability and Corruption: Political Institutions Matter." World Bank Policy Research Working Paper No. 2708. Washington.

Lee, Grace O. M. 1997. "The Succession Crisis in Hong Kong's Civil Service." *Issues and Studies,* 33, no. 8: 49–62.

Lee, Hong Yung. 1983. "Deng Xiaoping's Reform of the Chinese Bureaucracy." In *The Limits of Reform in China,* ed. Ronald A. Morse, 19–37. Boulder, Colo.: Westview Press.

———. 1991. *From Revolutionary Cadres to Party Technocrats in Socialist China.* Berkeley: University of California Press.

Lee, Peter N. S. 1981. "The Causes and Effects of Police Corruption: A Case in Political Modernization." In *Corruption and Its Control in Hong Kong,* ed. Rance P. L. Lee, 167–198. Hong Kong: Chinese University Press.

———. 1990. "Bureaucratic Corruption during the Deng Xiaoping Era." *Corruption and Reform,* 5, no. 5: 29–47.

Lee, Rance P. L. 1981. "Incongruence of Legal Codes and Folk Norms." In *Corruption and Its Control in Hong Kong,* 75–104. Hong Kong: Chinese University Press.

Leff, Nathaniel H. 1964. "Economic Development through Bureaucratic Corruption." *American Behavioral Scientist,* 8, no. 3: 8–14.

Lethbridge, H. J. 1974. "The Emergence of Bureaucratic Corruption as a Social Problem in Hong Kong." *Journal of Oriental Studies,* 12, nos. 1–2: 17–29.

———. 1985. *Hard Graft in Hong Kong: Scandal, Corruption, the ICAC.* Hong Kong: Oxford University Press.

LeVine, Victor T. 1975. *Political Corruption: The Ghana Case.* Stanford, Calif.: Hoover Institution Press.

Levy, Richard. 1995. "Corruption, Economic Crime and Social Transformation since the Reforms: The Debate in China." *Australian Journal of Chinese Affairs,* no. 33: 1–25.

Li, Hongyi, Lixin Colin Xu, and Heng-Fu Zou. 2000. "Corruption, Income Distribution, and Growth." *Economics and Politics,* 12, no. 2: 155–182.

Li, Lianjiang. 2001. "Support for Anti-corruption Campaigns in Rural China." *Journal of Contemporary China,* 10, no. 29: 573–586.

Liew, Leong H. 1993. "Rent-Seeking and the Two-Track Price System in China." *Public Choice,* 77, no. 2: 359–375.

Lin, Danming. 1996. "Hong Kong's China-Invested Companies and Their Reverse Investment in China." In *Management Issues in China: Volume II, International Enterprises,* ed. John Child and Yuan Lu, 165–182. London: Routledge.

Lin, Yi-Min, and Zhanxin Zhang. 1999. "Backyard Profit Centers: The Private Assets of Public Agencies." In *Property Rights and Economic Reform in China,* ed. Jean C. Oi and Andrew G. Walder, 203–225. Stanford, Calif.: Stanford University Press.

Little, Walter, and Eduardo Posada-Carbó, eds. 1996. *Political Corruption in Latin America.* New York: St. Martin's Press.

Liu, Alan P. L. 1983. "The Politics of Corruption in the People's Republic of China." *American Political Science Review,* 77, no. 3: 602–623.

Lo, Sonny S. H. 1994. "Independent Commission Against Corruption." In *The Other Hong Kong Report 1994,* ed. Donald H. McMillen and Man Si-wai, 23–38. Hong Kong: Chinese University Press.

Lowenstein, Daniel H. 1985. "Political Bribery and the Intermediate Theory of Politics." *UCLA Law Review,* 32, no. 4: 784–851.

———. 1996. "When Is a Campaign Contribution a Bribe?" Paper presented at the annual meeting of the Midwest Political Science Association, Chicago, Apr. 18–20.

Lu, Xiaobo. 1997. "The Politics of Peasant Burden in Reform China." *Journal of Peasant Studies,* 25, no. 1: 113–138.

———. 2000a. "Booty Socialism, Bureau-preneurs, and the State in Transition." *Comparative Politics,* 32, no. 3: 273–294.

———. 2000b. *Cadres and Corruption: The Organizational Involution of the Chinese Communist Party.* Stanford, Calif.: Stanford University Press.

Lui, Francis T. 1985. "An Equilibrium Queuing Model of Bribery." *Journal of Political Economy,* 93, no. 4: 760–781.

Luo, Wei. 1998. *The 1997 Criminal Code of the People's Republic of China with English Translation and Introduction.* Chinese Law Series, vol. 1. Buffalo, N.Y.: William S. Hein and Co.

———. 2000. *The Amended Criminal Procedure Law and the Criminal Court Rules of the People's Republic of China with English Translation, Introduction, and Annotation.* Chinese Law Series, vol. 3. Buffalo, N.Y.: William S. Hein and Co.

Ma, Lilian Y. Y. 1991. "Corruption Offences in Hong Kong: Reverse Onus Clauses and the Bill of Rights." *Hong Kong Law Journal,* 21, no. 3: 289–331.

Ma, Stephen K. 1989. "Reform Corruption: A Discussion on China's Current Development." *Pacific Affairs,* 62, no. 1: 40–52.

Manion, Melanie. 1985. "The Cadre Management System, Post-Mao: The Appointment, Promotion, Transfer and Removal of Party and State Leaders." *China Quarterly*, no. 102: 203–233.

———. 1990. "Reluctant Duelists: The Logic of the 1989 Protests and Massacre." In *Beijing Spring, 1989: Confrontation and Conflict. The Basic Documents*, ed. Michel Oksenberg, Lawrence R. Sullivan, and Marc Lambert, xiii–xlii. Armonk, N.Y.: M. E. Sharpe.

———. 1993. *Retirement of Revolutionaries in China: Public Policies, Social Norms, Private Interests*. Princeton, N.J.: Princeton University Press.

———. 1994. "Survey Research in the Study of Contemporary China: Learning from Local Samples." *China Quarterly*, no. 139: 741–765.

———. 1996. "Corruption by Design: Bribery in Chinese Enterprise Licensing." *Journal of Law, Economics, and Organization*, 12, no. 1: 167–195.

———. 1998. "Issues in Corruption Control in Post-Mao China." *Issues and Studies*, 34, no. 9: 1–21.

Manzetti, Luigi. 2000. "Market Reforms without Transparency." In *Combating Corruption in Latin America*, ed. Joseph S. Tulchin and Ralph H. Espach, 130–172. Washington, D.C.: Woodrow Wilson Center Press.

Mao Zedong. 1949. "Preserve the Style of Plain Living and Hard Struggle." In *Selected Readings from the Works of Mao Tsetung*, 362–363. 5 Mar. Excerpt from Report to Second Plenary Session of the Seventh Central Committee of the Communist Party of China. Beijing: Foreign Languages Press [1971].

Mason, T. David. 1994. "Modernization and Its Discontents Revisited: The Political Economy of Urban Unrest in the People's Republic of China." *Journal of Politics*, 56, no. 2: 400–424.

Mauro, Paolo. 1995. "Corruption and Growth." *Quarterly Journal of Economics*, 110, no. 3: 681–712.

———. 1997. "The Effects of Corruption on Growth, Investment, and Government Expenditure: A Cross-Country Analysis." In *Corruption and the Global Economy*, ed. Kimberly Ann Elliott, 83–107. Washington, D.C.: Institute for International Economics.

Miller, William L., Ase B. Grodeland, and Tatyona Koshechkina. 2001. *A Culture of Corruption: Coping with Government in Post-Communist Europe*. Budapest: Central European University Press.

Mulvenon, James. 1998. "Military Corruption in China: A Conceptual Examination." *Problems of Post-Communism*, 45, no. 2: 12–21.

———. 2001. *Soldiers of Fortune: The Rise and Fall of the Chinese Military-Business Complex, 1978–1998*. Armonk, N.Y.: M. E. Sharpe.

Murphy, Kevin M., Andrei Schleifer, and Robert W. Vishny. 1993. "Why Is Rent-Seeking So Costly to Growth?" *American Economic Review*, 83, no. 2: 409–414.

Myers, James T. 1985. "China: The 'Germs' of Modernization." *Asian Survey*, 25, no. 10: 981–997.

———. 1987. "Another Look at Corruption: Lessons of the Career of the 'God of Fortune'." *Issues and Studies*, 23, no. 11: 28–49.

———. 1989. "China: Modernization and 'Unhealthy Tendencies'." *Comparative Politics*, 21, no. 2: 193–213.

Myrdal, Gunnar. 1968. "Corruption—Its Causes and Effects." In *Asian Drama: An Inquiry into the Poverty of Nations,* vol. 2, 937–958. New York: Twentieth Century Fund.

Nathan, Andrew J. 1990. *China's Crisis: Dilemmas of Reform and Prospects for Democracy.* New York: Columbia University Press.

Newman, David, and David L. Weimer. 1997. "The Credibility of the PRC Commitment to a Market Economy in Hong Kong: Hypotheses and Evidence." *Economics and Politics,* 9, no. 3: 251–280.

North, Douglass C. 1990. *Institutions, Institutional Change, and Economic Performance.* Cambridge: Cambridge University Press.

North, Douglass C., and Barry R. Weingast. 1989. "Constitutions and Commitment: The Evolution of Institutions Governing Public Choice in Seventeenth-Century England." *Journal of Economic History,* 49, no. 4: 803–832.

Nossiter, T. J. 1975. *Influence, Opinion and Political Idioms in Reformed England: Case Studies from the Northeast, 1832–74.* Hassocks, England: Harvester Press.

Nye, J. S. 1967. "Corruption and Political Development: A Cost-Benefit Analysis." *American Political Science Review,* 61, no. 2: 417–427.

O'Brien, Kevin J., and Lianjiang Li. 1999. "Campaign Nostalgia in the Chinese Countryside." *Asian Survey,* 39, no. 3: 375–393.

Ocampo, Luis Moreno. 2000. "Structural Corruption and Normative Systems: The Role of Integrity Pacts." In *Combating Corruption in Latin America,* ed. Joseph S. Tulchin and Ralph H. Espach, 53–70. Washington, D.C.: Woodrow Wilson Center Press.

Oi, Jean C. 1989. "Market Reforms and Corruption in Rural China." *Studies in Comparative Communism,* 22, nos. 2–3: 221–233.

Oldenburg, Philip. 1987. "Middlemen in Third-World Corruption: Implications of an Indian Case." *World Politics,* 39, no. 4: 508–535.

O'Leary, Cornelius. 1962. *The Elimination of Corrupt Practices in British Elections, 1868–1911.* Oxford: Clarendon Press.

Ostergaard, Clemens Stubbe. 1986. "Explaining China's Recent Political Corruption." *Corruption and Reform,* 1, no. 1: 209–233.

Ostergaard, Clemens Stubbe, and Christina Petersen. 1991. "Official Profiteering and the Tiananmen Square Demonstrations in China." *Corruption and Reform,* 6, no. 2: 87–107.

Peerenboom, Randall. 2002. *China's Long March toward Rule of Law.* Cambridge: Cambridge University Press.

Pei, Minxin. 1999. "Will China Become Another Indonesia?" *Foreign Policy,* no. 116: 94–109.

Pope, Jeremy. 1999. "Enhancing Accountability and Ethics in the Public Sector." In *Curbing Corruption: Toward a Model for Building National Integrity,* ed. Rick Stapenhurst and Sahr J. Kpundeh, 105–116. Washington, D.C.: World Bank, Economic Development Institute.

Prevention of Bribery Ordinance (Chapter 201). 1971. Hong Kong. 14 May.

Quah, Jon S. T. 1989. "Singapore's Experience in Curbing Corruption." In *Political Corruption: A Handbook,* ed. Arnold J. Heidenheimer, Michael Johnston, and Victor T. Le Vine, 841–853. New Brunswick, N.J.: Transaction Publishers.

———. 1995. "Controlling Corruption in City-States: A Comparative Study of Hong Kong and Singapore." *Crime, Law, and Social Change,* 22, no. 4: 391–414.

———. 1999. "Corruption in Asian Countries: Can It Be Minimized?" *Public Administration Review,* 59, no. 6: 483–494.

Rawski, Thomas G. 2002. "How Fast Is China's Economy Really Growing?" *China Business Review,* Mar.–Apr.: 40–43.

Report of the ICAC Review Committee. 1994. Mimeo. Hong Kong. Dec.

Rocca, Jean-Louis. 1992. "Corruption and Its Shadow: An Anthropological View of Corruption in China." *China Quarterly,* no. 130: 402–416.

Root, Hilton. 1989. "Tying the King's Hands: Credible Commitments and Royal Fiscal Policy During the Old Regime." *Rationality and Society,* 1, no. 2: 240–258.

Rose-Ackerman, Susan. 1978. *Corruption: A Study in Political Economy.* New York: Academic Press.

———. 1999. *Corruption and Government: Causes, Consequences, and Reform.* Cambridge: Cambridge University Press.

Rowen, Henry S. 2001. "The Growth of Freedoms in China." Stanford University, Institute for International Studies, Asia/Pacific Research Center Working Paper. Apr. Stanford, Calif.

Royal Hong Kong Police Force. 1952–53 to 1972–73. *Annual Departmental Report.* Hong Kong: Government Printer.

Sandholtz, Wayne, and William Koetzle. 2000. "Accounting for Corruption: Economic Structure, Democracy, and Trade." *International Studies Quarterly,* 44, no. 1: 31–50.

Sands, Barbara N. 1990. "Decentralizing an Economy: The Role of Bureaucratic Corruption in China's Economic Reforms." *Public Choice,* 65, no. 1: 85–91.

Sayer, Geoffrey Robley. 1975. *Hong Kong 1862–1919: Years of Discretion.* Hong Kong: Hong Kong University Press.

Schelling, Thomas. 1960. *The Strategy of Conflict.* Cambridge: Harvard University Press.

Schuman, Howard, and Stanley Presser. 1981. *Questions and Answers in Attitude Surveys: Experiments on Question Form, Wording, and Context.* Orlando, Fla.: Academic Press.

Scott, Ian. 1989. *Political Change and the Crisis of Legitimacy in Hong Kong.* Honolulu: University of Hawaii Press.

Scott, James C. 1972. *Comparative Political Corruption.* Englewood Cliffs, N.J.: Prentice-Hall.

Sedigh, Shahrzad, and Alex Muganda. 1999. "The Fight against Corruption in Tanzania." In *Curbing Corruption: Toward a Model for Building National*

Integrity, ed. Rick Stapenhurst and Sahr J. Kpundeh, 151–177. Washington, D.C.: World Bank, Economic Development Institute.

Sedigh, Shahrzad, and Augustine Ruzindana. 1999. "The Fight against Corruption in Uganda." In *Curbing Corruption: Toward a Model for Building National Integrity,* ed. Rick Stapenhurst and Sahr J. Kpundeh, 179–205. Washington, D.C.: World Bank, Economic Development Institute.

Seligson, Mitchell A. 2002. "The Impact of Corruption on Regime Legitimacy: A Comparative Study of Four Latin American Countries." *Journal of Politics,* 64, no. 2: 408–433.

Shan, Weijian. 1992. "The Hybrid System and Continued Marketization of the Chinese Economy." *China Economic Review,* 3, no. 1: 57–74.

Shen, George. 1993. "China's Investment in Hong Kong." In *The Other Hong Kong Report 1993,* ed. Choi Po-king and Ho Lok-sang, 425–454. Hong Kong: Chinese University Press.

Shleifer, Andrei, and Robert W. Vishny. 1993. "Corruption." *Quarterly Journal of Economics,* 58, no. 3: 599–617.

Siu, Yat-ming. 1999. "New Arrivals: A New Problem and an Old Problem." In *The Other Hong Kong Report 1998,* ed. Larry Chuen-ho Chow and Yiu-kwan Fan, 201–228. Hong Kong: Chinese University Press.

Skeldon, Ronald. 1990–91. "Emigration and the Future of Hong Kong." *Pacific Affairs,* 63, no. 4: 500–523.

———. 1991. "Emigration, Immigration and Fertility Decline: Demographic Integration or Disintegration?" In *The Other Hong Kong Report 1991,* ed. Sung Yun-wing and Lee Ming-kwan, 233–258. Hong Kong: Chinese University Press.

———. 1994a. "Hong Kong in an International Migration System." In *Hong Kong Becoming China: The Transition to 1997.* Vol. 5, *Reluctant Exiles? Migration from Hong Kong and the New Overseas Chinese,* 21–51. Armonk, N.Y.: M. E. Sharpe.

———. 1994b. "Immigration and Emigration: Current Trends, Dilemmas and Policies." In *The Other Hong Kong Report 1994,* ed. Donald H. McMillen and Man Si-wai, 165–186. Hong Kong: Chinese University Press.

———. 1995. "Immigration and Population Issues." In *The Other Hong Kong Report 1995,* ed. Stephen Y. L. Cheung and Stephen M. H. Sze, 303–316. Hong Kong: Chinese University Press.

Smart, Josephine. 1994. "Business Immigration to Canada: Deception and Exploitation." In *Hong Kong Becoming China: The Transition to 1997.* Vol. 5, *Reluctant Exiles? Migration from Hong Kong and the New Overseas Chinese,* ed. Ronald Skeldon, 98–119. Armonk, N.Y.: M.E. Sharpe.

Solinger, Dorothy J. 1984. *Chinese Business under Socialism: The Politics of Domestic Commerce.* Berkeley: University of California Press.

Speville, B. E. D. de. 1999. "The Experience of Hong Kong, China, in Combating Corruption." In *Curbing Corruption: Toward a Model for Building National Integrity,* ed. Rick Stapenhurst and Sahr J. Kpundeh, 51–58. Washington, D.C.: World Bank.

Stone, Brewer S. 1993. "*Tanwu fubai* and *kaifang*: Corruption and China's Opening to the International Economy." Paper presented at the Annual Meeting of the Association for Asian Studies, Los Angeles, Mar. 25–28.

Sun, Yan. 1991. "The Chinese Protests of 1989: The Issue of Corruption." *Asian Survey,* 31, no. 8: 762–782.

———. 1999. "Reform, State, and Corruption: Is Corruption Less Destructive in China Than in Russia?" *Comparative Politics,* 32, no. 1: 1–20.

Tanner, Murray Scot. 1994. "The Erosion of Communist Party Control over Lawmaking in China." *China Quarterly,* no. 138: 381–403.

Tanner, Murray Scot, with Michael J. Feder. 1993. "Family Politics, Elite Recruitment, and Succession in Post-Mao China." *Australian Journal of Chinese Affairs,* no. 30: 89–119.

Teiwes, Frederick C. 1978. *Elite Discipline in China: Coercive and Persuasive Approaches to Rectification, 1950–1953.* Canberra: Contemporary China Institute, Australian National University.

Theobald, Robin, and Robert Williams. 2000. "Combating Corruption in Botswana: Regional Role Model or Deviant Case?" In *Corruption and Democratisation,* ed. Alan Doig and Robin Theobald, 117–134. London: Frank Cass.

Tirole, Jean. 1996. "A Theory of Collective Reputations (with Applications to the Persistence of Corruption and to Firm Quality)." *Review of Economic Studies,* 63, no. 1: 1–22.

Transparency International. 2004. Corruption Perceptions Index. Internet Center for Corruption Research at http://www.gwdg.de/~uwvw/icr.htm. Last retrieved June 2004.

Treisman, Daniel. 1999. "Decentralization and Corruption: Why Are Federal States Perceived to Be More Corrupt?" Paper presented at the 95th Annual Meeting of the American Political Science Association, Atlanta, Sept. 2–5.

———. 2000. "The Causes of Corruption: A Cross-National Study." *Journal of Public Economics,* 76, no. 3: 399–458.

Tseng, Choosin. 1996. "Foreign Direct Investment from the People's Republic of China." In *Business Transformation in China,* ed. Henri-Claude de Bettignies, 85–114. London: International Thomson Business Press.

Wang, Shaoguang. 1995. "The Rise of the Regions: Fiscal Reform and the Decline of Central State Capacity in China." In *The Waning of the Communist State: Economic Origins of Political Decline in China and Hungary,* ed. Andrew G. Walder, 87–113. Berkeley: University of California Press.

Wang, Zhonghui. 1995. "Township Public Finance and Its Impact on the Financial Burden of Rural Enterprises and Peasants in Mainland China." *Issues and Studies,* 31, no. 8: 103–121.

Wedeman, Andrew. 1996. "Politics and Corruption." In *China Review 1996,* ed. Maurice Brosseau, Suzanne Pepper, and Tsang Shu-ki, 61–94. Hong Kong: Chinese University of Hong Kong Press.

———. 1997a. "Looters, Rent-Scrapers, and Dividend Collectors: The Political Economy of Corruption in Zaire, South Korea, and the Philippines." *Journal of Developing Areas,* 31, no. 4: 457–478.

——. 1997b. "Stealing from the Farmers: Institutional Corruption and the 1992 IOU Crisis." *China Quarterly*, no. 152: 805–831.

——. 2000. "Budgets, Extra-budgets, and Small Treasuries: Illegal Monies and Local Autonomy in China." *Journal of Contemporary China*, 9, no. 25: 489–511.

Weder, Beatrice, and Aymo Brunetti. 1998. "Another Tale of Two Cities: A Note on Institutions in Hong Kong and Singapore." Mimeo. University of Basel.

Wei, Shang-Jin. 2000. "Why Does China Attract So Little Foreign Direct Investment?" In *The Role of Foreign Direct Investment in East Asian Economic Development*, ed. Takatoshi Ito and Anne O. Krueger, 239–261. Chicago: University of Chicago Press.

White, Gordon. 1996. "Corruption and the Transition from Socialism in China." *Journal of Law and Society*, 23, no. 1: 149–169.

White, Lynn T., III. 1988. "Changing Concepts of Corruption in Communist China: Early 1950s Versus Early 1980s." In *Changes and Continuities in Chinese Communism*. Vol. 2, *The Economy, Society, and Technology*, ed. Yu-ming Shaw, 316–353. Boulder, Colo.: Westview Press.

——. 1989. *Policies of Chaos: The Organizational Causes of Violence in China's Cultural Revolution*. Princeton, N.J.: Princeton University Press.

Whitehead, Laurence. 1983. "On Presidential Graft: The Latin American Experience." In *Corruption: Causes, Consequences and Control*, ed. Michael Clarke, 163–189. London: Pinter.

Wong, Fanny. 1997. "The Civil Service." In *The Other Hong Kong Report 1997*, ed. Joseph Y. S. Cheng, 71–100. Hong Kong: Chinese University Press.

Wong, Jeremiah K. H. 1981. "The ICAC and Its Anti-Corruption Measures." In *Corruption and Its Control in Hong Kong*, ed. Rance P. L. Lee, 46–72. Hong Kong: Chinese University Press.

Wong, John. 1994. "Power and Market in Mainland China: The Danger of Increasing Government Involvement in Business." *Issues and Studies*, 30, no. 1: 1–12.

Wong, Kar-Yiu. 1992. "Inflation, Corruption, and Income Distribution: The Recent Price Reform in China." *Journal of Macroeconomics*, 14, no. 1: 105–123.

Wong, Siu-lun. 1992. "Emigration and Stability in Hong Kong." *Asian Survey*, 32, no. 10: 918–933.

Yang, Mayfair Mei-hui. 1989. "The Gift Economy and State Power in China." *Comparative Studies in Society and History*, 31, no. 1: 25–54.

——. 1994. *Gifts, Favors, and Banquets: The Art of Social Relations in China*. New York: Cornell University Press.

Ye, Jianying. 1979. Speech at meeting in celebration of the thirtieth anniversary of the founding of the People's Republic of China. *Beijing Review*, no. 40 (29 Sept.): 7–32.

Young, Graham. 1984. "Control and Style: Discipline Inspection Commissions Since the 11th Congress." *China Quarterly*, no. 97: 24–52.

Zafanolli, Wojtek. 1988. "A Brief Outline of China's Second Economy." In *Trans-

forming China's Economy in the Eighties. Vol. 2, *Management, Industry and the Urban Economy,* ed. Stephen Feuchtwang, Athar Hussain, and Thierry Pairault, 138–155. Boulder, Colo.: Westview Press.

Zhang Peitian. 1995. "Investigating and Prosecuting Official Corruption in China: The Minjiang Case." Translated by Weiping Wang, examined and ed. Sarah Biddulph. Mimeo. University of Melbourne.

Works in Chinese

Central Committee. Feb. 1952. Dui zhong xiao tanwu fenzi chufen wenti de zhishi (jielu) (Instructions on punishment of small and middle corrupt elements [excerpts]). In *Zhong wai fan fubai shiyong quanshu* (Complete book on Chinese and comparative anticorruption work), compiled by Liang Guoqing, Ye Feng, and Hu Jinguang, 714. Beijing: Xinhua chubanshe, 1994.

———. 29 Feb. 1980. Guanyu dangnei zhengzhi shenghuo de ruogan zhunze (Standards for inner-party political life). In *Zhongguo gongchandang dangnei fagui xuanbian, 1978–1996* (Chinese communist party inner-party regulations, 1978–1996), compiled by Central Committee General Office of Laws and Regulations, Central Discipline Inspection Commission Office of Laws and Regulations, and Central Organization Department General Office, 41–56. Beijing: Falü chubanshe, 1996.

———. 11 Jan. 1982. Jinji tongzhi (Urgent notice). In *Lianzheng shouce* (Handbook on clean government), 473–474. Beijing: Zhongguo renmin gongan daxue chubanshe, 1989.

———. 1 June 1988. Guanyu dang he guojia jiguan bixu baochi lianjie de tongzhi (Notice on need for party and government agencies to maintain honesty). In *Lianzheng shouce* (Handbook on clean government), 11–12. Beijing: Zhongguo renmin gongan daxue chubanshe, 1989.

———. 27 Feb. 1997. Zhongguo gongchandang jilü chufen tiaoli (shixing) (Chinese communist party regulations on party disciplinary action [for trial implementation]). In *Zhongguo gongchandang jilü chufen tiaoli* (Chinese communist party regulations on disciplinary action), compiled by Central Discipline Inspection Commission Office of Laws and Regulations, 2–39. Beijing: Zhongguo fangzheng chubanshe, 1997.

Central Committee and State Council. 13 Apr. 1982. Guanyu daji jingji lingyu zhong yanzhong fanzui huodong de jueding (Decision on a crackdown on serious criminal activities in the economic sphere). In *Cha chu "guandao" anjian shiyong fagui shouce* (Handbook of regulations and laws on investigation and punishment in cases of "official profiteering"), 20–30. Beijing: Falü chubanshe, 1989.

———. 28 July 1989. Guanyu jinqi zuo ji jian qunzhong guanxin de shi de jueding (Decision on actions in the near future to address some matters of concern to the masses). In *Jiaqiang lianzheng jianshe jiuzheng hangye bu zheng zhi feng zhengce fagui huibian* (Policies, regulations, and laws on building clean government and rectifying improper conduct), compiled by

Ministry of Supervision Bureau of Policy, Regulation, and Law, 54–56. Beijing: Falü chubanshe, 1991.

———. 5 Oct. 1993. Guanyu fan fubai douzheng jinqi zhua hao ji xiang gongzuo de jueding (Decision on some key aspects of work in the current struggle against corruption). In *Chachu jingji weifa fanzui zhengce fagui shouce* (Handbook of policies, regulations, and laws on investigation and punishment in cases of economic crimes), compiled by Supreme People's Procuratorate General Office, 29–31. Beijing: Falü chubanshe, 1996.

Central Committee General Office. 13 Aug. 1982. Guanyu chengzhi tanwu shouhui zui de buchong guiding (caoan) (jielu) (Supplementary provisions on punishments for the crimes of corruption and accepting bribes [draft] [excerpts]). In *Lianzheng shouce* (Handbook on clean government), 531–532. Beijing: Zhongguo renmin gongan daxue chubanshe, 1989.

Central Committee General Office and State Council. 5 Oct. 1993. Guanyu fan fubai douzheng jinqi zhua hao ji xiang gongzuo de jueding (Decision on some key aspects of work in the current struggle against corruption). In *Chachu jingji weifa fanzui zhengce fagui shouce* (Handbook of policies, regulations, and laws on investigation and punishment in cases of economic crimes), compiled by Supreme People's Procuratorate General Office, 29–31. Beijing: Falü chubanshe, 1996.

Central Committee General Office and State Council General Office. 26 Nov. 1985. Guanyu jiejue dangqian jiguan zuofeng zhong ji ge yanzhong wenti de tongzhi (Notice on resolving some current serious problems of workstyle in agencies). In *Baochi lianjie fandui fubai wenxian xuanbian* (Selected documents on countering corruption and maintaining clean government), ed. Supreme People's Procuratorate Editorial Group, 247–251. Beijing: Zhongguo zhengfa daxue chubanshe, 1989.

Central Discipline Inspection Commission. 14 July 1982. Guanyu jiuzheng dangqian chuli jingji fanzui anjian zhong cunzai de "zhong fa qing xing" xianxiang de tongzhi (Notice on rectifying the current practice of "giving priority to fines over criminal punishment" in handling cases of economic crime). In *Lianzheng shouce* (Handbook on clean government), 479–481. Beijing: Zhongguo renmin gongan daxue chubanshe, 1989.

———. 11 Sept. 1982. Xiang dang de di shi er ci quanguo daibiao dahui de gongzuo baogao (Work report to the 12th national party congress). *Xinhua yuebao*, no. 9 (1982): 42–48.

———. 10 Mar. 1983. Guanyu gongchandangyuan zai jingji lingyu zhong weifa fanzui de dangji chuli zanxing banfa (jielu) (Interim measures on party disciplinary action for communist party members who commit economic crimes [excerpts]). In *Jiaqiang lianzheng jianshe jiuzheng hangye bu zheng zhi feng zhengce fagui huibian* (Policies, regulations, and laws on building clean government and rectifying improper conduct), compiled by Ministry of Supervision Bureau of Policy, Regulation, and Law, 301–303. Beijing: Falü chubanshe, 1991.

———. 30 June 1987. Guanyu jianjue chachu gongchandangyuan suohui wenti de jueding (Decision on resolutely investigating and punishing communist party members who solicit bribes). In *Chachu jingji weifa fanzui zhengce fagui shouce* (Handbook of policies, regulations, and laws on investigation and punishment in cases of economic crimes), compiled by Supreme People's Procuratorate General Office, 222–223. Beijing: Falü chubanshe, 1996.

———. 30 Oct. 1987. Xiang dang de di shi san ci quanguo daibiao dahui de gongzuo baogao (Work report to the 13th national party congress). *Renmin ribao*, 5 Nov. 1987.

———. 12 May 1988. Zhongguo gongchandang jilü jiancha jiguan anjian jiancha gongzuo tiaoli (shixing) (Regulations on case investigation by Chinese communist party discipline inspection agencies [for trial implementation]). In *Fan fubai zhengce fagui shouce* (Handbook of anticorruption policies, regulations, and laws), compiled by Central Discipline Inspection Commission Office of Laws and Regulations and Office for Coordination of Supervisory Work, 317–328. Beijing: Zhongguo fangzheng chubanshe, 1994.

———. 28 Oct. 1989. Tigao ban an xiaolü fangzhi anjian jiya de zanxing banfa (Interim measures to improve efficiency and prevent delays in handling cases). In *Zhongguo gongchandang dangnei fagui xuanbian, 1978–1996* (Chinese communist party inner-party regulations, 1978–1996), compiled by Central Committee General Office Office of Laws and Regulations, Central Discipline Inspection Commission Office of Laws and Regulations, and Central Organization Department General Office, 594–596. Beijing: Falü chubanshe, 1996.

———. 1 July 1990. Guanyu gongchandangyuan zai jingji fangmian weifa weiji dangji chufen de ruogan guiding (shixing) (Provisions on party disciplinary action for communist party members who violate the law and discipline in the economic sphere [for trial implementation]). In *Zhongguo gongchandang dangnei fagui xuanbian, 1978–1996* (Chinese communist party inner-party regulations, 1978–1996), compiled by Central Committee General Office Office of Laws and Regulations, Central Discipline Inspection Commission Office of Laws and Regulations, and Central Organization Department General Office, 487–496. Beijing: Falü chubanshe, 1996.

———. 9 Oct. 1992. Xiang dang de di shi si ci quanguo daibiao dahui de gongzuo baogao (Work report to the 14th national party congress). *Renmin ribao*, 23 Oct. 1992.

———. 25 Mar. 1994. Zhongguo gongchandang jilü jiancha jiguan anjian jiancha gongzuo tiaoli (Regulations on case investigation by Chinese communist party discipline inspection agencies); and Zhongguo gongchandang jilü jiancha jiguan anjian jiancha gongzuo tiaoli shishi xize (Detailed rules for implementation of regulations on case investigation by Chinese communist party discipline inspection agencies). In *Zhongguo gongchandang dangnei fagui xuanbian, 1978–1996* (Chinese communist party inner-party regulations, 1978–1996), compiled by Central Committee General Office Office of Laws and Regulations, Central Discipline Inspection Commission Office of

Laws and Regulations, and Central Organization Department General Office, 652–672. Beijing: Falü chubanshe, 1996.

———. 9 Sept. 1997. Xiang dang de di shi wu ci quanguo daibiao dahui de gongzuo baogao (Work report to the 15th national party congress). In *Jiufeng gongzuo nianjian 1990–1997* (Yearbook on rectifying workstyle, 1990–1997), ed. State Council Office to Rectify Improper Conduct, 896–904. Beijing: Fangzheng chubanshe.

Central Discipline Inspection Commission, Central Organization Department, and Ministry of Supervision. 8 Oct. 1993. Guanyu dangzheng jiguan xian (chu) ji yishang lingdao ganbu lianjie zilü "wutiao guiding" de shishi yijian (Opinions on implementation of "five provisions" on honesty and self-discipline for leading party and government officials at and above the county [division] level). In *Chachu jingji weifa fanzui zhengce fagui shouce* (Handbook of policies, regulations, and laws on investigation and punishment in cases of economic crimes), compiled by Supreme People's Procuratorate General Office, 32–34. Beijing: Falü chubanshe, 1996.

Central Discipline Inspection Commission, Supreme People's Court, Supreme People's Procuratorate, and Ministry of Public Security. 17 Sept. 1989. Guanyu jilü jiancha jiguan yu fayuan jianchayuan gongan jiguan zai cha chu anjian guocheng zhong huxiang tigong youguan anjian cailiao de tongzhi (Notice on the mutual provision of case materials by discipline inspection agencies, courts, procuratorates, and public security agencies in the course of investigating and handling cases). In *Zhongguo gongchandang dangnei fagui xuanbian, 1978–1996* (Chinese communist party inner-party regulations, 1978–1996), compiled by Central Committee General Office Office of Laws and Regulations, Central Discipline Inspection Commission Office of Laws and Regulations, and Central Organization Department General Office, 592–593. Beijing: Falü chubanshe, 1996.

Central Discipline Inspection Commission and Supreme People's Procuratorate. 21 Nov. 1988. Guanyu dang de jilü jiancha weiyuanhui yu guojia jiancha jiguan jianli lianxi zhidu de tongzhi (Notice on the establishment of a system to coordinate party discipline inspection committees and government procuratorates). In *Zhongguo gongchandang dangnei fagui xuanbian, 1978–1996* (Chinese communist party inner-party regulations, 1978–1996), compiled by Central Committee General Office Office of Laws and Regulations, Central Discipline Inspection Commission Office of Laws and Regulations, and Central Organization Department General Office, 585–586. Beijing: Falü chubanshe, 1996.

Central Discipline Inspection Commission Research Office, comp. 1996. *Dang feng lianzheng jianshe he jijian jiancha gongzuo ziliao ku 1993, 1994* (Building party style and clean government: Materials on discipline inspection and supervision, 1993 and 1994). Beijing: Zhongguo fangzheng chubanshe.

Central People's Government Council. 18 Apr. 1952. Zhonghua renmin gongheguo chengzhi tanwu tiaoli (Regulations of the People's Republic of China on punishment for the crime of corruption). In *Zhong wai fan fubai shiyong quanshu* (Complete book on Chinese and comparative anti-corruption work), compiled by Liang Guoqing, Ye Feng, and Hu Jinguang, 748–749. Beijing: Xinhua chubanshe, 1994.

Central People's Government Council Political Legal Committee Deputy Director (Peng Zhen). 18 Apr. 1952. Guanyu zhonghua renmin gongheguo chengzhi tanwu tiaoli caoan de shuoming (Discussion of regulations of the People's Republic of China on punishment for the crime of corruption). In *Zhong wai fan fubai shiyong quanshu* (Complete book on Chinese and comparative anticorruption work), compiled by Liang Guoqing, Ye Feng, and Hu Jinguang, 749–752. Beijing: Xinhua chubanshe, 1994.

Chen Wenbing, ed. 1993. *Zhongguo gongchandang xinglian fanfu lu 1921–1993* (Chronology of the Chinese communist party effort to promote clean government and oppose corruption 1921–1993). Beijing: Xiyuan chubanshe.

Commission on State Organ Establishment. 4 Nov. 1988. Jiancha bu "san ding" fangan (Plan for three measures for the Ministry of Supervision). In *"Zhonghua renmin gongheguo xingzheng jiancha tiaoli" jieyi* (Annotated "Regulations of the People's Republic of China on administrative supervision"), ed. Ministry of Supervision Bureau of Policy, Regulation, and Law, 176–182. Beijing: Zhongguo zhengfa daxue chubanshe, 1991.

Dong Chunjiang, and Ding Muying. 1993. "Zhijie shouli zhencha anjian gongzuo bu neng quxiao" (The work of directly accepting and investigating cases must not be eliminated). *Renmin jiancha*, no. 7: 57–58.

Fang Wen. 1996. *Tiannu* (Wrath of heaven). Hohhot, Inner Mongolia: Yuanfang chubanshe.

Fei Hongzhi, et al. 1991. *Lianzheng daguan* (Overview of clean government). Beijing: Changzheng chubanshe.

Gong Xiaobing, et al. 1991. *Tanwu huilu fanzui duice lun* (A study of measures to handle crimes of corruption and bribery). Beijing: Falü chubanshe.

He Qinglian. 1997. *Zhongguo de xianjing* (China's pitfall). Hong Kong: Mirror Books.

Hou Zongbin. 1995. Ting qu xinfang shi gongzuo huibao hou de jianghua (Talk after hearing work reports by offices of letters and visits). In *Jijian jiancha gongzuo wenjian xuanbian* (Documents on discipline inspection and supervision), compiled by Central Discipline Inspection Commission General Office, vol. 1, 436–440. Beijing: n.p. 15 March.

Hu Angang. 2001. "Fubai: zhongguo zui da de shehui wuran" (Corruption: China's biggest social pollution). In *Zhongguo: tiaozhan fubai* (China: Fighting against corruption), 34–66. Hangzhou: Zhejiang renmin chubanshe.

Hu Kangsheng, et al., eds. 1997. *Zhonghua renmin gongheguo xingfa jieyi* (Annotated criminal law of the People's Republic of China). Beijing: Falü chubanshe.

Huang Xiurong, and Liu Rongbing, eds. 1997. *Zhongguo gongchandang lianzheng fan fu shiji* (Record of the Chinese communist party's effort to build clean government and combat corruption). Beijing: Zhongguo fangzheng chubanshe.

Jiang Zemin. 1995. Zai Beijing shiwei changwei kuoda huiyi shang de jianghua (Talk at the enlarged meeting of the Beijing party standing committee). In *Jijian jiancha gongzuo wenjian xuanbian* (Documents on discipline inspection and supervision), compiled by Central Discipline Inspection Commission General Office, vol. 1, 84–86. Beijing: n.p. 27 Apr.

Li Peng. 1995. Zai Beijing shiwei changwei kuoda huiyi shang de jianghua (Talk at the enlarged meeting of the Beijing party standing committee). In *Jijian jiancha gongzuo wenjian xuanbian* (Documents on discipline inspection and supervision), compiled by Central Discipline Inspection Commission General Office, vol. 1, 87–89. Beijing: n.p. 27 Apr.

Li Xueqin. 1997. "Ruhe pingjia fan fubai douzheng de chengxiao" (How to evaluate results in the anticorruption struggle). *Neibu wengao* (Internal manuscripts), no. 1: 21–22.

Li Xueqin, et al., comps. 1993. *Xin zhongguo fan fubai tongjian* (Survey of the effort to counter corruption in new China). Tianjin: Tianjin renmin chubanshe.

Liang Guoqing, Ye Feng, and Hu Jinguang, eds. 1994. *Zhong wai fan fubai shiyong quanshu* (Complete book on Chinese and comparative anticorruption work). Beijing: Xinhua chubanshe.

Liu Sheng. 1996. "Fan tanwu yu gongzhong canyu" (Fighting corruption and mass public participation). *Jiancha lilun yanjiu* (Studies in supervision), no. 1: 21–24.

Lu Yun. 1998. "Guo you qiye fubai xianxiang tan yuan" (Exploring the causes of corruption in state-owned enterprises). *Dang jian yanjiu nei can* (Internal reference studies on party building), no. 4: 2–5.

Luo Ji, et al., eds. 1996. *Tanwu zui* (The crime of corruption). Beijing: Zhongguo jiancha chubanshe.

Ministry of Finance. 30 Dec. 1986. Guanyu fa mo caiwu he zhuihui zangkuan zangwu guanli banfa (Measures on management of confiscated assets and recovered stolen funds and goods). In *Chachu jingji weifa fanzui zhengce fagui shouce* (Handbook of policies, regulations, and laws on investigation and punishment in cases of economic crimes), compiled by Supreme People's Procuratorate General Office, 310–315. Beijing: Falü chubanshe, 1996.

Ministry of Supervision. 1993. *Zhongguo jiancha nianjian 1987–1991* (Yearbook on Chinese supervisory work 1987–1991). Beijing: Zhongguo zhengfa daxue chubanshe.

Ministry of Supervision Bureau of Policy, Regulation, and Law. 1991. "Zhonghua renmin gongheguo xingzheng tiaoli" jieyi (Annotated "Regulation on administrative supervision of the People's Republic of China"). In *"Zhonghua renmin gongheguo xingzheng tiaoli" jieyi* (Annotated "Regulations of the People's Republic of China on administrative supervision"), 1–97. Beijing: Zhongguo zhengfa daxue chubanshe.

National People's Congress Standing Committee. 8 Mar. 1982. Guanyu yancheng yanzhong pohuai jingji de zuifan de jueding (Decision on severe punishment of criminals for seriously undermining the economy). 5th National People's Congress, 22d session. In *Chachu jingji weifa fanzui zhengce fagui shouce*

(Handbook of policies, regulations, and laws on investigation and punishment in cases of economic crimes), compiled by Supreme People's Procuratorate General Office, 62–63. Beijing: Falü chubanshe, 1996.

———. 21 Jan. 1988. Guanyu chengzhi tanwu zui huilu zui de buchong guiding (Supplementary provisions on punishment for the crimes of corruption and bribery). 6th National People's Congress, 24th session. In *Chachu jingji weifa fanzui zhengce fagui shouce* (Handbook of policies, regulations, and laws on investigation and punishment in cases of economic crimes), compiled by Supreme People's Procuratorate General Office, 64–67. Beijing: Falü chubanshe, 1996.

National People's Congress Standing Committee Working Committee on the Legal System, Office on the Criminal Law, ed. 1997. *Zhonghua renmin gongheguo xingfa shiyi* (Explanation of the criminal law of the People's Republic of China). Beijing: Falü chubanshe.

Qi Peiwen. 1995. Cha ban anjian gongzuo zhong ying zhuyi bawo de ji ge wenti: Qi Peiwen tongzhi zai quanguo sheng qu shi jijian jiancha anjian jiancha gongzuo yantao hui shang de jianghua (Some priority issues to grasp in investigation and handling of cases: Speech of comrade Qi Peiwen at the conference of provinces, regions, and municipalities on discipline inspection and supervisory case investigation). In *Jijian jiancha gongzuo wenjian xuanbian* (Documents on discipline inspection and supervision), compiled by Central Discipline Inspection Commission General Office, vol. 1, 549–574. Beijing: n.p. 31 July.

Qin Xingmin. 2000. "Xianxing tanwu huilu zui jubao zhidu de gongneng ji qi wanshan" (Functions and improvement of the current system of reporting crimes of embezzlement and bribery). In *Fubai he zhapian fanzui de chengzhi yu fangfan: guoji jiancha guan lianhe hui di si jie nianhui ji huiyuan dahui (zhong fang huiyuan) lunwen ji* (Prevention and punishment of criminal corruption and fraud: Papers [Chinese participants] from the fourth annual meeting of the international association of prosecutors), ed. Chinese Research Institute on Procuratorial Theory and Chinese Association of Procurators, 97–103. Beijing: Zhongguo jiancha chubanshe.

Ren Zhizhong. 1992. "Jianzhu ye huilu fanzui de tedian ji zhencha duice" (Features of bribery in the construction business and measures to investigate it). *Renmin jiancha* (People's procuracy), no. 3: 14–15.

Sheng Liangang, ed. 1996. *Chengzhi jingji fanzui falü fenjie shiyong shouce* (Handbook on laws applicable to the punishment of economic crimes). Beijing: Renmin fayuan chubanshe.

Small Group on Revision of the Party Constitution. 12 Oct. 1992. Guanyu zhongguo gongchandang zhangcheng (xiuzheng an) de shuoming (Explanations on communist party of China constitution [amended version]). In *Zhongguo gongchandang dangnei fagui xuanbian, 1978–1996* (Chinese communist party inner-party regulations, 1978–1996), compiled by Central Committee General Office of Laws and Regulations, Central Discipline Inspection Commission Office of Laws and Regulations, and Central Organization Department General Office, 25–33. Beijing: Falü chubanshe, 1996.

Song Yantong. 1998. "Dui xian yishang lingdao ganbu weiji weifa qingkuang de diaocha yu sikao" (Survey and reflections on violations of law and discipline by leaders at and above the county level). *Dang jian yanjiu neican* (Internal reference studies on party building), nos. 1–2: 20–21.

State Council. 15 July 1987. Guanyu zai xian yi shang difang ge ji renmin zhengfu sheli xingzheng jiancha jiguan de tongzhi (Notice on the establishment of administrative supervisory agencies in local governments at and above the county level). In *"Zhonghua renmin gongheguo xingzheng jiancha tiaoli" jieyi* (Annotated "Regulations of the People's Republic of China on administrative supervision"), ed. Ministry of Supervision Bureau of Policy, Regulation, and Law, 158–162. Beijing: Zhongguo zhengfa daxue chubanshe, 1991.

State Council Office to Rectify Improper Work Conduct. 1995. Guanyu 1994 nian di si ci hangye fengqi wenjuan diaocha qingkuang de baogao (Report on findings from the fourth survey on workstyle, conducted in 1994). In *Jijian jiancha gongzuo wenjian xuanbian* (Documents on discipline inspection and supervision), compiled by Central Discipline Inspection Commission General Office, vol. 2, 1087–1091. Beijing: n.p. 6 Jan.

Sun Qian, ed. 1990. *Guojia gongzuo renyuan zhiwu fanzui yanjiu* (On crimes involving abuse of office by state functionaries). Beijing: Zhongguo jiancha chubanshe.

Sun Tonghui, and Zhang Min, eds. 1995. *Zhongyang jiwei zhongyang jianwei gongzuo jishi* (Record of the work of the central committee discipline inspection commission and central committee control commission). Beijing: Zhongguo fangzheng chubanshe.

Supreme People's Court, and Supreme People's Procuratorate. 2 Nov. 1984. Guanyu dangqian banli daoqie anjian zhong juti ying yong falü de ruogan wenti de jieda (Reply to certain questions about concrete application of the law in the current handling of cases of theft). In *Jiancha shouce (1984–1985)* (Procuratorial handbook [1984–1985]), compiled by Supreme People's Procuratorate Research Office, 45–51. Beijing: Zhongguo jiancha chubanshe, 1991.

———. 8 July 1985. Guanyu dangqian banli jingji fanzui anjian zhong juti ying yong falü de ruogan wenti de jieda (shixing) (Reply to certain questions about concrete application of the law in the current handling of cases of economic crime [for trial implementation]). In *Xin zhongguo fan fubai tongjian* (Survey of the effort to counter corruption in new China), compiled by Li Xueqin et al., 811–816. Tianjin: Tianjin renmin chubanshe, 1993.

———. 14 Mar. 1987. "Guanyu nuoyong gongkuan gui geren shiyong huozhe jinxing feifa huodong yi tanwu lunchu de wenti" de xiugai buchong yijian (Supplementary opinions on revision of "the question of punishing as corruption the misappropriation of public funds for personal use or to engage in illegal activities"). In *Xin zhongguo fan fubai tongjian* (Survey of the effort to counter corruption in new China), compiled by Li Xueqin et al., 819–820. Tianjin: Tianjin renmin chubanshe, 1993.

———. 15 Aug. 1989. Guanyu tanwu shouhui touji daoba deng fanzui fenzi bixu zai xianqi nei zishou tanbai de tonggao (Notice of a limited time period in which criminals who have engaged in corruption, acceptance of bribes, speculation and profiteering, and other crimes must confess and turn themselves in to authorities). In *Xin zhongguo fan fubai tongjian* (Survey of the effort to counter corruption in new China), compiled by Li Xueqin et al., 825–826. Tianjin: Tianjin renmin chubanshe, 1993.

———. 18 Aug. 1989. Zui gao renmin fayuan he zui gao renmin jianchayuan fuze ren jiu fabu "guanyu tanwu shouhui touji daoba deng fanzui fenzi bixu zai xianqi nei zishou tanbai de tonggao" da jizhe wen (Responsible people at the Supreme People's Court and the Supreme People's Procuratorate answer journalists' questions about "Notice of a limited time period in which criminals who have engaged in corruption, acceptance of bribes, speculation and profiteering, and other crimes must confess and turn themselves in to authorities"). In *Xin zhongguo fan fubai tongjian* (Survey of the effort to counter corruption in new China), compiled by Li Xueqin et al., 827–829. Tianjin: Tianjin renmin chubanshe, 1993.

———. 22 Aug. 1989. Guanyu zhixing "tonggao" di er tiao youguan guiding de jiti yijian (Concrete opinions on implementing relevant regulations in the second article of the "notice"). In *Xin zhongguo fan fubai tongjian* (Survey of the effort to counter corruption in new China), compiled by Li Xueqin et al., 829–830. Tianjin: Tianjin renmin chubanshe, 1993.

———. 14 Sept. 1989. Guanyu zhixing "tonggao" de ruogan wenti de dafu (Answers to certain questions on implementing the "notice"). In *Xin zhongguo fan fubai tongjian* (Survey of the effort to counter corruption in new China), compiled by Li Xueqin et al., 830. Tianjin: Tianjin renmin chubanshe, 1993.

———. 6 Nov. 1989. Guanyu zhixing "guanyu chengzhi tanwu zui huilu zui de buchong guiding" ruogan wenti de jieda (Reply to certain questions about implementation of "supplementary provisions on punishment for the crimes of corruption and bribery"). In *Chachu jingji weifa fanzui zhengce fagui shouce* (Handbook of policies, regulations, and laws on investigation and punishment in cases of economic crimes), compiled by Supreme People's Procuratorate General Office, 154–159. Beijing: Falü chubanshe, 1996.

———. 11 Dec. 1992. Guanyu banli daoqie anjian juti yingyong falü de ruogan wenti de jieshi (Explanation of certain issues in application of the law in handling cases of theft). In *Chachu jingji weifa fanzui zhengce fagui shouce* (Handbook of policies, regulations, and laws on investigation and punishment in cases of economic crimes), compiled by Supreme People's Procuratorate General Office, 164–171. Beijing: Falü chubanshe, 1996.

Supreme People's Procuratorate. 18 Aug. 1982. Guanyu tanwu zui zhuisu shixiao wenti de fuhan (Reply on the issue of statute of limitations for the crime of corruption). In *Chachu jingji weifa fanzui zhengce fagui shouce* (Handbook of policies, regulations, and laws on investigation and punishment in cases of economic crimes), compiled by Supreme People's Procuratorate General Office, 300. Beijing: Falü chubanshe, 1996.

———. 25 Dec. 1982. Guanyu zai banli tanwu shouhui deng jingji fanzui anjian zhong zhengque yunyong mianyu qisu de ji dian yijian (xiugai gao) (Some opinions on the correct application of exemption from prosecution for cases of embezzlement of public assets, bribery, and other economic crimes [revised draft]). In *Lianzheng shouce* (Handbook on clean government), 487–489. Beijing: Zhongguo renmin gongan daxue chubanshe, 1989.

———. 25 Nov. 1988. Renmin jianchayuan jubao gongzuo ruogan guiding (shixing) (Some provisions on reporting work for procuratorates [for trial implementation]). In *Zhongguo falü nianjian 1990* (1990 yearbook on Chinese law), 699–701. Beijing: Zhongguo falü nianjian chubanshe, 1990.

———. 18 July 1996. Renmin jianchayuan jubao gongzuo guiding (Provision on reporting work for procuratorates). *Xin fagui yuekan* (New laws and regulations), no. 10 (1996): 19–22.

Supreme People's Procuratorate Chief Procurator (Huang Huoqing). 6 Dec. 1982. Zui gao renmin jianchayuan gongzuo baogao (Report on the work of the Supreme People's Procuratorate). *Renmin ribao* (People's daily), 17 Dec. 1982.

Supreme People's Procuratorate Chief Procurator (Yang Yichen). 3 Apr. 1985. Zui gao renmin jianchayuan gongzuo baogao (Report on the work of the Supreme People's Procuratorate). *Renmin ribao* (People's daily), 16 Apr. 1985.

———. 8 Apr. 1986. Zui gao renmin jianchayuan gongzuo baogao (Report on the work of the Supreme People's Procuratorate). *Renmin ribao* (People's daily), 20 Apr. 1986.

———. 6 Apr. 1987. Zui gao renmin jianchayuan gongzuo baogao (Report on the work of the Supreme People's Procuratorate). In *Zhongguo jiancha nianjian 1988* (Procuratorial yearbook of China 1988), 21–26. Beijing: Zhongguo jiancha chubanshe, 1989.

Supreme People's Procuratorate Chief Procurator (Liu Fuzhi). 29 Mar. 1989. Zui gao renmin jianchayuan gongzuo baogao (Report on the work of the Supreme People's Procuratorate). In *Zhongguo jiancha nianjian 1990* (Procuratorial yearbook of China 1990), 13–20. Beijing: Zhongguo jiancha chubanshe, 1991.

———. 25 Oct. 1989. Guanyu jiancha jiguan kaizhan fan tanwu huilu douzheng qingkuang de baogao (Report on the struggle against corruption and bribery by procuratorates). In *Zhongguo jiancha nianjian 1990* (Procuratorial yearbook of China 1990), 20–27. Beijing: Zhongguo jiancha chubanshe, 1991.

———. 29 Mar. 1990. Zui gao renmin jianchayuan gongzuo baogao (Report on the work of the Supreme People's Procuratorate). In *Zhongguo jiancha nianjian 1991* (Procuratorial yearbook of China 1991), 7–15. Beijing: Zhongguo jiancha chubanshe, 1992.

———. 6 Nov. 1990. Zai quanguo jiancha zhang gongzuo huiyi shang de baogao (Report at the national meeting of chief procurators). *Zhongguo jiancha nianjian 1991* (Procuratorial yearbook of China 1991), 214–224. Beijing: Zhongguo jiancha chubanshe, 1992.

———. 3 Apr. 1991. Zui gao renmin jianchayuan gongzuo baogao (Report on the work of the Supreme People's Procuratorate). In *Zhongguo jiancha nianjian 1992* (Procuratorial yearbook of China 1992), 27–35. Beijing: Zhongguo jiancha chubanshe, 1993.

———. 28 Mar. 1992. Zui gao renmin jianchayuan gongzuo baogao (Report on the work of the Supreme People's Procuratorate). In *Zhongguo jiancha nianjian 1993* (Procuratorial yearbook of China 1993), 6–11. Beijing: Zhongguo jiancha chubanshe, 1994.

———. 28 Mar. 1993. Zui gao renmin jianchayuan gongzuo baogao (Report on the work of the Supreme People's Procuratorate). In *Zhongguo jiancha nianjian 1994* (Procuratorial yearbook of China 1994), 17–22. Beijing: Zhongguo jiancha chubanshe, 1995.

Supreme People's Procuratorate Chief Procurator (Zhang Siqing). 28 Oct. 1993. Guanyu jiancha jiguan zai fan fubai douzheng zhong jizhong jingli cha ban da an yao an qingkuang de baogao (Status report on the concentration of efforts by procuratorial agencies to investigate and handle cases involving big sums and senior officials in the course of the anticorruption struggle). In *Zhongguo jiancha nianjian 1994* (Procuratorial yearbook of China 1994), 17–11. Beijing: Zhongguo jiancha chubanshe, 1995.

———. 15 Mar. 1994. Zui gao renmin jianchayuan gongzuo baogao (Report on the work of the Supreme People's Procuratorate). In *Zhongguo jiancha nianjian 1995* (Procuratorial yearbook of China 1995), 25–34. Beijing: Zhongguo jiancha chubanshe, 1996.

———. 13 Mar. 1995. Zui gao renmin jianchayuan gongzuo baogao (Report on the work of the Supreme People's Procuratorate). In *Zhongguo jiancha nianjian 1996* (Procuratorial yearbook of China 1996), 27–36. Beijing: Zhongguo jiancha chubanshe, 1997.

———. 12 Mar. 1996. Zui gao renmin jiancha yuan gongzuo baogao (Report on the work of the Supreme People's Procuratorate). *Zhonghua renmin gongheguo zuigao renmin jianchayuan gongbao* (Bulletin of the Supreme People's Procuratorate of the People's Republic of China), nos. 1–2 (1996): 3–9.

———. 11 Mar. 1997. Zui gao renmin jianchayuan gongzuo baogao (Report on the work of the Supreme People's Procuratorate). *Zhonghua renmin gongheguo zui gao renmin jianchayuan gongbao* (Bulletin of the Supreme People's Procuratorate of the People's Republic of China), 1997, no. 2: 52–59.

———. 10 Mar. 1998. Zui gao renmin jianchayuan gongzuo baogao (Report on the work of the Supreme People's Procuratorate). *Zhongguo jiancha nianjian 1999* (Procuratorial yearbook of China 1999), 1–9. Beijing: Zhongguo jiancha chubanshe, 2000.

Supreme People's Procuratorate Chief Procurator (Han Zhubin). 10 Mar. 2000. Zuo gao renmin jianchayuan gongzuo baogao (Report on the work of the Supreme People's Procuratorate). *Zhonghua renmin gongheguo zui gao renmin jianchayuan gongbao* (Bulletin of the Supreme People's Procuratorate of the People's Republic of China), no. 2: 13–20.

———. 10 Mar. 2001. Zui gao renmin jianchayuan gongzuo baogao (Report on the work of the supreme people's procuratorate). *Zhonghua renmin gongheguo zui gao renmin jianchayuan gongbao* (Bulletin of the Supreme People's Procuratorate of the People's Republic of China), 2001, no. 2: 4–9.

———. 11 Mar. 2003. Zui gao renmin jianchayuan gongzuo baogao (Report on the work of the Supreme People's Procuratorate). Supreme People's Procuratorate at http://www.spp.gov.cn/baogao. Last retrieved May 2003.

Tong Baoyu. 1991. "1988 nian jiancha jiguan kaizhan jubao gongzuo de qingkuang" [Development of public reporting work in procuratorates in 1988]. In *Zhongguo jiancha nianjian 1989* (Procuratorial yearbook of China 1989), 14–15. Beijing: Zhongguo jiancha chubanshe.

Wang Guang. 1995. Zai xi nan xi bei jiu sheng qu jijian jiancha xinxi gongzuo zuotanhui shang de jianghua (Talk at the conference of nine southwest and northwest provinces and regions on discipline inspection and supervisory information work). In *Jijian jiancha gongzuo wenjian xuanbian* (Documents on discipline inspection and supervision), compiled by Central Discipline Inspection Commission General Office, vol. 1, 441–456. Beijing: n.p. 9 Mar.

Wang Hongguang. 1994. "Dang wei—tuidong tupo da yao an de hexin liliang" (Party committees—The key force in promoting a breakthrough in big and important cases). *Renmin jiancha* (People's procuracy), no. 11: 28–29.

Wang Xiaoguang. 25 Nov. 1989. Zai quan guo jiancha zhang gongzuo huiyi shang guanyu sixiang zhengzhi gongzuo de baogao (Report on political and ideological work at the national work conference of chief procurators). In *Zhongguo jiancha nianjian 1990* (Procuratorial yearbook of China 1990), 230–236. Beijing: Zhongguo jiancha chubanshe, 1991.

Wei Jianxing. 20 Jan. 1995. Shenru gongzuo hen zhua luoshi nuli qude fan fubai douzheng xin chengjiu (Deepen work, resolutely grasp implementation, and make efforts to achieve new results in the anticorruption struggle). In *Jijian jiancha yewu fagui zhengce xuanbian* (Policies, regulations, and laws on discipline inspection and supervision), compiled by Central Discipline Inspection Commission Office of Regulation and Law and Ministry of Supervision Bureau of Regulation and Law, no. 1, 47–65. Beijing: Zhongguo fangzheng chubanshe, 1995.

———. 9 Aug. 1995. Zai quan guo sheng qu shi jijian jiancha anjian jiancha gongzuo yantao hui shang de jianghua (Talk at the conference of provinces, regions, and municipalities on discipline inspection and supervisory case investigation). In *Jijian jiancha gongzuo wenjian xuanbian* (Documents on discipline inspection and supervision), compiled by Central Discipline Inspection Commission General Office, vol. 1, 575–583. Beijing: n.p., 1995.

———. 24 Jan. 1996. Zai zhonggong zhongyang jilü jiancha weiyuanhui di liu ci quanti huiyi shang de jianghua (Talk at the 6th plenary meeting of the Central Discipline Inspection Commission). In *Jijian jiancha yewu fagui zhengce xuanbian* (Policies, regulations, and laws on discipline inspection and supervision), compiled by Central Discipline Inspection Commission Office of Regulation and Law and Ministry of Supervision Bureau of Regulation and Law, no. 2, 88–105. Beijing: Zhongguo fangzheng chubanshe, 1996.

———. 12 Jan. 2000. Jianding xinxin jiaqiang lidu shenru tuijin dangfeng lianzheng jianshe he fan fubai douzheng (Strengthen confidence and forces, deepen and promote the building of clean government and the struggle against corruption). In *Xingzheng jiancha gongzuo wenjian xuanbian* (Selected documents on administrative supervisory work), compiled by Central Discipline Inspection Commission Office of Regulation and Law and Ministry of Supervision Bureau of Regulation and Law, 1–17. Beijing: Zhongguo fangzheng chubanshe, 2001.

———. 25 Dec. 2000. Jiada zhiben lidu henzhua gongzuo luoshi qude fan fubai douzheng de xin chengxiao (Augment forces to get at the root of the problem, resolutely implement work measures to realize new results in the struggle against corruption). In *Jijian jiancha yewu fagui zhengce xuanbian* (Selected policies, regulations, and laws on discipline inspection and supervision), compiled by Central Discipline Inspection Commission Office of Regulation and Law and Ministry of Supervision Bureau of Regulation and Law, 657–667. Beijing: Zhongguo fangzheng chubanshe, 2001.

Wei Pingxiong, and Wang Ranji, eds. 1992. *Tanwu huilu zui de rending yu duice* (Determining and countering the crimes of corruption and bribery). Beijing: Qunzhong chubanshe.

Wen Shengtang. 1996. "1995 nian zhongguo de fan fubai" (The anticorruption effort in China in 1995). In *1995–1996 nian zhongguo shehui xingshi fenxi yu yuce* (Chinese society in 1995–96: Analysis of the situation and forecast), ed. Jiang Liu, Lu Xueyi, and Dan Tianlun, 97–111. Beijing: Zhongguo shehui kexue chubanshe.

———. 1997. "1996–1997 nian de fan fubai douzheng" (The struggle against corruption in 1996–97). In *1996–1997 nian zhongguo shehui xingshi fenxi yu yuce* (Chinese society in 1996–97: Analysis of the situation and forecast), ed. Jiang Liu, Lu Xueyi, and Dan Tianlun, 106–123. Beijing: Zhongguo shehui kexue chubanshe.

———. 2003. "2002 nian fan fubai douzheng de xin jinzhan" (New progress in the anticorruption struggle in 2002). In *Shehui lanpi shu 2003 nian: zhongguo shehui xingshi fenxi yu yuce* (Blue book of Chinese society 2003: Analysis of the situation and forecast), ed. Ru Xin, Lu Xueyi, and Li Peilin, 99–110. Beijing: Shehui kexue wenxian chubanshe.

Wu Baoliang. 1998. "Dui fan fubai wenti de renshi he sikao" (A consideration of the problem of anticorruption). *Lilun dongtai* (Theoretical trends), no. 1365: 1–11.

Xu Qing. 1997. "Guanyu zhiding he shishi 'lianzheng zhunze' de ji ge wenti" (Issues in the drafting and implementation of "standards of integrity"). *Dangjian yanjiu neican* (Internal reference studies of party building), no. 9: 2–12.

Xu Shaowei, and Nie Shaolin. 1994. "Wei shenme yixie qunzhong dui fan fubai chengguo rentong chengdu di" (Why is it that some masses have a low estimation of results in the anti-corruption effort?). *Neibu wengao* (Internal manuscripts), no. 20: 22–24.

Yan Tao. 1997. "Dang nei jiandu yao zhenzheng ying qi lai" (Supervision within the party must be genuinely strengthened). *Neibu wengao* (Internal manuscripts), no. 6: 21–24.

Yan Yuhe. 1995. "Zhichi jiancha gongzuo shi dangwei yi burong ci de zhize" (Party committees are duty-bound to support procuratorial work). *Renmin jiancha* (People's procuracy), no. 1: 34–35.

Yang Shuang. 1996. "Fan fubai: qingshi yanjun dai gaige" (Anticorruption effort: A grim situation awaiting reform). In *1996–1997 nian zhongguo fazhan qingkuang yu qushi* (1996–1997 situation and development trends in China), ed. Weng Jieming, Zhang Ximing, Zhang Tao, and Qu Kemin, 74–91. Beijing: Zhongguo shehui chubanshe.

Ye Huilun, and Yu Bing, eds. 1996. *Nuoyong gongkuan zui* (The crime of misappropriation of public funds). Beijing: Zhongguo jiancha chubanshe.

Yuan Yue. 1997. "1996–1997 nian zhongguo chengshi shehui wending yu fazhan zhuangkuang de gongzhong xintai fenxi" (Public views on urban stability and urban development in 1996–97). In *1996–1997 nian zhongguo shehui xingshi fenxi yu yuce* (Chinese society in 1996–97: Analysis of the situation and forecast), ed. Jiang Liu, Lu Xueyi, and Dan Tianlun, 80–90. Beijing: Zhongguo shehui kexue chubanshe.

Zhang Leike, and Liu Jian, eds. 1992. *Gaige kaifang zhong de lianzheng jianshe* (Building clean government under reform and opening). Beijing: Zhongguo jiancha chubanshe.

Zhang Siqing, et al., eds. 1991. *Zhonghua renmin gongheguo jiancha yewu quanshu* (Complete book on procuratorial work in the People's Republic of China). Changchun: Jilin renmin chubanshe.

Zhao Hongzhu. 1995. Jiaqiang lingdao banzi jianshe tigao ganbu duiwu suzhi wei jijian jiancha gongzuo tigong you li de zuzhi baozheng (Strengthen the building of leadership groups, improve the quality of the cadre corps, provide a beneficial organizational guarantee for discipline inspection and supervisory work). In *Jijian jiancha gongzuo wenjian xuanbian* (Documents on discipline inspection and supervision), compiled by Central Discipline Inspection Commission General Office, vol. 1, 173–189. Beijing: n.p. 10 Apr.

Zhong Jiwen. 1997. "Jingti fubai xianxiang de zizhang manyan" (Guard against the growth and spread of corruption). *Dang jian yanjiu neican* (Internal reference studies on party building), no. 4: 12, 8.

Zhongguo falü nianjian 1989–2001 (Yearbook on Chinese law 1989–2001). 1990–2001. Beijing: Zhongguo falü nianjian chubanshe.

Zhongguo gongchandang dangzhang (Chinese communist party constitution). 11 Sept. 1982. Beijing: Renmin chubanshe, 1987.

———. 18 Oct. 1992. In *Zhongguo gongchandang dang nei fa gui xuanbian (1978–1996)* (Chinese communist party inner-party regulations, 1978–1996), compiled by Central Committee General Office of Laws and Regulations, Central Discipline Inspection Commission Office of Laws and Regulations, and Central Organization Department General Office, 1–23. Beijing: Falü chubanshe, 1996.

Zhongguo jiancha nianjian 1988–2001. (Procuratorial yearbook of China, 1988–2001). 1989–2002. Beijing: Zhongguo jiancha chubanshe.

Zhonghua renmin gongheguo xingfa (Criminal law of the People's Republic of China). 1 July 1979. 5th National People's Congress, 2d session. In *The Criminal Law and the Criminal Procedure Law of the People's Republic of China,* 65–109. Beijing: Foreign Languages Press, 1984.

Zhonghua renmin gongheguo xingfa (Criminal law of the People's Republic of China). 14 Mar. 1997. 8th National People's Congress, 5th session. Beijing: Falü chubanshe, 1997.

Zhonghua renmin gongheguo xingshi susong fa (Criminal procedure law of the People's Republic of China). 1 July 1979. 5th National People's Congress, 2d session. In *The Criminal Law and the Criminal Procedure Law of the People's Republic of China,* 111–214. Beijing: Foreign Languages Press, 1984.

Zhonghua renmin gongheguo xingshi susong fa (Criminal procedure law of the People's Republic of China). 17 Mar. 1996. 8th National People's Congress, 4th session. Beijing: Falü chubanshe, 1996.

Author Index

Subject Index

1854 Corrupt Practices Prevention Act, 18
1867 Second Reform Act, 18
1872 Ballot Act, 18
1883 Corrupt and Illegal Practices Act, 18
1884 Third Reform Act, 18
1885 Redistribution of Seats Act, 18
1979 Criminal Law, 140–148, 173, 174, 181, 233n30, 237n58, 242n28
1997 Criminal Law, 91, 112, 122, 129, 140–148, 171, 228n24, 230n7, 233nn30,31, 235n51, 236n56, 237n59, 238n68, 241n16
"1997 quick buck syndrome," 74, 79, 82

Advisory Committee on Corruption, 31, 32, 49, 217n13
Agricultural Bank, 107
Amnesty for past corruption, 41, 44; public opinion against, 220n32
Anhui province, 160, 205
Anti-Corruption Branch. *See* Anti-Corruption Office
Anticorruption Bureau. *See* Anticorruption General Bureau
Anticorruption campaigns: definition of, 90, 96, 119, 127, 131, 147, 160–163; in Maoist era, 156–160; as enforcement strategy, 168–199, 207, 238n71
Anticorruption General Bureau, 87, 135, 148; renaming of, 122
Anti-Corruption Office (ACO), 33, 39, 57,

217n11; creation of, 31; separation from police force, 32; public confidence in, 34–36, 44; reports of corruption to, 216n11
Arbitrage in the form of official profiteering *(guandao)*, 99
Asian financial crisis, 75, 79, 224n54
Attorney General's Office, 217n12

Beliefs: role of, 1, 5, 13, 19, 28, 57, 77, 105, 224n52; changes in, 3, 26, 35, 44, 200, 222n41; distortion of, 20; sources of, 222n39
Bill of Rights, 216n7
Blair-Kerr, Justice Alastair, 29, 34, 216n8
Bribery: definition of, 39, 143; statistics on, 87, 91, 97, 126, 158, 164–167, 227n8, 239n8; sums involved, 87, 103, 112–113, 128–129, 187, 238n69; organizational, 103–104, 112–113, 228n25, 236n55; in subcontracting, 104
Bureaucratic commerce: corruption as, 96, 103, 116, 117; definition of, 97; development of, 98; profits from, 99–101; policy roots of, 100; popular salience of, 110, 112, 118, 203
Business cycles, 75, 80

Cater, Sir Jack, 35, 37, 38, 40, 41
Central Discipline Inspection Commission (CDIC), 84, 121, 123, 131, 133, 206,